D0486303

GOVERNANCE IN A
GLOBALIZING
WORLD

Visions of Governance for the 21st Century

Why People Don't Trust Government
Joseph Nye Jr., Philip Zelikow, and David King
(1997)

democracy.com? Governance in a Networked World
Elaine Ciulla Kamarck and Joseph Nye Jr.
(1999)

GOVERNANCE IN A GLOBALIZING WORLD

Joseph S. Nye Jr.
John D. Donahue
Editors

VISIONS OF GOVERNANCE
FOR THE 21ST CENTURY
Cambridge, Massachusetts

BROOKINGS INSTITUTION PRESS
Washington, D.C.

ABOUT BROOKINGS

The Brookings Institution is a private nonprofit organization devoted to research, education, and publication on important issues of domestic and foreign policy. Its principal purpose is to bring knowledge to bear on current and emerging policy problems. The Institution maintains a position of neutrality on issues of public policy. Interpretations or conclusions in Brookings publications should be understood to be solely those of the authors.

Copyright © 2000
Visions of Governance for the 21st Century

All rights reserved. No part of this publication may be reproduced or transmitted in any form or by any means without permission in writing from the Brookings Institution Press, 1775 Massachusetts Avenue, N.W., Washington, D.C. 20036 (www.brookings.edu).

Library of Congress Cataloging-in-Publication data

Governance in a globalizing world / Joseph S. Nye Jr. and John D. Donahue, editors.
    p.   cm.
Includes bibliographical references and index.
ISBN 0-8157-6408-1 (cloth)   ISBN 0-8157-6407-3 (pbk.)
1. Globalization.   2. State, The.   I. Nye, Joseph S.   II. Donahue, John D.
JZ1318 .G68 2000   00010678
327.1'01dc21   CIP

9 8 7 6 5 4 3 2

The paper used in this publication meets minimum requirements of the American National Standard for Information Sciences—Permanence of Paper for Printed Library Materials: ANSI Z39.48-1992.

Typeset in Adobe Garamond

Composition by R. Lynn Rivenbark
Macon, Georgia

Printed by R. R. Donnelley and Sons
Harrisonburg, Virginia

To the memory of

Raymond Vernon

Contents

Preface

GLOBALIZATION is at once a rallying cry, a riddle, and a Rohrshach test. Traditionalists lament it. Investors exploit it. Pundits dissect it or debunk it. But what *is* globalization? Is it mostly a matter of money, or microbes, or media, or something else altogether? Is it new or a durable trend discernible only when history's more distracting dramas quiet down? What propels globalization? Will it deepen divides between the world's winners and losers or reshuffle the deck with wider opportunity? How is it altering the challenges of governance within and among nation-states? And how can public leaders come to terms with governance in a globalizing world?

These are the issues we address in this volume. *Governance in a Globalizing World* emerged from a series of discussions orchestrated through the Visions of Governance for the 21st Century project. Like all Visions efforts, this book is deeply and deliberately interdisciplinary, including chapters by political scientists, economists, historians, information technology analysts, and sociologists. This thematic and disciplinary diversity is essential to any effort to come to grips with a multifaceted phenomenon like globalization. At the same time, this book extends deep roots into the real world, as befits a product of Harvard's professional school of government. Abstraction and technicality—while they cannot be wholly banished without skimping on substance—are kept to a minimum. Our aim is to present a set of perspectives that is at once sound and useful, to stimulate scholars while informing practitioners.

We have divided *Governance in a Globalizing World* into three main sections, preceded by an introductory chapter. The first section examines globalization from several angles—economic, military, and cultural—and tracks established and emerging trends. The second section explores globalization's effect on national governance, in general terms (such as legal transplantation or the spread of administrative reform) and through highlighting specific nations and groups of nations. The last section inverts the telescope to explore the effect of governance on globalization, discussing the roles of nongovernmental organizations, information policy, and the logic of governance for a global economy.

The Visions of Governance project—as an instrument of the John F. Kennedy School of Government's central mission—has sought from the start to clarify questions that matter for democracy. Since the initiative began in 1996, its scholars have lent data, discipline, and structure to crucial public conversations about the ongoing challenges of self-government. Previous Visions volumes include *Why People Don't Trust Government* (1997) and *democracy.com? Governance in a Networked World* (1999). This volume extends that franchise and also marks the start of a publishing partnership with the Brookings Institution Press.

We thank the volume's contributors, along with many other colleagues who offered advice, criticism, and encouragement to the authors (in various forms, in various settings) as they drafted and refined their contributions. We also thank Lynn Akin and Neal Rosendorf for their indispensable assistance. This stage of the Visions of Governance project has benefited from the generosity of the Christian A. Johnson Endeavor Foundation, the Daniel and Joanna S. Rose Fund, the Herbert S. Winokur Fund for Public Policy, the Parker Gilbert Montgomery Endowment, Kenneth G. Lipper, and the Xerox Foundation, which we gratefully acknowledge. And we owe a special debt to Elaine Ciulla Kamarck, the previous director of the Visions project, under whose stewardship this effort was launched.

Governance in a Globalizing World is dedicated to Raymond Vernon, who earned his reputation as an eminent scholar of globalization decades before the theme came into vogue. Ray's death, just as this book began to take shape, cost us a colleague of rare energy, honesty, and acuity. One of our titles bears his name; both of our minds (like those of so many others) bear his mark.

JOSEPH S. NYE JR.
Don K. Price Professor of Public Policy
Dean, John F. Kennedy School of Government

JOHN D. DONAHUE
Raymond Vernon Lecturer in Public Policy
Director, Visions of Governance
for the 21st Century

GOVERNANCE IN A GLOBALIZING WORLD

1

ROBERT O. KEOHANE
JOSEPH S. NYE JR.

Introduction

G LOBALIZATION became a buzzword in the 1990s, as "interdependence" did in the 1970s. Sometimes, it seems to refer to anything that the author thinks is new or trendy. But globalization, as this
book shows, refers to real changes of fundamental importance. These
changes have profound implications for politics as well as for economics,
military activities, and the environment. In this book we ask three fundamental questions. One, how are patterns of globalization evolving in the
first part of the twenty-first century? Two, how does this affect governance,
previously closely associated with the nation-state? Three, how might globalism itself be governed?

Globalization will affect governance processes and be affected by them.
Frequent financial crises of the magnitude of the crisis of 1997–99 could
lead to popular movements to limit interdependence and to a reversal of
economic globalization. Chaotic uncertainty is too high a price for most
people to pay for somewhat higher average levels of prosperity. Unless some
aspects of globalization can be effectively governed, it may not be sustainable in its current form. Complete laissez-faire was not a viable option during earlier periods of globalization and is not likely to be viable now. The
question is not—will globalization be governed?—but rather, *how* will
globalization be governed?

Defining Globalism

Globalism is a state of the world involving networks of interdependence at multicontinental distances.[1] These networks can be linked through flows and influences of capital and goods, information and ideas, people and force, as well as environmentally and biologically relevant substances (such as acid rain or pathogens). Globalization and deglobalization refer to the increase or decline of globalism. In comparison with interdependence, globalism has two special characteristics:[2]

—Globalism refers to networks of connections (multiple relationships), not simply to single linkages. We would refer to economic or military interdependence between the United States and Japan but not to globalism between the United States and Japan. U.S.-Japanese interdependence is part of contemporary globalism but by itself is not globalism.

—For a network of relationships to be considered "global," it must include multicontinental distances, not simply regional networks. Distance is of course a continuous variable, ranging from adjacency (for instance, between the United States and Canada) to opposite sides of the globe (for instance, Britain and Australia). Any sharp distinction between "long-distance" and "regional" interdependence is therefore arbitrary, and there is no point in deciding whether intermediate relationships— say, between Japan and India or between Egypt and South Africa—would qualify. Yet "globalism" would be an odd word for proximate regional relationships. Globalization refers to the shrinkage of distance but on a large scale. It can be contrasted with localization, nationalization, or regionalization.

Some examples may help. Islam's quite rapid diffusion from Arabia across Asia to what is now Indonesia was a clear instance of globalization; but the initial movement of Hinduism across the Indian subcontinent was not, according to our definition. Ties among the countries of the Asia-Pacific Economic Cooperation Forum (APEC) qualify as multicontinental interdependence, because these countries include the Americas as well as Asia and Australia; but the Association of Southeast Asian Nations (ASEAN) is regional.

Globalism does not imply universality. At the turn of the millennium, a quarter of the American population used the World Wide Web compared with one hundredth of 1 percent of the population of South Asia. Most people in the world today do not have telephones; hundreds of millions of people live as peasants in remote villages with only slight connections to world markets or the global flow of ideas. Indeed, globalization is accompanied by increasing gaps, in many respects, between the rich and the poor. It does not imply homogenization or equity.[3] As Jeffrey Frankel and Dani Rodrik show in their chapters, an integrated world market would mean free flows of goods, people, and capital, and convergence in interest rates. That is far from the facts. While world trade grew twice as fast and foreign direct investment three times as fast as world output in the second half of the twentieth century, Britain and France are only slightly more open to trade (ratio of trade to output) today than in 1913, and Japan is less so. By some measures, capital markets were more integrated at the beginning of the century, and labor is less mobile than in the second half of the nineteenth century when 60 million people left Europe for new worlds.[4] In social terms, contacts among people with different religious beliefs and other deeply held values have often led to conflict.[5] Two symbols express these conflicts: the notion of the United States as the Great Satan, held by Islamic fundamentalism in Iran; and student protestors' erection in Tiananmen Square in China, in 1989, of a replica of the Statue of Liberty. Clearly, in social as well as economic terms, homogenization does not follow necessarily from globalization.

The Dimensions of Globalism

Interdependence and globalism are both multidimensional phenomena. All too often, they are defined in strictly economic terms, as if the world economy defined globalism. But other forms of globalism are equally important. The oldest form of globalization is environmental: climate change has affected the ebb and flow of human populations for millions of years. Migration is a long-standing global phenomenon. The human species began to leave its place of origin, Africa, about 1.25 million years ago and reached the Americas sometime between 30,000 and 13,000 years ago. One of the most important forms of globalization is biological. The first smallpox epidemic is recorded in Egypt in 1350 B.C. It reached China in 49 A.D., Europe after 700; the Americas in 1520, and Australia in 1789.[6] The plague or Black Death originated in Asia, but its spread killed a quarter to a third of the population of Europe between 1346 and 1352. When Europeans journeyed to the New World in the fifteenth and sixteenth centuries they carried pathogens that destroyed up to 95 percent of the indigenous population.[7] Today, human impact on global climate change could affect the lives of people everywhere. However, not all effects of environmental globalism are adverse. For instance, nutrition and cuisine in the Old World benefited from the importation of such New World crops as the potato, corn, and the tomato.[8]

Military globalization dates at least from the time of Alexander the Great's expeditions of 2,300 years ago, which resulted in an empire that stretched across three continents from Athens through Egypt to the Indus. Hardest to pin down, but in some ways the most pervasive form of globalism, is the flow of information and ideas. Indeed, Alexander's conquests were arguably most important for introducing Western thought and society, in the form of Hellenism, to the eastern world.[9] Four great religions of the world—Buddhism, Judaism, Christianity, and Islam—have spread across great distances over the past two millennia; and in this age of the Internet other religions such as Hinduism, formerly more circumscribed geographically, are doing so as well.[10]

Analytically, we can differentiate dimensions according to the types of flows and perceptual connections that occur in spatially extensive networks:

—Economic globalism involves long-distance flows of goods, services, and capital, and the information and perceptions that accompany market exchange. It also involves the organization of the processes that are linked to these flows: for example, the organization of low-wage production in Asia for the U.S. and European markets. Indeed, some economists define globalization in narrowly economic terms as "the transfer of technology and capital from high-wage to low-wage countries, and the resulting growth of labor-intensive Third World exports."[11] Economic flows, markets, and organization, as in multinational firms, all go together. In chapter 2, Jeffrey Frankel describes the current state of economic globalism.

—Military globalism refers to long-distance networks of interdependence in which force, and the threat or promise of force, are employed. A good example of military globalism is the "balance of terror" between the United States and the Soviet Union during the cold war. Their strategic interdependence was acute and well recognized. Not only did it produce world-straddling alliances, but either side could have used intercontinental missiles to destroy the other within thirty minutes. It was distinctive not because it was totally new, but because the scale and speed of the potential conflict arising from interdependence were so enormous. In chapter 3, Graham Allison explains how military and other forms of globalism are changing conceptions of security.

—Environmental globalism refers to the long distance transport of materials in the atmosphere or oceans or of biological substances such as pathogens or genetic materials that affect human health and well-being. Examples include the depletion of the stratospheric ozone layer as a result of ozone-depleting chemicals; human-induced global warming, insofar as it is occurring; the spread of the AIDs virus from central Africa around the world beginning at the end of the 1970s. As in the other forms of globalism, the transfer of information is important, both directly and through the movement of genetic material and indirectly as a result of inferences made on the basis of material flows. Some environmental globalism may be entirely natural—the earth has gone through periods of warming and cooling since before the human impact was significant—but much of the recent change has been induced by human activity, as William C. Clark describes in chapter 4.

—Social and cultural globalism involves movements of ideas, information, and images, and of people—who of course carry ideas and information with them. Examples include the movement of religions or the diffusion of scientific knowledge. An important facet of social globalism involves imitation of one society's practices and institutions by others: what some sociologists refer to as "isomorphism."[12] Often, however, social globalism has followed military and economic globalism. Ideas and information and people follow armies and economic flows, and in so doing, transform societies and markets. At its most profound level, social globalism affects the consciousness of individuals and their attitudes toward culture, politics, and personal identity. Indeed, as Neal M. Rosendorf describes in chapter 5, social and cultural globalism interacts with other types of globalism, since military and environmental, as well as economic, activity convey information and generate ideas, which may then flow across geographical and political boundaries. In the current era, as the growth of the Internet reduces costs and globalizes communications, the flow of ideas is increasing independent of other forms of globalization. Deborah Hurley and Viktor Mayer-Schoenberger explore the information dimensions of social globalism in chapter 6.

One could imagine other dimensions. For example, political globalism could refer to that subset of social globalism that refers to ideas and information about power and governance. It could be measured by imitation effect (for example, in constitutional arrangements or the number of democratic states) or by the diffusion of government policies, or of international regimes. Legal globalism could refer to the spread of legal practices and institutions to a variety of issues, including world trade and the criminalization of war crimes by heads of state. Globalization occurs in other dimensions as well—for instance, in science, entertainment, fashion, and language.

One obvious problem with considering all these aspects of globalism to be dimensions on a par with those we have listed is that when categories proliferate, they cease to be useful. To avoid such proliferation, therefore, we treat these dimensions of globalism as subsets of social and cultural globalism. Political globalism seems less a separate type than an aspect of any of our four dimensions. Almost all forms of globalization have political implications. For example, the World Trade Organization (WTO), Non-Proliferation Treaty (NPT), Montreal Convention, and United Nations Educational, Scientific, and Cultural Organization are responses to economic, military, environmental, and social globalization.

In the aftermath of Kosovo and East Timor, ideas about human rights and humanitarian interventions versus classical state sovereignty formulations were a central feature of the 1999 UN General Assembly. UN Secretary General Kofi Annan argued that in a global era, "The collective interest is the national interest," and South African President Thabo Mbeki stated that "the process of globalization necessarily redefines the concept and practice of national sovereignty." President Abdelaziz Bouteflika of Algeria, the head of the Organization of African Unity, replied that he did not deny the right of northern public opinion to denounce breaches of human rights, but "sovereignty is our final defense against the rules of an unequal world," and that "we [Africa] are not taking part in the decision-making process."[13] These were debates about the political implications of social and military globalization, rather than about political globalization as distinct from its social and military dimensions.

The division of globalism into separate dimensions is inevitably somewhat arbitrary. Nonetheless, it is useful for analysis, because changes in the various dimensions of globalization do not necessarily co-vary. One can sensibly say, for instance, that "economic globalization" took place between approximately 1850 and 1914, manifested in imperialism and in increasing trade and capital flows between politically independent countries; and that such globalization was largely reversed between 1914 and 1945. That is, economic globalism rose between 1850 and 1914 and fell between 1914 and 1945. However, military globalism rose to new heights during the two world wars, as did many aspects of social globalism. The worldwide influenza epidemic of 1918–19, which took 21 million lives, was propagated by the flows of soldiers around the world.[14] So did globalism decline or rise between 1914 and 1945? It depends on the dimension of globalism one is referring to. Without an adjective, general statements about globalism are often meaningless or misleading.

Thick Globalism: What's New?

When people speak colloquially about globalization, they typically refer to recent increases in globalism. Comments such as "globalization is fundamentally new" only make sense in this context but are nevertheless misleading. We prefer to speak of globalism as a phenomenon with ancient roots and of globalization as the process of increasing globalism, now or in the past.

The issue is not how old globalism is, but rather how "thin" or "thick" it is at any given time.[15] As an example of "thin globalization," the Silk Road provided an economic and cultural link between ancient Europe and Asia, but the route was plied by a small group of hardy traders, and the goods that were traded back and forth had a direct impact primarily on a small (and relatively elite) stratum of consumers along the road. In contrast, "thick" relations of globalization involve many relationships that are intensive as well as extensive: long-distance flows that are large and continuous, affecting the lives of many people. The operations of global financial markets today, for instance, affect people from Peoria to Penang. "Globalization" is *the process by which globalism becomes increasingly thick.*

Often, contemporary globalization is equated with Americanization, especially by non-Americans who resent American popular culture and the capitalism that accompanies it. In 1999, for example, some French farmers protecting "culinary sovereignty" attacked McDonald's restaurants.[16] Several dimensions of globalism are indeed dominated today by activities based in the United States, whether on Wall Street, in the Pentagon, in Cambridge, in Silicon Valley, or in Hollywood. If we think of the content of globalization being "uploaded" on the Internet, then "downloaded" elsewhere, more of this content is uploaded in the United States than anywhere else.[17] However, globalization long predates Hollywood and Bretton Woods. The spice trade and the intercontinental spread of Buddhism, Christianity, and Islam preceded by many centuries the discovery of America, much less the formation of the United States. In fact, the United States itself is a product of seventeenth- and eighteenth-century globalization. Japan's importation of German law a century ago, contemporary ties between Japan and Latin

American countries with significant Japanese-origin populations, and the lending by European banks to emerging markets in East Asia also constitute examples of globalization not focused on the United States. Hence, globalism is not intrinsically American, even if its current phase is heavily influenced by what happens in the United States.

Globalism today is America-centric, in that most of the impetus for the information revolution comes from the United States, and a large part of the content of global information networks is created in the United States. However, the ideas and information that enter global networks are downloaded in the context of national politics and local cultures, which act as selective filters and modifiers of what arrives. Political institutions are often more resistant to transnational transmission than popular culture. Although the Chinese students in Tiananmen Square in 1989 built a replica of the Statue of Liberty, China has emphatically not adopted U.S. political institutions. Nor is this new. In the nineteenth century, Meiji reformers in Japan were aware of Anglo-American ideas and institutions but deliberately turned to German models because they seemed more congenial.[18] For many countries today, as Frederick Schauer shows, Canadian constitutional practices, with their greater emphasis on duties, or German laws, restrictive of racially charged speech, are more congenial than those of the United States.[19] And Kamarck's chapter shows that the current wave of imitation of government reform started in Britain and New Zealand, not the United States.

The central position of the United States in global networks creates "soft power": the ability to get others to want what Americans want.[20] But the processes are in many respects reciprocal, rather than one way. Some U.S. practices are very attractive to other countries—honest regulation of drugs, as in the Food and Drug Administration (FDA); transparent securities laws and practices, limiting self-dealing, monitored by the Securities and Exchange Commission (SEC). U.S.-made standards are sometimes hard to avoid, as in the rules governing the Internet itself. But other U.S. standards and practices—from pounds and feet (rather than the metric system) to capital punishment, the right to bear arms, and absolute protection of free speech—have encountered resistance or even incomprehension. Soft power is a reality, but it does not accrue to the United States in all areas of life, nor is the United States the only country to possess it.

Is there anything about globalism today that is fundamentally different? Every era builds on others. Historians can always find precursors in the past for phenomena of the present, but contemporary globalization goes "faster, cheaper and deeper."[21] The degree of thickening of globalism is giving rise to increased density of networks, increased "institutional velocity," and increased transnational participation.

Economists use the term "network effects" to refer to situations in which a product becomes more valuable once many other people also use it. This is why the Internet is causing such rapid change.[22] Joseph Stiglitz, former chief economist of the World Bank, argues that a knowledge-based economy generates "powerful spillover effects, often spreading like fire and triggering further innovation and setting off chain reactions of new inventions. . . . But goods—as opposed to knowledge—do not always spread like fire."[23] Moreover, as interdependence and globalism have become thicker, the systemic relationships among different networks have become more important. There are more interconnections among the networks. As a result, "system effects" become more important.[24] Intensive economic interdependence affects social and environmental interdependence, and awareness of these connections in turn affects economic relationships. For instance, the expansion of trade can generate industrial activity in countries with low environmental standards, mobilizing environmental activists to carry their message to the newly industrializing but environmentally lax countries. The resulting activities may affect environmental interdependence (for instance, by reducing cross-boundary pollution) but may generate resentment in the newly industrializing country, affecting social and economic relations.

The extensivity of globalism means that the potential connections occur worldwide, sometimes with unpredictable results. Even if we thoroughly analyzed each individual strand of interdependence between two societies, we might well miss the synergistic effects of relationships between these linkages between societies.

Environmental globalism illustrates the point well. When scientists in the United States discovered chlorofluorocarbons (CFCs) in the 1920s, they and many others were delighted to have such efficient chemicals available for refrigeration (and other purposes) that were chemically inert, hence not subject to explosions and fires. Only in the 1970s was it suspected, and in the 1980s proved, that CFCs depleted the stratospheric ozone layer, which protects human beings against harmful ultraviolet rays. The environmental motto, "Everything is connected to everything else," warns us that there may be unanticipated effects of many human activities, from burning of carbon fuels (generating climate change) to genetically modifying crops grown for food.

As William C. Clark's chapter shows, environmental globalism has political, economic, and social consequences. Discoveries of the ozone-depleting properties of CFCs (and other chemicals) led to this issue being put on international agendas, intranational, international, and transnational controversies about it, and eventually a series of international agreements, beginning at Montreal in 1987, regulating the production and sale of such substances. These agreements entailed trade sanctions against violators, thus affecting economic globalism. They also raised people's awareness of ecological dangers, contributing to much greater transnational transmission of ideas and information (social globalism) about ecological processes affecting human beings.

Another illustration of network interconnections is provided by the impact, worldwide, of the financial crisis that began in Thailand in July 1997. Unexpectedly, what appeared first as an isolated banking and currency crisis in a small "emerging market" country, had severe global effects. It generated financial panic elsewhere in Asia, particularly in Korea and Indonesia; prompted emergency meetings at the highest level of world finance and huge "bail-out" packages orchestrated by the International Monetary Fund; and led to a widespread loss of confidence in emerging markets and the efficacy of international financial institutions. Before that contagious loss of confidence was stemmed, Russia had defaulted on its debt (in August 1998), and a huge U.S.-based hedge fund, Long-Term Capital Management, had to be rescued suddenly through a plan put together by the U.S. Federal Reserve. Even after recovery had begun, Brazil required a huge IMF loan, coupled with devaluation, to avoid financial collapse in January 1999.

The relative magnitude of foreign investment in 1997 was not unprecedented. Capital markets were by some measures more integrated at the beginning than at the end of the twentieth century. The net outflow of capital from Britain in the four decades before 1914 averaged 5 percent of gross domestic product, compared with 2 to 3 percent for rich countries today.[25] The fact that the financial crisis of 1997 was global in scale also had precursors: "Black Monday" on Wall Street in 1929 and the collapse of Austria's Credit Anstalt bank in 1930 triggered a worldwide financial crisis and depression. (Once again, globalism is not new.) Financial linkages among major financial centers have always been subject to the spread of crisis, as withdrawals from banks in one locale precipitate withdrawals elsewhere, as failures of banks in one jurisdiction lead to failures even of distant creditors. Nevertheless, despite the greatly increased financial sophistication of this era compared with the interwar period, the crisis was almost totally unanticipated by most economists, governments, and international financial institutions. The World Bank had recently published a report entitled "The Asian Miracle" (1993), and investment flows to Asia rose rapidly to a new peak in 1996 and remained high until the crisis hit. In December 1998 Federal Reserve Board Chairman Alan Greenspan said, "I have learned more about how this new international financial system works in the last twelve months than in the previous twenty years."[26] As David Held and others argue, sheer magnitude, complexity, and speed distinguish contemporary globalization from earlier periods.[27]

There are also interconnections with military globalism. In the context of superpower bipolarity, the end of the cold war represented military deglobalization. Distant disputes became less relevant to the balance of power. But the rise of social globalization had the opposite effect. Humanitarian concerns interacting with global communications led to dramatization of some conflicts and military interventions in places like Somalia, Bosnia, and Kosovo. At the same time, other remote conflicts such as Southern Sudan, which proved less accessible, were largely ignored. At the tactical level, the asymmetry of global military power and the interconnections among networks raise new options for warfare. For example, in devising a strategy to stand up to the United States, some Chinese officers are proposing terrorism, drug trafficking, environmental degradation, and computer virus propagation. They argue that the more complicated the combination—for example, terrorism plus a media war plus a financial war—the better the results. "From that perspective, 'Unrestricted War' marries the Chinese classic *The Art of War* by Sun Tzu, with modern military technology and economic globalization."[28]

The general point is that the increasing thickness of globalism—the density of networks of interdependence—is not just a difference in degree from the past. Thickness means that different relationships of interdependence intersect more deeply at more different points. Hence, effects of events in one geographical area, on one dimension, can have profound effects in other geographical areas, on other dimensions. As in scientific theories of "chaos," and in weather systems, small events in one place can have catalytic effects, so that their consequences later and elsewhere are vast.[29] Such systems are very difficult to understand, and their effects are therefore often unpredictable. Furthermore, when these are human systems, human beings are often hard at work trying to outwit others, to gain an economic, social, or military advantage precisely by acting in an unpredictable way. As a result, we should expect that globalism will be accompanied by pervasive uncertainty. There will be a continual competition between increased complexity, and uncertainty, on the one hand; and efforts by governments, market participants, and others to comprehend and manage these increasingly complex interconnected systems, on the other.

Globalization and Levels of Governance

By governance, we mean the processes and institutions, both formal and informal, that guide and restrain the collective activities of a group. Government is the subset that acts with authority and creates formal obligations. Governance need not necessarily be conducted exclusively by governments and the international organizations to which they delegate authority. Private firms, associations of firms, nongovernmental organizations (NGOs), and associations of NGOs all engage in it, often in association with governmental bodies, to create governance; sometimes without governmental authority.

Contrary to some prophetic views, the nation-state is not about to be replaced as the primary instrument of domestic and global governance. There is an extensive literature on the effects of globalism on domestic governance, which in our view reaches more nuanced conclusions (summarized below). Instead, we believe that the nation-state is being supplemented by other actors—private and third sector—in a more complex geography. The nation-state is the most important actor on the stage of global politics, but it is not the only important actor. If one thinks of social and political space in terms of a nine-cell matrix, more governance activities will occur outside the box represented by national capitals of nation-states (figure 1-1).

Not only is the geography of governance more complex, but so are its modalities at all three levels. As Lawrence Lessig argues, governance can be accomplished by law, norms, markets, and architecture. Taking a local example, one can slow traffic through a neighborhood by enforcing speed limits, posting "children at play" signs, charging for access, or building speed bumps in the roads. Lessig describes an Internet world in which governance is shifting from law made by governments to architecture created by companies. "Effective regulation then shifts from lawmakers to code writers."[30] At the same time, private firms press governments for favorable

Figure 1-1. *Governance Activities*

	Private	Governmental	Third sector
Supranational	TNCs	IGOs	NGOs
National	Firms	Central	Nonprofits
Subnational	Local	Local	Local

legal regimes domestically and internationally, as do actors from the third sector. The result is not the obsolescence of the nation-state but its transformation and the creation of politics in new contested spaces.

Many writers in talking about the governance of globalism use what Hedley Bull referred to as the "domestic analogy."[31] It is commonplace for people to think of global governance as global government, because the domestic analogy is so familiar. Michael Sandel, for instance, argues that just as the nationalization of the American economy in the nineteenth century led to the nationalization of American government in the Progressive era, globalization of the world economy should lead to world government.[32] But the structure of federalism already existed in the United States, and it rested on a common language and political culture. (And even that did not prevent a bloody civil war in the middle of the century.)

Another example is the UN World Development Report, which portrays global governance in terms of strengthening UN institutions. It calls, for example, for a bicameral General Assembly, an investment trust that will redistribute the proceeds of taxes on global transactions, and a global central bank.[33] But it is state structures, and the loyalty of people to particular states, that enable states to create connections among themselves, handle issues of interdependence, and resist amalgamation, even if it might seem justified on purely functional grounds. Hence, world government during our lifetimes seems highly unlikely, at least in the absence of an overwhelming global threat that could only be dealt with in a unified way. In the absence of such a threat, it seems highly unlikely that peoples in some two hundred states will be willing to act on the domestic analogy for well into the new century. World government might or might not be desirable—we think it could have many adverse consequences—but in any event, it is hardly likely to be feasible.

Although we think world government is infeasible, we are not complacent about the effects of globalization without some coherent means of governance. Karl Polanyi made a powerful argument that the inability of polities to cope with the disruptive effects of nineteenth century globalization helped cause the great disturbances of the twentieth century—communism and fascism.[34] Along similar lines, Jeffrey Williamson has more recently documented how the "late nineteenth-century globalization backlash made a powerful contribution to interwar deglobalization."[35] Without regulation—or what was traditionally known as "protection"—personal insecurity for many individuals can become intolerable. As Polanyi, with his dramatic flair, put it, "To allow the market mechanism to be sole director of the fate of human beings and their natural environment . . . would result in the demolition of society."[36]

If world government is unfeasible and laissez-faire a recipe for a backlash, we need to search for an intermediate solution: a set of practices for governance that improve coordination and create safety valves for political and social pressures, consistent with the maintenance of nation-states as the fundamental form of political organization. Such arrangements will, we argue, involve a heterogeneous array of agents—from the private sector and the third sector as well as from governments. And the governmental agents will not necessarily be operating on orders from the "top levels" of governments. The efficacy of these agents will depend on the networks in which they are embedded and their positions in those networks. And no hierarchy is likely to be acceptable or effective in governing networks.

One could refer very generally to the governance structures we envisage as "networked minimalism." Networked—because globalism is best characterized as networked, rather than as a set of hierarchies. Minimal—because governance at the global level will only be acceptable if it does not supersede national governance and if its intrusions into the autonomy of states and communities are clearly justified in terms of cooperative results.

To speak of "networked minimalism" is, of course, not to solve the problems of global governance but merely to point toward a generic response to them. In particular, such a phrase begs the question of accountability, which is crucial to democratic legitimacy.

Globalization and Domestic Governance

The literature on the effect of globalism on governance is extensive. The most persuasive work, it seems to us, converges on a number of general conclusions that suggest that nation-states will continue to be important; indeed, that the internal structures of states will be crucial in their ability to adapt to globalization and its effects on them.

First, it is important not to overstate the extent of the change in the near future. As Frankel and Rodrik point out, global economic integration has a long way to go. From a strictly economic point of view, this can be considered "inefficiency." But from a political-economy perspective, it might be called a "useful inefficiency" that provides a buffer for domestic political differences while allowing openness to the global economy. With time and market integration, this useful inefficiency will be eroded. National political systems have strong effects that are not easily erased by technology. For example, John Helliwell's studies show that even in North America, national boundaries have a powerful effect on economic activity. Toronto trades ten times as much with Vancouver as it does with Seattle. Electronic commerce is burgeoning, but is still a small fraction of the total even in the United States. Geoffrey Garrett points out that despite talk of vanishing policy autonomy, "Globalization has not prompted a pervasive policy race to the neoliberal bottom among the OECD countries, nor have governments that have persisted with interventionist policies invariably been hamstrung by damaging capital flight."[37]

Second, although globalization may have powerful impacts on distributional politics and inequality, these impacts are not as clear with respect to contemporary globalization as they are, in retrospect, for the nineteenth century. Universal propositions about rising inequality and "the poor getting poorer" are too simple. First, one must distinguish between domestic and international inequality. In general, from the Heckscher-Ohlin theorem, we should expect increasing inequality in rich countries (capital and high-skill labor, the abundant factors, should benefit at the expense of unskilled labor), but we should expect, at least to some degree, increasing equality—at least as far as labor employed in the market sector is concerned—in developing countries. As Grindle's chapter shows, reality may be more complicated than theory—and the nature of the political system and institutional weakness may be decisive in developing countries; but the point is, our baseline economic expectations should be different in rich and poor countries.

In economic terms, low-priced labor in poorer countries benefits from trade and migration; low-priced labor in richer ones suffers. This was certainly true in the late nineteenth century, given the magnitude of migration. Jeffrey Williamson concludes that "the forces of late nineteenth-century convergence included commodity price convergence and trade expansion, technological catch-up, and human-capital accumulation, but mass migration was clearly the central force."[38] In some relationships—such as that between Britain and the United States—the Heckscher-Ohlin effect was significant; but in others, it was not very important: "Heckscher and Ohlin may have gotten the sign right, but they were not very relevant when it came to magnitudes."[39]

Contemporary globalization is driven so much less by labor migration than in the nineteenth century that the contemporary implications of Williamson's argument are ambiguous. Globalization in the form of trade between rich and poor countries is likely to increase income inequality in rich countries, as Heckscher and Ohlin would have predicted.[40] However, in the nineteenth century, capital movements had the opposite effect, since they went largely to high-wage countries with unexploited natural resources.[41] The United States is a huge capital-importer now, despite being a high-wage country. So on an international basis, this form of globalization could be creating divergence rather than convergence. Migration, which generates convergence, is significant now but not nearly as important as it was in the nineteenth century.[42] And other potential causes of rising inequality exist in rich countries—technology and the changing composition of the labor force in particular. Frankel's chapter reports common estimates that trade may account for between 5 and 33 percent of the increase in wage gaps. We are not qualified to sort out these issues; but it is worth noting that such estimates in the analytical economic literature do not prevent "globalization," writ large, from bearing political blame for increasing income inequality. Even if skill-biased technological change is the primary cause of the increase in income inequality in rich countries during the past three decades, globalization is going to be politically contentious.[43]

Third, the impact of globalization on the state varies substantially by political-economic system.[44] One way of thinking about these issues is in terms of "production systems." In market systems, globalization leads to income inequality as market prices are bid up for skilled labor, and as the division of labor expands. In social democratic welfare states, transfer payments limit income inequality, but unemployment results.[45] In Japanese-style systems, globalization puts pressure on the lifetime employment system and other provisions for providing welfare through the corporation rather than the state. The overall point is that globalization interacts with domestic politics; it is neither true that globalization produces the same effects everywhere (much less destroys the welfare state, or destroys state power)[46], nor that globalization is irrelevant. Multiple feasible paths may be taken to deal with the effects of globalization, depending on history, structures, attitudes—the notion of a single "golden straitjacket" is not viable.

Does globalism weaken state institutions? The answers vary by the type of state and the type of function. It is true that market constraints on states are greater than three decades ago, but the effects vary greatly. France, Germany, and Sweden feel market pressures, but the core of their welfare state remains strong. Some less developed countries, however, feel market pressures but do not have strong safety nets or governmental institutions to begin with. Transnational mobility of capital and skilled labor undercut powers of taxation. Transnational communications and the Internet make it more difficult and costly for authoritarian police to control citizens. In some instances, differential development may stimulate ethnic tensions that can overwhelm the institutions of the state. And as Grindle points out, some less developed countries may have such weak institutions (for whatever historical and cultural reasons) that their leaders are unable to cope with the new challenges posed by globalization. For other developing countries, however, economic globalism has strengthened state institutions by creating a more robust economic base—witness the development of Singapore, Malaysia, or Korea. And as Saich's chapter shows, China is a special case. Linda Weiss argues that there is more of a transformation of state functions than a weakening of the state.[47] Our major conclusion about how globalism affects domestic governance is one of caution. Certainly, strong effects occur, but generalizations about the effect of globalism on the nation-state vary with the size, power, and domestic political culture of the states involved.

From the perspective of governance, what is striking about the last half of the twentieth century is the relative *effectiveness* of efforts by states to respond to globalization. The welfare state was a major step. Whether Polanyi's narrative about the inability of polities to cope with the disruptive effects of nineteenth-century globalization is correct or not, such views were widely held. After World War II, a compromise was struck in rich countries that Ruggie has called "embedded liberalism."[48] The price of an open economy was a social safety net. Rodrik has shown that openness and the welfare state are highly correlated. Coupled with the welfare state was the development of international regimes in areas such as finance and trade, designed to promote cooperation among states. The result in the last half of the twentieth century was a remarkable period in which economic growth was remarkably strong, despite periods of recession, and in which many economies became progressively more open to others' products and capital flows.

The big question is whether the coming era of economic globalization is different, because of changes in the degree of interdependence leading to fundamental transformations; or because of the information revolution.[49] In the view of Kenneth Waltz, the more things change, the more they remain the same. "Challenges at home and abroad test the mettle of states. Some states fail, and other states pass the tests nicely. In modern times, enough states always make it to keep the international system going as a system of states. The challenges vary; states endure."[50] In sharp contrast, some writers declare that as an externally sovereign actor, the state "will become a thing of the past."[51] And prophets of the Information Age argue that global cyberspace is replacing territorial space and making national governmental controls impossible.

When rapid, fundamental change is mixed with stability, it is hard to draw the balance easily. To say that states endure is to overlook the emergence of other significant actors and the constraints that they may impose on state autonomy. But to say that "everything is different" overlooks the fact that modern states are resilient and resourceful. While it is true that boundaries are becoming more porous, and some controls more problematic, the future of domestic governance is not so simple. The Internet was initially structured by hackers with a libertarian antigovernment culture, but commerce is rapidly changing the net. Commercial procedures for authentication of credentials are creating a framework that allows private regulation, and the presence of large commercial entities provides targets for an overlay of public regulation.[52]

As in the economic literature on globalism and the nation-state, the answer is unlikely to be that "everything is changed," or that nothing is. The question may be less one of erosion or maintenance of authority than of changes in how we think about space. While the messages of global electronic commerce cross borders freely, the processes by which they are produced often involve a reconfiguration of physical space. Sassen refers to a "relocation of politics" from national capitals to global cities constituting a "new economic geography of centrality, one that cuts across national boundaries and across the old North-South divide."[53]

Our expectation is that governance will remain centered in the nation-state. State power will remain crucially important, as will the distribution of power among states. Whether the United States remains dominant, or is successfully challenged by others, will fundamentally affect globalism and its governance. However, the image of "the state" may become increasingly misleading as agencies of states are linked in networks to private and third sector actors. Transgovernmental networks will become more important, as will transnational relations of all kinds.[54] As Brown and others describe in their chapter, mixed coalitions will occur as parts of governments and NGOs may ally against other parts of governments allied with transnational corporations. Global networks will become more complex. As Coglianese, Hurley, and Mayer-Schoenberger argue, governance will require extensive networked cooperation, and hierarchical rules are likely to become less effective.

The Governance of Globalism: Regimes, Networks, Norms

Global governance is not the same as world government, and the domestic analogy is not adequate. The world system of the twenty-first century is not merely a system of unitary states interacting with one another through diplomacy, public international law, and international organizations. In that model, states as agents interact, constituting an international system.[55] But this model's focus on the reified unitary state fails sufficiently to emphasize two other essential elements of the contemporary world system: *networks* among agents, and *norms*—standards of expected behavior—that are widely accepted among agents. We can think of this international system as the *skeleton* of the contemporary world system—essential to the functioning of the whole system—but not as a whole system. It therefore is a helpful simplified model with which we can to begin is to ask about global governance, although it by no means provides us with the basis for a comprehensive account.

Governments' Responses to Problems of Governance

A worthwhile first cut at the problem is to see it as a response to problems and opportunities faced by states. States devise international institutions to facilitate cooperation, which they seek to achieve their own purposes. Broadly speaking, this is a rational-functional account, in the sense that anticipation of effects explains.[56] Interests within states are affected by the actions of other states and actors, and therefore a "demand for international regimes" develops.[57] That is, governments become willing to exchange some of their own legal freedom of action to have some influence on the actions of these other actors. Whether this involves "giving up sovereignty" is a legal issue that depends on the arrangement made. Besides purely domestic interests, transnational actors (corporations, NGOs) develop an interest in making transborder transactions more predictable and press for arrangements that do so. This functional explanation plausibly accounts for the existence of the hundreds of intergovernmental organizations and regimes that govern issues ranging from fur seals to world trade. It may also help to explain efforts to govern the international use of force stretching from the Hague peace treaties at the end of the nineteenth century through the League of Nations to the UN Charter and Security Council.

Only some of these governance patterns are global, and none of them corresponds to the image of "world government" promoted by world federalists in the past and derided by governments and academic experts alike during the past several decades. There are examples of formal global governance through multilateral institutions, in which states create international regimes and cede some power to intergovernmental organizations to govern specified issues. Such delegation to broadly defined institutions takes place for trade policy (in the World Trade Organization) and financial and development policy (notably, the International Monetary Fund [IMF] and the World Bank). More limited delegation is evident in environmental policy, for example, to institutions governing chemicals depleting the ozone layer or to fisheries outside the territorial zones of states. The global role of international institutions dedicated to protection of human rights is increasing—a trend that will be accentuated if the International Criminal Court becomes a reality. At the global level, what we find is not world government but the existence of regimes of norms, rules, and institutions that govern a surprisingly large number of issues in world politics. The islands of governance are more densely concentrated among developed states, but they often have global extension.

Importantly, governments' responses to increases in globalism need not take the form of initiating or supporting multilateral regimes on a global level. Indeed, three other responses are particularly evident:

—Unilateral. Some unilateral responses are isolationist and protection-ist with the effect of diminishing globalism. Others' unilateral actions may increase global governance. Particularly interesting is the acceptance by states of the standards developed by others. This process ranges on a scale from voluntary to highly coercive. Unilateral acceptance of common stan-dards can be highly voluntary—for example, when states and firms outside the United States learned how to conform to Y2K standards created (at greater cost) in the United States, or when they copy others' political arrangements to solve domestic problems that they have themselves iden-tified. Adoption of common standards can be partially voluntary, as when states adopt generally accepted accounting principles, make their books more transparent, or establish regulatory agencies that imitate those of other countries.[58] In this case, the degree of voluntariness is limited by the fact that foreign investment or other benefits might be withheld by pow-erful external actors if such actions were not taken. Further toward the coercive end of the continuum are such phenomena as IMF conditionality, linked closely to acceptance of macroeconomic views that correspond to those of the "Washington consensus." Finally, powerful states may simply impose standards on the weak as Britain did with antislavery in the nine-teenth century.[59]

—Where broad consensus is difficult or too costly, states may seek to construct bilateral or "minilateral" regimes with a few like-minded part-ners.[60] Hundreds of bilateral tax treaties exist. The Basle agreements on banking adequacy provide another example. One consequence of such a strategy may be to change the status quo point, therefore making nonpar-ticipants worse off, and perhaps forcing them to join arrangements that are worse than the original status quo.[61]

—Regional. States may see themselves as better able to cope with global forces if they form regional groupings. Within a region, mutual recognition of one another's laws and policies may promote cooperation without exten-sive harmonization of laws. The recent strengthening of the European Union (EU) provides the principal example of such regionalism.

Our focus is on multilateral cooperation at the global level, although much that we say is relevant to "minilateral" or regional regimes. We believe that the patterns of multilateral cooperation that predominated in the second half of the twentieth century are changing and will have to change further if multilateral cooperation is to be successful in a rapidly globalizing world. To make this argument, however, we need first to describe two important sets of changes that are occurring—in the agents active on issues of international and transnational public policy and in the norms that are thought relevant to multilateral cooperation.

New Agents in Networks

The actors in world politics cannot simply be conceived of as states. Private firms, NGOs, and subunits of governments can all play independent or quasi-independent roles. These agents help to create or exacerbate the dilemmas of diffusion of power, transparency, and deadlock, afflicting international organizations. But they may also play a crucial role in governance. When they do, they operate as parts of networks.

Because the rapidly declining cost of communication is reducing the barriers to entry, other actors are becoming more involved in many governance arrangements that are not controlled by executives or legislatures of states. In other words, global governance involves both private sector and "third sector," or NGOs, actors as well as governments:

TRANSNATIONAL CORPORATE NETWORKS. Transnational corporations respond to the absence of governance by providing their own governance forms. Airlines and computer firms form alliances with one another to gain competitive advantages. Other examples include commodity chains, producer driven or buyer driven.[62] Many crucial standard-setting exercises are private. In the chemical industry, "responsible care" standards, for example, are designed to head off national-level or international-level governance.[63] In cyberspace, commercially crafted codes have a powerful impact on issues such as privacy, property rights, and copyright law. Private rules about how an offer is accepted "may or may not be consistent with the contract rules of a particular jurisdiction. . . . Local governments lose control over the rules and the effective rule-maker shifts to cyber space."[64]

NGOs. In the last decade of the twentieth century, the number of international NGOs grew from 6,000 to 26,000, ranging in size from the Worldwide Fund for Nature with 5 million members to tiny network organizations. As described in the chapter by L. David Brown and others, they provide services, mobilize political action, and provide information and analysis. As a group, they provide more aid than the whole UN system. Besides providing services, others play lobbying and mobilization roles. About 1,500 NGOs signed an anti-WTO protest declaration that was circulated online in 1999, including groups from both rich and poor countries. Technically oriented groups offer sophisticated analysis and information that affected the verification system of the Chemical Weapons Treaty and the negotiations over global climate change.[65] In the eyes of some analysts, the real losers in this power shift are less obviously governments than intergovernmental institutions that lack political leverage over policymakers and whose public image tends to be faceless and technocratic.

The relations of the three sectors in governance should not be analyzed solely in isolation, much less in zero sum terms. State responses to the forces of globalism are supplemented by private and nongovernmental actors, some of which compete and some of which complement state actions. Transnational corporations may replace legislative functions of states. For example, when Nike or Mattel creates codes of conduct governing their subcontractors in less developed countries, they may be imposing codes that would not have passed the legislatures of Honduras or India (and which those governments would have opposed at the WTO).

Similarly, companies may bypass the judicial branch of host governments because they regard them as slow or corrupt. More and more often commercial contracts are written with provisions for commercial arbitration to keep them out of national courts. The International Chamber of Commerce plays a large role. Some governments, however, are pleased when private rating agencies like Moody's or Standard and Poor's create ratings that lead foreign corporations to follow standards and procedures not necessarily in domestic law.

Some governments and parts of governments may also be pleased when NGOs influence agenda setting and press other governments for action. An important example is provided by the succession of UN-sponsored international conferences on women and issues, such as birth control, of particular interest to women. NGOs have taken the lead in promoting this agenda, but governments and the United Nations have also been active.[66] Or consider the effects of Transparency International in exposing corruption. In other instances, NGOs form coalitions with some governments against others: witness the landmine treaty in which Canada drew support against the United States. Some NGOs participate regularly in sessions of some intergovernmental organization such as the Organization for Economic Cooperation and Development or the World Bank. In some instances, such as human rights and refugees, they supply crucial information to governments as well as help provide services. Foundations play a similar role.

Trisectoral partnerships are also becoming more explicit.[67] Transnational corporations and NGOs sometimes work together and sometimes with

IGOs to provide services. Citibank uses local NGOs to provide micro-finance in Bangladesh. In 1998 Kofi Annan proposed a global compact in which corporations joined with the United Nations to support development and improved labor standards. The International Chamber of Commerce has offered its support. Other innovations include the World Commission on Dams, which consists of four commissioners from governments, four from private industry, and four from NGOs. And in the governance of Internet domain names, the U.S. government helped create ICANN, an NGO that supplements but also works with private companies. The government turned to the NGO form because it feared that a formal IGO would be too slow and cumbersome in dealing with rapidly developing issues related to Internet domain names.

In short, areas of intergovernmental coordination exist in a competitive and cooperative relationship with private and third sector actors that provide some governance for several issues in global politics. Notably, in many of these arrangements the quasi-judicial capabilities and "soft legislative" capabilities, as exemplified in the development of soft law and norms, have moved ahead much faster than "hard legislative" or executive capabilities. The formal, obligatory rules of IGOs are established by states, but the IGOs themselves are becoming more important interpreters of their own rules, and often the operational rules go well beyond those that are formally obligatory. Meanwhile, the formal governance structures of IGOs remain quite weak and are often beset by deadlock.

Norms

Changes in agency are an important part of contemporary changes in governance of global issues. NGOs and private sector actors, operating in various competing networks, have become increasingly important. But there is something more. As constructivist theorists point out, changing ideas frame and channel interests. Convergence on knowledge, norms, and beliefs is a prelude to convergence on institutions and processes of governance.[68] Transnational communications, coupled with political democracy, promote the development of global norms as a backdrop against which the islands of governance stand out.

Changes in norms can be seen as part of the development of an incipient civil society. It is not entirely new. Nineteenth-century antislavery movements involved transnational ideas as well as domestic politics.[69] The spread of science is another early example. Examples in the twentieth century include the development of human rights ideology in the second half of the century. As Sassen points out, "Self determination is no longer enough to legitimate a state; respect for international human rights codes is also a factor."[70] Since the end of the cold war, the broad acceptance of liberal market forces is another example. In sharp contrast to the 1970s demands for a statist "new international economic order," when a newly created Group of 20 rich and poor countries met in 1999, the discussion was over details, not the desirability, of a neoliberal financial system.[71] Pressures on traditional territorial sovereignty in the security area derive largely from human rights and humanitarian norms (at odds with traditional sovereignty norms), and they remain hotly contested. After Secretary General Annan's September 1999 speech to the General Assembly, the head of the Organization for African Unity expressed alarm that a right to humanitarian intervention threatened "our final defence against the rules of an unequal world," and in the United States a former official predicted "war, at least with the Republican Party."[72]

Soft power rests on the attractiveness of some actors, and their principles, to others. Soft power is therefore relative to norms: it is those actors who conform to widely admired norms that will gain influence as a result. It is hard to pinpoint specific changes in domestic law and practice that are directly affected by changes in norms. However, clearly, in areas such as human rights and the role of sovereignty, global norms are changing at a dramatic pace. Sovereignty is up for grabs in a way that has not been the case since the seventeenth century. The fact that it was criticized by Secretary General Annan—the leader of an intergovernmental organization whose Charter rests solidly on the Westphalian conception of sovereignty—reveals striking evidence of normative change.

Norms do not operate automatically but through the activities of agents in networks. Even binding international law does not meet with automatic and universal compliance. Even less automatic are the effects of soft law. As Tony Saich shows in his chapter China may have signed the International Convention on the Protection of Civil and Political Rights, hoping to avoid serious internal consequences, just as the Soviet Union signed onto "Basket Three" of the Helsinki Convention in 1975. Whether these norms will actually change policies, or undermine the legitimacy of regimes, depends on how agents operate: for instance, on the "boomerang effects" discussed by Keck and Sikkink.[73]

To understand global governance for the twenty-first century, we will have to go well beyond understanding multilateral cooperation among states. We will have to understand how agents, in networks—including agents that are organizationally parts of governments as well as those who are not—interact in the context of rapidly changing norms. Governance is likely to be fragmented and heterogeneous. Whatever else it is, it is unlikely to be based on the domestic analogy.

The Club Model of Multilateral Cooperation: At Risk

Multilateral cooperation has been remarkably extensive, indeed unprecedented, in the latter half of the twentieth century. Beginning with the Bretton Woods conference of 1944, key regimes for governance have operated like "clubs." Cabinet ministers or the equivalent who were working on the same issues, initially from a relatively small number of relatively rich countries, got together to make rules. Trade ministers dominated GATT; finance ministers ran the IMF; defense and foreign ministers met at NATO; central bankers at the Bank for International Settlements. They negotiated in secret, then reported their agreements to national legislatures and publics. It was difficult for outsiders to understand the actual positions taken in negotiations, how firmly they were held, and the bargaining dynamics that produced compromises. Within the framework of these procedures, as Michael Zurn comments, "The opportunity of strategic manipulation of information is wide open to decision-makers."[74]

From the perspective of multilateral cooperation, this club model can be judged a great success. The world seems more peaceful, more prosperous, and perhaps even environmentally somewhat cleaner than it would have been without such cooperation. However, the very success of multilateral cooperation has generated increased interdependence—now in the form of "globalization"—that threatens to undermine it. Technology and market growth are reducing technological and economic barriers between countries and between issues, thus eroding the politically useful inefficiency described above. The organizations formerly run by clubs of rich country ministers have expanded their memberships to include many developing countries, which demand participation. Their leaders are often ambivalent about the regimes, suspicious about the implications of rich country leadership, and resentful of the existence of club rules, made by the rich, that they did not help to establish. Furthermore, globalization has generated a proliferation of non-state agents, including business firms, business associations, labor unions, and NGOs, all clamoring to make their voices heard. The Seattle meetings of the WTO, in November 1999, indicated the difficulties that a combination of heterogeneous state objectives and activism by NGOs can create for international trade negotiations. Diffusing power increases legitimacy but makes it harder to make any clear decisions. As Harlan Cleveland once put it, how do you get everyone into the act and still get action?

At the same time, international institutions have faced increasing demands for accountability, which implies transparency. Here the source of the pressure is not increases in membership and a corresponding diffusion of capabilities but rather the incursion of domestic norms of democratic accountability into the international arena. A large and growing literature argues that international institutions do not meet the procedural standards of democracy, particularly for transparency, as a necessary condition for accountability.[75] Some of this literature begs the question of to whom accountability is owed, and the degree to which accountability and transparency are indirect in some domestic democratic arrangements—witness the Supreme Court and the Federal Reserve in the United States. Nonetheless, even though international organizations are ultimately accountable to (mostly) democratically elected member governments, the international bureaucrats are more remote than national bureaucracies. The chain of connection to elections is more indirect. Moreover, delegates to such institutions, though instructed by and accountable to elected officials in democracies, often act in the privacy of the clubs built around their issues and related institutions. Quite naturally, as such clubs control more important resources and values, demands for transparency and more direct participation increase. Europeans, many of whom see their institutions evolving toward a domestic model, have taken the lead in the debate on transparency, accountability, and the "democratic deficit," and their chief target has been the European Union.

The situation with global regimes is more problematic because they are more remote from the domestic analogy than is the European Union. The WTO, for example, has been a recent target of criticisms that it is undemocratic. Yet on a first approximation, it conforms with democratic principles relatively well. The secretariat is small and weak. The WTO is highly responsive to the (mostly) elected governments of its member states. Furthermore, it defers to them. Indeed, its dispute settlement procedures provide space for national democratic processes while still protecting the system of world trade. If pressures within a democracy cause a country to derogate from its agreements, a WTO panel can authorize compensation for others rather than see a tit-for-tat downward spiral of retaliation. It is like a fuse in the electrical system of a house. Better the lights go out than the house burns down. Better to make some concessions to the domestic politics of trade than to see a downward spiral of tit-for-tat retaliation that makes everyone worse off as in the 1930s.

Yet the WTO notably lacks transparency and has therefore been charged with violating democratic accountability. Again, the question is account-ability to whom? Trade officials and their elected superiors may know what is happening and be held accountable for what happens in the WTO, but officials and groups based in issues such as labor and the environment are demanding more transparency and participation. Charges of unaccount-ability and lack of democracy are instruments used to pry open access to— or in some cases to destroy—the club from which they have been excluded in the past.

IGOs can move incrementally and can interpret their mandates—inso-far as their secretariats and leading states can build alliances with crucial private sector and third sector actors. But they cannot make large formal moves forward in the absence of support either from a broad consensus about their proper purposes or from political institutions that can give them definitive guidance, based on a wide expression of social views. As a result of the constraints and opportunities that they face, international organizations, like the WTO, tend to be dominated by small networks of professionals who can modify their informal rules and practices and some-times develop a body of case law. The club model helps to overcome dead-lock that accompanies the diffusion of power. What is missing? The legit-imating activity of broadly based politicians speaking directly to domestic publics. This may have mattered less in the past when issues were less linked, and accountability of trade ministers to parliaments was sufficient to provide legitimacy. But with the linkage of issues, there is a need for the involvement of politicians who can link specific organizations and policies with a broader range of public issues through electoral accountability. In that sense, some global institutions are accused of developing a "democra-tic deficit" that could become a source of political weakness.

It is not easy to fix this type of "democratic deficit," in part because it is difficult to identify the political community that is relevant for direct par-ticipation, and in part because the functional club model has been the basis for effective international cooperation over the last half century. Indeed, a *lack of transparency to functional outsiders,* under the old club model, was a key to political efficacy. Protected by lack of transparency, ministers could make package deals that were difficult to disaggregate or even sometimes to understand. For instance, after the U.S. Congress deconstructed the trade agreements made during the Kennedy Round (1967), implementing unilateral modifications to bargains that had been reached, America's trade partners demanded modifications in internal U.S. practices as a condition for the next trade round. The political response in the United States was a "fast-track" procedure, agreed to by Congress, that limited its power to pick apart agreements. In effect, Congress agreed to "tie itself to the mast," as it sailed past specific protectionist sirens. It agreed to immunize international bargains from disaggregation in return for European, Japanese, and Canadian willingness to negotiate further reductions in trade barriers. Cooperation on international trade benefited, but labor and environmentalist interests whose power was reduced by the practice have reacted strongly against it and the associated international institution.

A fundamental problem of multilateral cooperation and democratic governance is how to increase transparency and accountability without subjecting all deals to deconstruction and unwinding. The mixed quality of contemporary social globalization makes such governance particularly difficult now. In one sense, social globalization has increased dramatically during the past decade. As discussed below, the creation of the Internet has coincided with an apparent fourfold increase in the number of NGOs. That is, *transnational social activity* is increasing dramatically. However, as Pippa Norris shows in her chapter, another dimension of potential social globalization—*collective identity*, or solidarity—remains at negligible levels, although it can be argued that a weak sense of identity is developing in the OECD and in the European Union. Lower transaction costs, coupled with a lack of a sense of political community or authoritative political institutions, will make it easier to pick packages apart than to put them together.

These problems for interstate cooperation are accentuated when states seek to deal with relationships across issue-areas, defined as clusters of issues, such as those relating to trade. As described above, globalization is increasing the density and interaction among networks. The islands of governance can no longer be kept isolated. As trade becomes more important, for instance, it has more implications for labor standards or the natural environment. It is also a subject of higher levels of social globalism: more awareness and more potential mobilization, as in the Seattle WTO meetings. Among issue-areas, globalization is producing increased real connections. But at the level of governance, there is little linkage among issue-areas. Overarching bodies such as the United Nations are weak. The International Labor Organization sets labor standards but lacks effective sanctions. For that reason, rich country trade unions want labor standards dealt with in the WTO, and many poor countries such as India resist it. Nothing plays the integrative role that occurs within well-ordered nation-states.

It might appear as if intergovernmental deadlock would lead to a stalemate in the current system of disaggregated global governance; and in the wake of the failure of the Seattle WTO meetings, various alarms to this effect have been sounded. Indeed, it does seem that the post-1945 model of cooperation through intergovernmental regimes is under serious pressure. Traditionally, international regimes have been constructed, within the complex system of the world political economies, as "decomposable hierarchies."[76] The parallel is with the nation-state as a hierarchy, so that individuals within it only interact politically through their governments. In this model—characteristic of the second half of the twentieth century, at least in formal terms—international regimes, with particular states as members, were established to govern "issue-areas." Some of these regimes were open to universal membership; others were selective or required meeting a set of standards imposed by the original participants. These regimes, thus defined by membership and issues, were "decomposable" from the rest of the system. Their members constructed rules—either in the form of traditional international law or as sets of established but less obligatory practices known as "soft law"—to govern their relationships within the issue-area. This model of separate clubs worked well, but globalization now generates so many linkages among issues that it raises challenges to the decomposition of issue-areas. One way to see the problem posed by globalization is that the hierarchies—both the national governments and established international regimes—are becoming less "decomposable," more penetrable, less hierarchic. It is more difficult to divide a globalized world political economy into decomposable hierarchies on the basis of states and issue-areas as the units.

The foregoing review has identified four key problems that threaten the club model of multilateral cooperation that has worked relatively well for the past half century. The number and heterogeneity of states in the system have increased severalfold. New entities—particularly business firms and associations, labor unions, and NGOs—have become more active participants in the multilateral policy process. Democratic societies demand accountability and transparency, and these demands are often based on a domestic analogy that conflicts with club practices. But most important, increasingly close linkages among issue-areas pose difficulties for international regimes organized by issue-area. It becomes harder to maintain the grounds for exclusion of some outsiders from the club. New strategies will be needed to supplement the old club model if multilateral cooperation is to thrive in the twenty-first century.

These strategies will have to be consistent with the new global politics, in which IGOs will have to share power with the private sector and with NGOs. Agents will be connected to one another in networks and will work through a variety of competing and cooperating coalitions, but none of the components will be subordinate to another. We should not see these agents, networks and organizations as in opposition to unitary states: on the contrary, they will participate in transnational-transgovernmental networks with governmental officials, often pitted against other transnational-transgovernmental networks with different purposes.[77] Mixed or trisectoral coalitions are becoming more common in world politics. But global politics is unlikely to be dominated by multilateral intergovernmental cooperation alone. Seen from a transgovernmental perspective, the WTO is a club of trade ministers working with rules that have served well in that issue-area. But it becomes more problematic when one considers issue linkages, the "trade and . . ." issues. Environment and labor ministers, for example, do not have a seat at the table. In other words, some relevant publics have no direct voice—only an indirect voice through national legislatures and executives. Thus the demonstrations at Seattle, incoherent and self-interested though they were, had a point. The participants wanted more direct access to the arena where their interests were being affected. In principle, this could be solved by linkages among UN organizations—UNEP and ILO—but they do not have similar strength. And even if they did, issues of accountability would be raised, since effective decisionmaking would still be distant from democratic legislatures.

Some cooperation with NGOs might help to alleviate the concern about accountability, although careful choices of NGO and roles would be important to preserve the effectiveness of the IGO. For example, some NGOs might be invited not to participate directly in trade negotiations, but they could be given observer status at WTO Council meetings where rules are discussed or given the right to file amicus briefs in dispute settlement cases.[78] The World Bank has been relatively successful in co-opting NGOs. More than seventy NGO specialists (mostly from technically proficient organizations) work in Bank field offices. "From environmental policy to debt relief, NGOs are at the center of World Bank policy. . . . The new World Bank is more transparent, but is also beholden to a new set of special interests."[79] Environmental NGOs have played effective roles at UN conferences. Whether this would work for other organizations is an open question. The democratic legitimacy of NGOs is not established simply by their claims to be part of "civil society." Obviously, the legitimacy of favored NGOs could be called into question by co-optation; and excluded NGOs are likely to criticize those that are included for "selling out." Political battles among NGOs will limit a co-optation strategy. Nonetheless, without some form of NGO representation, it seems unlikely that the islands of multilateral governance will be able to maintain their legitimacy.

The political patterns that will emerge are difficult, indeed impossible, to foresee. But it is important to be cautious about projecting trendlines. For instance, the recent dramatic increases in the activities of NGOs does not necessarily mean that they will become increasingly powerful. Actions generate reactions. One result of deadlock, if it occurs, could be the movement of decisionmaking to new forums, less subject to democratic participation. That is, an ironic result of NGO activity could be institutional changes that reduce the efficacy of public protests and media campaigns. For example, we could see a continued increase in the legalization of international institutions. In the absence of legislative action, judiciaries and other tribunals may extend their interpretations of rules into rulemaking. The European Court of Justice is a prime example.[80] Its ability to avoid reversals of its rulings by governments is enhanced by legislative deadlock: no unanimous coalition can be organized to repeal ECJ rulings. On a less extensive basis, the judicial organs of the WTO have been making rules (for example, on trade-environment issues) that could not have been adopted by the WTO's Council. Of course, legalization could be stymied or reversed by powerful political movements. The point is not that legalization is inevitable or even likely, but that the dynamics of political change are often nonlinear and often surprising in terms of democratic theory.

Democracy and Global Governance

Democracy is government by the people. In simplified form, this has meant the majority of the people (though with protections for individuals and minorities in liberal democracies). Historically, democracy has meant government by the majority of the people who regard themselves as a political community. The key question for global governance is, who are "we the people" when there is no sense of political identity and community, and the political world is organized largely around a system of unequal states?

In thinking about legitimacy, it may be helpful to separate the inputs and outputs of democratic government. On the input side, elections determine ruling majorities. But what are the boundaries of the relevant electoral constituencies in which votes are held? If the moral claim for democracy rests on the worth and equality of individuals, then a basic rule is one person, one vote. One state, one vote is not democratic because a Maldive Islander would have 1,000 times the voting power of a citizen of China. A cosmopolitan view, however, that treats the globe as one constituency implies the existence of a political community in which citizens of 198 states would be willing to be continually outvoted by a billion Chinese and a billion Indians. As Norris shows in her chapter, there is no evidence that national identities are changing in a manner that would make that feasible for a long time to come. In the absence of such a community, the extension of domestic voting practices to the world scale would make little normative sense even if it were feasible. Most meaningful voting, and associated democratic political activities, occurs within the boundaries of nation-states that have democratic constitutions and processes. Minorities are willing to acquiesce to a majority in which they may not participate directly because they feel they participate in some larger community. This is clearly absent at the global level and creates severe normative as well as practical problems for the input side of global democracy.

At the same time, voting is not the only feature of the input side of democracratic government. Many democratic theorists would argue that people should have a voice on issues that have important effects on their lives, and that voice is raised frequently in the long intervals between elections. The mechanisms stretch from polls to protests. The boundaries for this type of input are less clearly defined than in electoral constituencies. A public space is an identifiable set of issues, and the public is the group of people who communicate and agitate over their shared externalities in that space—sometimes at local and sometimes at transnational levels. In this sense of shared externalities, there may be some global publics even if there is no global community. In a well-functioning domestic democracy, the various aspects of political inputs—popular activity, media attention, pluralist interest-group lobbying, parties, elections and formal legislation—are articulated together. There is a clear pathway by which laws can be created; and when laws are enacted, regular procedures and organizations exist to implement, amend, and change those laws. This is the procedural basis for democratic legitimacy.

Internationally, however, the link between popular activity and policy is severely attenuated. Public meetings, such as recent UN-sponsored conferences on the role of women in society, have not led to formal rules that have obligatory status ("hard law"). The resolutions of such conferences are typically susceptible to contrasting interpretations or can simply be ignored by recalcitrant governments. These meetings affect public views on a global basis and help mobilize domestic and transnational movements, but they do not provide clear "hooks" to change policy. For instance, Agenda 21, adopted at the Rio Conference on Sustainable Development, is very soft law: it does not have treaty status, and it obliges no one. And despite the UN Convention on Eliminating Discrimination against Women, most of the norms revolving around women's rights have not been codified into treaties that have universal or near-universal validity.

In a well-functioning domestic democracy, popular politics and the organization of interest groups lead directly to legislation and to the implementation of such legislation. These connections are lacking at the international level. As we have seen, those intergovernmental organizations that do make binding rules often lack the democratic legitimacy that comes from having transparent procedures, institutional arrangements that facilitate accountability, and activities by politicians seeking re-election by appealing to publics. At the same time, the private and NGO sectors that agitate about political issues internationally do not have any greater claim to democratic legitimacy. Despite their claims to represent civil society, they tend to be self-selected and often unrepresentative elites. The disjunction between international arrangements facilitating such public involvement, and multilateral cooperation on binding decisions, leads to disputes over legitimacy and dangers of stalemate in intergovernmental institutions. As we have seen, this disjunction cannot be solved simply by adopting the domestic voting model at a global level.

The legitimacy of governments is not determined solely by the procedures used on the input side. Substantive outputs also matter. Citizens are concerned about security, welfare, and identity. When these substantive outputs are missing, procedural democracy on the input side is often not sufficient. Legitimacy of democratic government rests on procedures and on effectiveness in producing valued outputs. If the challenges to their democratic legitimacy on the input side lead to increased stalemate, global institutions may also lose whatever legitimacy has accrued to them through their role in facilitating effective substantive intergovernmental coopera-tion. At the same time, it also implies that if some changes can be made on the input side, even though they fall well short of the procedures implied by the domestic analogy, there may be some residual legitimacy in the effectiveness on the output side.

This suggests the need for a more appropriate measure for judging democratic legitimacy than the so-called democratic deficit based on the domestic analogy. The development of appropriate normative theory for judging global institutions will be an important part of the development of global governance. It is unlikely that the literature based on the European Union with its close links to the domestic analogy is appropriate for global institutions for reasons given above. Nor will new theories based on the potential for direct voting in cyberdemocracy be sufficient. One can imag-ine technology enabling the world to engage in frequent plebiscites that collect the votes of vast numbers of people interested in an issue. But it is more difficult to envisage the effective processes of deliberation in the absence of a community that would make such voting meaningful in a normative sense. With time, such obstacles may be overcome and practices gradually develop, but that is not imminent.

In the interim it will be important to develop more modest normative principles and practices to enhance transparency and accountability not only of IGOs but of corporations and NGOs that constitute global gov-ernance today. For example, increased transparency is important to accountability, but transparency need not be instantaneous or com-plete—witness the delayed release of Federal Reserve Board hearings or the details of Supreme Court deliberations. Similarly, accountability has many dimensions, only one of which is reporting up the chain of dele-gation to elected leaders. Markets aggregate the preferences (albeit unequally) of large numbers of people, and both governments and transnational corporations are accountable to them. Professional associ-ations create and maintain transnational norms to which IGOs, NGOs, and government officials can be judged accountable. The practice of "naming and shaming" of transnational corporations with valuable brand names by NGOs and the press also provides a sort of accountability. Similarly, the naming and shaming of governments engaged in corrupt practices helps create a type of accountability. While trisectoral coopera-tion and mixed coalitions are to be welcomed, competition among sec-tors and among mixed coalitions is useful for transparency and account-ability. Even in a democracy like the United States, the best solution to the problem of the iron triangles of bureaucrats, interest groups, and sub-committee legislators is competition and publication in the press.

Transgovernmental and trisectoral networks are sometimes praised for being able to act much more quickly and effectively than IGOs, but they are inherently less subject to democratic or quasi-democratic accountability.[81] Informal coordination can be quicker than following formal procedures, but it leaves fewer traces. The agents themselves may be quite insulated from public pressure, insofar as they include private firms, associations of firms, and independent or quasi-independent regulatory agencies. Transgovernmental politics could become special interest group politics on a world scale. Furthermore, it is unlikely that states will turn over major decisionmaking activities, creating hard law, to transgovernmental and trisectoral networks. Such networks are likely to be an increasingly important part of the global policy process, and their effectiveness will be welcome, but it will be important to develop appropriate ways to judge their transparency and accountability without resorting to the claims of direct democracy or a simple domestic analogy.

Conclusions: Globalism and Governance

Globalization is strongly affecting domestic governance, but it is far from making the nation-state obsolete as some prophets claim. The existence of "useful inefficiencies" and the persistence of national political traditions and cultures means that the state will remain the basic institution of governance well into the century. But domestic polities will be under pressure from the erosion of economic inefficiency, tensions around the redistribution and inequality that accompany economic globalization, and the increasing roles of transnational and third sector actors. The compromise of embedded liberalism that created a social safety net in return for openness was successful in the second half of the twentieth century but is under new pressure. That compromise was the basis for Bretton Woods institutions that (along with other regimes) governed " issue islands" in world politics. As Rodrik shows, this compromise worked to combine economic globalization with some domestic autonomy for democratic politics. Now, for reasons we have suggested, that system is under challenge. This does not mean that it must be discarded, but that new strategies will be necessary to resolve the dilemma of efficacy versus legitimacy that we have described.

Rulemaking and rule interpretation in global governance have become pluralized. Rules are no longer a matter simply for states or intergovernmental organizations. Private firms, NGOs, subunits of governments, and the transnational and transgovernmental networks that result, all play a role, typically with central state authorities and intergovernmental organizations. As a result, any emerging pattern of governance will have to be networked rather than hierarchical and must have minimal rather than highly ambitious objectives. "Networked minimalism" seeks to preserve national democratic processes and embedded liberal compromises while allowing the benefits of economic integration.

Networked minimalism is only a broad principle of governance—more a matter of what not to try (hierarchy and intrusiveness in domestic politics) than what to do. If multilateral cooperation is to continue, any networked arrangements will have to solve the classic governance problem of reaching legitimate decisions. The club model, based on decomposable sets of issues, reached decisions, but they are increasingly challenged. Somehow, the more diverse actors—more states, private sector actors, NGOs—that are now involved in global public policy will have to be brought into the system.[82] Cross-sectoral partnerships of government (and IGO), private, and third sector organization may provide part of a solution, but they still pose problems. More nuanced approaches to transparency and accountability of both international institutions and networks will be an important part of understanding global governance.

As Applbaum shows in his chapter, it is important not to think of legitimacy solely in terms of majoritarian voting procedures. Many parts of the American constitution (such as the Supreme Court) and political practice would fail that test. Democratic legitimacy has a number of sources, both normative and substantive. Legitimacy in international regimes will derive in part from delegation from elected national governments but also from effectiveness and transnational civil society. New modes of ensuring public participation, not relying entirely on elections, will have to be found. But insofar as major societies are democratic, legitimacy will depend on the popular views that international governance practices are consistent with democratic norms. Some form of transparency and accountability will be crucial. And since the legitimacy of global decisions will probably remain shaky for many decades, it will be crucial also to relax the pressure on multilateral institutions by preserving substantial space for separate domestic political processes—what in the language of the European Union is referred to as "subsidiarity." The practices of the WTO in allowing domestic politics to sometimes depart from international agreements without unraveling the whole system of norms are a useful example.

It is possible that the political base of intergovernmental organizations and international regimes will be too weak to sustain high levels of governance: that the need for international regimes will exceed the supply. Deadlock and frustration could result. But the results of such deadlock are not clear. They could lead to a move away from such institutions for governance, back to the state, limiting globalism, as occurred after 1914. But that is not likely. They could lead in other directions—toward the development of quasi-judicial processes internationally, "soft legislation," and effective governance of specific issue—areas by transnational and transgovernmental networks. What is not likely is a mere repetition of the past or a return to a world of isolated nation-states. Globalism is here to stay. How it will be governed is the question.

Notes

1. Much of the material in this section is drawn from chapter 10 of Robert O. Keohane and Joseph S. Nye, *Power and Interdependence,* 3d ed. (Addison-Wesley, 2000).

2. Robert O. Keohane and Joseph S. Nye, *Power and Interdependence: World Politics in Transition* (Little, Brown, 1977; Harper Collins, 2d ed., 1989).

3. United Nations Development Program (UNDP), *Human Development Report* (Oxford University Press, 1999).

4. Keith Griffin, "Globalization and the Shape of Things to Come," in *Macalester International: Globalization and Economic Space,* vol. 7, Spring 1999, p. 3; and "One World?" *Economist,* October 18, 1997, pp. 79–80.

5. Samuel P. Huntington, *The Clash of Civilizations and the Remaking of World Order* (Simon and Schuster, 1996).

6. Nicolo Barquet and Pere Domingo, "Smallpox: The Triumph over the Most Terrible of the Ministers of Death," *Annals of Internal Medicine,* October 15, 1997, pp. 636–38.

7. Jared Diamond, *Guns, Germs and Steel: The Fates of Human Societies* (W.W. Norton, 1998), pp. 202, 210; and William H. McNeill, *Plagues and Peoples* (London: Scientific Book Club, 1979), p. 168. See also Alfred W. Crosby, *Ecological Imperialism: The Biological Expansion of Europe, 900–1900* (Cambridge: Cambridge University Press, 1986).

8. Alfred Crosby, *The Columbian Exchange: Biological and Cultural Consequences of 1492* (Greenwood Press, 1972).

9. John P. McKay and others, *A History of Western Society,* 4th ed. (Houghton Mifflin, 1991), pp. 106–07.

10. Arjun Appuradai, *Modernity at Large* (University of Minnesota Press, 1996).

11. Paul Krugman, *The Return of Depression Economics* (Norton, 1999), p. 16.

12. John W. Meyer and others, "World Society and the Nation-State," *American Journal of Sociology,* vol. 103 (July 1997), pp. 144–81.

13. "U.N. Oratory: Pleas for Help, Pride in Democracy,"*New York Times,* September 21, 1999, p. A12; "U.N. Chief Wants Faster Action to Avoid Slaughter in Civil Wars," *New York Times,* September 21, 1999, p. A12; and "General Assembly U.N. Chief Champions Security Council-Backed Humanitarian Intervention," *Financial Times* (London), September 21, 1999, p. 1.

14. Diamond, *Guns, Germs and Steel,* p. 202.

15. David Held and others, *Global Transformations: Politics, Economics and Culture* (Stanford University Press 1999), pp. 21–22.

16. "Fearful over the Future, Europe Seizes on Food," *New York Times,* August 29, 1999, sec. 4, p. l.

17. Professor Anne-Marie Slaughter of Harvard University Law School used the expressions of "uploading" and "downloading" content, at John F. Kennedy School of Government Visions Project Conference on Globalization, Bretton Woods, N.H., 1999.

18. Richard Storry, *A History of Modern Japan* (Harmondsworth, UK: Penguin, 1960), pp. 115–16; and Hioaki Sato, "The Meiji Government's Remarkable Mission to Learn from Europe and Japan," *Japan Times,* October 14, 1999.

19. Frederick Schauer, "The Politics and Incentives of Legal Transplantation," paper presented at John F. Kennedy School of Government Visions Project Conference on Globalization, 1999.

20. Joseph S. Nye Jr. *Bound to Lead: The Changing Nature of American Power* (Basic Books, 1990), pp. 31–32.

21. Thomas Friedman, *The Lexus and the Olive Tree: Understanding Globalization* (Farrar Straus Giroux, 1999), pp. 7–8.

22. "A Semi-Integrated World," *Economist,* September 11, 1999, p. 42.

23. Joseph Stiglitz, "Weightless Concerns," *Financial Times* (London), February 3, 1999, op-ed page.

24. Robert Jervis, *System Effects: Complexity in Political and Social Life* (Princeton University Press, 1997).

25. "One World?" *Economist,* October 18 1997, p. 80.

26. Greenspan quoted in Friedman, *The Lexus and the Olive Tree,* p. 368.

27. Held and others, *Global Transformations,* p. 235.

28. "China Ponders New Rules of 'Unrestricted War,'" *Washington Post,* August 8, 1999, p. l.

29. M. Mitchell Waldrop, *Complexity: The Emerging Science at the Edge of Order and Chaos* (Touchstone Books, 1992).

30. Lawrence Lessig, *Code and Other Laws of Cyberspace* (Basic Books, 1999), pp. 88, 207.

31. Hedley Bull, *The Anarchical Society : A Study of Order in World Politics* (Columbia University Press, 1977), p. 46.

32. Michael J. Sandel, *Democracy's Discontents* (Harvard University Press, 1996), pp. 338 ff.

33. UNDP (United Nations Development Program), *Human Development Report 1999* (Oxford University Press, 1999).

34. Karl Polanyi, *The Great Transformation* (Rinehart, 1944).

35. Jeffrey G. Williamson, "Globalization and the Labor Market: Using History to Inform Policy," in Philippe Aghion and Jeffrey G. Williamson, eds., *Growth, Inequality and Globalization* (Cambridge University Press, 1998), p. 193.

36. Polanyi, *The Great Transformation,* p. 73.

37. Geoffrey Garrett, *Partisan Politics in the Global Economy* (Cambridge, UK: Cambridge University Press, 1998), p. 183.

38. Williamson, *Globalization and the Labor Market,* p. 168.

39. Ibid., p. 142.

40. Adrian Wood, *North-South Trade, Employment and Inequality* (Oxford: Clarendon Press, 1994).

41. Williamson, "Globalization and the Labor Market," p.168.

42. George Borjas, *Heaven's Door: Immigration Policy and the American Economy* (Princeton University Press, 1999).

43. Dani Rodrik, *Has Globalization Gone Too Far?* (Washington: Institute for International Economics, 1997); and Robert Lawrence, *Single World, Divided Nations* (Brookings, 1996).

44. Robert O. Keohane and Helen V. Milner, *Internationalization and Domestic Politics* (Cambridge University Press, 1996); and Suzanne Berger and Ronald Dore, eds., *National Diversity and Global Capitalism* (Cornell University Press, 1996).

45. Amartya Sen, *Development as Freedom* (Knopf, 1999).

46. See Linda Weiss, *The Myth of the Powerless State* (Cornell University Press, 1998); Garrett, *Partisan Politics*; and Rodrik, *Has Globalization Gone Too Far?*

47. Weiss, *The Myth of the Powerless State.*

48. John G. Ruggie, "International Regimes, Transactions and Change: Embedded Liberalism in the Postwar Economic Order," in Stephen D. Krasner, ed., *International Regimes* (Cornell University Press, 1983).

49. Keohane and Nye, *Power and Interdependence,* 3d ed., chaps. 9, 10.

50. Kenneth N. Waltz, "Globalization and Governance," *PS, Political Science & Politics* (December 1999), p. 697.

51. Wolfgang Reinicke, "Global Public Policy," *Foreign Affairs* (November–December 1997), in Waltz, "Globalization and Governance," p. 697.

52. Lessig, *Code and Other Laws,* chap. 4.

53. Saskia Sassen, *Cities in a World Economy,* 2d ed. (Thousand Oaks: Pine Forge Press, 2000).

54. See Robert O. Keohane and Joseph S. Nye Jr., *Transnational Relations and World Politics* (Harvard University Press, 1974); and Anne-Marie Slaughter, "The Real New World Order," *Foreign Affairs* (September–October 1997), pp. 183–97.

55. Kenneth N. Waltz, *Theory of International Politics* (Addison-Wesley, 1979).

56. Robert O. Keohane, *After Hegemony: Cooperation and Discord in the World Political Economy* (Princeton University Press, 1984).

57. Robert O. Keohane, "The Demand for International Regimes," in Stephen D. Krasner, ed., *International Regimes* (Cornell University Press, 1983), pp. 141–71.

58. Meyer and others, "World Society and the Nation-State"; Martha Finnemore, *National Interests in International Society* (Cornell University Press, 1996); and Martha Finnemore, "Sovereign Default and Military Intervention," unpublished paper, 2000.

59. Chaim D. Kaufmann and Robert A. Pape, "Explaining Costly International Moral Action: Britain's Sixty-Year Campaign against the Atlantic Slave Trade," *International Organization* (Autumn 1999), pp. 631–68.

60. Miles Kahler, "Multilateralism with Small and Large Numbers," *International Organization* (Summer 1992), pp. 681–709.

61. Thomas Oatley and Robert Nabors, "Redistributive Cooperation: Market Failure, Wealth Transfers, and the Basle Accord," *International Organization* (Winter 1998), pp. 35–54.

62. Gary Gereffi and Miguel Korzeniewicz, eds., *Commodity Chains and Global Capitalism* (Greenwood Press, 1994).

63. Ronie Garcia-Johnson, *Exporting Environmentalism: US Multinational Chemical Corporations in Brazil and Mexico* (MIT Press, 2000).

64. Lessig, *Code and Other Laws of Cyberspace*, p. 197.

65. "After Seattle: The Nongovernmental Order," *Economist*, December 11, 1999, p. 21.

66. Margaret Keck and Kathryn Sikkink, *Activists beyond Borders: Advocacy Networks in International Politics* (Cornell University Press, 1998).

67. Wolfgang H. Reinicke, "The Other World Wide Web: Global Public Policy Networks," *Foreign Policy* (Winter 1999–2000), pp. 44–57.

68. Sheila Jasanoff, private note to authors, January 2000.

69. Keck and Sikkink, *Activists beyond Borders*; Kaufmann and Pape, "Explaining Costly International Moral Action."

70. Sassen, *Cities in a World Economy*, p. 96.

71. "Lively Debate at First G-20 Talks," *Financial Times*, December 17, 1999, p. 11.

72. "Head of OAU Opposes Call by Annan," *Financial Times*, September 21, 1999, p. 5; and "Kofi Annan Unsettles People as He Believes U.N. Should Do," *New York Times*, December 31, 1999, p. A1.

73. Keck and Sikkink, *Activists beyond Borders*, n. 70.

74. Michael Zurn, "Democratic Governance beyond the Nation State: The EU and Other International Institutions," unpublished paper, 2000, pp. 16–17.

75. Zurn, "Democratic Governance."

76. Herbert A. Simon, *The Sciences of the Artificial*, 3d ed. (MIT Press, 1996).

77. Keohane and Nye, *Transnational Relations*.

78. Daniel C. Esty, "Non-Governmental Organizations at the World Trade Organization: Cooperation, Competition, or Exclusion," *Journal of International Economic Law*, vol. 123 (Fall 1998), pp. 709–30.

79. "After Seattle," p. 21.

80. Karen J. Alter, "Who Are the 'Masters of the Treaty?' European Governments and the European Court of Justice," *International Organization* (Winter 1998), pp. 121–48; and Anne-Marie Slaughter, "Governing the Global Economy through Government Networks," in Michael Byers, ed., *The Role of Law in International Politics* (Oxford: Oxford University Press, 2000).

81. Slaughter, "Governing the Global Economy through Government Networks"; Reinicke, "The Other World Wide Web."

82. Wolfgang H. Reinicke, *Global Public Policy: Governing without Government* (Brookings, 1998).

PART I

Trends in
Globalization

2

JEFFREY FRANKEL

Globalization of the Economy

Economic globalization is one of the most powerful forces to have shaped the postwar world. In particular, international trade in goods and services has become increasingly important over the past fifty years, and international financial flows over the past thirty years. This chapter documents quantitatively the process of globalization for trade and finance. It then briefly goes beyond the causes of international economic integration to consider its effects, concluding that globalization is overall a good thing, not just for economic growth but also when noneconomic goals are taken into account.

The two major drivers of economic globalization are reduced costs to transportation and communication in the private sector and reduced policy barriers to trade and investment on the part of the public sector. Technological progress and innovation have long been driving the costs of transportation and communication steadily lower. In the postwar period we have seen major further cost-saving advances, even within

The author would like to thank Jagdish Bhagwati, Ash Carter, Farhad Rassekh, Dani Rodrik, Pierre Sauve, Ira Shapiro, Rob Stavins, Arvind Subramanian, Daniel Tarullo, and Alan Winters for comments.

ocean shipping: supertankers, roll-on-roll-off ships, and containerized cargo. Between 1920 and 1990 the average ocean freight and port charges per short ton of U.S. import and export cargo fell from $95.00 to $29.00 (in 1990 dollars). An increasing share of cargo goes by air. Between 1930 and 1990, average air transport revenue per passenger mile fell from $0.68 to $0.11. Jet air shipping and refrigeration have changed the status of goods that had previously been classified altogether as not tradable internationally. Now fresh-cut flowers, perishable broccoli and strawberries, live lobsters, and even ice cream are sent between continents.[1] Communications costs have fallen even more rapidly. Over this period the cost of a three-minute telephone call from New York to London fell from $244.65 to $3.32. Recent inventions such as faxes and the Internet require no touting.

It is easy to exaggerate the extent of globalization. Much excited discussion of the topic makes it sound as though the rapid increase in economic integration across national borders is unprecedented. Some commentators imply that it has now gone so far that it is complete; one hears that distance and national borders no longer matter, that the nation-state and geography are themselves no longer relevant for economic purposes, and that it is now as easy to do business with a customer across the globe as across town. After all, has not the World Wide Web reduced cross-border barriers to zero?

It would be a mistake for policymakers or private citizens to base decisions on the notion that globalization is so new that the experience of the past is not relevant, or that the phenomenon is now irreversible, or that national monetary authorities are now powerless in the face of the global marketplace, or that the quality of life of Americans—either economic or noneconomic aspects—is determined more by developments abroad than by American actions at home.

It is best to recognize that at any point in history many powerful forces are working to drive countries apart, at the same time as other powerful forces are working to shrink the world. In the 1990s, for example, at the same time that forces such as the Internet and dollarization have led some to proclaim the decline of the nation-state, more new nations have been created (out of the ruins of the former Soviet bloc) than in any decade other than the decolonizing 1960s, each with its own currencies and trade policies.[2] The forces of shrinkage have dominated in recent decades, but the centrifugal forces are important as well.

Two Benchmarks for Measuring Economic Integration

The overall post–World War II record of economic integration across national borders, powerful as it has been, is, in two respects, not as striking as widely believed. The first perspective is to judge by the standard of 100 years ago. The second is to judge by the standard of what it would mean to have truly perfect global integration.

Judging Globalization 2000 by the Standard of 1900

The globalization that took place in the nineteenth century was at least as impressive as the current episode. The most revolutionary breakthroughs in transportation and communication had already happened by 1900—for example, the railroad, steamship, telegraph, and refrigeration. Freight rates had fallen sharply throughout the century. An environment of political stability was provided by the Pax Britannica, and an environment of monetary stability was provided by the gold standard. Kevin O'Rourke and Jeffrey Williamson show that, as a result of rapidly growing trade, international differences in commodity prices narrowed dramatically.[3]

It is inescapable to invoke a particularly famous quote from John Maynard Keynes: "What an extraordinary episode in the progress of man that age was which came to an end in August 1914! . . . The inhabitant of London could order by telephone, sipping his morning tea in bed, the various products of the whole earth . . . he could at the same time and by the same means adventure his wealth in the natural resources and new enterprise of any quarter of the world."[4]

The world took a giant step back from economic globalization during the period 1914–1944. Some of the causes of this retrogression were isolationist sentiments in the West that followed World War I, the monetary instability and economic depression that plagued the interwar period, increases in tariffs and other trade barriers including most saliently the adoption by the U.S. Congress of the Smoot-Hawley tariff of 1930, the rise of the fascist bloc in the 1930s, and the rise of the communist bloc in the 1940s. All of these factors pertain to barriers that were created by governments, in contrast to the forces of technology and the private marketplace, which tend to reduce barriers. As a result, the world that emerged in 1945 was far more fragmented economically than the world that had turned to war in 1914.

The victors, however, were determined not to repeat the mistakes they had made at the time of the first world war. This time, they would work to promote economic integration in large part to advance long-term political goals. To govern international money, investment, and trade, they established multilateral institutions—the International Monetary Fund, World Bank, and General Agreement on Tariffs and Trade.[5] The United States initially led the way by reducing trade barriers and making available gold-convertible dollars.

By one basic measure of trade, exports or imports of merchandise as a fraction of total output, it took more than twenty-five years after the end of World War II before the United States around 1970 reached the same level of globalization that it had experienced on the eve of World War I. This fraction continued to increase rapidly between 1971 and 1997—reaching about 9 percent today, still far lower than that in Britain throughout the late and early twentieth centuries. By other measures, some pertaining to the freedom of factor movements, the world even by the turn of the millennium was no more integrated than that of the preceding turn of the century.[6]

Most people find it surprising that trade did not reattain its pre–World War I importance until the early 1970s. The significance of the comparison with 100 years ago goes well beyond factoids that economic historians enjoy springing on the uninitiated. Because technological know-how is irreversible—or was irreversible over the second millennium, if not entirely over the first—there is a tendency to see globalization as irreversible. But the political forces that fragmented the world for thirty years (1914–44) were evidently far more powerful than the accretion of technological progress in transport that went on during that period. The lesson is that nothing is inevitable about the process of globalization. For it to continue, world leaders must make choices of the sort made in the aftermath of World War II, instead of those made in the aftermath of World War I.

Judging by the Globalization 2000 Standard of Perfect International Integration

Perhaps perfect economic integration across national borders is a straw man. (The reader is likely to think so by the end of this chapter, even if he or she did not at the beginning.) But straw men have their purposes, and in this case ample rhetoric exists to justify the interest. A good straw man needs to be substantial enough to impress the crows and yet not so substantial that he can't be knocked flat. On both scores the proposition of complete international integration qualifies admirably.

Consider again the basic statistics of trade integration—a country's total exports of goods and services, or total imports, as a fraction of GDP. With the rapid increase in services included, these ratios now average 12 percent for the United States. The current level of trade likely represents a doubling from 100 years ago. As remarkable as is this evidence of declining transportation costs, tariffs, and other barriers to trade, it is still very far from the condition that would prevail if these costs and barriers were zero. More sophisticated statistics below will document this claim. But a very simple calculation is sufficient to make the point. U.S. output is about one-fourth of gross world product. The output of producers in other countries is thus about three-fourths of gross world product. If Americans were prone to buy goods and services from foreign producers as easily as from domestic producers, then foreign products would constitute a share of U.S. spending equal to that of the spending of the average resident of the planet. The U.S. import-GDP ratio would equal .75. The same would be true of the U.S. export-GDP ratio. And yet these ratios are only about one-sixth of this hypothetical level (12 percent /75 percent = one-sixth). In other words, globalization would have to increase another sixfold, as measured by the trade ratio, before it would literally be true that Americans did business as easily across the globe as across the country.

Other countries are also a long way from perfect openness in this sense. The overall ratio of merchandise trade to output worldwide is about twice the U.S. ratio. This is to be expected, as other countries are smaller. For the other two large economies—Japan and the European Union considered as a whole—the ratio is closer to the U.S. level. In almost all cases, the ratio falls far short of the level that would prevail in a perfectly integrated world.[7] In figure 2-1, the vertical dimension represents the share of a country's output that is sold to its fellow citizens, rather than exported. The downward movement for most countries illustrates that they have become more open over the past 130 years. (One can also see that the integration trend was interrupted during the interwar period.) The United States is still far from perfect openness: the share of output sold at home is disproportionate to the share of world output. Other countries have a higher ratio of trade to GDP than the United States as a result of being smaller and less self-sufficient. Nonetheless, they are similarly far from perfect openness.

Figure 2-1. *Country Size (Share of World Output) versus Closedness (Sales at Home/Total Output)*

Share of output sold at home

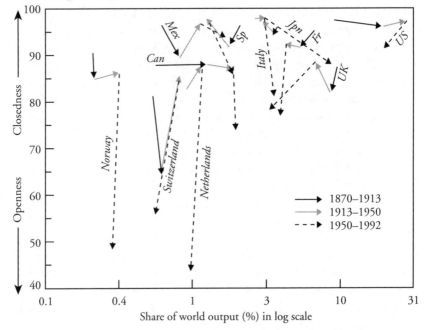

Share of world output (%) in log scale

Source: Author's calculations and data from Angus Maddison, *Monitoring the World Economy* (Paris: Development Center of the Organization for Economic Cooperation and Development, 1995).
Note: Closedness = $(1 - (x/GDP))*100$.

Why is globalization still so far from complete? To get an idea of the combination of transportation costs, trade barriers, and other frictions that remains yet to be dismantled, we must delve more deeply into the statistics.

Statistical Measures of Economic Integration

It can be instructive to look at direct measures of how some of the barriers to transborder integration have changed during the twentieth century—the level of tariffs on manufactures as an illustration of trade policy, or the price of a trans-Atlantic telephone call as an illustration of technological change in communications and transportation. Nevertheless, the political and physical determinants are too numerous and varied to be aggregated into a few key statistics that are capable of measuring the overall extent of integration in trade or finance. Tariff rates, for example, differ tremendously across commodities, and there is no single sensible way to aggregate them. The situation is even worse for nontariff barriers. Alternative possible measures of the importance of tariffs and other trade barriers have very low correlation with each other.[8]

A comprehensive measure of shipping costs for a country's trade is the ratio of c.i.f. trade value (measured as the cost to the importing country, including insurance and freight) to f.a.s. or f.o.b. trade value (measured as it leaves the exporting country as "free alongside ship" or "free on board"). The margin for U.S. trade fell from about 9.5 percent in the 1950s to about 6 percent in the 1990s. (The average worldwide is under 4 percent.) But this probably understates the decline in shipping costs. The reason is that the composition of trade has changed, and c.i.f. margins vary widely across commodities and across trading partners.[9]

It is more rewarding to look at summary measures of the *effects* of cross-border barriers on the patterns of trade and investment than to look at measures of the barriers themselves. Two sorts of measures are in use: those pertaining to quantities and those pertaining to prices.

Measures of quantities might appear more direct: "just how big are international flows?" But economists often prefer to look at price measures. In the first place, the quality of the data is often higher for prices than quantities. (This is particularly true of data on international financial markets—the data on the prices of foreign securities are extremely good, the data on aggregate international trade in securities are extremely bad.) In the second place, even at a conceptual level, international differentials in the prices of specific goods or specific assets, which measure the ability of international arbitrage to hold these prices in line, are more useful indicators of the extent of integration in a causal sense. Consider the example of U.S. trade in petroleum products. It is not especially large as a percentage of total U.S. output or consumption of petroleum products. And yet arbitrage ties the price of oil within the United States closely to the price in the world market. Even a pair of countries that records no bilateral oil trade whatsoever will find that their prices move closely together. It is the absence of barriers and the *potential* for large-scale trade that keeps prices in line and makes the markets integrated in the most meaningful sense, not the magnitude of trade that takes place.

The Ability of Arbitrage to Eliminate International Differentials in Goods Prices

According to basic economic theory, arbitrage, defined as the activity of buying an item in a place where it is cheap and simultaneously selling the same item where it is expensive, should drive prices into equality. Its failure to do so perfectly is a source of repeated surprise to economists (though perhaps to nobody else). Often the explanation is that the commodities in question are not in fact identical. Brand names matter, if for no other reason than matters of retailing, warranty, and customer service. A BMW is certainly not the same automobile as a Lexus, and even a BMW sold in Germany is not the same as a BMW sold in the United States (different air pollution control equipment, for example). When the comparison across countries uses aggregate price indexes, as in standard tests of "purchasing power parity," it is no surprise to find only weak evidence of arbitrage.[10] The finding of international price differentials is more surprising in the case of nondifferentiated non-brand-name commodities such as standardized ball bearings. Tests find that price differentials for specific goods are far larger across national borders than they are within countries. Exchange rate variability is a likely culprit.[11]

Even more surprising is the paucity of evidence of a tendency for price differentials to diminish over the long sweep of history. Kenneth Froot, Michael Kim, and Kenneth Rogoff have obtained data on prices in England and Holland since the year 1273 for eight commodities (barley, butter, cheese, eggs, oats, peas, silver, and wheat).[12] Deviations from the so-called Law of One Price across the English Channel are no smaller or less persistent now than they were in the past, even though technological progress has certainly reduced the cost of shipping these products dramatically. Evidently other forces have counteracted the fall in transport costs; candidates are trade barriers under Europe's Common Agricultural Policy and volatility in the exchange rate between the guilder and the pound.[13]

Factors Contributing to Home-Country Bias in Trade

Geography in general—and distance in particular—remain far more important inhibitions to trade than widely believed.

DISTANCE. Distance is still an important barrier to trade and not solely because of physical shipping costs. The effects of informational barriers are

observed to decrease with proximity and with linguistic, cultural, historical, and political links. We might call it social distance. Hans Linnemann
called it "psychic distance," and Peter Drysdale and Ross Garnaut named
it "subjective resistance."[14]

Among many possible proofs that distance is still important, one of the
simplest is the observed tendency toward geographical agglomeration of
industries. The tendency for industry to concentrate regionally is evidence
both of costs to transportation and communication and of increasing
returns to scale in production.

The agglomeration occurs even in sectors where physical transport costs
are negligible, as in financial services or computer software. Financial firms
concentrate in Manhattan and information technology firms concentrate
in Silicon Valley. The reason they choose to locate near each other is not
because they are trading physical commodities with each other and wish to
save on shipping costs. Rather, face-to-face contact is important for
exchanging information and negotiating deals.

The importance of distance is also revealed by analysis of data on prices
of goods in different locations. If transport costs and other costs of doing
business at a distance are important, then arbitrage should do a better job
of keeping prices of similar goods in line when they are sold at locations
close together rather than far apart. Charles Engel and John Rogers study
prices in fourteen consumption categories for twenty-three Canadian and
U.S. cities.[15] They find that the distance between two North American
cities significantly affects the variability of their relative prices.

Similar results emerge by looking at trade quantities rather than prices.
The gravity model says that trade between a pair of countries is inversely
related to the distance between them, and proportional to the product of
their sizes, by analogy with Newton's law of gravitational attraction. It fits
the data remarkably well and is well founded in the theory of trade in
goods that are imperfect substitutes. In part because data are so abundant
(a set of 100 countries offers $100 \times 99 = 9,900$ pairs of export observations), standard errors tend to be small.

Statistical estimates find highly significant effects of distance on bilateral
trade. When the distance between two countries is increased by 1 percent,
trade between them falls by 0.7 to 1.0 percent. This statistic, like the others that follow, pertains to the effect in isolation, holding constant other
effects on trade, such as the size of the trading partners. The wonderful
property of ordinary least squares regression analysis is that it is capable of
examining the independent effect of one factor at a time.[16]

OTHER GEOGRAPHICAL VARIABLES. Other physical attributes of location also have statistically significant effects. Landlocked countries engage in less trade by a factor of about one-third, holding other factors equal. Two countries that are adjacent to each other trade about 80 percent more than two otherwise similar countries.

LINGUISTIC AND COLONIAL FACTORS. Linguistic barriers remain an impediment to trade. Two countries that speak the same language trade about 50 percent more than two otherwise similar countries. The multitude of languages is one of the reasons why economic integration remains far from complete in the European Union.

Colonial links have also been important historically. In 1960, the year when the break-up of the largest colonial empires began in earnest, trade between colonies and the colonial power was on average two to four times greater than for otherwise similar pairs of countries.[17] This effect, already reduced from an earlier peak in the colonial era, has continued to decline in the 1970s and 1980s. But it has not disappeared. Indeed, if small dependencies are included in the sample, then two units that share the same colonizer still trade on average an estimated 80 percent more with each other than two otherwise similar countries (as recently as 1990). In addition, if one of the pair is the colonial mother country, trade is five to nine times greater than it would otherwise be.[18]

MILITARY FACTORS. The effects on bilateral trade of politico-military alliances, wars, have also been examined. Theoretically and empirically (in the gravity framework) trade is generally higher among countries that are allies and lower among countries that are actual or potential adversaries. Understandably, if two countries are currently at war, there is usually a negative effect on trade. It runs as high as a 99 percent reduction in 1965. More typical is an 82 percent reduction in 1990.[19]

FREE TRADE AREAS. Regional trading arrangements reduce tariffs and other trade barriers within a group of countries, though there is a range from mild preferential trading arrangements to full-fledged economic unions. Often the members of such groups are already tightly linked through proximity, common language, or other ties. But even holding constant for such factors, in the gravity model, the formation of a free trade area is estimated on average to raise trade by 70 to 170 percent.[20] A serious common market, such as the European Union, can have a bigger effect. Nevertheless, in each of the EU member countries, a large bias toward trade within that country remains.

POLITICAL LINKS. A naive economist's view would be that once tariffs and other explicit trade barriers between countries are removed, and geographic determinants of transportation costs are held constant, trade should move as easily across national boundaries as within them. But this is far from the case in reality. If two geographic units belong to the same sovereign nation, such as France and its overseas departments, trade is roughly tripled. Thus political relationships among geographic units have larger effects on trade than such factors as explicit trade policies or linguistic barriers.

COMMON COUNTRY. Even after adjusting for distance (including non-contiguity) and linguistic barriers, all countries still exhibit a substantial bias toward buying domestic goods rather than foreign. Shang-Jin Wei estimates this bias for countries in the Organization for Economic Cooperation and Development; it has declined only very slowly over time and is still statistically significant (though the United States has the smallest bias of all).[21]

There would be some great advantages of having data at the level of states or provinces within countries. We would be able to ascertain how trade between two geographical entities is affected by their common membership in a political union. We have learned that when two geographical units share such links as speaking a common language, their bilateral trade is clearly boosted. It stands to reason that when two units share a common cultural heritage or legal system, their trade will be enhanced by even more. Data are not generally available on trade among U.S. states, Japanese prefectures, German länder, British counties, or French departments. But there do exist data on trade undertaken by Canadian provinces, among one another and with major American states. They show a strong intranational bias to trade. Ontario exports three times as much to British Columbia as to California, even though the latter has ten times as many people. (The figures are for 1988.)

John McCallum has applied the gravity model to trade among the provinces and states. The usual effects of size and distance show up.[22] The fascinating result is the effect of a dummy variable to represent when two states or provinces lie in the same country. Two such provinces trade twenty-two times as much with each other as would a province and a state that are otherwise similar but lie on opposite sides of the border. John Helliwell has updated this test to reflect data under the Canada-U.S. Free Trade Agreement. He finds that the intra-Canadian bias factor averages twenty-one for 1988–90.[23]

The result is reminiscent of the striking finding in "How Wide Is the Border?" by Engel and Rogers, that crossing the Canadian-U.S. border adds as much to the relative price variability between two cities as does traversing a physical distance of 2,500 to 10,000 miles within either country.[24] This tendency for Canadian provinces to trade with one another is all the more surprising because they tend to maintain trade barriers against one another, never having had the advantage of a Constitution like the one in the United States that reserves trade policy exclusively for the federal level. Reasons for the intra-Canadian bias in trade include the ease of doing business within the same legal system, an integrated media and advertising sector, nationwide store chains, and an East-West railroad network. John Helliwell and John McCallum "suspect that the answers lie in a whole host of educational and geographic ties based on migration and family ties and supported by networks of transportation, communication and education, along with portability of health care and pension rights—if not completely of beer."[25] Presumably the sources of intranational bias are even stronger for other countries that do not share the cultural proximity and liberalized trade relations of Canada and the United States.

CURRENCIES. There has long been reason to suspect that the existence of different currencies, and especially the large fluctuation in the exchange rates between currencies since the break-up of the Bretton Woods monetary system in 1971, has been a barrier to international trade and investment. Exchange rate fluctuations are clearly related to the failures of the law of one price observed in goods markets. When it is observed that, for example, Canadians and Americans trade far more with their countrymen than with each other, in a context where trade barriers, geography, and linguistic barriers have been eliminated, the currency difference is one of the prime suspects. Until recently, however, it has been difficult to find strong evidence that currency factors discourage trade and investment. The gravity model has now been used for this purpose.[26] It turns out that eliminating one standard deviation in exchange rate variability—for example, from its mean of 7 percent to zero—raises trade between a pair of countries by an estimated 13 percent. Furthermore, Rose has found that going all the way and literally adopting a common currency has a much bigger effect; it multiplies trade by an additional 3.5 times.[27]

Promoting trade and finance is one of several motivations for the recent adoption of common currencies or currency boards by roughly twenty countries over the past decade (including the eleven members of the European Economic and Monetary Union in 1999). At the same time, however, approximately the same number of new currencies have come into existence, as a result of the breakup of the former Soviet bloc.

Measures of Financial Market Integration

The delegates who met at Bretton Woods in 1944 had a design for the world monetary system that explicitly did not accord financial markets the presumption that was accorded trade in goods, the presumption that international integration was unambiguously good and that barriers should be liberalized as rapidly as possible. Although economic theory can make as elegant a case in favor of free trade in assets as for free trade in goods and services, the delegates had been persuaded by the experience of the 1930s that some degree of controls on international capital movements was desirable. It was not until the final 1973 breakdown of the system of fixed exchange rates that Germany and the United States removed their capital controls. Japan and the United Kingdom kept theirs until the end of the 1970s, and most other European countries did not liberalize until the end of the 1980s. Many emerging-market countries also opened up to large-scale international capital movements in the 1990s (though the subsequent crises have convinced some observers that those delegates at Bretton Woods might have had it right in the first place).

Tests regarding financial markets show international integration that has increased tremendously over the past thirty years but that is less complete than often supposed. This generalization applies to quantity-based tests as well as to price-based tests.

It is true that the gross volume of cross-border capital flows has grown very large. Perhaps the most impressive and widely cited statistic is the gross volume of turnover in foreign exchange markets: $1.5 trillion per day worldwide, by April 1998, which is on the order of a hundred times greater than the volume of trade in goods and services. *Net* capital flows are for most purposes more interesting than gross flows, however. Net capital flows today are far smaller as a share of GDP than were pre–World War I net flows out of Great Britain and into such land-abundant countries as Argentina, Australia, and Canada.[28] Furthermore, Martin Feldstein and Charles Horioka argued in a very influential paper that net capital flows are far smaller than one would expect them to be in a world of perfect international capital mobility: a country that suffers a shortfall in national saving tends to experience an almost commensurate fall in investment, rather than making up the difference by borrowing from abroad.[29] Similarly, investors in every country hold far lower proportions of their portfolios in the form of other countries' securities than they would in a well-diversified portfolio, a puzzle known as home country bias.[30] Evidently, imperfect information and transactions costs are still important barriers to cross-country investment.

The ability of arbitrage to equate asset prices or rates of return across countries has been widely tested. One would expect that in the absence of barriers to cross-border financial flows, arbitrage would bring interest rates into equality. But the answer depends on the precise condition tested. Interest rates that have had the element of exchange risk removed by forward market cover are indeed virtually equated across national borders among industrialized countries, showing that they have few controls on international capital movements. But interest rates seem not to be equalized across countries when they are adjusted for expectations of exchange rate changes rather than for forward exchange rates, and interest rates are definitely not equalized when adjusted for expected inflation rates. Evidently, currency differences are important enough to drive a wedge between expected rates of return. Furthermore, residual transactions costs or imperfect information apparently affects cross-border investment in equities.[31] They discourage investors altogether from investing in some information-intensive assets, such as mortgages, across national borders. Furthermore, country risk still adds a substantial penalty wedge to all investments in developing countries.

In short, though international financial markets, much like goods markets, have become far more integrated in recent decades, they have traversed less of the distance to perfect integration than is widely believed. Globalization is neither new, nor complete, nor irreversible.

The Impact of Economic Globalization

What are the effects of globalization and its merits? We must acknowledge a lower degree of certainty in our answers. It becomes harder to isolate cause and effect. Moreover, once we extend the list of objectives beyond maximizing national incomes, value judgments come into play. Nevertheless, economic theory and empirical research still have much to contribute.

The Effect of Trade on the Level and Growth of Real Income

Why do economists consider economic integration so important? What are the benefits of free trade for the economy?

THE THEORETICAL CASE FOR TRADE. Classical economic theory tells us that there are national gains from trade, associated with the phrase "comparative advantage." Over the past two decades, scholars have developed a "new trade theory." It suggests the existence of additional benefits from trade, which are termed dynamic. We consider each theory in turn.

The classical theory goes back to Adam Smith and David Ricardo. Adam Smith argued that specialization—the division of labor—enhances productivity. David Ricardo extended this concept to trade between countries. The notion is that trade allows each country to specialize in what it does best, thus maximizing the value of its output. If a government restricts trade, resources are wasted in the production of goods that could be imported more cheaply than they can be produced domestically.

What if one country is better than anyone else at producing *every* good? The argument in favor of free trade still carries the day. All that is required is for a country to be *relatively* less skilled than another in the production of some good in order for it to benefit from trade. This is the doctrine of comparative advantage—the fundamental (if perhaps counterintuitive) principle that underlies the theory of international trade. It makes sense for Michael Jordan to pay someone else to mow his lawn, even if Jordan could do it better himself, because he has a comparative advantage at basketball over lawn mowing. Similarly, it makes sense for the United States to pay to import certain goods that can be produced more efficiently abroad (apparel, shoes, tropical agriculture, consumer electronics), because the United States has a comparative advantage in other goods (aircraft, financial services, wheat, and computer software).

This is the classical view of the benefits of free trade in a nutshell. Two key attributes of the classical theory are worth flagging. First, it assumes perfect competition, constant returns to scale, and fixed technology, assumptions that are not very realistic. Second, the gains from trade are primarily static in nature—that is, they affect the *level* of real income. The elimination of trade barriers raises income, but this is more along the lines of a one-time increase.

What of the "new trade theory"? It is more realistic than the classical theory, in that it takes into account imperfect competition, increasing returns to scale, and changing technology. It can be viewed as providing equally strong, or stronger, support for the sort of free trade policies that the United States has followed throughout the postwar period, that is, multilateral and bilateral negotiations to reduce trade barriers, than did the classical theory.[32]

To be sure, these theories say that, under certain very special conditions, one country can get ahead by interventions (for example, subsidies to strategic sectors), provided the government gets it exactly right and provided the actions of other countries are taken as given. But these theories also tend to have the property that a world in which everyone is subsidizing at once is a world in which everyone is worse off, and that we are all better off if we can agree to limit subsidies or other interventions.

Bilateral or multilateral agreements where other sides make concessions to U.S. products, in return for whatever concessions the United States makes, are virtually the only sorts of trade agreements the United States has made. Indeed, most recent trade agreements (like the North American Free Trade Agreement and China's accession to the WTO) have required much larger reductions in import barriers by U.S. trading partners than by the United States. The reason is that their barriers were higher than those of the United States to start with. But the natural implication is that such agreements raise foreign demand for U.S. products by more than they raise U.S. demand for imports. Hence the United States is likely to benefit from a positive "terms of trade effect." This just adds to the usual benefits of increased efficiency of production and gains to consumers from international trade.

Furthermore, even when a government does not fear retaliation from abroad for trade barriers, intervention in practice is usually based on inadequate knowledge and is corrupted by interest groups. Seeking to rule out all sector-specific intervention is the most effective way of discouraging rent-seeking behavior. Globalization increases the number of competitors operating in the economy. Not only does this work to reduce distortionary monopoly power in the marketplace (which is otherwise exercised by raising prices), it can also reduce distortionary corporate power in the political arena (which is exercised by lobbying).

Most important, new trade theory offers reason to believe that openness can have a permanent effect on a country's rate of growth, not just the level of real GDP. A high rate of economic interaction with the rest of the world speeds the absorption of frontier technologies and global management best practices, spurs innovation and cost-cutting, and competes away monopoly.

These dynamic gains come from a number of sources. They include the benefits of greater market size and enhanced competition. Other sources include technological improvements through increased contact with foreigners and their alternative production styles. Such contact can come, for example, from direct investment by foreign firms with proprietary knowledge or by the exposure to imported goods that embody technologies developed abroad. Each of these elements of international trade and interactions has the effect of promoting growth in the domestic economy. When combined with the static effects, there is no question that the efforts to open markets, when successful, can yield significant dividends.

THE EMPIRICAL CASE FOR TRADE. Citing theory is not a complete answer to the question, "how do we know that trade is good?" We need empirical evidence. Economists have undertaken statistical tests of the determinants of countries' growth rates. Investment in physical capital and investment in human capital are the two factors that emerge the most strongly. But other factors matter. Estimates of growth equations have found a role for openness, measured, for example, as the sum of exports and imports as a share of GDP. David Romer and I look at a cross-section of 100 countries during the period since 1960.[33] The study sought to address a major concern about simultaneous causality between growth and trade: does openness lead to growth, or does growth lead to openness? We found that the effect of openness on growth is even stronger when we correct for the simultaneity compared with standard estimates.

The estimate of the effect of openness on income per capita ranges from 0.3 to 3.0.[34] Consider a round middle number such as 1.0. The increase in U.S. openness since the 1950s is 0.12. Multiplying the two numbers together implies that the increased integration has had an effect of 12 percent on U.S. income. More dramatically, compare a stylized Burma, with a ratio close to zero, versus a stylized Singapore, with a ratio close to 100 percent. Our ballpark estimate, the coefficient of 1.0, implies that Singapore's income is 100 percent higher than Burma's as a result of its openness. The fact that trade can affect a country's growth rate—as opposed to affecting the level of its GDP in a "one-shot" fashion—makes the case for trade liberalization even more compelling.

One possible response is that this approach demonstrates only the growth benefits from geographically induced trade and need not necessarily extend to the effects of policy-induced trade.[35] But popular critics of globalization seem to think that increased international trade and finance is the problem, regardless of whether it comes from technological progress or government liberalization. As the critics make their arguments against government dismantling of policy barriers, they seldom specify that cross-border interactions attributable to geography or to technological innovations in transport are economically beneficial.

MACROECONOMIC INTERDEPENDENCE. Trade and financial integration generally increase the transmission of business cycle fluctuations among countries. Floating exchange rates give countries some insulation against one another's fluctuations. When capital markets are highly integrated, floating rates do not give complete insulation, as the post-1973 correlation among major industrialized economies shows. But international transmission can be good for a country as easily as bad, as happens when adverse domestic developments are in part passed off to the rest of the world. The trade balance can act as an important automatic stabilizer for output and employment, improving in recessions and worsening in booms.

Contagion of financial crises is more worrying. The decade of the 1990s alone abounds with examples: the 1992–93 crises in the European exchange rate mechanism, the "tequila crisis" that began with the December 1994 devaluation of the Mexican peso, and the crises in East Asia and emerging markets worldwide from July 1997 to January 1999. Evidently when one country has a crisis it affects others. There is now a greater consensus among economists than before that not all of the observed volatility, or its cross-country correlation, can be attributed to efficient capital markets punishing or rewarding countries based on a rational evaluation of the economic fundamentals. It is difficult to do justice in one paragraph to a discussion that is as voluminous and vigorous as the debate over the welfare implications of the swelling international capital flows. Still, the majority view remains that countries are overall better off with modern globalized financial markets than without them.[36]

The Effect of Trade on Other Social Goals

Many who fear globalization concede that trade has a positive effect on aggregate national income but suspect that it has adverse effects on other highly valued goals such as labor rights, food safety, culture, and so forth. Here we consider only two major values—equality and the environment— and briefly at that.[37]

INCOME DISTRIBUTION. International trade and investment can be a powerful source of growth in poor countries, helping them catch up with those who are ahead in endowments of capital and technology. This was an important component of the spectacular growth of East Asian countries between the 1960s and the 1990s, which remains a miracle even in the aftermath of the 1997–98 currency crises. By promoting convergence, trade can help reduce the enormous worldwide inequality in income. Most of those who are concerned about income distribution, however, seem more motivated by within-country equality than global equality.

A standard textbook theory of international trade, the Heckscher-Ohlin-Samuelson model, has a striking prediction to make regarding within-country income distribution. It is that the scarce factors of production will lose from trade, and the abundant factors will benefit. This means that in rich countries, those who have capital and skills will benefit at the expense of unskilled labor, whereas in poor countries it will be the other way around. The same prediction holds for international capital mobility (or, for that matter, for international labor mobility). It has been very difficult, however, to find substantial direct evidence of the predictions of the model during the postwar period, including distribution effects within either rich or poor countries. Most likely the phenomena of changing technology, intraindustry trade, and worker ties to specific industries are more important today than the factor endowments at the heart of the Heckscher-Ohlin-Samuelson model.[38]

In the United States, the gap between wages paid to skilled workers and wages paid to unskilled workers rose by 18 percentage points between 1973 and 1995 and then leveled off. The fear is that trade is responsible for some of the gap, by benefiting skilled workers more than unskilled workers. Common statistical estimates—which typically impose the theoretical framework rather than testing it—are that between 5 and 30 percent of the increase is attributable to trade. Technology, raising the demand for skilled workers faster than the supply, is the major factor responsible for the rest.[39] One of the higher estimates is that trade contributes one-third of the net increase in the wage gap.[40]

On a sample of seventy-three countries, Chakrabarti finds that trade actually reduces inequality, as measured by the Gini coefficient. This relationship also holds for each income class.[41]

Clearly, income distribution is determined by many factors beyond trade. One is redistribution policies undertaken by the government. In some cases such policies are initiated in an effort to compensate or "buy off" groups thought to be adversely affected by trade. But a far more important phenomenon is the tendency for countries to implement greater redistribution as they grow richer.

A long-established empirical regularity is the tendency for income inequality to worsen at early stages of growth and then to improve at later stages. The original explanation for this phenomenon, known as the

Kuznets curve, had to do with rural-urban migration.[42] But a common modern interpretation is that income redistribution is a "superior good"—something that societies choose to purchase more of, even though at some cost to aggregate income, as they grow rich enough to be able to afford to do so. If this is right, then trade can be expected eventually to raise equality, by raising aggregate income.

ENVIRONMENT. Similar logic holds that trade and growth can also be good for the environment, once the country gets past a certain level of per capita income. Gene Grossman and Alan Krueger found what is called the environmental Kuznets curve: growth is bad for air and water pollution at the initial stages of industrialization but later on reduces pollution as countries become rich enough to pay to clean up their environments.[43] A substantial literature has followed.[44] A key point is that popular desires need not translate automatically into environmental quality; rather government intervention is usually required to address externalities.

The idea that trade can be good for environment is surprising to many. The pollution-haven hypothesis instead holds that trade encourages firms to locate production of highly polluting sectors in low-regulation countries in order to stay competitive. But economists' research suggests that environmental regulation is not a major determinant of firms' ability to compete internationally.[45] Furthermore, running counter to fears of a "race to the bottom," is the Pareto-improvement point: trade allows countries to attain more of whatever their goals are, including higher market-measured income for a given level of environmental quality or a better environment for a given level of income. In a model that combines various effects of trade, including via the scale and composition of output, Werner Antweiler, Brian Copeland, and M. Scott Taylor estimate that if openness raises GDP by 1 percent, then it reduces sulphur dioxide concentrations by 1 percent. The implication is that, because trade is good for growth, it is also good for the environment.[46]

The econometric studies of the effects of trade and growth on the environment get different results depending on what specific measures of pollution they use. There is a need to look at other environmental criteria as well. It is difficult to imagine, for example, that trade is anything but bad for the survival of tropical hardwood forests or endangered species, without substantial efforts by governments to protect them.

The argument that richer countries will take steps to clean up their environments holds only for issues when the effects are felt domestically—

where the primary "bads," such as smog or water pollution, are external to the firm or household but internal to the country. Some environmental externalities that have received increased attention in recent decade, however, are global. Biodiversity, overfishing, ozone depletion, and greenhouse gas emissions are four good examples. A ton of carbon dioxide has the same global warming effect regardless of where in the world it is emitted. In these cases, individual nations can do little to improve the environment on their own, no matter how concerned their populations or how effective their governments. For each of the four examples, governments have negotiated international treaties in an attempt to deal with the problem. But only the attempt to address ozone depletion, the Montreal Protocol, can be said as yet to have met with much success.

Is the popular impression then correct, that international trade and finance exacerbates these global environmental externalities? Yes, but only in the sense that trade and finance promote economic growth. Clearly if mankind were still a population of a few million people living in pre-industrial poverty, greenhouse gas emissions would not be a big issue. Industrialization leads to environmental degradation, and trade is part of industrialization. But virtually everyone wants industrialization, at least for themselves. Deliberate self-impoverishment is not a promising option. Once this point is recognized, there is nothing special about trade compared with the other sources of economic growth: capital accumulation, rural-urban migration, and technological progress.

U.S. congressional opponents of the Kyoto Protocol fear that if the industrialized countries agreed to limit emissions of carbon dioxide and other greenhouse gases, there would be an adverse effect on American economic competitiveness vis-à-vis the developing countries, who are not yet covered by the treaty. This is partially true: those U.S. sectors that are highly carbon intensive, such as aluminum smelting, would indeed suffer adversely. But other U.S. sectors would be *favorably* affected by trade with nonparticipating countries. The real issue—the true reason why we need the developing countries to participate in a global climate change agreement—is that the industrialized countries would otherwise have very little effect on aggregate global emissions over the coming decades, even if they were willing to cooperate and to bear moderately high costs involved in restructuring their energy economies. But this point has nothing to do with trade. It would be the same in a world without economic globalization.

Summary of Conclusions

This chapter gives confident answers to questions about the extent and sources of economic globalization and moderately confident answers to some questions about its effects.

The world has become increasingly integrated with respect to trade and finance since the end of World War II, owing to declining costs to transportation and communication and declining government barriers. The phenomenon is neither new nor complete, however. Globalization was more dramatic in the half-century preceding World War I, and much of the progress during the last half-century has merely reversed the closing off that came in between. In the second regard, globalization is far from complete. Contrary to popular impressions, national borders and geography still impede trade and investment substantially. A simple calculation suggests that the ratio of trade to output would have to increase at least another six-fold before it would be true that Americans trade across the globe as readily as across the country. Such barriers as differences in currencies, languages, and political systems each have their own statistically estimated trade-impeding influences, besides the remaining significant effects of distance, borders, and other geographical and trade policy variables.

The chapter's discussion of the impacts of economic globalization has necessarily been exceedingly brief. Both theory and evidence are read as clearly supportive of the proposition that trade has a positive effect on real incomes. This is why economists believe it is important that the process of international integration be allowed to continue, especially for the sake of those countries that are still poor.

Effects on social values other than aggregate incomes can be positive or negative, depending on the details, and the statistical evidence does not always give clear-cut answers about the bottom line. In the two most studied cases, income distribution and environmental pollution, there seems to be a pattern whereby things get worse in the early stages of industrialization but then start to get better at higher levels of income. Societies that become rich in terms of market-measured output choose to improve their quality of life in other ways as well. It is possible that the same principle extends to noneconomic values such as safety, human rights, and democracy. In short, there is reason to hope that, aside from the various more direct effects of trade on noneconomic values, there is a general indirect beneficial effect that comes through the positive effect of trade on income.

Questions of international governance fall to the later chapters in this volume. But I will conclude with an observation on the subject of labor and environmental standards, which inspired fervent demonstrations at the November 1999 World Trade Organization meeting in Seattle. An international "trilemma" composed of sovereignty, regulation, and integration has been noted: countries can have any two of these three desirable goals, but they cannot have all three at once. Does this mean that globalization impedes sovereign countries from choosing their own labor and environmental regulations? Perhaps. But such cross-border concerns as child labor, endangerment of species, and emissions of greenhouse gases do not arise from international trade and investment. These problems would exist even without trade. The concerns arise from a noneconomic kind of globalization—having more to do with the transmission of information and ideas—considered in other chapters of this volume. Presumably the demonstrators do not favor shutting off this transmission. But in that case shutting off economic globalization would not help either.

Neither international trade nor global institutions such as the WTO are obstacles to addressing those concerns. To the contrary, the obstacle to multilateral efforts to protect the global environment, such as ratification of the Kyoto Protocol on Climate Change, *is precisely national sovereignty,* along with a failure of citizens of each country to agree among themselves on the priority that their society should place on environmental benefits. These two obstacles—obsession with national sovereignty and internal disagreements—are, ironically, as bad or worse in the United States as in other countries. The obstacle to international action on the environment is not, as most of the Seattle demonstrators appeared to believe, the *infringement* of sovereignty by multilateral institutions such as the WTO.

Notes

1. Jeffrey Frankel, *Regional Trading Blocs in the World Trading System* (Washington: Institute for International Economics, 1997), chap. 3; Paul Krugman, "Growing World Trade: Causes and Consequences," *Brookings Papers on Economic Activity,* no. 1 (1995), pp. 327–62. Krugman emphasizes that many of the most important technical advances occurred before 1870, such as steel-hulled ships, the screw propeller, and the trans-Atlantic telegraph. Cooper, "Comments" on Paul Krugman, "Growing World Trade: Causes and Consequences," *Brookings Papers on Economic Activity,* no. 1 (1995), pp. 363–68, argues that the technological progress of this century has had more of an effect than Krugman

admits, as do Michael Bordo, Barry Eichengreen, and Douglas Irwin, "Is Globalization Today Really Different Than Globalization a Hundred Years Ago?" *Brookings Trade Forum* (Brookings, 1999), pp. 1–65.

2. Alberto Alesina, Enrico Spolaore, and Romain Wacziarg, "Economic Integration and Political Disintegration," Working Paper 6163 (Cambridge, Mass.: National Bureau of Economic Research, September 1997), and *American Economic Review*, forthcoming. Alesina, Spolaore, and Wacziarg argue that the correlation between trade integration (as reflected in trade/GDP ratios), and political separatism (as reflected in the number of countries in the world), is a systematic pattern historically, attributable to the need for economies of scale. If countries can attain these economies of scale through international trade in an open global system, they need not attain them through political union with other countries.

3. But it is not always the case that "there is nothing new under the sun." Economic globalization in the nineteenth century *was* qualitatively different from what had come in preceding centuries, for example, in the Age of Exploration. Kevin O'Rourke and Jeffrey Williamson, "The Heckscher-Ohlin Model between 1400 and 2000: Why It Explained Factor Price Convergence, When It Did Not, and Why," Working Paper 7411 (Cambridge, Mass.: National Bureau of Economic Research, November 1999) show that by the relevant economic criteria the "big bang" of globalization is properly dated in the nineteenth century.

4. John Maynard Keynes, *The Economic Consequences of the Peace* (Harcourt, Brace, and Howe, 1920).

5. The conference at Bretton Woods, New Hampshire, in 1944 had proposed the creation of an International Trade Organization as the third of the institutions, the one to promote free trade. In this aspect, however, the U.S. Congress opted for a reprise of its rejection twenty-five years before of the president's League of Nations, dooming the ITO at conception. It was not until 1995 that the stopgap GATT in Geneva became a true international multilateral agency, the World Trade Organization.

6. Richard Baldwin and Philippe Martin, "Two Waves of Globalization: Superficial Similarities, Fundamental Differences," NBER Working Paper 6904 (January 1999) provide a cornucopia of data comparing postwar globalization with the earlier wave from 1820 to 1914.

7. The average country constitutes about 0.5 of 1 percent of world output. (There are about 180 members of the International Monetary Fund.) Thus in a fully globalized world, the average country would buy or sell 99.5 percent of its output abroad. Again, most economies fall far short of this degree of international integration. Singapore and Hong Kong are the only two exceptions. Their exports and imports are each more than 100 percent of GDP, which points up that the denominator of the ratio should really be a measure of gross sales, not a value-added measure like GDP. In other words, the statistic that globalization must increase sixfold before it is complete is an underestimate.

8. Lant Pritchett and Geeta Sethi, "Tariff Rates, Tariff Revenue, and Tariff Reform: Some New Facts," *World Bank Economic Review*, vol. 8 (January 1994), pp. 1–16.

9. Across commodities, the c.i.f. margin for U.S. trade ranges from a low of 0.7 percent for pearls and 0.8 percent for aircraft, to a high of 25.1 percent for salt, sulphur, earth, stone, and plastering material. Across U.S. trading partners, the c.i.f. margin ranges from

1.7 percent for Mexico to 25.8 percent for Guinea. For an elaboration of these statistics, see Frankel, *Regional Trading Blocs*, pp. 40–45.

10. The literature is surveyed by Kenneth Rogoff, "The Purchasing Power Parity Puzzle," *Journal of Economic Literature*, vol. 34 (June 1996), pp. 647–68.

11. Charles Engel, "Real Exchange Rates and Relative Prices: An Empirical Investigation," *Journal of Monetary Economics*, vol. 32 (August1993), pp. 35–50.

12. Kenneth Froot, Michael Kim, and Kenneth Rogoff, "The Law of One Price over 700 Years," Working Paper 5132 (Cambridge, Mass.: National Bureau of Economic Research, May 1995).

13. From 1870 to 1913, however, O'Rourke and Williamson, "The Heckscher-Ohlin Model," find a steady downward trend in the differential in wheat prices between Europe and the United States as the result of trade.

14. Hans Linnemann, *An Econometric Study of International Trade Flows* (Amsterdam: North-Holland, 1960); and Peter Drysdale and Ross Garnaut, "Trade Intensities and the Analysis of Bilateral Trade Flows in a Many-Country World," *Hitotsubashi Journal of Economics*, vol. 22 (1982), pp. 62–84.

15. Charles Engel and John Rogers, "How Wide Is the Border?" *American Economic Review*, vol. 86 (December 1996), pp. 1112–25.

16. The sources for the gravity estimates cited here, unless otherwise specified, are Frankel, *Regional Trading Blocs*; and Andrew Rose, "One Money, One Market: Estimating the Effect of Common Currencies on Trade," *Economic Policy*, vol. 30 (April 2000), pp. 7–46; Jeffrey Frankel and Andrew Rose, "An Estimate of the Effect of Currency Unions on Trade and Growth," conference on Currency Unions, organized by Alberto Alesina and Robert Barro, Hoover Institution, Stanford University, May 2000; and an early reference on the gravity model is Linnemann, *An Econometric Study*.

17. Ephraim Kleiman, "Trade and the Decline of Colonialism," *Economic Journal*, vol. 86 (September 1976), pp. 459–80.

18. The colonial relationship is defined as of 1945. (Before taking the exponent, the estimate is 1.75 in 1990, or 2.2 for 1970–90 pooled.)

19. Edward Mansfield, "Effects of International Politics on Regionalism in International Trade," in Kym Anderson and Richard Blackhurst, eds., *Regional Integration and the Global Trading System* (Harvester Wheatsheaf, 1993); Edward Mansfield and Rachel Bronson, "The Political Economy of Major-Power Trade Flows," in Edward Mansfield and Helen Milner, eds., *The Political Economy of Regionalism* (Columbia University Press 1997); and Joanne Gowa and Edward Mansfield, "Power Politics and International Trade," *American Political Science Review*, vol. 87 (June 1993), pp. 408–20.

20. Frankel, *Regional Trading Blocs*; and Rose, "One Money."

21. Shang-Jin Wei, "How Stubborn Are Nation States in Globalization?" Working Paper 5331 (Cambridge, Mass.: National Bureau of Economic Research, April 1996).

22. John McCallum, "National Borders Matter: Canada-U.S. Regional Trade Patterns," *American Economic Review*, vol. 85 (June 1995), pp. 615–23.

23. John Helliwell, *How Much Do National Borders Matter?* (Brookings, 1998).

24. Engel and Rogers, "How Wide Is the Border?"

25. John Helliwell and John McCallum, "National Borders Still Matter for Trade," *Policy Options/Options Politiques*, vol. 16 (July–August 1995), pp. 44–48.

26. Frankel, *Regional Trading Blocs,* pp. 135–39; and Jeffrey Frankel and Shang-Jin Wei, "Regionalization of World Trade and Currencies: Economics and Politics," in J. Frankel ed., *The Regionalization of the World Economy* (University of Chicago Press, 1997); and Rose, "One Money."

27. Rose, "One Money."

28. Alan Taylor, "International Capital Mobility in History: The Saving-Investment Relationship," Working Paper 5743 (Cambridge, Mass.: National Bureau of Economic Research, 1996).

29. Martin Feldstein and Charles Horioka, "Domestic Saving and International Capital Flows," *Economic Journal,* vol. 90 (1980): 314–29; and Jeffrey Frankel, "Measuring International Capital Mobility: A Review," *American Economic Review,* vol. 82 (May 1992), pp. 197–202, offers a short survey of the saving-investment and interest parity tests of financial integration.

30. Karen Lewis, "Puzzles in International Financial Markets," in Gene Grossman and Kenneth Rogoff, eds., *Handbook of International Economics,* vol. 3 (North Holland, 1995).

31. Country-specific sentiment seems to separate investors who reside in different countries. The price of a closed-end country fund traded in New York City differs widely from the "net asset value," the price of the basket of stocks traded in the country, which should be identical in value. Kenneth Froot and Emil Dabora, "How Are Stock Prices Affected by the Location of Trade," *Journal of Financial Economics,* vol. 53 (August 1999), pp. 182–216. Even in the case of what is virtually the identical company, Froot and Dabora show that Siamese twins like Royal Dutch/Shell exhibit imperfect integration, the price of Royal Dutch behaving as if it is part of the New York stock market and Shell as part of the London market.

32. Gene Grossman and Elhanan Helpman, *Innovation and Growth in the Global Economy* (MIT Press, 1991); and Elhanan Helpman and Paul Krugman, *Market Structure and Foreign Trade* (MIT Press, 1985).

33. Jeffrey Frankel and David Romer, "Does Trade Cause Growth?" *American Economic Review,* vol. 89 (June 1999), pp. 379–99.

34. The smaller estimate is the more relevant if one wishes to hold constant for such income determinants as investment, human capital, and initial (1960) income in order to isolate the direct effect of trade on income. But it leaves out, for example, any effect of openness that comes by way of investment, which is included in the larger number. The smaller estimate is the more relevant if one wishes to hold constant for such income determinants as investment, human capital, and initial (1960) income in order to isolate the direct medium-run effect of trade on income. But given the estimated speed of convergence, an effect of 0.3 over a twenty-five-year period translates into an effect of 1.2 in the long-run steady state. Douglas Irwin and Marko Tervio, "Does Trade Raise Income? Evidence from the Twentieth Century," preliminary draft (March 2000), going back as far as 1913, find large effects as well.

35. Dani Rodrik and Francisco Rodríguez, "Trade Policy and Economic Growth: A Skeptic's Guide to the Cross-National Evidence" (Harvard University, Kennedy School of Government, 2000); and National Bureau of Economic Research, *Macroeconomics Annual 2000* (Cambridge, Mass., forthcoming), have critiqued the empirical literature that finds an association between trade and growth.

36. There are many possible references. Maurice Obstfeld, "The Global Capital Market: Benefactor or Menace?" Working Paper 6559 (Cambridge, Mass.: National Bureau of

Economic Research, May 1998) also forthcoming in the *Journal of Economic Perspectives,* and Jeffrey Frankel, "Proposals Regarding Restrictions on Capital Flows," *African Finance Journal,* vol.1 (1999), pp. 92–104, each succinctly state the arguments for and against international capital mobility.

37. One of the most important arguments *in favor* of trade is also noneconomic—that it promotes peace and understanding and helps spread values like democracy and free markets that Americans prize. There is not enough space to discuss this argument here. This is probably just as well, as many opponents are under the illusion that free trade is a favor that Americans do to benefit other countries—a favor, for example, that was geopolitically necessary during the cold war but that the United States can no longer afford.

38. O'Rourke and Williamson, "The Heckscher-Olin Model," find that trade did have the major equalizing influence hypothesized on returns to labor, land, and capital in the nineteenth century, the period that the Heckscher-Ohlin theory was designed to explain.

39. For example, see Paul Krugman and Robert Lawrence, "Trade, Jobs and Wages," *Scientific American,* April 1994.

40. Though this is only 6 percent of the total unequalizing forces. The complication is that a large increase has occurred in the supply of skilled workers, which works to drive down their relative wage; thus the total unequalizing forces to be explained are more than 100 percent of the increase in the gap between skilled and unskilled wages. William Cline, *Trade, Jobs, and Income Distribution* (Washington: Institute for International Economics, 1997).

41. Avik Chakrabarti, "Do Nations That Trade Have a More Unequal Distribution of Income?" (University of Wisconsin, 2000).

42. Robert Barro, "Inequality, Growth, and Investment," Working Paper 7038 (Cambridge, Mass.: March 1999), includes references and updated statistical support for the relationship for many countries.

43. Gene Grossman and Alan Krueger, "Economic Growth and the Environment," *Quarterly Journal of Economics,* vol. 110 (1995), pp. 353–77.

44. Some revised data are not as supportive of the inverted U-shaped relationship between income and pollution. William Harbaugh, Arik Levinsohn, and David Wilson, "Reexamining the Empirical Evidence for an Environmental Kuznets Curve," NBER Working Paper 7711 (Cambridge, Mass.: National Bureau of Economic Research, May 2000). But the authors also find that trade per se has a beneficial effect, holding constant for income.

45. When deciding where to locate, multinational firms pay far more attention to such issues as labor costs and market access than to the stringency of local environmental regulation. J. A. Tobey, "The Effects of Domestic Environmental Policies on Patterns of World Trade: An Empirical Test," *Kyklos,* vol. 43 (1990), pp. 191–209; and Adam Jaffe and others, "Environmental Regulation and the Competitiveness of U.S. Manufacturing: What Does the Evidence Tell Us?" *Journal of Economic Literature,* vol. 33 (1995), pp. 132–63.

46. Werner Antweiler, Brian Copeland, and M. Scott Taylor, "Is Free Trade Good for the Environment?" Working Paper 6707 (Cambridge, Mass.: National Bureau of Economic Research, August 1998).

3

GRAHAM ALLISON

The Impact of Globalization on National and International Security

GLOBALIZATION is clearly a buzzword, perhaps the buzzword of the era. At the outset, it is useful to remind ourselves that it is essentially a conceptual construct, not a simple fact. As currently used, globalization is too often an ill-defined pointer to a disparate array of phenomena—frequently accompanied by heavy breathing that implies that behind these phenomena, or at their root, is some yet-to-be-discovered substance. (Recall Locke's definition of matter: "something I know not what.") As used by many popularizers today, it reminds me of a famous radio program called "The Shadow," whose lead line announced, "The Shadow has the power to cloud men's minds." Distinguishing between globalization, on the one hand, and globaloney, on the other, is a major challenge.

To assist in that task, let me propose a definition based on what one of my colleagues calls the "network metaphor." According to this metaphor, globalization should be thought of in terms of *identifiable networks*. Etymologically, networks are a conceptual extension of a simple object called a net, for example, a fishing net, in which connected strands cross at regular intervals. Linkages among nodes in a radio or television broadcasting system, or connected electronic components, become a network. Using this metaphor, globalization is thus defined as the creation or expansion of

The author wishes to thank Ben Dunlap for assistance in the preparation of this chapter.

an identifiable network around the globe. A global network connects points and people around the globe on some specified dimension or medium.

The significance of this definition becomes clearer if one contrasts globalization with regionalization, nationalization, solar-system-ization, or even universalization. Nationalization is understood as establishment of networks among points and people along specified dimensions across the nation; solar-system-ization as creation of networks along specific dimensions among points across a solar system.

In the case of networks, consider the telephone network or an electricity network or even the Internet. A network is defined in terms of specific connections among points or people who are parts of the network. Networks have an "architecture" that defines the specific nature of the relationship among units in the system. Three standard network architectures are the "hub and spokes" or "star," the grid, consisting of interconnected hubs, and the "bus" network, consisting of a single transmission link onto which various nodes are attached (figures 3-1, 3-2, 3-3). Air traffic originating from a single airport is an example of a hub and spokes network; electricity networks are an example of the grid architecture; the bus network is a commonly used Internet topology. Other examples from Internet topology include the "ring" and the "star-wired ring"—a combination of the star and ring configuration (figures 3-4, 3-5).

Earlier discussions of growing global interconnectedness produced the concept of "interdependence," meaning, essentially, reciprocal effects resulting from ties among different countries. Over time it became clear that interdependence captured only part of the story. Countries and actors in different countries are often interconnected on specific dimensions, and by virtue of this connectedness have reciprocal impacts on one another. But rarely are the effects of such interactions equal. Relative power, strength, or influence are also defining factors in relationships among countries or actors in different countries.

Using the concept of a global network, we can identify two key questions about globalization. First, what specific connection exists between which specific points in the system? Without specific connections among specific points around the globe on some specific dimensions, there is no globalization. Only points on the globe connected to the global system, for example, the Internet, participate in this specific global system. Second, we can ask about the *impact* of each unit in the system on other units. In a hub and spokes network, a central source of power, such as a

Figure 3-1. *The Star*

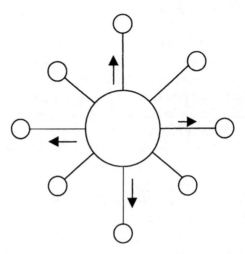

Figure 3-2. *The Grid*

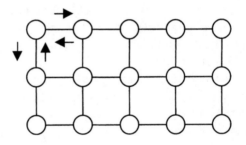

Figure 3-3. *The Bus*

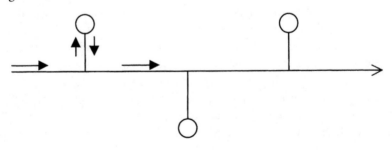

Figure 3-4. *The Ring*

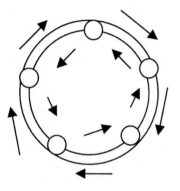

Figure 3-5. *The Star and Ring*

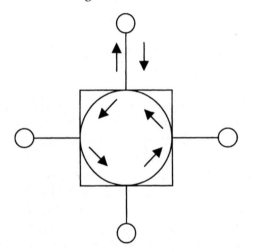

central power station, distributes electricity out through regional nodes to local consumers, with impact flowing in only one direction. Alternatively, in an electricity power grid, multiple generators distribute power among nodes in a network. The remarkably "democratizing" character of the Internet has often been noted for many legitimate reasons. For example, every participant in the system can generate messages to others; almost anyone with the know-how can create a web site; the World Wide Web as a whole is relatively unregulated; and search engines turn up results in a democratic manner. Nonetheless, differences in relative impact among users and servers or users and content providers or search engines are as large as the power differentials observed in most national systems.

Defining globalization in terms of specific global networks can allow us to avoid much of what appears to be globaloney about the great equalizer. Points around the globe that become connected to a global network along some dimension may benefit, as does a rural farmer when electricity comes to his farm. But no one imagines that the farmer's influence upon the power generator is equivalent to the generator's influence on him. Consider, similarly, the owner of a pharmaceutical factory in Sudan that became connected to a global positioning system plus a long-range delivery system for precision-guided munitions. This linkage made it possible for the president of the United States by a unilateral decision to destroy that facility in a matter of hours, bringing home to the factory owner the inequality of an unwelcome connectedness.

What Is Meant by "Traditional National and International Security Issues"

In the standard international relations textbooks, states are the principal actors in international relations, and the central issues for states are survival, integrity of national territory and institutions, freedom of action to preserve these core interests, and prosperity of the state and its citizens. Thus, for example, the Commission on America's National Interests on which I served started with the traditional national security one-liner from post–World War II U.S. strategy, namely, "to preserve the U.S. as a free nation with our fundamental institutions and values intact."[1] The modern version says "to safeguard and enhance the well being of Americans in a free and secure nation," thus recognizing prosperity as well as survival and security as core objectives.

Again, note big differences between great and small powers and thus among strategies available for dealing with challenges to these core objectives. Note also that there can be conflict among these objectives, for example, as shown by the current European experience in submerging sovereign control of currencies in favor of a European Central Bank in the hope of enhancing prosperity. Similarly, to ensure survival and territorial integrity the weak frequently sacrifice independence of action by aligning with stronger powers.

Thus traditional security issues include war and peace, especially among great powers; balances of power and alliances; imperialism; international economic relations including access to critical materials, trade, investments, and currencies; international law; and international institutions. The so-called new agenda includes some issues that have emerged as technologies developed (for example, environmental consequences of production processes or biotech's contributions to affordable weapons of mass destruction) and some that states previously cared less about, particularly events within other states like civil wars and human rights.

The first issue of the leading journal in this field, *International Security*, published in 1976, offered a definition of international security that has proved a durable guide:

Nations are increasingly defining their security not only in the conventional modes of military strength, economic vigor, and governmental stability, but also in terms of capabilities previously less central: energy supplies, science and technology, food, and natural resources. . . . Today, global interdependence has forced transnational concerns—such as trade, terrorism, military supplies, and the environment—to be essential elements in the security considerations of any prospering society. . . . International security embraces all of those factors that have a direct bearing on the structure of the nation state system and the sovereignty of its members, with particular emphasis on the use, threat, and control of force.[2]

In sum, the dependent variable in this essay's inquiry includes states' survival, sovereignty, power, prosperity, and the principal instruments by which they protect and advance these interests.

What Are the Major Starting Theses, or Hypotheses, about the Impact of Globalization on Traditional National and International Security Issues?

Let us begin by considering the major theses presented by the most widely cited overview of this topic, in a book by David Held and others.[3] They offer six principal hypotheses about globalization and security issues.

—"The spread of military technology throughout the world means that as innovators develop and deploy cutting edge high-tech weapons, other states are forced to acquire the latest hardware and systems or pay the price of lagging behind in their military power and security."[4]

While the fact asserted is correct, it is neither new, nor global.

—"Fighting a war in the information age no longer requires the physical mobilization of societies; rather it requires an effective public relations policy that skillfully uses mass media to inform public opinion. Most of all war needs political acquiescence, since it is now capital intensive and potentially more circumscribed."[5]

Again, the assertion is correct, but it describes a development within some states, not a global truth. Moreover, the development cited is not a consequence of globalization.

—"The world is experiencing a new military-technological revolution (MTR) as information technologies transform existing military capabilities, the conduct of warfare, and the ability to project military force over considerable distances with great precision."[6]

MTR is an important, much discussed development in military capabilities that is extending the reach and discrimination of some states' military forces. States with intercontinental ballistic missiles (ICBMs) and nuclear weapons can attack all other points around the globe. Only one state, the United States, can apply discriminating force globally.

—"Real-time global communications systems make running a war easier, since leaders can supervise and intervene in military operations in the field to a degree never before possible."[7]

This is true for a state that has a global C^3 (command, control, and communication)—of which there is only one.

—"Increasing globalization of the civil industrial sectors involved in defense production, such as electronics or optics, compromises the traditional autonomy of national defense capability, since it makes the acquisition and use of weapons subject to the decisions and actions of other authorities or corporations beyond the scope of national jurisdiction."[8]

The phenomenon this proposition points to is occurring and could have major consequences for states that are essentially consumers of products or components from the information and genome revolutions. But for the United States, the much more significant development is the widening gap between civilian, market-driven technological development of chips, computers, genes, and so on, on the one hand, and government-owned or dominated development and application of those technologies, on the other.

—"Threats to national security are becoming both more diffuse and no longer simply military in character. Thus the proliferation of weapons of mass destruction poses a potential threat to all states."[9]

Again, this situation offers an important truth about weapons of mass destruction, but the connection to globalization is unclear.

Second, consider the major theses offered by Thomas Friedman's best seller in *The Lexus and the Olive Tree*, in his chapter on security and geopolitics.[10] Friedman presents four major propositions about impacts of globalization on security.

—Economic development and prosperity leads to peace between nations: "When a country reaches the level of economic development where it has a middle class big enough to support a McDonald's network, it becomes a McDonald's country. And people in McDonald's countries don't like to fight wars anymore, they prefer to wait in line for burgers."[11]

This provocative variant of the democratic peace theory, according to which argument democracies do not fight other democracies, was put to a test in the 1999 NATO air campaign against Serbia. McDonald's golden arches did not save downtown Belgrade. Economic globalization helps spread economic prosperity and technical change, but the impact of this development is less clear. Friedman acknowledges this later in his book, noting that "globalization, while it raises the costs of going to war for reasons of honor, fear, or interest, does not and cannot make any of these instincts obsolete."[12]

—Private international investors, not governments, provide the most significant sources of capital today, guided by the goal of profits, not ideology: "The bulls of the Electronic Herd do not write blank checks to win a country's love and allegiance; they write investment checks to make profits. And the Supermarkets and the Electronic Herd really don't care what color your country is outside any more. All they care about is how your country is wired inside, what level of operating system and software it's able to run, and whether your government can protect private property. Therefore, not only will the herd not fund a country's regional war or rebuild a country's armed forces after a war for free—the way the Superpowers would, just to win its allegiance—the herd will actually punish a country for fighting a war with its neighbors, by withdrawing the only significant source of growth capital in the world today."[13]

Here Friedman points to an important truth. International trade networks transcend traditional state sovereignty. Private international investors

seek predictable, and enforceable, rules of the game. As powerful independent sources of influence on nations and relations among nations, they
help shape the terms on which states participate in particular global networks. Thus the influence of GAAP (Generally Accepted Accounting
Practices, not the clothing store) on aspiring participants in global markets
is suggestive.

—Owing to the globalization of financial networks, states are more vulnerable to economic crisis spread from one region to another. "While
regional military crises get ghettoized today, what gets globalized are the
regional economic crises—like Mexico in the mid-1990s, Southeast Asia in
the late 1990s, and Russia at the end of the 1990s. The domino theory,
which once belonged to the world of politics, today belongs to the world
of finance."[14]

The domino theory has always been more metaphorical than analytical.
Generally, it covers an undifferentiated array of direct, indirect, psycho-
logical, and imagined connections that can be local, regional, or sometimes
even global. Capital markets are globally integrated, and thus events in one
country can affect others, both directly through instantaneous transfer of
funds and psychologically. Such impacts that trigger major disruptions in
an economy can undermine military capabilities, exacerbate secessionist
tendencies, or create vulnerability to external adversaries. These and other
results are richly illustrated by the Asian financial crisis of 1997–98, for
example, in Indonesia (which lost East Timor).

—Global connections give rise to new, less defined security threats.
"You still have to worry about threats coming from nation-states you are
divided from—Iraq, Iran, North Korea. But increasingly now you have to
be concerned with threats coming from those to whom you are connected—including over the Internet, through markets and from Super-
empowered individuals who can walk right in your front door."[15]

Globalized networks of communications, financial markets, and transportation increase states' vulnerability to threats from systems failures and
from nonstate actors.

Reflecting upon the questions posed, and arguments advanced by
Friedman, Held, and others, I offer for consideration eight hypotheses
about impacts of globalization on traditional national and international
security interests.

—Advances in technologies for identifying targets (global positioning
systems) and delivering explosives accurately to targets (missiles and laser-
guided bombs) and doing so in a matter of hours allows some states (par-

ticularly the United States) to reach out and destroy targets at virtually any point on the globe. This phenomenon has existed since the development of ICBMs with nuclear warheads, a capability developed by the United States, Russia, Britain, France, and China. The most recent developments allow the United States to achieve this result with non-nuclear conventional explosives delivered with high accuracy by smart bombs and cruise missiles. Among the consequences: weaker states are vulnerable to coercive threats and uses of force from distant powers in ways that would not have been possible earlier. This was demonstrated vividly by the U.S.-led NATO bombing of Serbia in 1999.

—Advances in technologies of massive destruction, especially biotechnology, that improve the destructive capabilities of biological agents, together with increased accessibility of nuclear weapons and weapons-usable nuclear material from the former Soviet Union, and globalized transportation networks make it possible for rogue states or transnational terrorists to cause destruction in strong states that would previously have been unimaginable.

Among the consequences: if or when Slobodan Milosevic, Osama bin Laden, or their equivalents place nuclear or biological devices in American cities, will the United States conduct an equivalent bombing campaign? Possible leakage of nuclear, biological, and chemical weapons technology and ever-increasing mobility of individuals as well as cargoes create new vulnerabilities even for strong states and stimulate them to take costly preventive measures against mass terrorism on their own soil.

—The erosion of state sovereignty and traditional protections from "interference in internal affairs" has multiple causes but is aggravated by globalization, particularly globalization of information about events in one state that matter to citizens of other states. "CNNization" allows citizens who are connected to a global television network to see for themselves events occurring almost anywhere around the world—and thus to judge that their interests are threatened or values offended. (A modern Bishop Berkley might ask, if a tree falls in the woods where no CNN camera is filming, does it make a sound?) In an attempt to justify what is now called humanitarian intervention, leaders such as Bill Clinton and Tony Blair advance universalist claims, disregarding UN rules that require Security Council approval of interventionist action. The issue has provoked debate among thoughtful leaders in the United Nations, such as Secretary General Kofi Annan, but has produced little consensus on what the new "rules of the game" should be.[16] Those who view international life through the lens of "realism" expect Rwanda and Kosovo to count simply as incidents in the long history of man's inhumanity to fellow human beings. Alternatively, those who view the world through more idealistic or optimistic lenses now hope that these test cases will be seen as significant steps forward in the (faltering but cumulative) construction of a "new new international order." In this scenario, some level of atrocities within a state provides sufficient justification for legitimate military intervention to stop such behavior. In either case the question remains, under what conditions, as assessed by what criteria and through what process can nations legitimately decide to intervene in the internal affairs of other states?

Among the consequences: increased consciousness of distant events that would earlier have passed unnoticed fuels demands, especially in rich democracies, for action. Accordingly, the pressure of public opinion in one nation may affect not only that government but also the government or citizens of another state. The American public's reactions to the plight of Albanians in Kosovo in March 1999 had direct consequences for the citizens and government of Yugoslavia. At the same time, actions that through American eyes seem obviously altruistic and humanitarian appear to many people in other countries hypocritical, hegemonic, neocolonial, or even neoimperialistic.

—"CNNization" allows citizens to watch war in their own living rooms, judge their military's performance on the battlefield or in the air, or assess flows of refugees or damage to civilians.

Among the consequences: war managers give increased emphasis to theatrics and manage perceptions (as in national politics). For example, in June 1999 NATO delayed its triumphal entry into Pristina airport in Kosovo until daylight in order to have appropriate light to allow TV coverage of NATO liberators. Under that night's cover of darkness, Russian troops beat them to the airport. More recently, having watched with amazement NATO's success in shaping opinion about the war in Kosovo, the Russian government and military made a rigorous, extensive, and largely successful effort to manage Russian perceptions of their latest war against Chechnya.

—Global networks in communication and trade make elites aware of superior goods and technologies. Consciousness creates demands for, and supply of, items that consumers in all societies prefer when made aware of them (from TVs and cell phones to Big Macs and blue jeans). Such demands spread "technologies"—physical and managerial—that have proved more efficient in producing prosperity, from internal combustion engines and integrated circuits to market-based private ownership, private rewards (on the basis of results rather than need) and private decisions about investment and production.

The consequences are multiple. Since economic performance and a society's technological base are the substructure of military capability, states seeking to develop military capabilities sufficient to ensure survival and independence have to go with the global flow of superior technologies. These include not only hardware but social software, like access to the Internet for a population that is able to develop software or participate in financial markets. Consider, for example, any Russian government's options today. Is there a viable alternative to seeking to join the global economy? President Vladimir Putin has answered unambiguously no. Larger implications of this proposition for democracy (as Francis Fukuyama has argued), for universal acceptance of ideas and ideals, and even for identity and interests deserve careful reflection.

—Global networks, particularly in economics, create demands by powerful players for predictability in interactions and thus for rules of the game that become, in effect, elements of international law.

Among the consequences: from GAAP to contracts that are enforceable under the commercial code of the state of New York to the World Trade Organization (WTO), international law advances inexorably.

—Consciousness of the extent to which terms and conditions of life for citizens within a state are shaped by actors beyond states (for example, multinational corporations or currency traders) produces, especially among weaker participants, demands for greater international governance. After protests in Seattle and Washington, D.C., "globalization" has been stigmatized. The processes of globalization naturally produce a backlash. The reasons for discontent are evident enough: globalization forces radical changes in countries and highlights national governments' inability to control their citizens' security and well-being.

Among the consequences: calls for international institutions that represent the interests of parties affected become increasingly plausible. Even financier George Soros, whom some regard as representative of the non-state actors shaping terms and conditions of life for citizens around the globe, has advocated building more effective transnational institutions of governance to help regulate the impact of globalizing economic forces.

—Transnational issues, such as illegal drug trade, terrorism, disease, smuggling, and organized crime, pose an increasing threat as global networks proliferate and strengthen. The *1999 Annual Report* of the U.S.

Secretary of Defense identifies transnational dangers as one of America's key security challenges. "The illegal drug trade and international organized crime, including piracy and the illegal trade in weapons and strategic materials, will persist, undermining the legitimacy of friendly governments, disrupting key regions and sea lanes, and threatening the safety of U.S. citizens at home and abroad. Finally, environmental disasters, uncontrolled flows of migrants, and other human emergencies will sporadically destabilize regions of the world." The report continues: "Increasingly capable and violent terrorists," it warns, "will continue to directly threaten the lives of American citizens and their institutions will try to undermine U.S. policies and alliances."[17]

Most networks can be used for both legitimate and illegitimate purposes. Globalization of networks means that the effects of illicit activities can be felt globally. For example, advances in telecommunications and shipping technology that have revolutionized international commerce also lower barriers and costs for terrorists or drug producers. The combination of globalization and the revolution in information technology have super-empowered individuals and groups all over the planet for pursuit of both creative and destructive aims. In addition, problems that are inherently transnational, such as environmental degradation and disease, naturally leap sovereign borders. Global communication and transportation networks spread transnational threats beyond immediate neighbors to distant nodes on the network.

Among the consequences: transnational problems, including economic, environmental, terrorist, cultural, criminal, and other threats to national security cannot be resolved by national means alone. Solutions require regional and even global mechanisms of cooperation and coordination. Thus, technologically driven creation of linkages among points around the globe on dimensions including information, communication, finance, trade, and the use of military power, create demands for supranational governance. How these demands can be addressed by political leaders accountable to narrower constituencies is globalization's enduring challenge to governance.

Notes

1. The Commission on America's National Interests, *America's National Interests* (Cambridge, Mass.: Belfer Center for Science and International Affairs, 2000), p. 15.

2. Center for Science and International Affairs, *International Security* (MIT Press, 1976).

3. David Held and others, *Global Transformations: Politics, Economics, and Culture* (Stanford University Press, 1999).

4. Held and others, *Global Transformations*, p. 104.

5. Ibid., p. 138.

6. Ibid.

7. Ibid.

8. Ibid.

9. Ibid., p. 102.

10. Thomas Friedman, *The Lexus and the Olive Tree* (Farrar, Strauss, and Giroux, 1999).

11. Ibid., p. 196.

12. Ibid., p. 197.

13. Ibid., p. 201.

14. Ibid., p. 204.

15. Ibid., p. 211.

16. See Kofi Annan, "Human Rights and Humanitarian Intervention in the Twenty-First Century," in Samantha Power and Graham Allison, eds., *Realizing Human Rights: Moving from Inspiration to Impact* (St. Martin's Press, forthcoming).

17. U.S. Department of Defense, *Report of the Secretary of Defense to the President and the Congress* (1999).

4

WILLIAM C. CLARK

Environmental Globalization

IN THIS EXPLORATION of environmental globalization, I adopt much of the conceptual framework for globalization from chapter 1 by Robert O. Keohane and Joseph S. Nye Jr., in this volume. In particular, I use their distinction between "globalism" as a condition or state of affairs and "globalization" as a process of increasing globalism. I share their conceptualization of globalism as consisting of networks of connections among actors (state and nonstate) at multicontinental distances, mediated through an open-ended variety of flows including people, information and ideas, force, capital, goods, and materials. This chapter also follows a line of thought that Keohane and Nye attribute to David Held, acknowledging globalism's ancient, if generally "thin," roots and focusing attention on identifying the processes—which they call processes of globalization—through which those roots become increasingly "thick."[1] This "thickening" of globalism is a usefully ambiguous image that, following Keohane and Nye, I use in my characterization of the extent of environmental globalization to direct attention toward possible increases in the variety, strength, and density of long distance relationships among actors, the number of actors entrained in those relationships, and the velocity of change in society that those changed relationships help to induce.[2]

Within a broad conceptual framework that focuses on intercontinental networks of relationships among social actors, three sorts of linkages stand out as important for understanding how the environment figures in relations among actors at multicontinental scales. The first, which I label "environmental stuff," addresses ways in which the flow of energy, materials, and organisms through the environment couples the actions of people in one place with the threats and opportunities faced by people long distances away. The second linkage, "environmental ideas," addresses ways in which people invoke the environment in structuring their relations with other people long distances away. The third linkage, "environmental governance," addresses the changing configuration of actors, norms, and expectations that have emerged as societies have wrestled with the globalization of environmental stuff and ideas.

The Globalization of Environmental "Stuff"

It is easy to point to examples of environmental stuff that have come to figure in relations among actors at intercontinental scale: plague germs, radioactive fallout from atmospheric tests of nuclear weapons, greenhouse gas emissions, and a few others would be on most people's lists. To build a critical understanding of the extent, prospects, and significance of environmental globalization, however, it is necessary go beyond selective lists to a systematic treatment of what kinds of linkages might be involved in environmental globalization, and to an empirical analysis of which of those linkages have mattered. Such a systematic treatment must begin with an understanding of the earth as a system.

As understanding of the earth system has emerged during the last two decades, it has revealed the planet's environment to be shaped by complex linkages among atmosphere, ocean, soil, and biota (figure 4-1). One common thread weaving through these systems is the flow of energy that drives the circulation of oceans and atmosphere, generates the climate, powers photosynthesis and surrounds us with light, heat, and ionizing radiation. Tightly coupled with the flow of energy is the global hydrological cycle. Another common thread is the flow of the major chemical compounds of carbon, nitrogen, oxygen, sulfur, and phosphorus. Finally, modern views of the earth system recognize the ubiquitous influence of life on the planet's interacting flows of energy and materials. One such form of life—our own species—is now recognized to constitute a significant force in shaping the planet's environment, even as it is shaped in turn by the world it has helped to create. The result of these multiple interactions is a

Figure 4-1. *Earth System Processes*

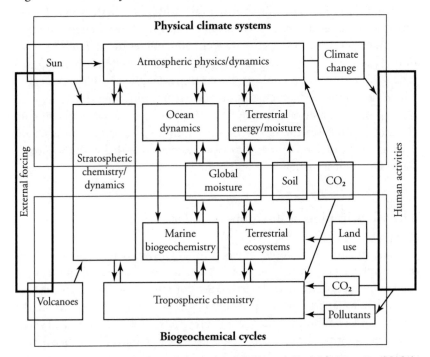

Source: Adapted from figure 2.4.2 of National Aeronautics and Space Administration (NASA), *Earth Systems Science Overview: A Program for Global Change* (also known as the Bretherton Report) (1986).

Note: This figure shows relationships among the biological, chemical, geophysical, and social processes characterizing the earth system.

complex system of *change*—change over temporal scales ranging from seconds to billions of years, and over spatial scales extending from the local to the global. The individual processes underlying these changes in the earth system span a comparable range of scales, from the acute and local turbulence of tornados to the slow and global tectonics of continental drift (figure 4-2).

Energy Linkages

The nature of the earth system—before and after the rise of our own species—is such that disturbances to the planet's energy budget at local scales can cascade upscale to create large-scale impacts half a planet away. The theoretical foundations and potential implications of such "teleconnections" were grasped nearly a half-century ago by John von Neumann who characterized them with his evocative image of a "butterfly effect" on world weather. Today, they are at the heart of forecasting efforts focused on the El Nino–Southern Oscillation phenomenon, where changes in sea-surface temperatures in the Pacific Ocean's eastern tropics are reflected in changes in India's monsoons, and in episodes of increased heat or drought as far away as northeastern North America, the east coast of South America, and Africa.[3] Numerous additional natural teleconnections of transcontinental scale have also been documented, including decadal North Atlantic oscillation in sea-level pressure that influences such diverse phenomena as winter temperatures in Siberia, the cod stock of the northwest Atlantic, and the mass balance of European glaciers.[4] As far as we know, all of these teleconnections are natural phenomena. They nonetheless clearly have the potential for bringing environment into relations among human actors at an intercontinental scale. Moreover, there are good reasons to suspect that some of these long distance teleconnections could be—and indeed may have been—altered by human activities that affect climate or the hydrologic cycle.[5]

Material Linkages

Although alteration of natural climatic teleconnections through human activities could well turn out to be the most dramatic aspect of environmental globalization in the future, two other aspects of long range linkages of environmental stuff have mattered more for human affairs of the past and present: flows of material and flows of biota.

Many materials in the earth system are involved in only modest movement and thus link the fates of human actors over only local to continental scales. These local effects may be extremely important, such as the effect of soil erosion on downstream neighbors or of factory emissions on nearby towns or regions. But they are not the stuff of globalization. In general, it is only through entrainment in the large-scale circulation of the atmosphere, or through intentional transport by humans, that material transport becomes significant in the relationships among actors at transcontinental distances.

Intercontinental transport by way of human conveyance of environmentally hazardous materials such as biocides and toxic wastes has been a

Figure 4-2. *Earth System Scales*

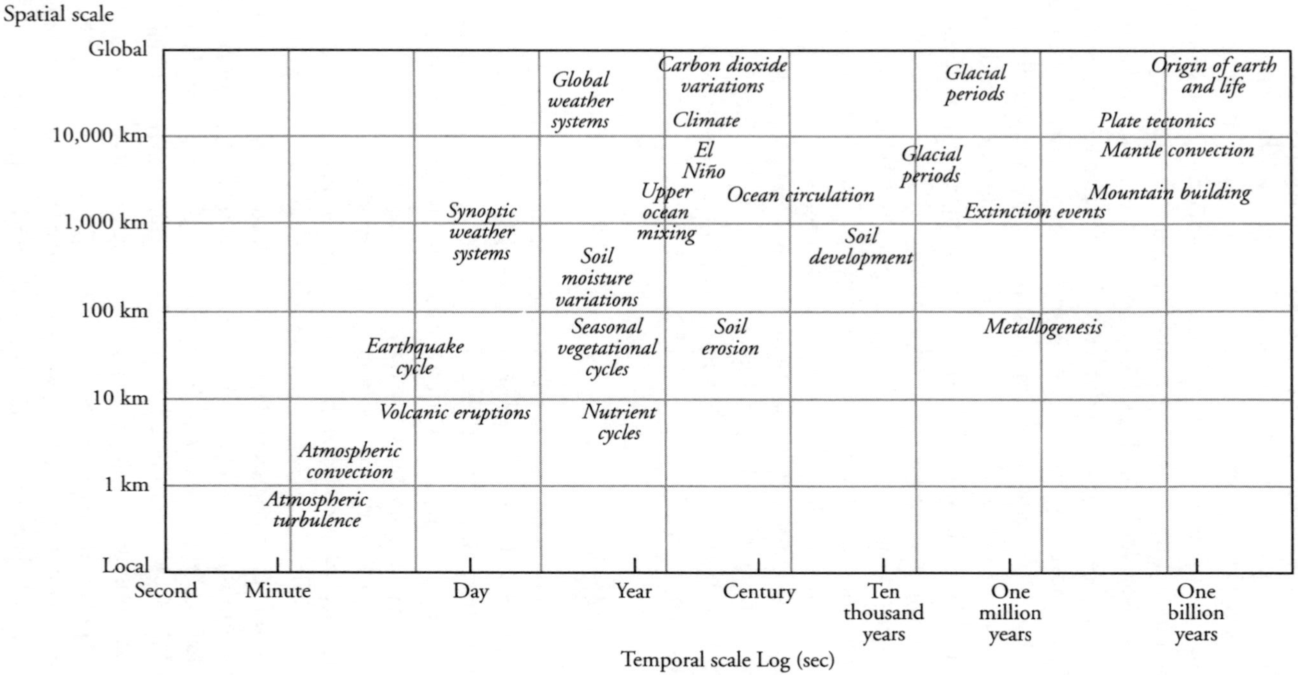

Spatial scale

Spatial scale	Second	Minute	Day	Year	Century	Ten thousand years	One million years	One billion years
Global				*Global weather systems*	*Carbon dioxide variations* / *Climate*		*Glacial periods*	*Origin of earth and life*
10,000 km			*Synoptic weather systems*					*Plate tectonics* / *Mantle convection* / *Mountain building*
1,000 km				*Soil moisture variations* / *Upper ocean mixing*	*El Niño* / *Ocean circulation*	*Soil development*	*Glacial periods* / *Extinction events*	
100 km			*Earthquake cycle*	*Seasonal vegetational cycles*	*Soil erosion*		*Metallogenesis*	
10 km			*Volcanic eruptions*	*Nutrient cycles*				
1 km		*Atmospheric convection*						
Local		*Atmospheric turbulence*						

Temporal scale Log (sec)

Source: Adapted from figure 2.3 of NASA, *Earth Systems Science Overview: A Program for Global Change* (also known as the Bretherton Report).
Note: This figure shows relationships among the time and space scales of the earth system processes depicted in figure 4-1. The axes are logarithmic.

subject of increasing attention in recent years.[6] There is no question that such transport has grown dramatically in the postwar period. Part of the reason has been the increasing trade of such materials in a globalizing economy; part has been the implementation of local regulations that increase incentives to send environmentally offensive materials elsewhere. Several well-publicized scandals involving "dumping" of such materials from countries of the North to countries in the South has led to such transport becoming more subject—at least in principle—to international monitoring and regulation. Nonetheless, at present the use and disposal of such materials remains largely local, with only a small fraction (far less than 10 percent for toxic wastes) actually shipped over transcontinental distances.

By far the most important—and most rapidly changing—way in which the environment figures in intercontinental relations today involves increases in the kinds and amounts of material entrained in the global circulation of the atmosphere. Most materials do not remain in the atmosphere long enough to travel over intercontinental distances but are instead precipitated out by gravity, dissolved in or absorbed on precipitation, or chemically transformed into something else. Nonetheless, a few gases such as carbon monoxide (CO) and dioxide (CO_2), methane (CH_4), nitrous oxide (N_2O), tropospheric ozone (O_3), and the chlorofluorocarbons (CFCs) are sufficiently long lived to become distributed and to affect the environment many thousands of kilometers from their point of emission.[7] Others, among them the so-called persistent organic pollutants (POPs), are sufficiently prone to revolatilize upon deposition that, through multiple transport episodes, they end up connecting midlatitude industrial societies with arctic haze or poisoned penguins.[8] Finally, sufficiently fine particles of even heavy materials such as lead can travel intercontinental distances, as evidenced by the occasional deposition of Saharan sand in Europe and industrial lead emissions in Greenland glaciers. In fact, if produced in sufficient quantities and sought with sufficient ingenuity, almost any material will have enough mass in the long "tail" of its distance distribution to build up measurable impacts at global scales.

Sometimes, natural processes introduce sufficient quantities of material into local environments to have global impacts. A well-known example is the precipitation of Europe and North America's "year without a summer" through the chilling effects of sulfate aerosols injected into the stratosphere by the 1815 eruption of the Tambora volcano in Indonesia. Besides such naturally caused linkages, however, emissions of a number of materials capable of sustaining long distance transport have increased dramatically in the postwar period.[9] The potential for environmental change figuring significantly in relations among actors at intercontinental scales is growing accordingly—very much a phenomenon of the past fifty years.

Whether that potential is realized depends, of course, on whether the actors involved are sensitive or vulnerable to, or otherwise concerned with, the consequences of long range material transport. Modern research and monitoring *might* have shown that much of the environment's potential for long range transport was not grounds for much concern. The history of discoveries during the past half-century is almost uniformly one of surprising revelations that the impacts of long distance transport of materials are more complex and potentially pernicious than originally supposed.[10] Discoveries of the 1960s included the global distribution and impacts of strontium-90 produced in atmospheric weapons testing, and of DDT used for pest control. The 1970s added attention to stratospheric ozone depletion driven by chlorofluorocarbons and other halogenated compounds that are potential catalysts of ozone destruction and have long enough chemical lifetimes to pass into the stratosphere. The possibility of global climate warming driven by increased emissions of the long-lived carbon dioxide had been known since the nineteenth century. By the 1980s, however, concern increased substantially as it became clear that additional contributions from the long-lived greenhouse gases methane, nitrous oxide, and the chlorofluorocarbons, could accelerate and magnify the carbon dioxide effect. The past decade has provided even more pathways of concern, ranging from disruptions of the global nitrogen cycle to global reductions in the capacity of the atmosphere to cleanse itself, thus leading to even faster global increases in the concentrations of most pollutants.[11] Recognition of the potential for environmental surprises through intensified global material flows is only likely to increase.[12]

Biotic Linkages

Most organisms spend their lives confined to relatively small parts of the subcontinental ranges that define the limits of most species' fit with the environment. These organisms come into the play of intercontinental relations among human actors only when previously isolated species are linked through new or intensified transport processes. A few organisms, however, naturally migrate over transcontinental distances. These include a few insects, a larger number of ocean-dwelling fish and mammals, and a significant fraction of birds from the temperate zones.[13] Their migrations provide a direct and often significant biotic link among human societies at transcontinental distances—links that can be broken through disruption of natural migratory patterns.

The most dramatic globalization in biotic linkages has involved the occasional movement (usually aided by human transportation processes) of pest or disease organisms from their native habitats to places where they have never been and where the resident people, or other biota we value, have evolved no protection from the invader. Disease epidemics, other forms of pest outbreaks, and repression or elimination of native species are often the result. Several excellent historical studies have traced the impacts on world affairs of transcontinental disease migrations.[14] Active programs of research and monitoring are in place to reduce the prospects of such unwanted migrations occurring in the future. Long range invasions by other "exotic" organisms are also significant, with perhaps 20 percent of some continental floras now represented by relatively recent immigrants.[15] The impacts of such long distance invasions are extensive, representing a major cause of land use transformation and species extinction.[16] Data on rates of invasion are sparse but suggest a rapid acceleration of incidence and extent owing to increases in commerce, tourism, and travel in general.[17] As one perceptive analysis has observed, "Human transport of species around the Earth is homogenizing the Earth's biota."[18]

A second way in which long distance movements of organisms have affected intercontinental relations among human actors is through the interruption by one group of regular migrations that another group depends on or otherwise values. This can involve harvest of the migratory organism (for example, salmon) or alteration of the habitat on which the migratory organism depends (for example, destruction of the Middle American wintering grounds of North American songbirds). Relations among actors regarding harvest of migratory species have long been subject to treaties and related arrangements, though increasingly the mobility of the harvester, rather than the harvested organism, makes the issue a subject of intercontinental relations.[19] The implications for intercontinental migratory species of local habitat destruction were somewhat later to be appreciated and regulated.[20] Understanding of these complex linkages is incomplete and controversial, as with the current debate over the relation between Middle American deforestation and the possible decline in songbird populations of northeastern North America.[21] The available evidence nonetheless suggests an accelerating trend in the frequency and impact of such disruptions.[22]

Interacting "Stuff"

There has always been a degree of globalism in the ways in which relationships among human actors have been mediated by flows of environmental stuff including energy, materials, and biota. What is new is the dramatic thickening of those relationships over the past half-century, a thickening brought on primarily by the increasing numbers, consumption, and economic connectivity of the world's human population. This thickening means that more and more kinds of human activities, undertaken by more and more people in more and more parts of the world, are imposing more and more impacts on other people at transcontinental scales. Moreover, those impacts are increasingly interactive. To take only one of the most graphic recent examples, it has been shown that climate warming and acidification combine to lower dissolved organic matter concentrations in lakes, which in turn allows deeper penetration of UV-B radiation and its concomitant impacts on life. The enhanced UV-B damage is larger than, and exacerbates, that attributable to ozone depletion in the stratosphere.[23] More generally, a recent report by the U.S. National Research Council concluded that "most of the individual environmental problems that have occupied most of the world's attention to date are unlikely in themselves to prevent substantial progress in [meeting social goals] over the next two generations. . . . More troubling in the medium term . . . are the environmental threats arising from multiple, cumulative and interactive stresses, driven by a variety of human activities."[24]

The Globalization of Environmental Ideas

How have ideas about the environment figured in people's shaping of their relations with one another at intercontinental scales? How has the role of environmental ideas in mediating such relations changed through time?

Managing Planet Earth

It is tempting to answer these questions from a straightforward rational actor perspective. From such a perspective, the growing evidence of globally connected environmental stuff would have been expected to lead to the emergence of a demand for comparably global environmental policy and management. To a significant degree, this appears to be happening. For example,

Richard Benedick, U.S. negotiator for the Montreal Protocol on Substances That Deplete the Ozone Layer, writes of a "new paradigm" for diplomatic approaches to challenges like ozone depletion in which "no single country or group of countries, however powerful, could effectively solve the problem. Without far-ranging cooperation, the efforts of some nations to protect the ozone layer would be undermined."[25] A substantial enterprise of international environmental research, monitoring, and assessment—addressing issues ranging from climate change to whale preservation—has indeed emerged devoted to the task of advancing this new paradigm through the shaping of globally consensual scientific knowledge about cause and effect on which enlightened management of the global commons can be based.[26] An almost equally ambitious effort is seeking to promulgate globally good practices and policy instruments that can make the overall effort to grapple with global environmental linkages more effective and efficient.[27]

All of these initiatives benefit from modern trends enhancing the rate and extent of information transfer. Relevant new scientific findings now diffuse around the globe in hours or days rather than years and decades. Moreover, contemporary environmental issues with an intercontinental dimension now move onto the agendas of public and political elites virtually simultaneously around the world.[28] The net result is that changing ideas about the global character of environmental linkages have fostered a surprisingly rational-looking—if still incomplete—response in research, development, and policy around the world. Moreover, this global process of social learning shows every sign of accelerating, taking place today at rates that may be an order of magnitude faster than those described by Richard Cooper for the global translation of ideas into action in the realm of infectious diseases and quarantine a century ago.[29]

Purity and Danger

There is much to be gained for people as well as the environment from the rationalization of efforts to manage global environmental change. That said, however, the role of ideas about the environment in structuring relations among actors at long distances has almost certainly been a great deal more complicated than Benedick's "new paradigm" suggests. We are given some useful warning as to *how* complex through accounts by anthropologists such as Mary Douglas who have shown the many ways in which environment emerges as an instrument for structuring social relations—for distinguishing "pure" from "polluted" people, or "safe" from "dangerous" practices—in both "primitive" and "modern" societies.[30] To see how such structuring has occurred in the presumably less primitive circumstances that concern us here, we need look no further than one of the earliest intercontinental environmental initiatives: the overseas wildlife conservation efforts of the nineteenth century.[31]

In the late 1800s, the increasingly rare big game animals of Africa and India were being hunted by sportsmen of the North and by the (indigenous) herders and hunters of the South. By defining the big animals as rare and endangered species that needed—in the global interest—to be conserved, the sportsmen conservationists essentially rendered the aims of the local people illegitimate and unjustifiable. This ultimately resulted in white men sitting in exclusive European clubs excluding the local herders and hunters (now "poachers") from the use of their own lands, all justified in terms of new environmental concerns rather than old colonial "rights." Without question, any number of breathtakingly wonderful species of large mammals have survived into the twenty-first century because of such conservation efforts. But equally clearly, environmental ideas of conservation also became, intentionally or not, an extension of transcontinental colonialism by another name.

This story of "white hunter" conservation is not merely a historical curiosity. With intentions at least equally good, modern biodiversity advocates are pushing for the identification of a few "hot spots" around the world that—on the basis of their measured species richness—merit international intervention to preserve them from uses other than those that maximize habitat protection. The debate over whether past emissions of greenhouse gases by a (relatively) few prosperous northerners ought to be weighed equally in international management regimes with the present or future emissions of a great many more relatively poor southerners is simultaneously about structuring humanity's relationships with global nature, and humanity's relationships with its global self. To be sure, the management programs advocated by the modern conservationists and pollution negotiators are generally less racist and more participatory than those of their predecessors. The fact remains, however, that environmental ideas are increasingly being used to structure power relations among actors at intercontinental scales, just as they always have been used to structure those social relationships in more local circumstances. The globalization of environmental ideas is thus at least as much a social and political story as it is a physical one.

Sustainable Development

One set of ideas has emerged during the past two decades that shows some prospect of bridging the gulf sketched above between science- and politics-based concepts of global environmental change. These are the ideas of "sustainable development," a varied and vague set of concepts nonetheless sharing a normative commitment, in the words of the 1987 Brundtland Commission, to "a new era of economic growth, one that must be based on policies that sustain and expand the environmental resource base."[32] Ideas of sustainability do contain a place for the classic transcontinental environmental concerns about climate change and ozone depletion. But they go beyond these global environmental issues to incorporate a globally shared but locally situated set of concerns about meeting human needs for food security, energy, industrial production, habitation, and resource conservation in environmentally sustainable ways.[33] Perhaps even more significant, ideas about sustainability have come to incorporate a more articulate stance on preferred means as well as ultimate ends. In particular, they reflect a growing consensus that effective efforts to rationalize human aspirations and environmental limits over the long run require not only an understanding of globalization but also a commitment to democratization—to effective mobilization of civil society from the grass roots upward in efforts to promote sustainability.[34]

Sustainability ideas—integrating concerns for environmental and economic well-being, as well as both global and local perspectives—were central to the 1992 UN Conference on Environment and Development and have resonated deeply and widely around the world during the past decade. For many people—in the private as well as governmental and nongovernmental sectors—they are emerging as the preferred frame of reference for structuring relationships around the joint themes of environmental, economic, and democratic globalization.[35]

The Globalization of Environmental Governance

Environment has also come to figure in relations among actors at intercontinental scale through the globalization of environmental governance.[36] Most obviously, global governance relationships include the formal treaties among states governing intercontinental environmental issues. More generally, they include a wide range of relationships governing the interactions within and between governments, businesses, and environmental advocates around the world. Examples range from voluntary corporate standards of environmental practice embodied in the International Standards Organization's ISO 14000 or the "Responsible Care" initiative,[37] to the pressures placed by Greenpeace on Shell Oil's Nigerian operations.

The matrix on the changing role of governance developed by Nye and his colleagues (figure 4-3) provides a useful template for systematizing the consideration of how different actors have been entrained in this process.

Government

At the nation-state level, the single greatest contribution to globalization may well be the copying of environmental regulations from one country to another. This effect has not, to my knowledge, been quantified at a global scale. But the degree to which national environmental regulations converge across countries has been remarked upon by a number of scholars.[38] At a more formal level, more than 150 international environmental treaties have now been signed, almost two-thirds of them since World War II and half since 1970. Many of these treaties are of limited scope or regional scale. But substantial agreements of intercontinental scope now exist covering aircraft engine emissions, climate change, ozone layer protection, shipment of hazardous chemicals and pesticides, discharges at sea, sea bed mining, whaling, biodiversity, migratory species, rare and endangered species, wetlands, desertification, plant genetic resources, tropical timber, and nuclear safety.[39] These function with varying degrees of efficacy, but at their best have brought about measurable change in the pressures placed by human activities on the environment.[40] Additional commitments among nation-states have taken the form of modest financial transfers, usually bilateral in character, which may total several billion U.S. dollars a year— a quantity approximately equal to that provided by the multilateral development banks.[41] These aid amounts grew through the 1980s, but plateaued after the Rio conference in 1992 and, for a number of sources, have declined in recent years.

Intergovernmental organizations have played a significant role in environmental globalization since the emergence of international conservation organizations in the nineteenth century.[42] Today, an array of permanent and ad hoc intergovernmental environmental organizations perform

Figure 4-3. *The Changing Role of Governance*

	Private	Public	Third sector
Supranational	Transnational corporations	Intergovernmental organizations	Nongovernmental organizations
National	National corporations	Twentieth-century model	National nonprofits
Subnational	Local businesses	State-local government	Local groups

Source: Adapted from figure 1-1, Robert O. Keohane and Joseph S. Nye Jr., in this volume.

Note: This figure shows relationships between the organizational scale (vertical axis) and the sectoral composition of principal governance roles at the beginning of the twenty-first century, emphasizing the diversification of significant governance roles beyond the dominant place of national governance in the "twentieth-century model."

a wide array of functions ranging from the coordination of research and monitoring, through the provision of scientific assessment and the promotion of international conventions, to implementation support and compliance assurance. This is not the place to review the burgeoning literature on such organizations and their effectiveness.[43] But it is abundantly clear that the networks of connections running through intergovernmental organizations dealing with environmental issues have thickened appreciably during the past several decades. They have done so in part by reaching out into organizations (for example, the World Bank) and regimes (for example, international trade) that previously took little account of environmental linkages among states. And they have developed a deepening level of professionalism and skill. In the process, many of them have become slow moving and conservative in the ways of large bureaucracies everywhere. A central question for them in the coming decades is whether they will retain an important role in environmental globalism or, instead, be displaced by the more agile nongovernmental organizations that have increasingly joined them on the international environmental stage.

Nongovernmental Actors, Public and Private

Significant intercontinental governance initiatives dealing with the environment have also been launched within the private sector. Besides the examples given above, groups such as the World Business Council for Sustainable Development and the International Chamber of Commerce have activities under way on all continents ranging from education and lobbying to the promulgation of voluntary standards and codes of conduct. Many individual firms with multinational operations have also brought environmental norms and considerations into their standard operating procedures. These measures are often harmonized across operations areas with the effect of transplanting high environmental standards from some parts of the world into others where governmental action on the environment has lagged behind.

Of the three actor groups represented on the Nye governance matrix, the one to have undergone the greatest change vis-à-vis the environment is surely the "third sector" of nongovernmental organizations. Such organizations have existed for a century or more. But it is only in recent decades, and particularly since the great success of the NGOs in shaping the Rio Conference on Environment and Development in 1992, that their numbers have blossomed. An accurate count of which international nongovernmental organizations (INGOs) deal exclusively or primarily with environmental issues is hard to come by. But many do. And many is a lot indeed. More than 25,000 INGOs are now listed by the Union of International Organizations; 20,000 of these did not exist a decade ago.[44] Of the 25,000 at least a thousand operate at intercontinental or global scale. The INGO community has shown a remarkable ability to utilize emerging information technologies and to be fast on its feet in convening ad hoc coalitions to address issues. They have been adept at derailing international initiatives, as at the Seattle WTO meetings, but also at getting things onto international agendas, as at the Rio conference. What remains to be seen is whether they can deliver on the agendas that they have helped establish. Recent experience in the wake of the UN Environment Conference (Rio) and Population Conference (Cairo) suggest that this may be more difficult than is generally appreciated, with states unwilling to deliver on agendas set for them by the INGOs.

Advocacy Networks and Discourse Coalitions

Finally, a unique and possibly most significant feature in the recent evolution of environmental governance may be the emergence of actor networks that cut across the conventional divisions of the Nye matrix.
Increasingly, we are finding the "action" on environment-development
issues to lie with coalitions of actors, united by their advocacy of particular programs but not constrained within particular sectors or even levels of governance. This has been observed as a general trend in transnational governance by Kathryn Sikkink and Margaret E. Keck, but seems
particularly strong in the environmental field.[45] We hardly have names
for these "advocacy coalitions," and scholarship has only begun to
explore their activities and effectiveness in the international realm. What
little we do know, however, suggests that they involve networks cutting
across not only actors but also scales. The result is globe-spanning networks of knowledge and practice, connected to multiple local action
coalitions that are individually attuned to the politics and ecology of particular places. Ronnie Lipschutz has perceptively named these governance structures "global civil society" and sees them at the core of any
serious prospect for dealing with global environmental issues.[46] Contemporary trends in problem areas as different as the provision of urban
settlements and the raising of rural agricultural productivity bear out this
view.[47] How, and whether, such multiscalar, multiactor governance structures can be accommodated in our emerging concepts of globalism and
globalization seems an appropriately weighty question on which to end
this section.

So What?

This initial survey confirms the unremarkable observation that environment today figures in the intercontinental dimensions of world affairs.
How strongly it has come to figure for some is suggested by UN Secretary
General Kofi Annan's *Millennium Report* to the General Assembly, in
which he describes the global agenda as of securing "freedom from want,
freedom from fear, and the freedom of future generations to sustain their
lives on this planet."[48] If we choose to make the qualifying condition for
"environmental globalism" the existence of a rich network of environmentally mediated linkages among actors at multicontinental distance,

then environmental globalism is unequivocally a salient feature of modern society.

Moreover, environmental globalization—viewed as the "thickening" of such environmental globalism—is surely under way. The following observations can be applied to the "thickening" criteria of David Held noted at the beginning of this chapter.[49]

—The number and variety of actors involved in intercontinental environmental affairs have soared, especially since the hallmark UN Conference on Environment and Development in 1992. This has been true not only for governmental organizations at all levels but also for private sector groups, "third sector" NGOs, and an increasing array of advocacy coalitions cutting across all of the conventional governance scales and actor groups.

—The extent of intercontinental environmental linkages—their "variety, strength, and density"—seems also to be on the rise. Whether measured by the richness of our knowledge about the global environment, the number of environmental treaties, the amount of environmentally conditioned aid or investment, the reach of environmental "news," or the "clout" carried by environmental arguments in world affairs, it is impossible to imagine that the past decade has not seen a "thickening" of globalization in comparison with the decades before.

—Whether there has been an increase in the "velocity" of change in society associated with the other dimensions of environmental globalization is more problematical. This is a conceptually muddy question and an empirically difficult one. What is certainly true is that the rate of change of many kinds of global environmental stuff and of new environmental actors on the intercontinental stage continues to accelerate, and that the early 1990s witnessed unprecedented, rapid growth in the buildup of institutions dealing with intercontinental environmental governance. Whether that extraordinary burst of social change can (or should) be sustained into the twenty-first century remains to be seen.

The fact of environmental globalization having been established, however, the question remains of whether, or how, it matters. If, for example, we treat "globalism" as a case of long distance complex interdependence, with the requirement that multicontinental linkages between actors be "reciprocal and costly," then it is not at all clear that there is much strictly *environmental* globalism at all.[50] As an example of the potential difficulty, one need merely consider that poster child of globally oriented environmentalists: climate change. For the past decade and more, this issue figured prominently in global environmental discussions initiated by principal actors of the OECD countries and their relatives. (This formulation admittedly relegates the U.S. Congress to a role as a less-than-principal actor in international environmental affairs, but that is another issue). However, recent surveys of environmental priorities around the world show clearly that for most of humanity, "costly" concerns remain local issues such as water contamination, urban pollution, deforestation, and soil erosion.[51] Climate change, ozone depletion, and saving the whales just do not figure prominently in these actors' views of the world. Their representatives participate in global climate negotiations, coalitions, and the like not because they perceive the global movement of environmental stuff as particularly costly to them, much less because they have much prospect of inflicting reciprocal costs on those responsible for emitting the stuff in the first place. Rather, they participate in part as an effort to reframe the global discourse so that their interests and concerns are better represented. They seek to increase the likelihood that any efforts they may be "asked" to undertake on behalf of other people's concerns for global climate may become linked to intercontinental commitments to help in addressing their (locally) costly problems. This calculus may not fit well into our analytic conceptualizations of (environmental) globalization. But it may nonetheless be the calculus with which many actors in the world are strategizing about their engagement in global affairs.

My own guess is that what I have called the "environmental stuff" dimension of globalism—the long distance movement of carbon dioxide, exotic diseases, and toxic chemicals—will not be the most important way in which environment figures in relations among actors at intercontinental distance in the coming decade. Instead, I expect that the dimension of "environmental ideas" will most affect world affairs, especially the globalization of ideas associated with sustainable development.

Whatever one thinks of the particular phrase, the ideas of sustainability have integrated environmental, economic, social, and political dimensions of human relations, rather than separating them. They have encompassed, earlier and more completely than most perspectives, the transcendent importance of thickening networks of connections—of interactions among multiple human activities and environmental consequences—in shaping the problems and opportunities before us. Finally, they have also emphasized the importance of local or regional institutions, mobilization, and initiatives in addressing the complex interactions among these multiple dimensions of human endeavor. At the same time, however, they have accepted—indeed embraced—the essential role played by global scale networks of knowledge and advocacy for advancing such local agendas.

To the extent that the view sketched above is even partially correct, the real "action" in environmental governance for the next several decades may occur more and more at regional rather than global or national scales. For scientific research suggests that at the regional scale multiple environmental pressures will coalesce to form distinctive "faces" or "syndromes" of global change. And political experience increasingly demonstrates that it is at subnational scales that civil society is most energetically and effectively mobilizing to reassert democratic answers to how development and environment should be balanced for particular people and groups. If such locally grounded but globally embedded ideas emerge as among the most significant dimensions of globalization in the coming decades, our thinking about the nature of globalization and its implications for governance will have a long—if potentially exciting—way to go in keeping up with events.

Notes

1. David Held and others, *Global Transformations: Politics, Economics and Culture* (Stanford University Press, 1999), pp. 21–22.

2. I do not, however, treat globalism as a long distance version of Keohane and Nye's "complex interdependence," since that would definitionally restrict globalism to networks of long distance linkages that are "reciprocally costly." See Robert O. Keohane and Joseph S. Nye, *Power and Interdependence,* 2d ed. (Scott, Foresman and Co., 1989). As I will show later on, in the pluralistic, uncertain, complex world of contemporary environmental affairs, the question of "how costly to whom?" is often at the heart of political debate. For example, what eventually turns out to be perceived as costly by most actors will initially be viewed as costly by only a few. As suggested by the case of stratospheric ozone depletion in the 1970s, some of the most interesting dynamics of globalization will lie in elevating such issues to the global agenda. The reverse is also true—issues generally asserted by many actors as "costly" will turn out not to be so—consider the global concern for "nuclear winter" in the mid-1980s. Similarly, even issues believed by some actors to be costly will not appear so to others, as in contemporary debates about climate change. The processes by which the perception of costliness is contested may turn out to be more informative in understanding environmental "globalism" and "globalization" than the "fact" of costliness itself.

Questions of how actors lacking the conventional aspects of power might gain "reciprocal" leverage to counter environmental pressures imposed by others is also what much of environmental politics is about. Much of the action in globalization of the environment consists of those on the receiving end of pollution trying to find ways to demonstrate, or impose, or threaten, reciprocal costs on the producers. This was, for example, the essence of the European debates on transboundary acid rain in the 1970s and 1980s. Not uncommonly, given the huge discrepancies in resources among actors considered at the global scale, such efforts to impose reciprocal costs fail for extended periods. When they do succeed, they are often imposed through some dimension of globalism other than the environment—for example, trade—and would therefore be missed if an analysis of *environmental* linkages is restricted to those that are reciprocal in and of themselves.

For the reasons cited, I decided that restricting this initial exploration of environmental globalization to only those relationships that are uncontroversially "costly and reciprocal" would be unhelpful, however it may have served in Keohane and Nye's initial work on complex interdependence. Whether our larger understanding of globalization is best served by a conceptual framework restricted to the long distance version of "costly and reciprocal" complex interdependence remains an open question.

3. National Research Council (NRC), Committee on Global Change Research, *Global Environmental Change: Research Pathways for the Next Decade* (National Academy Press, 1999), chap. 3.

4. National Research Council, *Global Environmental Change*, pp. 141–47.

5. Ibid., p. 151.

6. This paragraph draws on K. Krummer, *International Management of Hazardous Wastes: The Basel Convention and Related Legal Rules* (Clarendon Press, 1995); Jonathan Krueger, "What's to Become of Trade in Hazardous Wastes? The Basel Convention One Decade Later," *Environment*, vol. 41, no. 9 (1999), pp.11–21; and William Clark, "Learning to Manage Hazardous Materials," *Environment*, vol. 41, no. 9 (1999), p. i.

7. The importance of long range transport of tropospheric ozone has only recently become widely appreciated. See, for example, Daniel J. Jacob, Jennifer A. Logan, and Prashant P. Murti, "Effect of Rising Asian Emissions on Surface Ozone in the United States," *Geophysical Research Letters*, vol. 26 (1999), pp. 2175–78.

8. United Nations Environment Program (UNEP), *Report of the Second Session of the Criteria Expert Group for Persistent Organic Pollutants*, UNEP/POPS/INC/CEG/2/3 (Vienna, June 1999).

9. Robert W. Kates and others, "The Great Transformation," in B. L. Turner and others, *The Earth as Transformed by Human Action* (Cambridge University Press, 1990), chap. 1.

10. William C. Clark and others, "Acid Rain, Ozone Depletion and Climate Change: An Historical Overview," in Social Learning Group, *Learning to Manage Global Environmental Risks* (MIT Press, 2001), chap. 2.

11. National Research Council, *Global Environmental Change*; Paul J. Crutzen and Thomas E. Graedel, "The Role of Atmospheric Chemistry in Environment-Development Interactions," in William C. Clark and R. E. Munn, eds., *Sustainable Development of the Biosphere* (Cambridge University Press, 1986), pp. 213–51; and Peter Vitousek and others, "Human Alteration of the Global Nitrogen Cycle: Causes and Consequences," *Issues in Ecology*, vol. 1 (1997) (http://esa.sdsc.edu/issues.htm [January 14, 2000]). An additional globalizing influence can occur through the emission of substances such as methane that *deplete* the atmospheric concentrations of chemicals such as the hydroxl radical (OH) that normally serve as a "detergent," reacting with other chemicals to render them water soluble or otherwise more likely to be removed from the atmosphere.

12. Robert Kates and William Clark."Expecting the Unexpected?" *Environment,* vol. 38, no. 2 (1996), pp. 6–11, 28–34.

13. Scott Weidensaul, *Living on the Wind: Across the Hemisphere with Migratory Birds* (North Point Press, 1999); and Douglas Stotz and others, *Neotropical Birds: Ecology and Conservation* (University of Chicago Press, 1996). Weidensaul argues that 25 percent or so of North America's temperate birds pass the nonbreeding season in the tropics, primarily Middle America. Note that the potentially longer distance migrations that would have brought these birds further south into the Amazon Basin were relatively rare.

14. William McNeill, *Plagues and Peoples* (Doubleday, 1976); Alfred Crosby, *Ecological Imperialism: The Biological Expansion of Europe, 900–1900* (Cambridge University Press, 1986); and Jared Diamond, *Guns, Germs and Steel: The Fates of Human Societies* (Norton, 1997).

15. M. Rejmanek and J. Randall, *Madrono,* vol. 41(1994), p. 161.

16. Peter Vitousek and others, "Human Domination of the Earth's Ecosystems," *Science,* vol. 277 (1997), pp. 494–99, esp. p. 498.

17. Richard N. Mack and others, "Biotic Invasions: Causes, Epidemiology, Global Consequences and Control," *Issues in Ecology,* no. 5 (2000) (http://esa.sdsc.edu/issues5.htm [January 14, 2000]); J. A. Drake and H. A. Mooney, eds., *Biological Invasions: A Global Perspective* (Wiley, 1986); and V. H. Heywood, ed., *Global Biodiversity Assessment* (Cambridge University Press, 1995).

18. Vitousek and others, "Human Domination," p. 498.

19. For example, the International Conventions for the Regulation of Whaling (ICRW, Washington, 1946) and for the Conservation of Atlantic Tuna (ICCAT, Rio de Janeiro, 1966).

20. See, for example, the Conventions on the Conservation of Migratory Species of Wild Animals (CMS, Bonn, 1979) and on Wetlands of International Importance (Ramsar, 1971).

21. Scott K. Robinson, "The Case of the Missing Songbirds," *Consequences,* vol. 3 (1997), (http://www.gcrio.org/Consequences/vol3no1/toc.html [January 14, 2000]); and Brian A. Maurer and Marc-Andre Villard, "Continental Scale Ecology and Neotropical Migratory Birds: How to Detect Declines amid the Noise," *Ecology,* vol. 77 (1996), pp.1–2.

22. Heywood, *Global Biodiversity Assessment.*

23. Eville Gorham, "Lakes under a Three-Pronged Attack," *Nature,* vol. 381 (1996), pp. 109–10; N. D. Yan and others, "Increased UV-B Penetration in a Lake owing to Drought-Induced Acidification," *Nature,* vol. 381 (1996), pp. 141–43.

24. National Research Council, Board on Sustainable Development, *Our Common Journey: A Transition toward Sustainability* (National Academy Press, 1999), p. 8.

25. Richard Benedick, *Ozone Diplomacy* (Harvard University Press, 1991), p. 4.

26. German Advisory Council on Global Change, *World in Transition: The Research Challenge* (Springer Verlag, 1997).

27. Lynton K. Caldwell, *International Environmental Policy: From the Twentieth to the Twenty-First Century,* 3d ed. (Duke University Press, 1996).

28. Miranda A. Schreurs and others, "Issue Attention, Framing and Actors: An Analysis of Patterns across Arenas," in Social Learning Group, *Learning to Manage Global Environmental Risks* (MIT Press, 2001), chap. 14.

29. Richard N. Cooper, "International Cooperation in Public Health as a Prologue to Macroeconomic Cooperation," in *Can Nations Agree? Issues in International Economic Cooperation* (Brookings, 1989).

30. Mary Douglas and Aaron Wildavsky, *Risk and Culture: An Essay on the Selection of Technical and Environmental Dangers* (University of California Press, 1982).

31. The account draws from William Adams, *Green Development* (Routledge, 1992). Similar themes, from a contemporary political economy perspective, are central to Keith Pezzoli, *Human Settlements and Planning for Ecological Sustainability: The Case of Mexico City* (MIT Press, 1998).

32. World Commission on Environment and Development, *Our Common Future* (Oxford University Press, 1987), p. 1.

33. National Research Council, *Our Common Journey*.

34. See, for example, Pezzoli, *Human Settlements*; and Ronnie Lipschutz, *Global Civil Society and Global Environmental Governance* (SUNY Press, 1996); and Suparb Pas-ong and Louis Lebel, "Implications of Political Transformation in Southeast Asia for Environmental Governance," *Environment* (forthcoming).

35. Indicatively, the most recent report of the U.S. National Academy of Science on global environmental change was framed in terms of sustainable development ideas (see note 31). The UN Environment Program's new *Global Environmental Outlook—2000* report describes the state of human development and environment, not either alone. UNEP, *Global Environmental Outlook—2000* (Earthscan, 1999).

36. I focus on governance rather than *institutions* in order to sustain a conceptual framework focused on relations among actors. Organizations involved in global environmental affairs operate as agents of change, that is, as actors. Shared norms among actors—another component of many concepts of institutions—are treated in the preceding category of *ideas*. My use of *governance* is meant to direct attention to the relationships or linkages through which one actor constrains or motivates the actions of another. See also Pas-ong and Lebel, "Implications of Political Transformation."

37. See the description on the Chemical Manufacturers' Association web site: http://www.cmahq.com/ (January 14, 2000).

38. For example, Lennart J. Lundvist, *The Hare and the Tortoise: Clean Air Policies in the United States and Sweden* (University of Michigan Press, 1980); Ronald Brickman and others, *Controlling Chemicals: The Politics of Regulation in Europe and the United States* (Cornell University Press, 1985); David Vogel, *National Styles of Regulation: Environmental Policy in Great Britain and the United States* (Cornell University Press, 1986); and Sonia Boehmer-Christiansen and Jim Skea, *Acid Politics: Environmental and Energy Policies in Britain and Germany* (Belhaven Press, 1991).

39. See Helge O. Bergesson and Georg Parmann, *Green Globe Year Book of International Co-operation on Environment and Development* (Oxford University Press, 1997, and other years), for a description of the treaties and an account of their status.

40. See Oran R Young, ed., *The Effectiveness of International Environmental Regimes: Causal Connections and Behavioral Mechanisms* (MIT Press, 1999); David Victor and others, eds., *The Implementation and Effectiveness of International Environmental Commitments: Theory and Practice* (MIT Press, 1998); Robert O. Keohane and Mark A. Levy, eds., *Institutions for Environmental Aid* (MIT Press, 1996); and Peter M. Haas and others, eds.,

Institutions for the Earth: Sources of Effective International Environmental Protection (MIT Press, 1993).

41. Wendy Franz, "Appendix," in Keohane and Levy, *Institutions for Environmental Aid.*

42. See Caldwell, *International Environmental Policy.*

43. See note 40.

44. http://www.uia.org/ (January 14, 2000).

45. Margaret E. Keck and Kathryn Sikkink, *Activists beyond Borders: Advocacy Networks in International Politics* (Cornell University Press, 1998).

46. Lipschutz, *Global Civil Society.*

47. Pezzoli, *Human Settlements*; and Karen Litfin, *The Greening of Sovereignty in World Politics* (MIT Press, 1998).

48. Kofi Annan, secretary general of the United Nations, statement to the General Assembly on presentation of his Millennium Report, *We the Peoples: The Role of the United Nations in the 21st Century, 3 April, 2000,* UN Doc. SG/SM/7343, GA/9705 (April 3, 2000).

49. Held, *Global Transformations.*

50. See note 2.

51. UNEP, *Global Environmental Outlook—2000.*

5

NEAL M. ROSENDORF

Social and Cultural Globalization: Concepts, History, and America's Role

Social and cultural globalization is arguably the broadest, farthest-reaching dimension of the phenomenon, if we limit our examination of globalization to the human experience. It is deeply intertwined with the other dimensions identified by Keohane and Nye in chapter 1 of this volume. As the cultural theorist John Tomlinson puts it, "The huge transformative processes of our time that globalization describes cannot be properly understood until they are grasped through the conceptual vocabulary of culture; likewise . . . these transformations change the very fabric of cultural experience and, indeed, affect our sense of what culture actually is in the modern world."[1]

Military globalization entails the movement of people and often social-political structures, often temporarily, but sometimes long term or even permanently—think of imperial Rome, for example, and the cities and towns it established or vastly expanded from Britain to North Africa to the Middle East and Central Asia. The same holds true for the other great global military-colonial expansions that preceded or followed Rome—Alexander's Greece, the Islamic Ummayad Caliphate, Spain, Britain, and France. Indeed, even the threat of nuclear annihilation during the cold war, which did not entail the movement of troops, had a significant cultural globalizing effect—disparate peoples the world over shared the same anxiety that they could be snuffed out with the push of a few buttons.[2]

The economic dimension is as much about the movement of social values and intellectual structures as it is about money and trade. Consider, for example, the linkage that Max Weber drew between the Protestant worldview and capitalism in his famous work on the subject.[3] Now consider the increasing global pervasiveness of capitalism as the dominant economic system in the twenty-first century. As capitalism expands its reach, so do at least some of the social, political, and intellectual forces that lie behind it, such as the rule of law, meritocratic advancement, the vaunting of philosophical instrumentalism (for example, "politics is the art of the possible") and pragmatism, and enhanced social and political status for an entrepreneurial bourgeoisie at the expense of traditional ruling classes. Consider as well the more explicit, but ultimately no more pervasive, political-social-cultural agenda of capitalism's great twentieth century challenger, communism. Indeed, both Adam Smith and Karl Marx posited their systems as ultimately universal in scope.

And as for that part of environmental globalization that is the product of human as opposed to natural forces (unless one considers humans simply one more facet of the natural world), pandemics to name one example, are largely the product of long-distance travel and immigration. A significant part of global warming, to name another, is attributable to our species' ceaseless productive and consumptive endeavors, from fire building to factories to freeways clogged with sport utility vehicles.

Many of these interrelated dimensions are dealt with separately in other chapters in this volume. But even without them, social and cultural globalization still leaves plenty to contemplate: information, art and entertainment, religion and philosophy, social organization and hierarchy, language, politics, and immigration, to name some of the key aspects.

To attempt to deal even cursorily with each of these elements of social and cultural globalization in turn would result in a chapter that takes up most of this book. Thus, for the sake of practicability I begin by briefly sketching a general historical and thematic trajectory of this dimension. The balance of this chapter examines the single most important factor influencing contemporary and near-future social and cultural globalization: the global cultural power of the United States.

American culture is not by any means the only one with a global reach in the contemporary world. Sociologist Yogesh Atal notes, for example, that "the culture of India—the country of my belonging—has reached several countries throughout the world."[4] Indian art, music, film, cuisine, and even religion (primarily through the Hindu offshoot Hare Krishna faith) have found audiences and have been subject to local reinterpretation (the most famous example being the Beatles' cross-fertilization with sitar maestro Ravi Shankar) throughout the world. But nonetheless, like it or not the United States is the pacesetter in much of the global social-cultural realm, in part because the United States has unparalleled access to the means of producing and disseminating its ideas and life-style around the world, and in part because the United States possesses a unique set of cultural and historical attributes that are enablers of this dissemination. This does not mean that the world is being stampeded to cultural homogeneity, but it does mean that in more and more corners of the world American culture must be reckoned with on a regular basis, as an element alongside local culture.

Cultural Globalization—What It Entails and What It Doesn't

What exactly does social and cultural globalization entail? The imposition by hegemons of social and cultural forms and artifacts on subalterns? Or convergence and admixture that affect all participants? Is the result the homogenization of culture? Or does a negotiation take place between hegemon and subaltern that leaves local cultures distinctive, if modified?

The short answer to all of these questions is yes. Interestingly, though, the least consistently pervasive variety of social-cultural globalization, hegemonic imposition, is the one that typically excites the greatest concern. During various historical epochs one can find examples of a dominant power forcefully exerting its culture upon recipient societies. Imperial Rome, for example, spread Greco-Roman art, architecture, laws, entertainments, and transportation networks to link all and sundry together across three continents. Yet Rome, containing a powerful element of cultural syncretism at its core (present in the seminal blending of Tarquinian-Etruscan and Greek influences that gave birth to the Roman city-state) was itself culturally acted upon by its far-flung imperial possessions. One of the most powerful manifestations of this flow of culture from periphery to metropole occurred in the realm of religion. In metropolitan Rome one could eventually find significant cults devoted to, in addition to its resident pantheon of Greek-inspired deities, Asia Minor's Mithras, Egypt's Osiris, Judea's Yahweh (there was a considerable number of Gentile "God Fearers" who aligned themselves with welcoming Jewish congregations), and Judea's other manifestation of the divine, Jesus Christ. And yet, for all the regularizing of societal, physical, and legal structures that occurred across the Empire (epitomized by the declaration of all persons within the Empire as citizens of Rome during the reign of Caracalla in the early third century CE), the individual regions did not all become mere copies of Rome. Most of them retained unique local characteristics, including language, religion, family, and other hierarchical structures, although the Roman presence certainly had an impact on the coloration of these characteristics.[5]

This complex set of social-cultural interactions, which would to a greater or lesser extent mark the formal and informal imperia of Spain, France, Britain, and the United States, has been described as *hybridization* by such sociologists as Jan Nederveen Pieterse (this is not meant as an apologia for colonialism—the formal imperial powers forcefully and often brutally asserted the primacy of their cultures). While Pieterse accepts that the idea of "cultural synchronization" (another way of expressing the idea of homogenization) is relevant, he has concluded that "it is fundamentally incomplete." He asks, "How do we come to terms with phenomena such as Thai boxing by Moroccan girls in Amsterdam, Asian rap in London, Irish bagels, Chinese tacos and Mardi Gras Indians in the United States?" Pieterse's answer is that "cultural experiences, past or present, have not simply been moving in the direction of cultural uniformity and standardization."[6] Arjun Appuradai flatly states that "globalization is not the story of cultural homogenization."[7]

Roland Robertson uses the term *unicity*, as contrasted with "uniformity," to describe a world in which individual societies negotiate their existence, identities, and actions in the context of an overarching "single place."[8] Others have employed the term *glocalization* to describe a similar concept "that takes into account the local, national, regional, and global contexts of intercultural communicative processes."[9] Yogesh Atal believes that while in the colonial period insular regions were opened up via the "single aperture" of a dominant power, the end of colonialism has brought "multiple apertures," "connecting these societies with a number of other societies—both developed and developing."[10]

National and subnational cultures are in a continual state of varying degrees of change as they come into contact with other cultures. The contemporary Arab Near and Middle East, for example, is the sum not only of indigenous cultures but of the varying degrees of influence imparted by the cultures of ancient Greece and Rome, the Byzantine and Persian Sasanian Empires, medieval and modern Europe, and now the United States. Indeed, medieval Arab preeminence in sciences such as astronomy was predicated on a conscious synthesizing of Greek, Persian, and Indian scientific traditions.[11] Yet no one would argue that the region has ceased to have a distinctive set of cultural identities that set it apart from the rest of the world.

Some Historical Perspective

Roland Robertson's "single place" has been a long time coming. That humans have a mere two legs and move at a correspondingly slow rate compared with most large nonprimate mammals has not stopped us from being champion globe-trotters. From the time genus *homo* appeared on the scene about 1.7 million years ago he began wandering. By somewhere between 20,000 and 13,000 years ago the latest version of *homo, sapiens sapiens*, had reached the Western Hemisphere, effectively spanning the world.[12] Yet while evidence is mounting that there may have been subsequent intermittent contacts between the Eastern and Western Hemispheres aside from the undisputed Norse expeditions, seemingly almost exclusively in the form of forays from the former to the latter, peoples living in the two halves of the globe were effectively isolated from each other in terms of any lasting cultural impact until Christopher Columbus and his successors during the Age of European Exploration permanently linked together the Old and New Worlds.[13]

Hence when we speak of cultural globalization in the period before 1492, we are referring to phenomena that occurred within the still vast confines of the continents of the Eastern Hemisphere. Using the "multicontinental distances" criterion for globalization posited by Keohane and Nye in chapter 1, we can identify such "thin" globalizing phenomena as Alexander the Great's empire, which brought with it Hellenic culture, and which simultaneously "opened to Greek thinkers the vision of a politically and culturally unified world, a possibility which previously appeared to them neither practical nor desirable"[14]; the Roman empire and its Byzantine successor[15]; the Ummayid Caliphate, which spread Islam from Spain to Cairo to India and beyond; the West Asian trade routes of the Tarim Basin and the Turfan Oasis, which spread silk and other goods, an amalgam of religious traditions, and a dim mutual awareness across empires spanning from the Atlantic Ocean to the China Sea.[16] Indeed, the Silk Road provides a quintessential example of how "throughout history ideas and technologies have spread along trade routes, and that merchants have been among their prime transmitters."[17]

Part of what made these globalizing elements "thin" is that distances that
we would consider inconsequential were huge—it was a Herculean task to
attempt to communicate information at a rate of fifty miles per day.[18]
Additionally, Hellenization and Romanization most dramatically affected
official physical infrastructures (for example, buildings and squares devoted
to official duties) and the aesthetics, thought, and life-styles of elite strata of
the local population. For example, Egypt was ruled for centuries by the
Greek Ptolemies, and Alexandria contained the fabulous library commis-
sioned by Alexander the Great. But ordinary Egyptians lived most aspects of
their lives as they had prior to the arrival of their conquerors.[19] The
Ummayads had what was arguably the most enduring effect on their conquests with the permanent transplantation of their religion and, in much of
the empire, language (at the very least for liturgical purposes).[20]

Perhaps the most pervasive form of pre-1492 globalization, and certainly the longest lasting, is the spread of Christianity and Islam across sections of Europe, Asia, and Africa (the Jews as a people ranged far and wide
through the Eastern hemisphere, but after the ascendancy of the other two
major Western religions Judaism ceased to compete actively for converts.)[21]
A key difference between the spread of these religions and that of other
globalizing forms was that it was not confined to elite strata. By a combination of the wide appeal of the message and eventually the imposition of
the theologies by rulers as state religions, variants of Christianity and Islam
were embraced across the societal spectrum, with poor as well as rich wor-
shipping the same God. This of course would not keep Christians from
killing Christians or Muslims other Muslims, but a common set of beliefs
did provide a starting point for developing some common ideas about
issues such as ethics and morality.

In the wake of the Columbian expeditions a new era of cultural globalization occurred, largely as the product of colonialism. The globalization
process had now become truly "global" in that it spanned the planet. The
collision of Western expansionism and large-scale societies in the Americas,
Africa, and West, Central, and East Asia necessitated a complex cultural
negotiation between invader and invaded. Over the next four centuries
millions of people, free and enslaved, traveled thousands of miles to live,
work, kill, die, and intermingle with one another and with native peoples.
Until the nineteenth century it was primarily Europeans and Africans who
were transplanted, after which significant numbers of East and South
Asians, mainly Chinese and Indians, joined the ranks of multicontinental
immigrant groups.

Information and transportation technologies were the handmaiden of this dramatic enlargement of the sphere of social-cultural globalization. The invention of writing allowed ideas to be transmitted outside the bounds of real time, far beyond the scope of the spoken voice. The printing press with movable type greatly increased the volume of available written material while reducing its cost.[22] Small and lightweight, broadsides, pamphlets, and books could travel long distances. And better ships made possible an enlarged transport perimeter of people, ideas, and goods. Circa 1000 CE Norse longboats could barely island-hop their way across the waters of the North Atlantic to reach North America, so that its sailors could hold onto temporary settlement by their fingernails. But the ship-building and navigation technology of the late fifteenth century and beyond facilitated long distance ocean voyages with ever-larger crew complements and room left over for significant cargo transport.[23] Books, manufactured goods, and foodstuffs could find their way around the world. Aside from the purely economic impact, this promoted the exportation and the importation of such cultural artifacts as books and printing presses, clothing materials, household furnishings, and the ingredients of novel cuisine. Over time elites in Europe and in the United States embraced the aesthetics of *Chinoiserie* and *Japonoiserie*; later, elites in India and Japan embraced elements of the life-styles of Western gentlefolk. Spanish, Portuguese, French, and especially English became multicontinental languages in the wake of the seafaring colonizers. The colonizers ironically planted the seeds of the demise of their empires by exporting to their subject peoples the powerful liberating ideologies of nationalism and socialism.

The Age of Simultaneity

Yet, while an ever-enlarging segment of formerly isolated peoples were taking note of and being culturally affected by one another with widely varying degrees of enthusiasm, it would have required a great conceptual leap for them to think about what was going on in distant realms *at that moment*. The steamship and clipper ship significantly reduced transoceanic travel time, but travel time was still reckoned in weeks. However, the telegraph, the telephone, the phonograph, and, a bit later, motion pictures and radio provided a revolution in perceived immediacy that greatly intensified the experience of other cultures. They added back the element of real time, whether actual or simulated (as in the case of recordings and motion pictures), to long-distance communication. (Air travel, and especially passenger jet transport, would underline the sense of long distance real-time connectedness, but electric communication was the key to closing the gap.) The cultural historian Stephen Kern describes this as *simultaneity*, in which far-flung peoples, united by instantaneous communication technologies, experience a shared sense of experience of time and space.[24] Simultaneity, with its predication upon revolutionary scientific innovations, is a hallmark of the period lasting from the late nineteenth century to the present and provides a dividing line between this period and earlier historical epochs of cultural globalization.

The *Titanic* disaster provides a dramatic early example of simultaneity in action. The liner struck an iceberg at 11:40 p.m. on April 14, 1912; at 12:15 a.m. the captain sent out a distress call on the ship's wireless; at 1:06 a.m. the *Carpathia* picked up the signal and steamed toward the fatally wounded *Titanic*; by 1:20 a.m. the news of the maritime catastrophe was being transmitted telegraphically around the world. By the next morning, millions of people on several continents were grieving, bound together by the telegraph, telephone, and newspapers that immediately printed the electronically gathered news on high-speed presses.[25]

The past century has seen an intensification and a broadening of the franchise of simultaneity (a manifestation of thickening globalization) by way of radio, television, communication satellites, fiber optics, and computers. However, the period is most appropriately considered a historical unity, with subdivisions as new technologies and lower costs have facilitated an ever-increasing perception of simultaneous interconnectedness.

Let us contemplate the following tableau of cultural globalization in the new millennium: New Year's Eve 2000 festivities from around the world were being televised live in the United States on CNN and PBS, among other venues. During the late morning hours of December 31, 1999, on the American eastern seaboard, one could take in the fireworks, tolling of bells, and entertainment extravaganzas as East Asia moved into the first hours of January 1, 2000. Viewers could witness a technological marvel as video linkups shifted with dizzying speed from country to country.

Whether or not these revelers across the planet knew it, they were experiencing perhaps the single most dramatic example in human history to date of Kern's simultaneity. And what did this simultaneity bring to millennium's eve television audiences around the world? In the midst of all the celebratory tumult, one moment offered an encapsulation of the preponderant element of contemporary cultural globalization. As the new century dawned in Singapore, a local pop star with bleached blond hair and chic black clothes danced across a huge stage lustily singing the hit Latin-U.S. pop song "Living La Vida Loca" to a cheering crowd. PBS's commentator wryly observed, "It seems that no corner of the globe is safe from Ricky Martin." An East Asian vocalist was singing a bilingual Spanish-English tune by an Hispanic-American pop singer made famous worldwide by the distribution muscle of U.S.-based Columbia records, itself a subsidiary of Japan's Sony Corporation—and his game New Year's effort was being broadcast live to, among other places, the United States. This moment demonstrated not only communication technology's capacity to disseminate information and link people together but also the ubiquity and protean adaptability of American culture. This linking of ever-improving communications technology and American popular culture has been a key motif of twentieth century cultural globalization, and it is shaping up to be similarly important for much of the new century as well.

The Global Power of American Popular Culture

While Stuart Hall goes too far in equating cultural globalization with Americanization (and hence with homogenization), he is indisputably correct when he describes the contemporary global cultural sphere as "dominated by the visual and graphic arts . . . dominated by television and by film, and by the image, imagery, and styles of mass advertising."[26] It is the realm of popular culture, and it is here that the United States possesses a great advantage over all other states.

The United States in the twenty-first century will in all likelihood be the single greatest force in global culture at least to the extent it was in the twentieth century and probably more so. Based on historical precedents, the United States will rapidly come to dominate any new mass communications medium that develops, and the United States will not lose ground in any of the areas in which it already dominates. This dominance will be recession proof and up to a point, diplomatic disaster proof. This turn of events is likely because the United States built up such an overwhelming mastery of communication and entertainment technology and software in the twentieth century; the United States possesses unique qualities that provide awesome sinews of power in this realm; and there are no comers on the horizon—and there probably will not be.[27] The United States has maintained a commanding lead in the global communications entertainment race virtually from the time it joined it in earnest (owing to a combination of American entrepreneurial pluck and such helpful exogenous circumstances as World Wars I and II). And now Michael Jordan, *Baywatch*, Nike, McDonald's, Disney, Britney Spears, Ted Turner, and Bill Gates are the latest standard bearers and consolidators of this position.

Popular culture understood as a product of mass society originated in the United States, in the aftermath of the Civil War. Phenomena that were uniquely combined at the time (and in some ways, with variations, up to the present) in the United States shaped popular culture's form: "rapid industrialization, growing urbanization, the newly freed black masses, the influx of immigrants from eastern and southern Europe, the onset of universal compulsory education, and the creation of new means of mass communication."[28]

The Anglo-American colonies that would eventually become the United States were multiethnic and multicultural from the outset. In 1700, between the Hudson and Delaware rivers the population included Dutch, English, German, Jewish, French, Walloon, African, Swedish, and Scottish settlers.[29] As one study has put it, America "always faced a need to create a normative culture more or less non-threatening to most members of the society. To the extent that such a culture 'transcended' the imperatives of specific differences between diverse American cultures it was, thereby, also becoming a most suitable product for export."[30] And if America was multicultural in its earliest incarnation, by the turn of the twentieth century it was a staggering melange of peoples gathered from the four corners of the earth—by 1910, 75 percent of the populations of New York, Chicago, Cleveland, and Boston were immigrants or their children[31]—that caused many Americans of Northern European Protestant descent to fret about "race suicide."[32] Most of these people worked hard, made a relatively high wage compared with workers in other countries, and had the time and inclination to spend some part of that wage on entertainment and leisure. This situation has largely continued down to the present day.

Unsurprisingly, given its demographic makeup, the United States has been strongly receptive to external cultural influences, which have in many cases been incorporated into the fabric of American culture. Often, one culture's contributions have been mixed with those of others to make particularly potent hybrids. The combination of African and Celtic folk music, for example, resulted in such popular musical idioms as blues, country western, and rock and roll. Hollywood has welcomed generations of expatriate artists, such as Fritz Lang, David Lean, Milos Forman, and John Woo, who have brought with them such cinematic traditions as German

Expressionism, English Romanticism, postwar Eastern European anti-authoritarianism, and Hong Kong's hyperkinetic ballets of stylized action. American popular culture is in a perpetual state of ferment. At the same time, because of the myriad "foreign" influences, there are universalistic elements that can strike chords of recognition throughout the world.

The combination of a huge, diverse potential market with technology geared to the wide dissemination of goods and services—factories that could churn out hundreds of automobiles daily, movie-making and projecting equipment, high-speed printing presses, and the like—and a powerful economic culture of entrepreneurship was, and continues to be, explosive. The men who created Hollywood, as well as some of the most prominent entrepreneurs in other culturally significant fields (Henry Ford, for example), were not drawn from American elites but were mainly from modest backgrounds and hence strongly attuned to the average public's tastes.[33]

Satisfying the varied tastes of the American public has turned out serendipitously to be a training ground for expansion into international markets. Will Hays, the first head of the Motion Picture Producers and Distributors of America [or MPPDA, the forerunner to the Motion Picture Association of America, or MPAA], once declared that "there is a special reason why America should have given birth and prosperous nurture to the motion picture and its world-wide entertainment. America in the very literal sense is truly the world state. All races, all creeds, all men are to be found here."[34] The American market's unique qualities aided the international movement of the nation's popular culture in general, as media analyst William Read explains:

> The basic skills and expertise that are so useful when expanding into various foreign markets have been largely acquired within the United States, which is not so much a single national market as a complex of submarkets . . . [M]ass communications in the United States has traditionally been imbued with a strong sense of localism. The trick of a few major mass media organizations has been to blend the local operations into countrywide schemes. The talent developed in doing this was subsequently applied abroad.[35]

This combination of training and common-touch subject matter and sensibilities has been potent indeed in American popular culture's success in reaching to international markets. Additionally, Americans spent the first third of the twentieth century aggressively developing and rapidly dominating information/communications and travel sectors necessary for the effective international dissemination of American pop/mass culture, including undersea cables, radio and wireless telegraphy, news services, and aviation.[36] Add to this the propensity of American cultural producers to employ, in the typical manner of American business, economies of scale, which reduce the per capita cost at the consumer end. Moreover, the enormous size of the domestic market for movies, television programs, music, automobiles, fashions, and a plethora of other American software and hardware cultural commodities means that American producers can ordinarily amortize their production costs at home, which in turn means that foreign distribution is highly profitable.

American popular culture has been the creature of private enterprise not only in its creation but for the most part in its international dissemination as well. On this point the United States stands in contrast to the other major industrialized states, whose governments have long posited themselves as not only economic advocates but aesthetic and ideological tribunes as well.[37] While most governments are currently preoccupied with protecting their cultural industries and institutions as much as they can— which is very little—from American preponderance, France in particular has continued to make strong efforts, on ideological and artistic grounds, to promote its cultural offerings, including television programs, to Francophone nations around the world.

The American government plays a minor supporting role in cultural dissemination in comparison with other states. This is not to say that the U.S. government has not helped in the dissemination process. The Departments of Commerce and State have long played a salutary role in aiding the American radio, news information, motion picture, and television industries to gain and keep footholds in foreign markets.[38] The government has had good reason to aid the American culture industries: they constitute, after the aerospace industry, the country's second biggest export income source. In 1992, for example, American entertainment exports to Europe alone amounted to $4.6 billion.[39]

Except for brief periods during World Wars I and II, during the first half of the twentieth century the American government made little attempt to influence the content or international dissemination of American popular culture.[40] The Motion Picture Export Association of America and other American popular cultural enterprises have often come to the U.S. government for aid in opening, keeping, and expanding foreign markets. But in such endeavors the private sector enterprises were and are almost invariably the driving force. When ex-entertainment lawyer Mickey Kantor fought hammer-and-tongs as U.S. trade negotiator to include audiovisual exports as an element of the free market General Agreement on Tariffs and Trade (GATT) negotiations in 1993, he illustrated vividly how the American government serves as a vigorous advocate of the American popular culture industries' primarily economically driven positions.[41]

America and Other States: Contrasts

Contrast the American paradigm with the historic situation among the U.S. potential international popular cultural rivals. France, Germany, and Japan, for example, are all culturally homogeneous, which is not conducive to honing the ability to gratify disparate audiences. (Britain, somewhat more heterogeneous and linked to the United States by a common language, has periodically been successful in pushing into the international pop cultural sphere, for example, pop bands from the Beatles to the Spice Girls and the (American-financed and distributed) James Bond movie series. The Soviet Union was extraordinarily heterogeneous, but it was dominated by a communist regime attempting to dictate taste, not satisfy it, while at the same time it was an old-style empire bound together by the coercive power of the Red Army—hardly an environment where multiethnically pleasing consumer culture was going to evolve.

Moreover, in other states a yawning chasm exists between the elites who produce the culture and the potential consumers. Media that in the United States would be considered first and foremost as popular culture transmitters, such as motion pictures and television, are viewed as high cultural venues—at least when properly utilized—by tastemakers in London, Paris, Berlin, and elsewhere (André Malraux, among his other vocations Charles de Gaulle's minister of culture, referred to cinema as "*par ailleurs*" ["moreover"] an industry.)[42] This has resulted in some excellent, artistically challenging, often government-subsidized movies, television programs, and music. More often, however, it has resulted in fare that is more than anything else patently uninteresting to the audiences of the country where it is produced, much less to potential audiences elsewhere.[43] As historian Emily Rosenberg has noted in relation to the American movie industry's quick move to international dominance in the early twentieth century, "In contrast to Europe's elitist films, America's movies always appealed to mass audiences. Created not out of the traditions of elite art but designed to entertain a diverse, multi-ethnic patronage at home, early American films were perfectly suited to a world market."[44]

Additionally, America's potential cultural rivals do not have the populations necessary to support single-handedly a huge, internationally oriented popular cultural industry—France, for example, the nation that has most emphatically posited itself as a global cultural alternative to the United States, has approximately one-fifth the population of the United States. The business cultures of these states, at least when it comes to popular culture, long combined with their relatively small populations to militate against developing economies of scale. This situation has changed somewhat in the past two decades of the twentieth century, but the change has occurred mainly as the result of foreign investment in American popular cultural businesses.[45] China and India, the world's most populous nations, have huge domestic markets, and indeed India's "Bollywood" film industry is in sheer output the largest in the world. But, while as noted earlier Indian culture *in toto* has found international audiences, its pop culture appeals primarily to Indians in India and around the world (although the late 1990s hit Anglo-American movie *Elizabeth*, about the English Tudor queen, was directed by an Indian filmmaker in the characteristic hyperdramatic, visually colorful Bollywood style).[46] The Chinese, whose pop cultural offerings are still often hobbled by official censorship, in general avidly consume whatever American pop culture they can get their hands on.

Language and Ideology

There are additional crucial ingredients to the international success of American popular culture from its earliest movement overseas. One is the English language. Great Britain's longtime global pre-eminence and far-flung imperial interests caused English to be widely disseminated from the eighteenth century on. The United States seconded and intensified this process as its media and business moved into the global sphere in the twentieth century. Aside from the push two of the world's most powerful nations gave to the language, English is linguistically uniquely suited to wide usage as a second language.[47]

Moreover, English eschews for the most part the distinction common in other languages between a scholarly or aristocratic high form and a vulgate, as well as differences between the written and spoken language. There is no analogue to the *Academie Francaise* establishing and maintaining a strict set of rules concerning spelling, grammar, usage, or the importation of foreign words.[48] English, drawing at its core from archaic German and French, with clear remnants of Latin and Greek, functions as a lexical sponge— Spanish, Indian, Yiddish, Chinese, Native American, and African words and phrases have found their way into usage. The lack of a "*Hoch Englisch*" and these multilingual cognates impart a positive ideological value to the language as well.

This leads us to the indispensable final element to the popularity, and hence power, of American popular culture: the image of the United States. American popular culture has transfixed the world since the late nineteenth century, when Buffalo Bill Cody took his Wild West show to Europe and beyond, through the rise of Hollywood and the first flood of images of American consumer culture and movie star glamor, through the post–World War II avalanche of U.S. goods and entertainment, up to a present where the television series *Baywatch*, the single most popular program in the world, depicts Southern California's beach culture (and since its move to Honolulu in fall 1999, Hawaii's) as the Elysian Fields with sand.[49] Throughout the twentieth century the United States has seemed to others exciting, exotic, rich, powerful, trend-setting—the cutting edge of modernity and innovation.[50]

American pop culture is by turns sexy and violent and glamorous and materialistic and romantic. Whether through entertainment or the marketing of consumer goods it is generally optimistic, vulgar, and democratic. Much of it vaunts individualism and antiauthoritarianism and the triumph of the disfranchised over the powerful. While there is much that is specifically "American" about American pop culture—whether it is Hollywood stars and settings such as New York or Los Angeles on film and television, the iconography of American sports and counterculture in fashion and even fast food, rock, and rap in their entirety—its universal themes, deliberately chosen for their commercial potency, translate extremely well from one culture to another.[51]

American pop culture depicts a United States in which the citizens are attractive, assertive, successful, well-dressed, funny, articulate, imaginative, free to speak their minds, able to realize their dreams. America is portrayed as ethnically diverse, exciting, fast paced, raucous, filled with wilderness and urban beauty, and powerful—economically, politically, and militarily.[52]

The potential rub is that the U.S. government has virtually no control over the content or quality of the entertainment and products that the private sector exports around the world.[53] That is often part of the attraction—American films that critique domestic society, for example, offer evidence of a great power unafraid of dissent. However, from time to time private-sector-generated gaffes can hurt the American national image, if only briefly: Coca-Cola's initially stonewalling response to reports in mid-1999 of its products sickening West Europeans, in the midst of the Kosovo crisis and U.S.-EU banana trade wars, was a further drag on American prestige in the region during a difficult period.[54]

How does the Internet fit into all this? In short, it is custom-made to play to American strengths and to advance the American idea. The United States goes further than any other country in protecting free speech. The First Amendment's categorical language affords little of the wiggle room even other Western states have to engage in censorship or other forms of information suppression. The Internet has been from its founding imbued with a powerful strain of radical libertarianism—it is arguably the latest manifestation of the radical Whig oppositional ideology, fearful of tyranny and fiercely suspicious of conspiracies against liberty, that historian Bernard Bailyn identified as central to political awareness in eighteenth-century America and to the forging of the United States.[55] Official U.S. attempts to legislate controls or limits over content have repeatedly been beaten back, and the technological limitations on filters and on monitoring user log-ons mean that virtually whatever Americans can view, most international users of the Internet can view as well.

And what is it that Internet users around the world want to view more than anything else? The pneumatic American sex symbol Pamela Anderson Lee videotaped *in flagrante delicto* with her rock guitarist husband. In 1998–99 "Pamela Anderson" was by far the phrase that received the most hits on the Internet—savvy net marketers noted this popularity and use the phrase as a link to unrelated products and services, including plumbing supplies. Estimates are that the B-movie actress's name and image generated some $77 million in revenues by April 1999 alone.[56] Free speech, entertainment, and entrepreneurship have been the engine of American global dominance in mass media, and the Internet will almost undoubtedly be no exception. Like other engines of American pop/mass cultural dissemination, the Internet is a loose cannon with the potential to embarrass the United States on occasion and to provide its rivals and enemies with a forum in which to compete. However, the United States, with an older and more explicitly codified commitment to free speech than any other state, is better prepared than most other states to handle the Internet's vicissitudes.

Nonetheless, for the foreseeable future motion pictures will be more significant than the Internet or even television and radio, as the most important medium of projecting American pop culture abroad. Outside the United States and a handful of other wealthy nations, the Internet is still the perquisite of elites. Falling prices will undoubtedly enlarge the sphere of users considerably. But most households around the world continue to lack telephone connections for modems or even electricity for televisions. As long as this reality persists, publicly shown motion pictures will be the key means of transmitting the American pop cultural dream abroad, of selling sly subversion, sex, and sneakers.

Indeed, even when every household on earth is wired for electricity, television, and Internet access, Hollywood will stand alone in supplying the dream: movies monumentalize icons, vistas, and even products by rendering them literally larger than life; television and the Internet, by contrast, reduce images down, make them workaday. Even HDTV and its enlarged format will not approach the myth-making size of a theater screen, and certainly not its near-universal accessibility. Radios are a small, cheap, and ubiquitous means of spreading pop music and advertising, but a picture is still worth a thousand words. Hollywood continues to be what it has always been: the American dream factory that figures such as Stalin and Goebbels could only dream admiringly of duplicating.[57]

Reversing the Poles of American Cultural Influence

Nonetheless, there is an element of negotiation between the American producers of pop culture and its international consumers that can go beyond even the concepts of hybridization, unicity, and glocalization described earlier in this chapter. In some cases other states will attempt to turn American pop culture to their own uses, either domestically or directed at the United States itself, or sometimes both. They can make these efforts either with the cooperation of American cultural producers, or on their own.

One recent example is the 1997 Walt Disney animated film *Mulan*, a retelling of an ancient Chinese epic about a female warrior. *Mulan* was produced in the aftermath of an imbroglio between Disney and Beijing over director Martin Scorsese's film biography of the Dali Lama, *Kundun*, released by the Disney subsidiary Miramax, which enraged the communist leadership with its depictions of Chinese brutality in Tibet and caused them to threaten to bar Disney from China (Disney's China strategy, among other things, includes long-range plans for a Chinese Disneyland). *Mulan* was given the customary high-profile Disney release with toy and other commercial tie-ins in the United States and around the world. China was portrayed more positively in an American film than ever before during communist rule, Beijing was propitiated, and Disney was allowed to continue operating in China.[58]

An even more recent example is provided by Serbia during the 1999 Kosovo conflict. First of all, in the manner of Saddam Hussein in Iraq in 1991, the Milosevic regime provided CNN and other American news organizations with virtually unimpeded access to Belgrade and Serbian targets and victims of NATO bombing, including within Kosovo itself. Second, pro-Serbian organizations made effective use of the Internet to push Belgrade's line and to sow doubts about the rationale behind the NATO action for anyone looking for "the other side of the story." Third, the bull's-eye logo worn on T-shirts by thousand of Serbs and their supporters was appropriated from the American Target Stores logo. Fourth, Serbian television incessantly broadcast such American films as *Wag the Dog, Apocalypse Now, The Great Dictator*, and *Schindler's List* in order to portray the American-led attack as the product of U.S. domestic politics, associate the attack with the madness of Vietnam, and equate NATO with the Nazis.

In the future there will undoubtedly be more examples of this phenomenon and potentially in more proactive ways than those described in the preceding examples. In my doctoral dissertation I examine how after World War II Spain's fascist Franco regime attempted to use American tourism to Spain and U.S. movie production in Spain to shore up their image in the United States and elsewhere and to help rebuild their shattered economy.[59] One could well imagine, for example, a post-Milosevic regime attempting to do the same for Serbia (indeed, Yugoslavia was a haven for Hollywood's foreign production work during the 1970s and 1980s), or a future Beijing regime irrevocably decided on political and economic rapprochement with the United States.[60]

American Pop Cultural Soft Power and Its Limits

America's dominance in popular cultural production has imparted to it what Joseph Nye describes as soft power—the power to persuade or co-opt, versus hard or coercive power. As Nye puts it, "Soft power is our ability to get what we want through attraction rather than coercion. When other countries want the same outcome we want, then we can get what we want without having to spend as much on coercion."[61] However, a cornerstone of realist international relations theory is that less powerful states will come together to restrain or even defeat a state whose power is seen as a universal threat. American soft power as embodied by its pop/mass culture will not by itself cause a major, sustained political backlash against the United States; it has not done so thus far, during a century of ever-increasing dominance in the area.

But now, for the first time, American hard power has come to match the soft power preponderance the United States has maintained for so long. Particularly in the military sphere the United States stands in its own realm, lacking serious challengers, spending $270 billion a year on defense versus, for example, considerably less than $35 billion apiece by the Russians and the Chinese. In the twenty-first century the United States will be what French Foreign Minister Hubert Vedrine refers to as the world's "hyperpower," lacking an effective counterbalance for the first time in both the hard and soft power spheres, and as such a perpetual source of anxiety to other states and blocs. The twinning of American soft and hard power preponderance has the potential to tip much of the world away from the extant but already eroded perception of the United States as a relatively benign global hegemon. Especially if the United States is seen as consistently too assertive in pushing its military and economic agenda, the optimistic, glamorous, and fun-loving America portrayed so effectively by Hollywood could be overwhelmed by an image of the United States as an overbearing, even dangerous, imperialist power that, to paraphrase Thucydides, does what it can and forces others to do what they must.

In this scenario soft power, yoked uncomfortably to a hard power perceived to be out of control, may come to be seen not as harmless entertainment and consumerism or even gentle persuasion by the average international consumer but as hard power in sheep's clothing. A number of writers have claimed that much of American pop/mass culture is so thoroughly reinterpreted in other countries that it loses its specifically American character and becomes effectively part of their own culture. This is undoubtedly true, up to a point. However, the Belgrade crowds that trashed the local McDonald's and rallied carrying placards decrying "Stop Nato-Cola" in the style of the familiar soft drink logo in the aftermath of NATO bombing of their city offered dramatic evidence that at the end of the day, and particularly in severe crisis periods, nobody forgets the source of their fast food, fashions, and films.[62]

Conclusion

In the early twenty-first century we have a world with a far greater degree of mutual, simultaneous cultural awareness than ever before, made possible by the extraordinary technological developments that have given us the twentieth and twenty-first century electronic information age. But cultural globalization, a millennia-old series of phenomena, has not resulted in cultural homogenization but rather in a far more complex process of interchange that can be variously termed hybridization, unicity, glocalization, and the like. The United States, perhaps the most intensively hybridized state on the planet, has not been remaking the world in its image during this period, but it has consolidated and maintained a preponderant position as the single greatest generator of culture intended for worldwide consumption.

This cultural output is disseminating elements of American ideology and life-styles that provide disparate audiences all over earth with a perceived sense of simultaneous connection to the United States. This pervasive selling of the American way undoubtedly provides the United States the benefits of the soft power that Nye describes, and it will likely continue to do so unless the rest of the world comes to see the United States as an ongoing threat to global stability. However, we should not go overboard in assuming the mesmerizing or transformative effects of American popular culture—many of the young paramilitaries in the former Yugoslavia, for example, have engaged in ethnic slaughter, that most un-American of activities, while clad in Levi's blue jeans and Nike sneakers. As more and more of the world becomes "wired," the awareness of and interchange with other cultures will undoubtedly increase. But it would likely take a cataclysmic development on the order of Ronald Reagan's half-joking Martian invasion scenario (which he asserted would instantly cause the United States and the USSR to put their differences aside) to provide the centripetal force to forge some single "global culture." The world will remain a more interesting place in the Martians' absence.

Notes

1. John Tomlinson, *Globalization and Culture* (University of Chicago Press, 1999), p. 1.

2. This anxiety and the hope for its resolution were famously embodied in President John F. Kennedy's June 1963 American University speech, delivered in the aftermath of the Cuban Missile Crisis, in which he declared, "We [the U.S. and the USSR] are both caught

up in a vicious and dangerous cycle in which suspicion on one side breeds suspicion on the other, and new weapons beget counter weapons. . . . If we cannot now end our differences, at least we can help make the world safe for diversity. For, in the final analysis, our most basic common link is that we all inhabit this small planet. We all breathe the same air. We all cherish our children's future. And we are all mortal." Quoted in Bernard A. Weisberger, *Cold War, Cold Peace: The United States and Russia since 1945* (American Heritage Press, 1985), p. 227.

3. Max Weber, *The Protestant Ethic and the Spirit of Capitalism*, trans. Talcott Parsons, revised introduction by Randall Collins, 2d Roxbury ed. (Roxbury, 1998).

4. Yogesh Atal, "One World, Multiple Cultures," in Jan Servaes and Rico Lie, eds., *Media and Politics in Transition: Cultural Identity in the Age of Globalization* (Leuven, Belgium: Acco, 1997), p. 20.

5. Ray Laurence and Joan Berry, eds., *Cultural Identity in the Roman Empire* (London: Routledge, 1998), chap. 1 and passim. To be sure, one could find thoroughly Romanized cities, such as Britain's Londinium and Gaul's Lugdunum (Lyon). Moreover, the thorough-going Romanization of central Spain in the aftermath of a brutal series of wars in the second and first centuries B.C.E. offers a dramatic example of Rome's capacity for deliberately eradicating local cultural attributes that it considered a threat to its control. J.P.V.D. Balsdon, *Romans and Aliens* (London: Gerald Duckworth and Co., 1979), pp. 60, 64–65; Donald R. Dudley, *The Romans, 850 B.C.–A.D. 337* (Alfred Knopf, 1970), pp. 61–62.

6 . Jan Nederveen Pieterse, "Globalization as Hybridisation," *International Sociology* (June 1994), p. 169.

7. Arjun Appuradai, *Modernity at Large: Cultural Dimensions of Globalization* (University of Minnesota Press, 1996), p. 11.

8. Roland Robertson, *Globalization: Social Theory and Global Culture* (London: Sage Publications, 1992), p. 6.

9. Marwan M. Kraidy, "The Global, the Local, and the Hybrid: A Native Ethnography of Glocalization," *Critical Studies in Mass Communication* (December 1999), p. 472.

10. Atal, "One World," p. 22.

11. Albert Hourani, *A History of the Arab Peoples* (Harvard Belknap Press, 1991), pp. 7–9, 201–02.

12. Jared Diamond, *Guns, Germs, and Steel: The Fate of Human Societies* (Norton, 1997), pp. 35–41.

13. For a recent overview of the increasingly blurred line between fantasy and fact in the current debate over pre-Columbian East-West contact in the Americas, see Mark K. Stengel, "The Diffusionists Have Landed," *Atlantic Monthly*, January 2000, pp. 35–48.

14. John H. Marks, *Visions of One World: Legacy of Alexander* (Four Quarters Publishing Co., 1985), p. 69; see as well Erich S. Gruen, *The Hellenistic World and the Coming of Rome*, vol. 2 (University of California Press, 1984).

15. Marks, *Visons of One World*; and Gruen, *The Hellenistic World.*

16. The so-called Silk Road (a late nineteenth-century term coined by the German geographer and geologist Ferdinand Richthofen) "was not one road, but many; it was actually a network of roads, generally going East and West but with spurs into southern Iran, the northern Eurasian steppe, and south over the Hindu Kush to the Indian subcontinent." Richard C. Foltz, *Religions of the Silk Road: Overland Trade and Cultural Exchange from Antiquity to the Fifteenth Century* (St. Martin's, 1999), pp. 1–2 and passim.

17. Foltz, *Religions of the Silk Road*, pp. 6–7.

18. Harold Lasswell, David Lerner, and Hans Speir, eds., *Propaganda and Communication in World History, vol. 1: The Symbolic Instrument in Early Times* (University Press of Hawaii, 1979), p. 10–11.

19. From the Roman vantage point, Egypt was divided into the cosmopolitan, Greco-Jewish Alexandria and a vast, mysterious hinterland inhabited by native Egyptians. Balsdon, *Romans and Aliens,* pp. 68–69.

20. Hourani, *A History of the Arab Peoples,* pp. 26–29.

21. For the competitive position of Judaism in the Roman world prior to the fifth century C.E., see, for example, Kenan T. Erim, Joyce Reynolds, and Robert Tannenbaum, eds., *Jews and God-Fearers at Aphrodisias: Greek Inscriptions with Commentary—Texts from the Excavations at Aphrodisias* (Cambridge, U.K.: Cambridge Philological Society, 1987), and Judith Lieu, John North, and Tessa Rajak, eds., *The Jews among Pagans and Christians in the Roman Empire* (London: Routledge, 1994).

22. Communications analysts Harold Lasswell, David Lerner, and Hans Speier posit that Gutenberg's innovation was "perhaps a more important event in human history than the geographical accident of Columbus. For, moveable type made possible the diffusion of reading and writing, resulting in the three R's—'reading, 'riting, 'rithmetic'—which became the distinctive feature of Western civilization and may yet become the premise of human survival on this planet." Lasswell, Lerner, and Speir, *Propaganda and Communication,* p. 16.

23. Diamond, *Guns, Germs, and Steel,* pp. 372–73. Of course, shipbuilding technology by itself was not a sufficient determinant of the globe-trotting impulse. China was well on the way to developing ships with an intercontinental range in the early fifteenth century—the fleet of Admiral Chen Ho ventured as far as Zanzibar in its ten voyages between 1405 and 1433. Yet China fatefully decided to ban the construction of long-range ships and forgo exploration and the active pursuit of foreign trade. As historian Paul Kennedy notes, Chen Ho's ships "might well have been able to sail around Africa and 'discover' Portugal several decades before Henry the Navigator's expeditions began earnestly to push south of Ceuta." Paul Kennedy, *The Rise and Fall of the Great Powers: Economic Change and Military Conflict from 1500 to 2000* (Random House, 1987), pp. 6–7.

24. Stephen Kern, *The Culture of Time and Space, 1880–1918* (Harvard University Press, 1983).

25. Ibid., chap. 3.

26. Stuart Hall, "The Local and the Global: Globalization and Ethnicities," in A. D. King, ed., *Culture, Globalization and the World System* (London: Macmillan, 1991), pp. 19–31.

27. France maintains a significant global cultural presence, primarily in Francophone states and substates (such as Quebec). However, its reach is limited beyond the Francophone world, and many of its offerings, as noted in the following text, are not necessarily of particular appeal to popular as opposed to elite audiences.

28. Martin W. Laforce and James A. Drake, *Popular Culture and American Life: Selected Topics in the Study of Popular American Culture* (Nelson-Hall, 1981), p. viii.

29. Bernard Bailyn, *The Peopling of British North America: An Introduction* (Vintage, 1985), pp. 95–97.

30. "Questions of Cultural Exchange: The NIAS Statement on the European Reception of American Mass Culture," in Rob Kroes and others, eds., *Cultural Transmissions and*

Receptions: American Mass Culture in Europe (Amsterdam: VU University Press, 1993), p. 323.

31. Bernard Bailyn and others, *The Great Republic: A History of the American People*, 4th ed. (DC Heath, 1992), p. 229.

32. See, for example, Madison Grant, *The Passing of the Great Race: Or, the Racial Basis of European History* (Charles Scribner, 1916).

33. For example, movie mogul Samuel Goldwyn, a.k.a. Shmuel Gelbfisz of Warsaw, the son of Chasidic Jewish parents who spent his early years in America as a glove salesman before becoming involved with the infant motion picture industry, was no connoisseur of high art. But he and his colleagues had a gut-level understanding of the tastes of average Americans, as well as a boundless appetite for making money satisfying those tastes. See, for example, A. Scott Berg, *Goldwyn* (Knopf, 1989), as well as Neal Gabler, *An Empire of Their Own: How the Jews Invented Hollywood* (Crown, 1988).

34. Will Hays Papers, II, reel 19, frame 1167 ff., quoted in John Trumpbour, "Death to Hollywood: The Politics of Film in the United States, Great Britain, Belgium, and France, 1920–1960," Ph.D. dissertation, Harvard University, 1996, p. 25.

35. William Read, *America's Mass Media Merchants* (Johns Hopkins University Press, 1976), p. 9.

36. Emily Rosenberg, *Spreading the American Dream: American Economic and Cultural Expansion, 1890–1945* (Hill and Wang, 1982), chap. 5.

37. The French government established the Alliance Française in 1883; Italy founded the Societá Dante Alighieri in 1889; the Germans formed the Goethe Institut, ironically, in 1932, months before the Nazi takeover; and the British Council was founded in 1934.

38. For the interwar period, see, for example, Rosenberg, *Spreading the American Dream*, chap. 5; Costigliola, *Awkward Dominion: American Political, Economic and Cultural Relations with Europe, 1919–1933* (Cornell University Press, 1984), chaps. 5–6; and Ian Jarvie, *Hollywood's Overseas Campaign: The North Atlantic Movie Trade, 1920–1950* (Cambridge, U.K.: Cambridge University Press, 1992); for the post–World War II period see, for example, Jarvie, *Hollywood's Overseas Campaign*; Trumpbour, "Death to Hollywood," chap. 3; Paul Swann, "The Little State Department: Washington and Hollywood's Rhetoric of the Postwar Audience," in David Ellwood and Rob Kroes, eds., *Hollywood in Europe: Experiences of a Cultural Hegemony* (Amsterdam: VU University Press, 1994).

39. Nestor Garcia Canclini, "North Americans or Latin Americans? The Redefinition of Mexican Identity and the Free Trade Agreements," in Emile G. McAnany and Kenton T. Wilkinson, eds., *Mass Media and Free Trade: NAFTA and the Culture Industries* (University of Texas Press, 1996), pp. 149–50.

40. Immediately after World War II, U.S. film industry officials then serving in the armed forces spearheaded an effort to prevent the film industries of the Axis countries, especially Germany's Ufa studio, from getting back on their feet, ostensibly for ideological reasons. But they were in fact restrained by the U.S. government from fully carrying out their plan. See, for example, Ian Jarvie, "Free Trade as Cultural Threat: American Film and TV Exports in the Post-War Period," in Geoffery Nowell-Smith and Steven Ricci, eds., *Hollywood and Europe: Economics, Culture, National Identity 1945–95* (London: BFI Publishing, 1998), pp. 36–38.

41. McAnany and Wilkinson, "Introduction," in McAnany and Wilkinson, *Mass Media and Free Trade*, pp. 3, 7; Garcia Canclini, also in McAnany and Wilkinson, pp. 149–54;

Richard Pells, *Not Like Us: How Europeans Have Loved, Hated, and Transformed American Culture since World War II* (Basic Books, 1997), pp. 273–77. Kantor actually lost the negotiations over unrestricted exportation of American cultural products to GATT participant nations, but he had fought a hard battle before giving in.

42. Geoffery Nowell-Smith, "Introduction," in Nowell-Smith and Ricci, eds., *Hollywood and Europe*, p. 6.

43. Pells, *Not Like Us*, pp. 210–11, 227.

44. Rosenberg, *Spreading the American Dream*, p. 100; Rosenberg's analysis is not far removed from the Motion Picture Association of America's assertions concerning the secret of American movies' unique international success. Author's interview with former MPEA Vice-President S. Frederick Gronich, November 7, 1995.

45. Cultural historian Victoria de Grazia contrasts the American and European modes of movie production in the interwar period: "The American cinema stood for major economies of scale, capital-intensive technologies, and standardization; it favored an action-filled cinematographic narrative focused on the star and pitched to a cross-class audience. Its promoters were professionals who were formed outside of traditional centers of culture, and who were closely attuned to the problem of marketing their products. By contrast, the European tradition was indentified with decentralized artisan-atelier shops and was associated with theatrical and dramatic conventions attuned to well-defined publics." De Grazia, "Mass Culture and Sovereignty," *Journal of Modern History* (March 1989), p. 61. Her point was no less accurate for much of the postwar period as well. In the 1980s and 1990s, however, Rupert Murdoch, an Australian with his headquarters in Britain, purchased the various arms of the Fox Corporation, Britain's EMI bought Capitol Records, and Germany's Bertelsmann Gmbh. acquired the Bantam, Doubleday, and Dell publishers, as well as the Literary Guild book club. Pells, *Not Like Us*, pp. 320–21. It is noteworthy that Rupert Murdoch has taken on American citizenship and that Bertelsmann CEO Thomas Middelhoff has referred to himself (at an appearance in 1999 at Harvard University's Kennedy School of Government) as "an American with a German passport," raising the question of whether foreign ownership of American media companies has simply resulted in the tail wagging the dog.

46. As well as Russians, who, interestingly enough, are longtime aficionados of the genre. (Ismail Merchant, "Kitschy as Ever, Bollywood Is Branching Out," *New York Times*, November 22, 1998, sec. 2, p. 15.) It should be noted that the Indian expatriate community constitutes a large audience—for example, in 1998 one Bollywood film, *Dil Se*, became the first Indian film to break into the British top ten. *Dil Se*'s success was followed by that of *Kuch Kuch Hota Hai*, which included scenes shot in Scotland. "Planet Bollywood," *Marketing Week*, London, March 18, 1999, p. 35.

47. English, explains media analyst Jeremy Tunstall, "contains a greater variety of pithy phrases and simple words from which to choose (compared with French, for example), and the English-language version is usually shorter than the version in any other language." English has a simpler grammar than other widespread languages—Spanish has fourteen separate tenses, for example, versus English's six. "English," declares Tunstall, "is the language best suited to comic strips, headlines, riveting first sentences, photo captions, dubbing, sub-titling, pop songs, hoardings, disc-jockey banter, news flashes, sung commercials." Jeremy Tunstall, *The Media Are American: Anglo-American Media in the World*

(London: Constable, 1977), p. 128; Christopher Kendris, *501 Spanish Verbs*, 3d ed. (Barron's, 1990), p. xx.

48. Tunstall, *The Media Are American*, p. 127.

49. California has long beguiled and bemused foreign observers: the Italian journalist Luigi Barzini referred to the state as "a clean new world, where everything is easy and permissible, where the embarrassing traditions and the errors of the past are forgotten, the empty slate on which to start writing anew." Christopher Isherwood wrote, "Out there, in the eternal lazy morning of the Pacific, days slip away into months, months into years . . . one might pass a lifetime . . . between two yawns, lying bronzed and naked on the sand." Both quotes drawn from Pells, *Not Like Us*, pp.165–66. It would have been interesting to see whether *Baywatch* would exert the same fascination for international viewers had production moved to Australia, as had originally been planned. "Its Economy Ailing, Hawaii Hangs Some Hopes on Hollywood," *New York Times*, May 17, 1999, p. A1.

50. See, for example, C. W. E. Bigsby, *Superculture: American Popular Culture and Europe* (London: Elek, 1975), pp. 12–13; Costigliola, *Awkward Dominion*, p. 167; and Pells, *Not Like Us*, pp. 163–68.

51. For example, *My Cousin Vinny*, a 1995 film comedy about a leather-jacketed, decidedly non-Ivy League lawyer from Brooklyn who uses street smarts to defend a murder suspect in a buttoned-down Southern town presided over by a Yale-alum judge, was a major hit in China when it dubbed Vinny the lowbrow but clever lawyer in a provincial dialect and the haughty judge in formal Mandarin.

52. In 1996's blockbuster science fiction movie *Independence Day*, U.S. Air Force F-16s blow alien warships out of the sky and save humankind. What chance would any earthly challenger have? Of course, this image of near-limitless power can backfire: for example, many Chinese honestly believe that with American technological sophistication the U.S. bombing of the Chinese Embassy in Belgrade could not have been an accident.

53. In 1955, for example, U.S. Ambassador to Italy Clare Boothe Luce attempted to have *Blackboard Jungle* banned from the Venice Film Festival because of its depiction of urban juvenile delinquency (she failed in her effort).

54. "When Its Customers Fell Ill, a Master Marketer Faltered," *New York Times*, June 30, 1999, p. A1.

55. Bernard Bailyn, *The Origins of American Politics* (Vintage Books, 1968), chap. 1.

56. "Net of Fame: Who Rules the Web? Pamela Anderson Lee, The B-Movie Actress," *Wall Street Journal*, April 13, 1999, p. A1.

57. Joseph Goebbels declared in 1940, "We must give [German] film a task and a mission in order that we may use it to conquer the world. Only then will we also overcome American film." Quoted in Eric Rentschler, *The Ministry of Illusion: Nazi Cinema and Its Afterlife* (Harvard University Press, 1996), p. 215; Josef Stalin stated flatly, "If I could control the medium of the American motion picture, I would need nothing else to convert the entire world to communism." Quoted in Trumpbour, "Death to Hollywood," p. 4. More recently, Chinese President Jiang Zemin lauded the profitability of the movie *Titanic*, a box office hit in China, to the Politburo, declaring, "Let us not assume that we can't learn from capitalism." *Guardian*, April 27, 1998, p. 10.

58. Of course, without access to Disney's internal documents on the subject, we cannot be completely certain that *Mulan* was produced expressly to mollify China's offended rulers.

However, there is a strong circumstantial correlation to be discerned between Beijing's anger over *Kundun* and Disney's choice of subject matter for its subsequent animated epic.

59. Neal M. Rosendorf, "A Study in the International Character and Influence of Hollywood: The Life and Times of Samuel Bronston, Epic Film Producer," Ph.D. dissertation, Harvard University, 2000, chaps. 6–9.

60. Which resulted in Hollywood productions such as "Force 10 From Navarone" (1979), starring Harrison Ford and Robert Shaw, which inaccurately depicted the Yugoslav pro-Royalist, anticommunist Chetnik resistance group as unalloyed Nazi collaborators during World War II—a precise reflection of ex-partisan leader Tito's long-standing propaganda campaign against his wartime rivals.

61. Joseph S. Nye Jr., "The Power We Must Not Squander," *New York Times*, January 3, 2000, p. 19; for a fuller description of soft power as a concept, see Joseph S. Nye Jr., *Bound to Lead: The Changing Nature of American Power* (Basic Books, 1990), pp. 31–33; 190–95.

62 . See, for example, Thomas L. Friedman, *The Lexus and the Olive Tree: Understanding Globalization* (Farrar, Straus, Giroux, 1999), chap. 10, in which he restates in earnest the "Golden Arches Theory of Conflict Resolution" that he first propounded somewhat tongue-in-cheek in 1996: no two countries have gone to war since both gained a McDonald's franchise. See as well James Watson, ed., *Golden Arches East: McDonald's in East Asia* (Stanford University Press, 1997); Tom O'Regan, "Too Popular by Far: On Hollywood's International Reputation," *Continuum*, vol. 5, no. 2 (1992); Pells, *Not Like Us*; and Richard Kuisel, *Seducing the French: The Dilemma of Americanization* (University of California Press, 1993).

6

VIKTOR MAYER-SCHÖNBERGER
DEBORAH HURLEY

Globalization
of Communication

THE "COMMUNICATIONS REVOLUTION" has become a ubiquitous
catchphrase. Reference to its globalizing force is common to the point
of triteness. But is a global communications revolution really happening?
And if so, why and to what extent? For philosopher Karl Popper, the ability
to communicate is the very foundation of "being human."[1] Human communication is not only fundamental, it is also rich. We are able to use a variety of senses to exchange our thoughts with one another. With the help of
media, we have been able to extend our communicative reach in space and
time to exchange ideas across distances and through the ages. In this broad
sense, the sense intended in this chapter, communication is not limited to a
particular medium or type of human interchange. It includes all information transmittals, whether the information is spoken, written, drawn, or
performed, whether it is relayed through analogue or digital means, whether
it is transmitted in traditional forms, like letters or books, or by way of a
computer, telephone, or any other communication appliance.

The invention of painting and writing were the first forms of such mediated communications. They proved to be powerful tools to transcend our
temporal and spatial limits. The rise of the book has been termed a "revolution," as have the invention of radio and television.[2] All three media had
profound societal impacts, which transcended national boundaries. The
printing revolution spread across Europe like a firestorm at the end of the

fifteenth century. Monarchs embraced the new medium of communication as much as they attempted to regulate it. For Benedict Anderson, books and especially newspapers were necessary preconditions for the consolidation of monarchies and the formation of nation-states, for they provided media through which citizens were able to communicate and, thereby, develop a sense of commonality and community.[3] Similarly, radio and television have been described as tools to establish Marshall McLuhan's "global village," through communication unconstrained by borders.[4]

From this perspective, current developments in information and communication technologies are just symbols of yet another "communication revolution," internationalizing the exchange of ideas and information, in the same way that books, radio, television, and many other communication inventions have done before. But certain inherent, unique qualities of the new information and communication technologies indicate that this "communication revolution" is different from previous ones.

Qualities of the New Information and Communication Technologies

In the following we concentrate on the four most important of these unique qualities of new information and communication networks.

Digitization

From the first ancient cave paintings to the mass-produced books, movies, telephone, and television, a particular medium has constrained the communication channel it established to a particular mode and type of message. Paintings are visual and cannot be listened to, a telephone conversation cannot be watched, and a movie cannot be felt. This inherent limitation has forced us to use a variety of different media to accommodate the many different modes of human communication.

Digitization changes this. By translating information into a universal binary code, any kind of communication can be handled through time and space by the same medium and transmitted through its infrastructure. Text, drawings, pictures, sounds and speech, video, and many other types of information, once they are translated into binary code, are transmittable through digital networks. Since different types of information can be sent over one and the same network, many traditionally distinct information and communication uses migrate from dedicated networks to this universal network, a development called "convergence." Such digital networks even break down the traditional categories of one-to-one (telephone, letter) and one-to-many (television) networks. For Nicholas Negroponte, digitization is so fundamental a development that he named his book *Being Digital*.[5]

The universal digital code is the most important of the unique qualities of the "new" information and communication technologies. It permits the construction of networks, which are not custom tailored to a particular kind of information flow but remain open and adaptable for any possible future use. But digitization would not have been practical without the power of information technologies to translate rich information flows into the digital code and back. As digitization is the theoretical precondition, dramatic increases in information processing power are the practical necessity to build integrated, digital, universal communication networks.

Information Processing

The development of information processing capacity and power from the early days of integrated circuits in the 1960s to the twenty-first century has been nothing short of breathtaking. In 1965, a young engineer, Gordon Moore, who would later cofound Intel, the world's largest producer of microprocessors, published a four-page article forecasting that the information processing capacity of microprocessors would double every eighteen months, while cost and power consumption would decrease with similar speed.[6] Termed "Moore's Law," his prediction still holds. Today, computing speed is literally millions of times faster than in 1965. Experts predict that processing speed and power will continue to at least double every eighteen months until the end of the twenty-first century's first decade. By then information processing with silicon switches of electric current will be replaced by optical or biological computing, but as far as we know today Moore's Law will still hold or be surpassed by even more dramatic increases. Information processing provides the power to transform ever-richer streams of information into digital code and back into human-absorbable forms, to permit it to be handled and transmitted across digital networks. Advances in storage and display further enhance this development. In the 1980s, a typical hard disk in a personal computer could store 20 million characters of text. By the end of the 1990s, such hard disks stored 20 billion characters of text, at a comparable price.

Bandwidth

Moore's Law pertains to the processing of data—the transformation of almost any kind of information into a binary code, its easy manipulation and storage, and its translation back into the analogue kind of information flows that our human senses can grasp. Processing information efficiently in millions of computers is quite useful. But what makes it even more useful is the ability to move information around. Transmission of digitized information over networks, the necessary complement to processing power, has kept pace. Indeed, network bandwidth—the amount of information capable of being transmitted over a network—does not just double every eighteen months, as Moore's Law predicts for processing speed and power, but triples every twelve months.[7] Every three years then, processing speed increases fourfold and transmission capabilities (and thus transmission speeds) a staggering twenty-sevenfold. Experts expect this annual tripling of bandwidth to continue for at least the next twenty-five years. Already, the prediction is called Gilder's Law and given a status comparable to Moore's Law.[8] Digital storage is so cheap and bandwidth so plentiful that a leading computer manufacturer announced in early 2000 that it would give each of its more than 30 million customers 20 million characters of free disk storage on its servers, accessible through the Internet to use for temporary storage, backup, or information sharing.[9]

Standards and Decentralized Architecture

Universality of code, substantial and rapidly increasing processing power, and network bandwidth created the fertile soil for another, fourth major quality of the new information and communication technologies. It permitted the logistical tasks of sending and receiving information to become part of the communication infrastructures, the networks, themselves. Historically, many communication networks were built around a few central organizational entities. Newspapers were written, edited, laid out, and printed in one place and depended only on a peripheral distribution network. The telephone network was controlled by central, regional, and local switches owned and operated by the phone company. Terrestrial television was originally produced at and transmitted from one location. Like the phone network, television networks are controlled by the television company, its affiliates, and business partners.

The most successful of all digital networks, the Internet, is built on an entirely different paradigm. The Internet's network is decentralized, almost by definition, because of the communication standards and protocols that it employs. It is built on the premise that all elements of the network, whoever owns and operates them, will work together to function seamlessly. If one element of the network fails, the Internet protocols are designed to find ways to circumvent the failing element, to "re-route" information flows around the trouble spot. Embedding this "routing" intelligence into the network was made possible only by virtue of the processing power available to millions of users and the bandwidth increases caused by advances in transmission technology, particularly but not limited to fiber optics. Technically, loosening central control over a communication network, like the Internet, necessitates crafting into the communication protocols and structures of the network, pragmatic means of network self-management and self-regulation. The Internet is the "living" example that such dispersal of control is not just technically feasible, but working—and working very well. The delegation of control to the communication elements of the communication structure requires, however, that these elements use a common communication standard. Such powerful universal communication standards, like the Internet's TCP/IP, were instrumental in making the Internet work. Often overlooked in this context is the important fact that these standards, including TCP/IP, have evolved outside established, government-controlled standardization bodies and transcended national boundaries. Unlike voltage, telephone plugs, and television standards, TCP/IP is not limited in its reach to a particular geographic region or cluster of states.[10] It has been adopted globally, not by votes in an official standardization body, but by the pragmatic choice of millions of Internet users.

Enhancements to these standards will ensure the Internet's viability well into the second decade of the twenty-first century and permit billions of new elements (or "nodes") to be added to the network.[11] Standardization, from binary code to the Internet's TCP/IP, also created tremendous opportunities for economies of scale in the creation and manufacturing of necessary hard- and software components, as well as the information content available on the network.

These four interconnected qualities—digitization, processing power (Moore's Law), network bandwidth (Gilder's Law), and networks with a globally standardized but decentralized communication architecture (such as TCP/IP)—taken together, give the current digital information and communication networks a character that transcends previous technological innovations. If revolutions are symbolized by rapid replacement compared with evolutionary, incremental modifications and additions, the current development in the communication arena qualifies as a particularly strong "communication revolution." Unlike previous communication technologies, digital integrated networks do not just add to the existing communication "mix," but cause substantial shifts of communication flows from old "dedicated" networks to the new universal net based on a globally accepted standard. Interconnecting digital networks is comparatively easy, owing to their universal code. Moreover, the benefits of adding new users to the network are profound (this network externality is often called Metcalfe's Law).[12] Consequently, digital networks feature an internal dynamic driving toward global interconnection.

How can we calibrate the growth of global communication and its consequences? Measuring digital networks and their use with traditional means turns out to be difficult because of the very qualities that these new networks are built on, including the lack of central control. Any collection of such facts, then, must by definition remain incomplete and considered with a grain of salt. But despite these shortcomings, the data available provide the first good glimpse at the breadth and width of the current global communication revolution.

Gauging the Global Communication Revolution

Three perspectives gauge the global communication revolution: network reach, content depth, and economic impact. Each of these provides a unique picture of the developments. Network reach looks at the expanding and changing landscape of digital networks. Content depth focuses on the increase of information volume accessible on the network. Economic impact adds the economic and business side to the evolving picture.

Network Reach

Digital communication networks drive the communication revolution. They are not just replacing their analogue counterparts but are permitting their own continuous adaptation to rapidly evolving user needs.

Television has traditionally been transmitted through airwaves—an analogue signal, centrally controlled. Cable later enabled more analogue channels to be brought into homes. The introduction of digital technology in the 1990s fundamentally altered this analogue setup. Direct-to-home (DTH) broadcasting satellites deliver many hundreds of digitally coded television channels to millions of homes, not only in the developed world, but similarly successfully in developing economies, such as in southeast Asia, India, and China.[13] Such satellites—transmitting from no government's terrain, into millions of cheap and small receivers on rooftops feeding individual households—create digital communication networks without the government control of traditional infrastructures.

Even incomplete International Telecommunications Union (ITU) statistics show an eightfold increase in DTH satellite receivers worldwide, from 4.4 million in 1988 to 33.4 million in 1995.[14] As growth continues apace, a recent study predicted that digital satellite television subscribers will outnumber cable subscribers in the United States by 2003.[15] In an attempt to keep up with this shift, cable television companies are busy "upgrading" their own networks from a centralized analogue topology to an all digital fiber-optic network employing the Internet's TCP/IP network standard.

Digital networks have also taken over mobile telephony. GSM, an all-digital cellular communication standard developed in Europe, has been hugely successful around the world. The structure of GSM permits its subscribers to use their phones in more than sixty countries by "roaming" in local networks abroad. GSM networks are interconnected and form a global network of networks, which provides almost seamless communication across borders and continents. Through digital cellular networks, mobile telephony has expanded dramatically, from 4.2 million subscribers worldwide in 1988 to 137 million in 1996.[16] The total number of subscribers increased to 400 million in 1999 and is expected to hit the one billion mark in 2004, surpassing, at that point, fixed phone line subscribers.[17] In some regions, such as Scandinavia, mobile phone use has reached almost 100 percent for certain age groups, with many people owning and using more than one cell phone.[18]

The success of cellular phones is not limited to industrialized nations. Southeast Asian tigers, developing countries, even conservative nations, such as Saudi Arabia, fully embrace the mobile phone boom.[19] Switching to a mobile digital phone network has a number of advantages for these countries. It spares them the expensive and tedious process of digging up the earth and laying fixed lines. It permits them to build their network incrementally and to react swiftly to rapidly growing demand. It introduces competition in markets dominated by previously state-controlled incumbents. In addition, countries such as Bangladesh have been able to create successful niche economies of cellular subscribers who rent their phones for others to use.[20]

With a GSM phone, subscribers are not limited to voice communication. Through the keypad, they can enter short text messages (SMS) and send them to other subscribers. SMS are very successful. One in four mobile phone users in the Netherlands, for example, regularly sends and receives textual communication by way of a mobile telephone, and numbers for Scandinavia and Germany are not far behind. According to a recent estimate, approximately one billion SMS messages are sent monthly in the German-speaking countries alone.[21] Similarly, Japanese cellular users can transmit small pictures and digitized photos to one another—not only extremely popular among the young generation but also exemplifying the universality of digital networks and the fact that all information can be transmitted across them once it has been digitized.[22] New additions to the cellular standards, such as the Wireless Application Protocol (WAP), already enable subscribers to access their e-mail or to browse the World Wide Web through their mobile phones. Cellular phone companies, like Nokia, estimate that by 2003 cellular revenues will be generated almost entirely by accessing digital information and predict that cellular voice telephony, reduced to an ancillary function, may be entirely free of charge. At that time, digital networks of mobile communication will have become fully integrated into the Internet.

The Internet, of course, is not one network but comprises all digital interconnected networks based on the TCP/IP standard of packet-switched information transmission. Referring to "the Internet," then, includes the entire infrastructure of these interconnected networks, a true "network of networks" and one, as the enhancement to mobile phone networks indicates, which will soon grow to encompass all kinds of digital "subnets." The growth of the Internet over the past decade has been nothing short of phenomenal. The number of Internet "hosts," that is, nodes in the global network, has increased exponentially, reaching 10 million in 1996 and exceeding 70 million by the end of the millennium (figure 6-1).

While no firm figures are available, experts estimate that more than 200 million people were connected to the Internet worldwide in Sep-

Figure 6-1. *Internet Domain Survey Host Count*

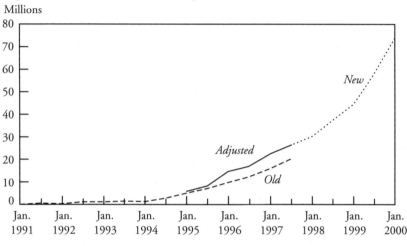

Source: Internet Software Consortium (www.isc.org).

tember 1999, with this number growing rapidly.[23] The Internet wave happened despite comparatively high costs of necessary hardware, particularly personal computers. The introduction of fully equipped personal computers (PCs) in the under $1,000 price range has opened the Internet to entire new classes of users, including lower-income populations in developed nations and users in developing countries. Embedding Internet connectivity into mobile phones, as WAP promises, and other cheap information appliances will arguably bring Internet access to huge numbers of additional people, especially in developing countries.

This digital network of networks offers open-ended media richness. User demand has undoubtedly been fueled by the World Wide Web, with its seamless integration of many different streams of information and communication. Providers of parts of the Internet's overall infrastructure have been busy adding bandwidth to the network, which is immediately utilized by users switching to more media-rich information offerings. To meet demand, in 1999 more than 4,000 miles of fiber optic cable were laid per day in the United States alone.[24]

Once seen as primarily a phenomenon of the developed world, the Internet has been embraced by many developing countries and transition economies as well. To be sure, the world map of Internet hosts still reveals the inequalities of information access. But it also shows that, at the beginning of the twenty-first century, the Internet has turned into a truly global information and communication network.

The global dimension of the Internet is furthered and supported by another unique feature of the net—its cost and billing structure. Since its inception, Internet traffic has been billed either as a flat fee or based on time and volume. Distance has never been a factor in the cost structure. Consequently, users are utterly oblivious to the location of their virtual communication partner or information resource. For them, it simply does not matter whether they are a hundred yards or 10,000 miles apart. Since, in contrast to telephony, distance is no cost factor, local information providers and communication partners enjoy no advantage over others located far away. Thus, going global for communication partners on the Internet is natural.

Content Depth

Expanding networks represent growth in the underlying infrastructure of modern information and communication technologies, but growth has extended to the information available online, the "content," as well. The structure of the World Wide Web has enabled information of vastly different types, location, and content to be linked together to create a web, whose sum—because of the embedded links—is bigger than its parts. The number of websites has increased at an even more staggering pace than the development of the Internet. In June 1993, barely 130 websites were online. Only three and one-half years later, Internet users could access over 650,000 sites.[25] Moreover, as total growth of data traffic over digital networks continues apace, and there is every indication it will, it overtook voice traffic on global telecommunication networks by 1998 and will eclipse it by approximately 2007.[26]

The breadth and depth of information content available online and the endless abilities to communicate globally have prompted users to spend more and more time on the net. In 1999 the average U.S. Internet user spent 12.1 hours per week online.[27] A 1999 study by the Kaiser Family Foundation showed that Internet use may substitute for television viewing among children.[28] Such changes in media use, prompted by the depth of content available on the net, have substantial implications, including economic ones.

Economic Impact

A third dimension of assessing the drastic changes caused by the current communication revolution is offered by the available economic and business data.

Digital networks have caused the global telecommunication market to grow to $600 billion in 1995.[29] The market is not only large but also grows at a rate well above the average growth rate of economies—8 percent from 1990 to 1995—even though this figure still includes growth-hampering old analogue networks.[30] Moreover, the capacity of these digital networks to embed routing intelligence in their structures has enabled telecommunication operators to accommodate this growth with fewer employees.[31] Despite substantial capital investments for digital infrastructures, therefore, telecommunication profits—and stock prices—have been soaring.

The impressive figures for infrastructure providers pale when compared with those of content providers on digital networks. Internet initial public offerings (IPOs) pushed the stock market to new heights. Start-ups such as Amazon, Ebay, Etoys or Freetrade, gained single, even double-digit billion dollar market valuations, surpassing many long-established global brands.[32] In 1999, this budding e-commerce industry produced revenues of $30 billion in the United States alone.[33] And this figure is bound to increase rapidly. "Living online," within the virtual worlds created by global information content providers, is already natural for young adults. A 2000 Forrester Research survey found that 34 percent of U.S. teenagers shop online.[34] *Time Magazine*, recognizing the ascent of this "information economy" based entirely on the global communication revolution, bestowed its highest laurels on Amazon's Jeff Bezos by voting him the "person of the year."[35] In addition, existing businesses around the world have started to realign themselves along the new digital frontier. Mergers, from small to gargantuan—such as AOL's with Time-Warner—are taking place to integrate networks and content horizontally and vertically.

The digital networks, with their communication infrastructures and rich, flexible content, have turned into important sources of economic growth. Value added per worker in IT-producing industries in the United States grew at an annual average of 10.4 percent in the 1990s, far higher than the rest of the country. Up to a full third of the entire annual growth in the United States in the last years of the twentieth century, some experts maintain, was generated just by the dramatic expansion in the "information economy."[36]

The vast and expanding network reach, the dramatically increasing breadth and depth of accessible content, and the astonishing economic growth and convergence provide three different kinds of indicators by which to gauge the unique ascent of the modern global digital networks. While an exact assessment of the communication revolution might require both temporal distance and measurement tools better suited for decentralized infrastructures, its overall importance need hardly be questioned.

Consequences

The consequences of this communication revolution are as profound as they are complex. Some of the most basic of these consequences will be felt by all societies affected, with governments forced to react to them. They range from the dependency on network infrastructures for societal growth and well-being to changes in the global economic order, from consequences for domestic governance to potential power shifts in international affairs.

Network Dependency

With digital networks taking an ever more prominent role in our daily lives, from work to leisure, our society as a whole will become more dependent on the network, its functioning and integrity. The 1980 ARPANET collapse, the nationwide saturation of the AT&T switching system in 1990, and the global havoc of the "iloveyou" virus in the spring of 2000 provide early glimpses of how dependent we have already become.[37] To make matters worse, the increase in dependency will coincide with an increase in vulnerability as the network standards are as robust and decentralized as they are insecure and open. To counter this insecurity, policymakers will have to coordinate efforts domestically and on a global scale, augmenting their policies with technological additions, such as encryption and digital signatures.

Despite these technological fixes, the fundamental openness of the networks will always leave it somewhat vulnerable to attacks. The simple provision of a regulatory framework for the use of tools adding network security will not suffice. Infrastructure protection and disaster prevention experts and law enforcement will have to understand the stakes. The most dangerous scenario might be one of hackers using a whole string of little-known security loopholes to bring down essential network parts in a domino effect that does not stop at borders.

Convergence and Mass Customization

Many associate the Internet with globalization, particularly in the business sector. There is no doubt that global networks supplement international trade and economic globalization, as they lower the cross-border transaction costs for advertising, marketing, and ordering. Globalization will receive a further boost from the Internet once a substantial part of the information traded globally is distributed over the network.

There is a second, highly important economic aspect of digital networks. They provide the framework for moving the economy from mass production to flexible production and mass customization. Mass production, symbolized by Henry Ford's assurance that customers could get the Model T car in any color they wanted so long as it was black, hinges on predicting demand, producing stock based on the prediction, and then using advertisement to stimulate demand for the products. Mass production is made possible in part by the ability of producers to "broadcast" their marketing information to a large number of potential customers. Existing media have been successfully employed for that purpose.

The digital networks permit a different model of production, which is, at least in theory, much more efficient. By using the networks' ability for two-way communication, producers now can query the consumers before they start production and ideally produce only what the consumers have already ordered. Mass customization, a concept made popular by Stan Davis in 1987 and theoretically refined by Joseph Pine, is now a leading strategy in the new economy.[38] Concrete consumer information leading to customized production substitutes for massive information outflows from producers to consumers. Already it has made it possible for large computer companies like Dell or Apple to offer their computers "built-to-order" on their websites, thus reducing overall inventory to as little as two days' supply—a huge efficiency gain given the steep and fast inventory depreciation in the computer sector. But mass customization is not limited to the manufacturing sector, it is almost a natural choice for information-oriented service sectors and the information media. The early 1990s predicted a world with 500 television channels. The success of the World Wide Web has shown that 500 channels do not carry the day, but, rather, a single highly customized stream of information for every user—"one channel for one."

This massive restructuring of the underlying business models in the new network economy poses many new and complex policy issues, including privacy and intellectual property, as the ability to control and use information becomes the source of wealth.

Virtual Communities

Global network reach, worldwide content formatting standards, and continuous drastic increases in bandwidth will create a ubiquitous information experience for an increasing number of users. The Internet pricing model, with its disregard for distance, will further facilitate this development. With the "information economy" moving from delivery of actual goods to delivery of information across networks, issues of product distribution infrastructures hampering current e-commerce businesses in developing economies will become less and less important. The "distances" of the digital networks will not be physical distances but bottlenecks in bandwidth and processing speeds. People will experience proximity and distance as the difference between a fast information server connected to the net with broad bandwidth and a small server linked to an unreliable and slow network link.

Traditional policymaking is based at least in part on the notion that states bind people together on the basis of geographic proximity. Almost the entire legal system of the world is premised on the notion of determinate location. Rules have a certain territorial reach and people within this reach are bound by them. But users of global digital networks will no longer experience geographic boundaries.[39] Instead, they will experience more and more boundaries of self-declared communities, created by users sharing similar interests or goals. These "virtual communities," a term made popular by Internet visionary Howard Rheingold in 1993, are not tied together by geographic proximity but by shared values, goals or experiences.[40] Moreover, while in most cases one can only be part of one physical community, there is no similar restriction for virtual communities. Thus unlike leaving a physical community, exiting a virtual community in most cases is much less costly for the individual.

Governance based on geographic proximity, territorial location, and exclusivity of membership to such physical communities will be fundamentally challenged by the advent of numerous non-proximity-based, overlapping virtual communities. A number of governance models for this new landscape have been suggested, from international law to community self-regulation, but how and how well these concepts may blend with the prevailing state-based governance model remains to be seen.

The Digital Divide

Digital networks are rapidly turning into tools of power. Access to the networks will be key to playing a role in the new economy. Technological breakthroughs, for example, in wireless communications, and Moore's Law may permit societies with currently limited network access capabilities to leapfrog into the information age. At the same time, access to networks like the Internet is not only dependent on the technological infrastructure. People desiring to access the net also need to know how to navigate and explore a still largely English, text-oriented web regardless of how easy the actual information access appliances will have become. Some predict that this education gap will bar a large percentage of the world's population, especially the socially disadvantaged, from the full benefits of the net, with the result of further exclusion. Overcoming the challenges implicit in such an analysis of a two-tier society will pose another serious governance issue.

While digital universal networks are neither the sole nor the primary force of globalization, they are intimately linked with the move toward globalization, both fueling it and being fueled by it. The societal consequences will be profound. Network dependency, the shift from mass production to mass customization, virtual communities, and the decline of the importance of geographic proximity as a defining element, as well as the potential harms of a global and societal digital divide, represent four domains of challenge for governance in the twenty-first century.

Notes

1. Karl Popper, *Alles Leben ist Problemlösen* (Riper, 1994), p. 22.
2. Elizabeth Eisenstein, *The Printing Revolution in Early Modern Europe* (Canto, 1983).
3. Benedict Anderson, *Imagined Communities* (London: Verso, 1983).
4. Marshall McLuhan, *Understanding Media* (McGraw-Hill, 1964).
5. Nicholas Negroponte, *Being Digital* (Knopf, 1995).
6. Gordon Moore, *Cramming More Components onto Integrated Circuits,* Electronics Serial (1965).
7. George Gilder, "Fiber Keeps Its Promise," *Forbes* ASAP, April 7, 1997, pp. 90–94.
8. Philips Evans and Thomas Wurster, *Blown to Bits* (Harvard Business School Press, 1999), p. 14.

9. "Apple Computer Announces Internet Strategy," January 4, 2000, www.apple.com.

10. Even the global DVD standard incorporates a geographic "region code," prohibiting U.S. DVDs to be played on European DVD players for copyright reasons.

11. Internet Protocol version 6 (Ipv6) specification, December 1998 (RTC 2460) and IP version 6 Addressing Architecture, July 1998 (RTC 2373).

12. Metcalfe is one of the inventors of the Ethernet protocol, which made possible the trends toward networks; his "law" is that the value of a network rises with the square of the number of participants. See generally Robert Metcalfe, *Packet Communication* (Thomson, 1996).

13. The success is not limited to Asian nations, but extends, for example, to Middle East countries. In 1995 Algeria already had more DTH satellite receivers (600,000) than Italy (479,000). International Telecommunications Union, *World Telecommunication Indicators Database*, 4th ed. (Geneva).

14. ITU, *World Telecommunication Indicators Database*, 4th ed.

15. "Digital DTH Subscribers to Outnumber Digital Cable Subscribers through 2003, according to 'Cahners In-Stat Group,'" *Business Wire*, October 19, 1999, online, Lexis Nexis Academic Universe, August 16, 2000.

16. ITU, *World Telecommunication Indicators Database*, 4th ed.

17. "The World in Your Pocket," *Economist*, October 9, 1999, *Telecommunications Survey*, p. 5.

18. "Cutting the Cord," *Economist*, October 9, 1999, *Telecommunications Survey*, p. 6.

19. South Korea added 1 million mobile subscribers in 1997 alone. "Testing Times for the Tigers," *Economist*, October 31, 1998. Israel has 28 mobile phones per 100 inhabitants, a rate exceeding that of mobile-savvy Denmark, and Lebanon sports 16 cellular subscribers per 100 inhabitants, about the same rate as Britain. "A Toy for Middle Eastern Times," *Economist*, April 10, 1999, p. 45.

20. "At the Back Beyond," *Economist*, October 9, 1999, *Survey Telecommunications*, p. 18.

21. "Das Handy als Briefträger," ORF ON, December 20, 1999; see also "In Search of Smart Phones," *Economist*, October 9, 1999, *Survey Telecommunications*, pp. 12, 16.

22. "The World in Your Pocket," p. 5.

23. Statistics available at www.nua.ie. [August 15, 2000].

24 . Evans and Wurster, "Blown to Bits," *Wired* 8.04, p.14; p. 82 reports that according to a study by KMI Corporation, "North American long distance carriers alone will deploy 6.8 million miles of optical fiber in 2000, four times the 1997 amount."

25. www.mit.edu/people/mkgray/net/internet-growth-summary.html [August 15, 2000].

26. Philip Mutooni and David Tennenhouse, "Modeling the Communication Network's Transition to a Data-Centric Model," presented at a conference on the Impact of the Internet on Communications Policy, Harvard Information Infrastructure Project, Harvard University, 1997.

27. Intelliquest Survey at www.intelliquest.com/press/release78.asp.

28. The Kaiser Family Foundation, *Kids and Media at the New Millennium* (November 1999).

29. ITU, *World Telecommunication Indicators Database*, 4th ed.

30. Ibid.

31. For example, full-time telecommunication staff in the United Kingdom decreased from 244,000 in 1988 to 141,000 in 1996; in the United States from 901,000 in 1988 to 897,000 in 1996; in Japan from 286,000 in 1988 to 213,000 in 1996; and in Germany from 233,000 in 1993 (post-unification) to 214,000 in 1996. ITU, *World Telecommunication Indicators Database*, 4th ed.

32. Priceline.com, a reverse auction site for airline tickets and hotel rooms, among other commodities, had a market valuation shortly after its IPO exceeding that of the three largest U.S. airlines taken together.

33. "Post-Holiday Survey Uncovers Where Online Shoppers Spent Their Money," Ernst & Young press release, January 3, 2000.

34. "Young Net Shoppers Soar Ahead of Online Adults," according to Forrester Research press release, February 23, 2000.

35. Joshua Casper Reno, "The Fast Moving Internet Economy Has a Couple of Competitors . . . and Here's the King: Jeffrey Preston Bezos—1999 Person of the Year," *Time Magazine*, December 27, 1999, pp. 50–55.

36. "The New Economy: Work in Progress," *Economist*, July 24, 1999, pp. 21–24.

37. For an impressive overview and analysis of the problem, see Peter Neumann, Computer-Related Risks (ACTI Press, 1995).

38. Stan Davis, *Future Perfect* (Addison-Wesley, 1987); and Joseph Pine, *Mass Customization* (ARS Press, 1993).

39. They may, however, experience cultural boundaries.

40. Howard Rheingold, *Virtual Community* (Addison-Wesley, 1993).

PART II

The Impact on Domestic Governance

7

PIPPA NORRIS

Global Governance and
Cosmopolitan Citizens

I N RECENT DECADES, a massive wave of globalization has expanded the
scale and speed of worldwide flows of capital, goods, people, and ideas
across national borders. "Globalization" is understood as a process that
erodes national boundaries, integrating national economies, cultures, technologies, and governance, producing complex relations of mutual interdependence. There continues to be dispute about the exact timing of the
phenomenon, the distinctiveness of the most recent wave, and its impact
in different spheres, but accounts point to a wide range of developments
contributing toward globalization in the late-twentieth century. As others
discuss in this book, communications have been transformed by the velocity and density of information flows and the extent of interconnectedness
by way of modern technologies, notably the Internet, reaching the mass
public as well as the elite.[1] Economies have been transformed by the rapid
expansion of financial markets, producing greater economic interdependence between states, such as the way that world exports of goods and services have almost tripled in real terms since the 1970s.[2] Perhaps the greatest change, however, has been the growth of multilayered governance and
the diffusion of political authority, with the role of the nation-state transformed by the development of regional trade blocs like the European
Union (EU), North American Free Trade Agreement (NAFTA), and

Association of South-East Asian nations (ASEAN); the growing role of international bodies like the World Trade Organization (WTO), United Nations (UN), and NATO; the burgeoning network of transnational non-governmental organizations (NGOs); and new norms and regulations of international and multilateral governance on issues ranging from trade to human rights and environmental protection.[3]

The impact of global governance upon national identities has raised many hopes and fears. On the one hand, theorists ranging from August Comte and John Stuart Mill to Karl Marx and Anthony Giddens have expressed optimism that humanity will eventually transcend national boundaries by moving toward a global culture and society. In this perspective, we can expect the globalization of markets, governance, and communications to strengthen a *cosmopolitan* orientation, broadening identities beyond national boundaries to a world community, and increasing awareness of the benefits of transnational collaboration within regional associations and international institutions.

Hence theorists such as Ohmae believe that we are witnessing the "end of the nation state," with the modern period representing a new historical era dominated by the growth of world market forces and the forces of Western consumerism, a tide against which national governments and economies have become increasingly powerless.[4] Anthony Giddens claims that contemporary globalization is historically unprecedented, reshaping modern societies, economies, governments, and the world order.[5] David Held argues that nation-states are drawing together by complex processes of interdependence on problems such as AIDS, migration, human rights, crime, trade, environmental pollution, and new challenges to peace, security, and economic prosperity that spill over national boundaries.[6] This process has gone furthest within the European Union, where the future of sovereignty and autonomy within nation-states has been most strongly challenged by European integration, but he argues that all of the world's major regions are affected, producing overlapping "*communities of fate.*" The association of nationalism with some of the most disruptive forces in twentieth-century history—from Hitler and Mussolini to recent conflict in the Balkans—has led many to applaud this development, although others deplore the loss of distinct national communities to the homogenizing cultural embrace of McDonald's, Disney, and Cable News Network (CNN).

Yet alternatively those who adopt a more skeptical perspective doubt whether the nation-state has been seriously weakened, and whether there is any evidence of an emerging "cosmopolitan identity" to replace the visceral appeals of nationalism. Structural developments in world economies and governance may have occurred without fundamentally eroding, indeed perhaps even strengthening, deep-rooted attitudes toward nationalism and the nation-state. In Anthony Smith's view, "We are still far from even mapping out the kind of global culture and cosmopolitan ideals that can truly supersede the world of nations."[7] Mann argues that, far from weakening nationalism, a reaction to globalization may have served to strengthen national identities.[8] Along similar lines, Hirst and Thompson argue that the nation-state retains its power in the modern era, and the main trend has been toward the growth of regional blocs, where nation-states remain the primary actors, not the emergence of a new world order that transcends states.[9]

What is the evidence to substantiate these arguments? The most systematic empirical work has examined whether nationalism has declined within the European Union. The process of economic and political integration, with people working, living, studying, and traveling in different member states, can be expected to have broken down some of the traditional cultural barriers between member states, particularly among the early joiners. Public opinion has been closely monitored in Eurobarometer surveys since early 1970. Successive studies have found that the public's identification with Europe has fluctuated over time, often in response to specific political events like the Maastricht agreement, the "mad cow" dispute, and the launch of the euro under the European Economic and Monetary Union (EMU). The process of European integration has been gradually strengthening, deepening, and widening the Union, yet there is little evidence that this process has generated a growing sense of European identity and community among its citizens, even among the public in long-standing member states like Germany.[10] Related attitudes also display a pattern of trendless fluctuations since the early 1970s, rather than growing public affection for the European project, including approval of EU policies, satisfaction with the performance of the Union, and confidence in EU institutions like the commission and Parliament. Persistent cross-national differences continue between states like Ireland and Belgium that are relatively positive across most indicators, and deep-seated Euro-skeptics like the British.[11] Moreover in the 1990s, British public opinion drifted in an ever more Euro-skeptic direction; almost half the public now opts for complete withdrawal.[12]

If there is little evidence of growing cosmopolitan identities within the EU, what is the situation elsewhere? We generally know far less about

trends in public opinion concerning other institutions of global governance, such as attitudes toward NATO, the UN, or World Trade Organization (WTO), in large part because systematic cross-national survey evidence is sparse beyond Western Europe, and largely nonexistent in most of
the developing world, although polls are available within particular countries.[13] One of the most thorough studies of attitudes toward international
organizations, by Philip Evert, suggests a similar pattern to that already
observed toward the EU. Evert found that support for the EU, NATO, and
the UN is essentially multidimensional, with attitudes influenced by
responses to specific issues and events, rather than being arrayed on a general continuum stretching from nationalism to internationalism. Fluctuations over time in the public's approval of NATO displayed no secular
trends, although there were also persistent differences in support between
member states.[14]

Therefore despite plausible theories that the rise of global governance
may lead toward growing cosmopolitanism, most of the available empirical studies lean toward a skeptical perspective. At least within Europe,
national publics vary significantly in their support for the institutions and
policies of the new world order, and the past thirty years have not seen the
rise of a more internationalist orientation. Nevertheless evidence remains
limited. We lack systematic comparative studies to understand trends in
many countries outside of the EU, particularly in the developing world,
and it remains possible that some underlying fundamental transformation
of national identities will take far longer to become apparent.

Evidence for Cosmopolitanism

The concepts of "cosmopolitan" and "national" identities are particularly
complex. In this study, "national identity" is understood to mean the existence of communities with bonds of "blood and belonging" arising from
sharing a common homeland, cultural myths, symbols and historical mem-
ories, economic resources, and legal-political rights and duties.[15] Nationalism can take "*civic*" forms, meaning ties of soil based on citizenship within
a shared territory and boundaries delineated by the nation-state, or it may
take "*ethnic*" forms, drawing on more diffuse ties of blood based on religious, linguistic, or ethnic communities.[16] National identities are usually
implicit and may only rise to the surface in response to an "other," in which
(rather like Simone de Beauvoir's *Second Sex*) we know what we are by

virtue of what we are not. Hence as a minority, Scottish nationalism is currently explicit and self-assertive, while English identity remains dormant
and inert, perhaps even slightly embarrassed.[17] In the modern world,
national identities underpin the state and its institutions exercising political authority within a given territory, although there are many multinational states like the United Kingdom as well as stateless nations like the
Kurds. *Nationalists* can be understood as those who identify strongly with
their nation-state, who have little confidence in multilateral and international institutions, and who favor policies of national economic protectionism over the free trade of goods and services.

     In contrast, *cosmopolitans* can be understood as those who identity more
broadly with their continent or with the world as a whole, and who have
greater faith in the institutions of global governance. The nationalism-
cosmopolitan dimension can be expected to crosscut traditional ideological cleavages, although there may be some overlap. If leaning rightward,
cosmopolitans can be expected to support policies designed to dismantle
protectionist economic barriers, while those on the left may favor other
measures like stricter global environmental regulations and greater spending on overseas aid. Cosmopolitans can be expected to be comfortable living and working in different countries, familiar with travel well beyond
their national boundaries, and fluent in languages, as well as connected to
international networks through global communications.[18] In previous eras
this process mainly influenced the elite, like the European aristocracy fin-
ishing their education in Paris and Rome on the eighteenth century Grand
Tour, but the most recent wave of globalization in communications may
have encouraged a resurgence of cosmopolitanism to spread well beyond
elite circles to the mass public.[19] If this hypothesis were correct, we would
expect to find that cosmopolitan identities would supplement traditional
national and ethnic allegiances, producing a broader identification with
neighboring countries, citizens, and regions of the world.

     What evidence would allow us to examine claims of a growing cos-
mopolitan consciousness? Previous analysis of public opinion toward these
issues has relied largely on the Eurobarometer, monitoring the fifteen
member states, as well as the annual International Social Survey Program
(ISSP), covering eighteen to twenty democracies.[20] These are invaluable
sources for monitoring trends over time, but the most comprehensive comparative data, which include a range of developing postcommunist and
postindustrial societies, are available from the World Values Survey.[21] The
1990–91 and 1995–97 waves are combined for this analysis, allowing the

comparison of seventy nations. The survey contains long-established democracies, consolidating regimes, and various types of authoritarian states, and includes societies ranging in per capita income from $300 to $30,000 a year. This study is still the only comparative survey that aims at global coverage, including 70 out of 174 independent nation-states in the world and the majority of the world's population. All the surveys used face-to-face interviews using a multistage random sample, and the data are weighted for analysis to compensate for obvious deviations from national populations.

One limitation of the survey is that the first wave in 1980–83 only included Western industrialized nations, so it cannot be used to study trends over time in postcommunist and developing societies. Cohort analysis can be employed, however, dividing the sample by decade of birth, to examine whether successive generations have become progressively more cosmopolitan in their orientations. Of course attitudes could be interpreted as a life-cycle effect, if younger people become more deeply rooted in their local or national communities as they age and settle down. We cannot resolve this issue with the available data, but it seems more plausible to understand age-related differences primarily as cohort effects, reflecting each generation's distinctive experiences of the major developments in international affairs in the twentieth century, as different generations acquire their attitudes and identities during their formative years prior to the Great War, the interwar era, or the postwar decades.

Public opinion can be monitored at three levels to distinguish among identification with the global community, confidence in the institutions of global governance, and approval of the policy mechanisms.[22] First, at the most diffuse level, theories suggest that the growth of global governance may have gradually eroded *national identities* and produced more cosmopolitans, understood as essentially "citizens of the world" with a broad internationalist outlook. Equally plausibly, theories suggest that globalization may have changed public attitudes toward the *institutions* of international and multilateral governance, notably the United Nations, which has rapidly expanded its role as an active player in peacekeeping operations, as well as the new regional associations like the EU, ASEAN, and NAFTA, which have strengthened economic links among member states. Lastly, at the most specific level, globalization may have altered public support for the *policy mechanisms* designed to dismantle national barriers, including policies promoting free trade and open labor markets for migrant workers.

The Erosion of National Identities

The strength of national and cosmopolitan identities is gauged by people's attachment to different territorial areas, an approach commonly used in previous studies.[23] In the World Values Surveys, people were asked the following:

"To which of these geographical groups would you say you belong first of all? And the next?

The locality or town where you live

The state or region of the country in which you live

Your country [The U.S, France, etc.] as a whole*

The continent in which you live [North America/Europe/Asia/Latin America, and so on]*

The world as a whole."

*[Each specific nation and continent substituted for these labels.]

People could give two responses, allowing overlapping and multiple identities if, for example, they feel they belong most strongly to their local community and then with their country, or if they identify with their country and then with their continent, and so on. The replies can be combined to provide a cosmopolitan identity scale ranging on a continuum from the most localized identities to the most cosmopolitan.[24]

Table 7-1 shows the response when people were asked their primary identification ("which geographic groups do you belong to *first of all?*"). The most striking finding to emerge is how far local and national identities remain far stronger than any cosmopolitan orientation. Almost half the public (47 percent) see themselves as belonging primarily to their locality or region of the country, while more than one-third (38 percent) say they identify primarily with their nation. Nevertheless, one-sixth of the public (15 percent) feels close to their continent or "the world as a whole" in their primary identity. The proportion of cosmopolitans is therefore small but not insignificant.

If we combine the first and second choices, altogether one-fifth of the public can be classified as pure localists, who identified only with their local-regional community (table 7-2). In contrast, only 2 percent are pure cosmopolitans, who expressed only a continental-world identity. The remainder had mixed multiple identities, for example, seeing themselves as belong to their region and country or to their country and continent. The overall results therefore serve to support the skeptical thesis that sees citizens as deeply rooted in their traditional communities, with strong ties of

Table 7-1. *Primary Type of Territorial Identity*
Percent

Profile	Variable	World-Continent	National	Local-Regional
All		15	38	47
Type of society	Postindustrial	15	41	44
	Postcommunist	16	32	53
	Developing	14	37	49
Cohort	1905–14	6	33	62
	1915–24	10	35	55
	1925–34	10	38	53
	1935–44	11	38	51
	1945–54	19	37	44
	1955–64	17	35	48
	1965–78	21	34	44
Continent	North America	16	43	41
	South America	17	37	45
	North Europe	11	36	53
	Northwestern Europe	13	25	62
	Southwestern Europe	13	23	64
	Eastern Europe	8	34	58
	Former Soviet Union	15	32	53
	Middle East	12	49	39
	Asia	13	32	55
	Africa	9	41	49
Education	Highest	18	42	40
	Lowest	7	29	64
Gender	Men	16	40	45
	Women	14	36	49

continued

blood and soil, despite (or even because of?) all the structural changes produced by globalizing forces.

How do attitudes vary by type of society? Perhaps the most common explanation for differences in the rise of cosmopolitanism regards the process of socioeconomic development as the primary driving force. Postmodernization theory certainly advances these claims. Traditional societies are facing increasing financial volatility and economic insecurities pro-

Table 7-1. *Primary Type of Territorial Identity (Continued)*
Percent

Profile	Variable	World-Continent	National	Local-Regional
Size of town	Low (less than 2,000)	11	34	55
	High (more than 500,000)	21	36	43
Type of culture	Northern European	12	36	53
	English	19	41	41
	Catholic European	13	24	64
	Confucian	5	44	52
	Central European	7	33	60
	Soviet	16	31	53
	Latin American	8	50	43
	Southeast Asian	8	29	63
	African	9	41	49
Postmaterialism	Materialist	12	38	50
	Mixed	16	39	45
	Postmaterialist	20	37	43
Type of democracy	Free	16	39	45
	Partly free	15	32	53
	Nonfree	10	32	58

Source: World Values Surveys combined waves 1990–91 and 1995–97, weighted data (N.147319).
Note: "To which of these geographical groups would you say you belong *first of all?*
    The locality or town where you live
    The state or region of the country in which you live
    Your country [*The U.S, France,* and so on] as a whole
    The continent in which you live [*North America/Europe/Asia/Latin America,* and so on]
    The world as a whole."

duced by opening up markets to global forces, illustrated by the East Asian financial crisis in 1997–99, throwing millions into unemployment and slowing down investments in Latin America. Since 1980, the majority of countries in Sub-Saharan Africa, many in Latin America, and most in transition have experienced disastrous failures in growth, with setbacks in human security and growing poverty.[25] Ronald Inglehart predicts that in a situation of growing insecurities traditional societies may experience a resurgence in feelings of nationalism and identification with the nation-state. In contrast, in postindustrial societies, with high levels of affluence

Table 7-2. *Multiple Territorial Identities*
Percent of total

Belong first (row)	Belong second (column)					
	Local	Region	Nation	Continent	World	All first
Local		15.5	17.5	1.0	2.6	36.7
Region	4.1		5.9	0.5	0.8	11.2
Nation	18.0	9.4		3.6	6.1	37.1
Continent	0.5	0.5	1.3		0.4	2.7
World	3.5	1.2	5.9	1.6		12.2
All second	26.1	26.6	30.6	6.8	9.9	100.0

Source: World Values Surveys combined waves 1990–91 and 1995–97, weighted data (N.147319).
Note: "To which of these geographical groups would you say you belong *first of all?* And the next?
   The locality or town where you live
   The state or region of the country in which you live
   Your country [*The U.S, France,* and so on] as a whole
   The continent in which you live [*North America/Europe/Asia/Latin America,* and so on]
   The world as a whole."

and economic growth during recent decades, Inglehart argues that the tendency is to transfer authority from the nation-state simultaneously downward toward more local and regional communities, as in Quebec, Scotland, and Catalonia, and also upward toward broader transnational ties.[26] If this account were correct, then we would expect cosmopolitanism to be most widespread in postindustrial societies. Countries like the United States, Germany, and the United Kingdom have been transformed most radically by the process of technological change, new communications, and open markets in goods and services, as well as by high levels of education and affluence produced by socioeconomic development. Nationalism can be expected to remain stronger in less developed societies, such as those in southeast Asia and Africa, as well as in postcommunist states struggling with the disruptive process of economic and political transitions in Central and Eastern Europe.

Table 7-1 shows how national identities vary in different types of societies.[27] The results show few major differences in cosmopolitan orientations among postindustrial, postcommunist, and developing societies, in contrast to Inglehart's hypotheses. Contrary to popular perceptions, nationalism proved weakest in postcommunist states, where local-regional identities prevail. Therefore globalization may well have had a differential impact on developed and developing countries, especially the "winners" and "losers" from the globalizations of markets, but it is not evident that so far this has affected the public's national identities.

Alternatively if the latest wave of globalization is a historical process, then plausibly the process of *generational* change may influence attitudes. As globalization is a gradual development, though one that has accelerated in the late twentieth century, it can be expected to affect the younger generation most strongly, brought up in a world of MTV, Yahoo, and McDonald's. In contrast, the prewar and interwar generation can be expected to retain stronger national allegiances and be most distrustful of the new forms of regional and global governance. The theory of postmodernization developed by Ronald Inglehart presents the strongest argument that pervasive structural trends are transforming the basic values of the younger generation; with the net result that intergenerational population replacement is producing cultural change.[28]

The results strongly confirm this thesis (table 7-1).[29] The oldest cohort, born at the turn of the last century, display by far the strongest nationalism while the younger cohorts, the baby boomers born after World War II, are most likely to have a sense of global identification. The generation gap means that cosmopolitans are more than three times as likely among the baby boomers than the pre–Great War generations. Moreover, this pattern was not just confined to postindustrial societies, as it was also equally evident among the younger cohorts in postcommunist and developing countries. If understood as a generational and not a life-cycle effect, and if we can extrapolate from these patterns, they provide important evidence that in the long term, secular trends will eventually reduce the balance of support for nationalism and move the public in a more cosmopolitan direction. The results suggest that the more optimistic scenarios of a global society and culture are indeed greatly exaggerated at present, but there is good evidence to believe that these hopes (and fears) may well be realized in the future as younger populations gradually replace older groups. The younger generations, backpacking with Eurail passes, volunteering for the Peace Corps, or working with environmental NGOs around the world, are most cosmopolitan in their orientation.

What are the other characteristics of the cosmopolitans? Table 7-1 shows that this group is broadly distributed by continent, although stronger in North and South America than in Europe, and weakest in Eastern Europe and Africa. Previous studies have emphasized that educational attainment is strongly associated with a sense of belonging to the European Union.[30] The comparison confirms that education strongly predicts a cosmopolitan identity, with twice as many people identifying with the world or continent in the highest than in the lowest educational group. There is a modest gender gap, with women marginally more localized than men. Not surprisingly, urbanization also has a significant impact, with far more localists in rural areas and more cosmopolitans living in large towns and cities. Among the cultural zones, cosmopolitanism was most clearly evident among those sharing an English-speaking background, while lower levels were found among those who shared a Confucian tradition. Postmaterial attitudes operated in the expected direction, with far more globalists among the postmaterialist category, while the type of democracy also had a modest association. We can conclude that perhaps the most significant indicator of an emerging cosmopolitan orientation comes from the generational patterns that we have observed, rather than from any major differences between postindustrial and developing societies. The postwar generation who grew up in conditions of relative peace and security seem most at home in the world, more comfortable with cosmopolitan identities than their fathers or grandfathers. Still it needs to be stressed that claims that we are all becoming citizens of the world remain exaggerated, since most people in most societies, continents, and cultures remain rooted in the older forms of belonging through their local community or nation-state.

Confidence in the Institutions of Global Governance

A related issue is how people feel about the new institutions of global governance, such as the World Trade Organization, the United Nations, or the European Commission. Attitudes toward the core institutions of representative democracy have received widespread attention in recent years, particularly research monitoring the erosion of confidence and trust in parliaments, parties, and governments.[31] We know far less about the trends in support for transnational levels of governance, still less how attitudes differ between postindustrial and developing societies.

If economic and political integration were contributing toward cosmopolitanism, we would expect this phenomenon to be most evident in states linked to others through strong regional associations. The member-states of the European Union could be expected to have gone furthest toward a transnational identity by developing a genuinely pan-European consciousness, where the Germans, French, and Italians come to see themselves as members of a common community with shared economic and political interests. The Community is the most ambitious attempt at transnational cooperation and integration. The 1992 Single European Act aimed to eliminate physical, technical, and fiscal frontiers among member states, reduce regional inequalities, harmonize rules governing working conditions, strengthen research and development, protect the environment, and facilitate monetary cooperation. The Maastricht Treaty, signed in 1992, and the Amsterdam Treaty in 1996, strengthens political as well as economic union, including common foreign and security policies. Economic and monetary union took a major step forward in January 1999 with the launching of the euro on the world currency market. If the process of European integration has influenced national identities we would expect to find stronger feelings of attachment to "Europe" in EU member states like Germany than in countries like Switzerland, Poland, and Bulgaria. Although less integrated politically, other trading blocs could play a similar role, such as ASEAN, the Southern Cone Common Market (Mercosur), NAFTA, and the Southern African Development Community.

To analyze how far people trusted international and multilateral organizations, the World Values Study asked the following:

"I am going to name a number of organizations. For each one, could you tell me how much confidence you have in them: is it a great deal of confidence, quite a lot of confidence, not very much confidence, or none at all?
——*The United Nations*
——*The European Union*"*
[**In all European countries; in other societies people were asked about the most important regional organization.]*[32]

The results in table 7-3 show the proportion that said they had "a great deal" or "quite a lot" of confidence. Overall in the early to mid-1990s the majority of the population (57 percent) expressed confidence in the United Nations, perhaps a remarkably high vote of support, while 44 percent trusted regional associations like the EU and NAFTA. One of the most striking findings of these results is that people trusted these global and regional institutions far more than their own domestic government, where overall only one-third of the public (34 percent) expressed any confidence. This difference was evident in postindustrial societies and particularly marked in postcommunist societies, where (at least pre-Kosovo) 27 percent trusted their domestic rulers, while 60 percent had confidence in the United Nations. If the growth of "critical citizens" has eroded support for

Table 7-3. *Support for United Nations and Regional Associations*
Percent with a "great deal" or "quite a lot" of confidence

Profile	Variable	United Nations	Regional associations
All		57	44
Type of society	Postindustrial	56	40
	Postcommunist	60	51
	Developing	59	52
Cohort	1905–14	43	36
	1915–24	54	44
	1925–34	51	37
	1935–44	53	39
	1945–54	53	38
	1955–64	52	38
	1965–78	60	49
Continent	North America	56	41
	South America	53	45
	North Europe	54	33
	Northwestern Europe	45	47
	Southwestern Europe	47	57
	Eastern Europe	51	42
	Former Soviet Union	61	53
	Middle East	47	45
	Asia	66	49
	Africa	61	57
Education	Highest	60	51
	Lowest	52	34
Gender	Men	54	43
	Women	60	44

continued

the core institutions of representative government like parties, parliaments, and executives in many established democracies, as argued elsewhere, it appears that this process has not yet undermined the public's confidence in the United Nations.[33]

Further analysis of the profile of those who supported the United Nations and regional associations in table 7-3 confirms many of the obser-

Table 7-3. *Support for United Nations and Regional Associations (Continued)*
Percent with a "great deal" or "quite a lot" of confidence

Profile	Variable	United Nations	Regional associations
Urbanization	Low (less than 2,000)	52	40
	High (more than 500,000)	57	49
Type of culture	Northern European	54	33
	English	51	36
	Catholic European	47	57
	Confucian	60	35
	Central European	39	46
	Soviet	60	52
	Latin American	70	54
	Southeast Asian	54	44
	African	61	57
Postmaterialism	Materialist	55	43
	Mixed	60	45
	Postmaterialist	52	41
Type of	Free	52	37
democracy	Partly free	60	53
	Nonfree	69	59

Source: World Values Surveys combined waves 1990–91 and 1995–97, weighted data (N.147319).
Note: "I am going to name a number of organizations. For each one, could you tell me how much confidence you have in them: is it a great deal of confidence, quite a lot of confidence, not very much confidence, or none at all?
The United Nations
The European Union"[a]
a. In all European countries; in other societies ask about the most important regional organization.

vations made earlier concerning a more cosmopolitan orientation. Again birth cohort is significantly associated with internationalism, with 60 percent of the sixties generation supporting the United Nations compared with only 43 percent of the pre–Great War generation, and there a parallel age gap was evident in levels of confidence in regional associations. Again, a more global perspective was associated with higher levels of educational and urbanization, although more women than men supported the United Nations. The type of government was also important, with the greatest support for the United Nations and for regional associations among nondemocratic states. Many possible factors could help to explain the crossnational variations that emerge, such as whether developing countries are major beneficiaries from aid flows and official development assistance from the United Nations, as well as the role of regional associations in promoting trade and export markets for member states.

Support for Globalization Policies

Lastly, at the most specific level, we can examine attitudes to see how far the public in different countries supports economic policies designed to promote globalization, such as those promoting free trade and the migration of labor. The following questions were asked:

[FREE TRADE] "Do you think it is better if:

Goods made in other countries can be imported and sold here if people want to buy them; or,

That there should be stricter limits on selling foreign goods here, to protect the jobs of people in this country."

[MIGRANTS] "How about people from other countries coming here to work. Which one of the following do you think the government should do?

—Let anyone come who wants to?

—Let people come as long as there are jobs available?

—Place strict limits on the number of foreigners who can come here?

—Prohibit people coming here from other countries?"

Table 7-4 shows that overall only one-third of the public favored free trade over protectionism, with most people preferring trade limitations to maintain jobs, and this pattern was found even in postindustrial societies during the relatively affluent mid-1990s. These attitudes may also have been fueled by concerns about the threat of unemployment, which remained fairly high throughout most of Western Europe in these years, as well as the experience of massive unemployment in the transition economies in Central and Eastern Europe. The public also opted to restrict immigration. Few (7 percent) supported the idea of open borders, so that anyone could enter to work, 38 percent favored allowing people to enter as long as jobs were available, 43 percent wanted to strictly limit the number of foreigners who could enter the country, while 12 percent would prohibit all entry.

The profile of those who support free market policies confirms a secular trend toward increasing support among younger cohorts. Again the

Table 7-4. *Support for Economic Free Trade and Labor Markets*
Percent approving

Profile	Variable	Free trade	Migrant labor
All		30	42
Type of society	Postindustrial	28	37
	Postcommunist	32	54
	Developing	31	39
Cohort	1905–14	15	31
	1915–24	17	32
	1925–34	20	36
	1935–44	26	44
	1945–54	31	46
	1955–64	34	46
	1965–78	40	52
Continent	North America	25	35
	South America	15	56
	North Europe	39	40
	Northwestern Europe	50	65
	Southwestern Europe	26	79
	Eastern Europe	31	37
	Former Soviet Union	33	55
	Middle East	15	38
	Asia	28	39
	Africa	38	34
Education	Highest	40	53
	Lowest	31	31

continued

youngest generation is almost three times as likely to support free trade as the oldest group (figure 7-1, table 7-5). Perhaps surprisingly, given the legacy of protectionism in the old Soviet Union, by the early to mid-1990s there is remarkably little difference in attitudes between postcommunist societies and Western countries. Education, urbanization, and postmaterial attitudes, observed earlier, are also consistent predictors of a more internationalist or free market orientation toward economic policy.

Table 7-4. *Support for Economic Free Trade and Labor Markets (Continued)*
Percent approve

Profile	Variable	Free trade	Migrant labor
Gender	Men	33	42
	Women	26	43
Size of town	Low (less than 2,000)	21	37
	High (more than 500,000)	37	54
Type of culture	Northern European	39	40
	English	26	38
	Catholic European	26	79
	Confucian	35	46
	Central European	39	54
	Soviet	32	54
	Latin American	21	32
	Southeast Asian	38	50
	African	38	34
Postmaterialism	Materialist	26	40
	Mixed	30	43
	Postmaterialist	34	46
Type of	Free	30	38
democracy	Partly free	33	54
	Nonfree	38	50

Source: World Values Surveys combined waves 1990–91 and 1995–97, weighted data (N.147319).

The Future of Cosmopolitan Citizenship

Other chapters in this book demonstrate that considerable evidence shows global trends in the free flow of goods, services, capital, people, ideas, and force. Yet we know far less about the consequences of these developments on public opinion. Has globalization increased the number of cosmopolitans, citizens of the world who feel comfortable traveling, living, and working within different societies, or in reaction has there been a resurgence of nationalism or even localism? Growing cultural globalism is often assumed, but beyond aggregate indicators, such as trends in news flows, movie receipts, or the number of McDonald's around the world (discussed in chapter 5), we know little about what it means for how people feel about the world and

Figure 7-1. *Cosmopolitan Attitudes by Cohort*

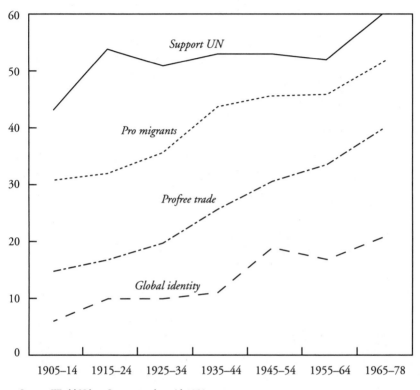

Source: World Values Surveys, early–mid-1990s.

whether structural changes have altered fundamental identities. As David McCrone and Paula Surridge remark, "National identity is one of the most discussed but least understood concepts of the late twentieth century."[34] The idea of cosmopolitanism is even more elusive and complex.

The results of this study are of the "cup half empty" or the "cup half full" variety. Interpretations of the evidence can be used to support both sides of the debate about nationalism. On the one hand, it is true that cosmopolitans remain a distinct minority, and most people remain strongly rooted to the ties of local, regional, and national communities that give people a sense of blood and belonging. When asked, more people are likely to see themselves as living in Berlin, Prague, or Athens, rather than sharing a more diffuse feeling of being Europeans, still less citizens of the world. The

Table 7-5. *Predictors of Support for Cosmopolitanism*

Cosmopolitan	Identity Local-global scale	Institutions Trust UN + regional association	Policies Support free trade + migrant labor	Coding
National development				
Level of human development	.15*	-.33*	-.10*	UNDP Human Development Index, 1997
Level of democratic development	.10*	-.31*	.05*	Freedom House 14-point Gastil Index
Years democratic	-.05*	-.18*	-.01	Years of continuous democracy
Social background				
Age	-.11*	-.08*	-.09*	Years old
Education	.05*	-.01*	.08*	9-point scale
Gender male	.05*	-.07*	.02*	Male (1)/female (0)
Urbanization	.10*	.09*	.08*	6-point scale of community size
HH income	-.01	-.01	.01	Household income (standardized)
Born in country	-.05*	-.03*	-.09*	Yes (1)/no (0)
Political attitudes				
National pride	.004	-.07*	.07*	4-item scale low (1) to high (4)
Rating of current political system	-.003	.19*	.11*	10-point scale low (1) to high (10)
Left-right party support	-.02*	-.05*	-.03*	Scaled from left (1) to right (10)
Postmaterialism	.12*	.02*	.25*	12-item scale. Postmaterialism = high
Constant	2.83	11.4	4.28	
Adjusted R^2	.052*	.088*	.130*	...
R	.227*	.296*	.361*	...

Source: World Values Survey.

Note: The dependent variables are those described in tables 7-1–7-4. The coefficients represent standardized beta coefficients in ordinary least-squares regression models.

* Significant at <.01 level.

globalization linking us through networks of mass communications, the flow of goods and capital, and the forces of mass tourism and travel has not yet destroyed local ties.

Yet, on the other hand, the most important indicators of cultural change found in this chapter are the persistent differences in international attitudes held by different generations. The more optimistic claims of some theorists concerning the decline of the nation-state and erosion of nationalism are not yet evident—but at the same time cohort analysis suggests that in the long term public opinion is moving in a more internationalist direction (figure 7-1). Most strikingly, almost one-fifth of the baby boomers born after World War II see themselves as cosmopolitan citizens of the globe, identifying with their continent or the world as a whole, but this is true of only one in ten of the group brought up in the interwar years, and of even fewer of the prewar generation. A similar generational divide is evident across the attitudes like support for the institutions of global governance and the policies of free trade and open labor markets. If this trend is maintained, we can expect to see a rising tide of popular support for globalization in future decades, through the gradual process of generational turnover. Growing urbanization and rising educational levels can also be expected to contribute toward this general development. This cultural shift has important implications for the democratic legitimacy of international organizations like the United Nations and the European Union, as well as for the gradual breakdown of some of the deep-rooted barriers dividing nation against nation. In short, the younger generation brought up in the postwar era is less nationalistic than its mothers and fathers, and it remains to be seen whether its children maintain this trend.

Notes

1. Pippa Norris, *A Virtuous Circle: Political Communications in Post-Industrial Democracies* (Cambridge University Press, 2000).

2. United Nations Development Program (UNDP), *Human Development Report 1999* (New York, 1999), p. 30.

3. For a discussion, see David Held and others, *Global Transformations: Politics, Economics and Culture* (Stanford University Press, 1999).

4. K. Ohmae, *The End of the Nation State* (Free Press, 1995).

5. Anthony Giddens, *The Consequences of Modernity* (Polity Press, 1990).

6. Held and others, *Global Transformations*, pp. 444–46.

7. Anthony Smith, "Towards a Global Culture?" in Michael Featherstone, ed., *Global Culture* (London: Sage, 1995).

8. M. Mann, "Has Globalization Ended the Rise and Rise of the Nation-State?" *Review of International Political Economy,* vol. 4 (1997).

9. P. Hirst and G. Thompson, *Globalization in Question: The International Economy and the Possibilities of Governance* (Polity, 1996).

10. Sophie Duchesne and Andrè-Paul Frognier, "Is There a European Identity?" in Oskar Niedermayer and Richard Sinnott, eds., *Public Opinion and Internationalized Governance* (Oxford: Oxford University Press 1995); Angelika Scheuer, "A Political Community?" in Hermann Schmitt and Jacques Thomassen, eds., *Political Representation and Legitimacy in the European Union* (Oxford: Oxford University Press 1999); and B. Nelson, D. Roberts and W. Veit, eds., *The Idea of Europe: Problems of National and Transnational Identity* (Oxford: Berg).

11. Pippa Norris, "The Political Regime," in *Political Representation and Legitimacy in the European Union.* See also Mattei Dogan, "The Decline of Nationalism within Western Europe," *Comparative Politics,* vol. 20 (1994), pp. 281–05.

12. Geoffrey Evans, "Europe: A New Electoral Cleavage?' in Geoffrey Evans and Pippa Norris eds., *Critical Elections: British Parties and Voters in Long-Term Perspective* (London: Sage, 1999); and Geoffrey Evans, "How Britain Views the EU," in Roger Jowell and others, *British Social Attitudes: The 15th Report* (Aldershot: Dartmouth/SCPR, 1998).

13. Although a detailed case study of the impact of NAFTA can be found in Ronald Inglehart, Neil Nevitte, and Migual Basanez, *Cultural Change in North America? Closer Economic, Political and Cultural Ties between the United States, Canada and Mexico* (De Gruyter, 1996).

14. Philip Evert, "NATO, the European Community, and the United Nations," in Oskar Niedermayer and Richard Sinnott, eds., *Public Opinion and Internationalized Governance* (Oxford: Oxford University Press, 1995).

15. There is a large literature on the concepts of nationalism and national identity. See, for example, Michael Ignatieff, *Blood and Belonging* (London: Chatto and Windus, 1993); Benedict Anderson, *Imagined Communities: Reflections on the Origin and Spread of Nationalism* (London: Verso); Anderson, *Banal Nationalism* (London: Sage, 1995); and Ernest Gellner, *Nations and Nationalism* (Oxford: Blackwell, 1983).

16. Anthony D. Smith, *National Identity* (London: Penguin, 1991), chap. 7. For a discussion of some of these issues, see Pippa Norris, "Ballots not Bullets: Testing Consociational Theories of Ethnic Conflict, Electoral Systems and Democratization," in Andrew Reynolds, ed., *Institutional Design, Conflict Management and Democracy,* forthcoming.

17. Bridget Taylor and Katarina Thomson eds., *Scotland and Wales: Nations Again?* (University of Wales Press, 1999).

18. For a more detailed discussion of this distinction see Pippa Norris, "Towards a More Cosmopolitan Political Science?" *European Journal of Political Research,* vol. 30, no. 1 (1997).

19. See Michael Featherstone, ed., *Global Culture* (London: Sage, 1995).

20. For an earlier study based on the ISSP module on nationalism, see, for example, Pippa Norris, "Global Communications and Cultural Identities," *Harvard International Journal of Press/Politics,* vol. 4, no. 4 (1999), pp. 1–7. The most thorough empirical work on orientations within Europe from 1973 to 1990 using the Eurobarometer surveys can be

found in Oskar Niedermayer and Richard Sinnott, *Public Opinion and Internationalized Governance* (Oxford: Oxford University Press, 1995).

21. The author is most grateful to the principal investigator, Ronald Inglehart, and all the collaborators on the World Values Surveys for release of this dataset.

22. David Easton, *A Framework for Political Analysis* (Prentice Hall, 1965); and Easton, "A Reassessment of the Concept of Political Support," *British Journal of Political Science,* vol. 5 (1975), pp. 435–57.

23. Ronald Inglehart, *The Silent Revolution: Changing Values and Political Styles among Western Nations* (Princeton University Press, 1977); and Sophie Duchesne and André-Paul Frognier, "Is There a European Identity?" in Oskar Niedermayer and Richard Sinnott, eds., *Public Opinion and Internationalized Governance* (Oxford: Oxford University Press, 1995).

24. Because of the size of the combined dataset (with more than 147,000 cases) all the differences between groups are statistically significant by conventional tests like ANOVA. As a result, tests of statistical significance are not reported in the presentation of the analysis.

25. UNDP, *Human Development Report 1999,* p. 99.

26. Ronald Inglehart, *Modernization and Post-Modernization* (Princeton University Press, 1997), pp. 303–05.

27. Developing societies were classified as those with a "medium" or "low" human development index in 1997. See UNDP, *Human Development Report 1999,* table 1, pp. 134–37.

28. Inglehart, *Modernization and Post-Modernization.*

29. The analysis is based on factor analysis not reported here.

30. Inglehart, *The Silent Revolution.*

31. Joseph S. Nye Jr., Philip Zelikow, and David C. King, eds., *Why People Don't Trust Government* (Harvard University Press, 1997); and Pippa Norris, ed., *Critical Citizens: Global Support for Democratic Governance* (Oxford: Oxford University Press, 1999).

32. For example, NAFTA (United States, Canada), Mercosur (Argentina, Brazil, Uruguay), Organization of African Unity (South Africa, Nigeria), South Asian Association for Regional Co-operation SAARC (India, Bangladesh), El Tratado de Libre Comercio (Mexico), ASEAN (Philippines), Organizacion de Estados Americanos (Dominican Republic), Andean Pact (Venezuela), and so on.

33. Norris, *Critical Citizens.*

34. David McCrone and Paula Surridge, "National Identity and National Pride," in Roger Jowell and others, eds., *British and European Social Attitudes, the 15th Report* (Aldershot: Ashgate, 1998).

8

MERILEE S. GRINDLE

Ready or Not:
The Developing World
and Globalization

THE GOVERNMENTS of developing countries, like their richer counterparts in the industrialized world, are seeking to reap more benefits
than costs from extensive changes in trade, financial markets, technological innovation, and new institutions and values. How successful can we
expect them to be?

Already, effective adaptations to globalization are well under way in a
number of developing countries. Some have increased their share of trade
in goods and services, and new technologies have created jobs and stimulated dynamic local economies. At a more general level, and as Jeffrey
Frankel points out in chapter 2, improvements in real incomes can be
expected as a consequence of global integration. Globalization is also
adding to the spread of more democratic governments and helping sustain
the legitimacy of those that have been created in recent years. Similarly, it
is adding pressure on governments and international institutions to commit resources to human capital development, institution building, and
environmental improvement. And, in virtually every developing country,
even the poorest, there are those whose lives have been enriched by
increased flows of goods, services, capital, and information.

Despite this good news, citizens of developing countries have more reasons to be apprehensive about the impact of globalization on their lives
than to be certain that they will benefit from it. In worst case scenarios,

globalization has the potential to cause economic dislocation, destruction of important social safety nets, accelerated environmental damage, loss of cultural identities, increased conflict, and the spread of disease and crime. Policymakers in poor countries have reason to worry that, despite their best efforts, globalization will constrict rather than expand the capacity to develop. They are certainly correct to be concerned that the gap between the North and the South will grow wider in the future. A powerful combination of difficult domestic challenges, international vulnerabilities, and more complex decisionmaking arenas lies behind their concerns.

In this chapter, I address the situation of poor countries as they confront globalization. Indeed, for many of them, opportunities for development are constrained by uncertain opportunities for economic growth, pervasive poverty, weak institutions, and limitations on the extent and distribution of technological innovation.[1] These conditions translate into vulnerabilities in a rapidly changing international context for development. To reverse these conditions at national and international levels, wise policymaking, effective implementation, and the creation of capable state institutions are essential. Yet, the political landscape facing policymakers has become more complex. How political elites maneuver within the increasingly stringent confines of international and domestic pressures for policy and policy results will determine, to a significant degree, the extent to which individual countries can counteract conditions that are marginalizing many of them from the benefits of globalization.

National and International Sources of Vulnerability

The benefits of globalization are not distributed equally among countries or populations. The world's poorest countries and poorest families are the least well positioned to benefit from the expansion of goods, services, capital, and information that characterizes this process of change. The sixty-three countries classified as low income are most at risk. These countries, with average per capita incomes of $760 in 1998, represent almost all countries in Africa and all of the most populous countries of South Asia and Asia. Together, they account for 3.5 billion of the world's 5.9 billion people.[2] In addition, low-income households in ninety-four middle-income countries—primarily in Latin America, the Middle East, North Africa, and Eastern Europe and Central Asia—are at greater risk of being left behind by rapid change than are their more affluent neighbors in the same countries. And, regardless of where they live, the 1.2 billion people who live on less than one dollar a day are the farthest from the jobs, improved opportunities, technology, and innovative ideas that globalization is creating.[3]

These countries and populations at risk have limited ability to tap into the advantages of globalization and equally limited capacity to avoid or negotiate away from some of its disadvantages. As suggested below, this is because domestic weaknesses as evidenced by low economic performance, widespread poverty, poorly functioning institutions, and technology gaps translate into international vulnerabilities that constrain the ability of developing countries to manage change.

Elusive Economic Growth

For the past two decades, improving economic policy to stimulate growth has been central to developing country policy agendas. In Latin America, Africa, and some parts of Asia, the debt crisis of the early 1980s set in motion a dynamic—and conflictful—period of economic policy change during which large numbers of state-led economies were replaced by more market-oriented ones. Even in countries in which the state fully dominated the economy, the extent of change has been remarkable. China began to liberalize its economy in the late 1970s and after 1989, former communist countries in eastern Europe and the Commonwealth of Independent States (CIS) started to move toward market systems. The East Asian financial crisis of 1997 encouraged a number of governments in that region, and those of countries elsewhere that were affected by the crisis, to alter policies and improve the performance of their financial institutions. Although the pace and depth of change varied significantly by country, by the end of the 1990s, most developing and transitional economies had implemented significant measures to liberalize domestic and international trade, lower tariff barriers, reduce the size and functions of the state, privatize a host of state-owned enterprises, and drastically cut back on subsidies to capital and labor.

In most countries, introducing a market economy also required major institutional innovations, such as the development of independent central banks and tax agencies, stock markets, and regulatory bodies for privatized industries and financial institutions.[4] In addition, many countries undertook institutional changes to improve legal guarantees for contracts and property rights, essential underpinnings of capitalist economies. In comparison with policy changes, most of which could be introduced and take effect in the short term, institutional changes required time and ongoing effort to train staff and alter the behavior of economic agents to reflect new rules for economic transactions.

Despite such important initiatives, almost twenty years of policy reform and institutional innovation have not been sufficient to deliver broadly on promises of improved economic growth. During the 1980s, when the economic crisis was at its height, GDP growth rates in many parts of the developing world stagnated or declined. The decade was particularly devastating for countries in Africa and Latin America, which produced average annual growth rates of 1.6 and 1.8 percent respectively.[5] Only East Asia (at an annual average of 8.0 percent) and parts of South Asia (at an average of 5.7 percent) demonstrated high and sustained growth during that period. In the 1990s, African countries continued to produce low growth and Latin American and Middle-Eastern countries to demonstrate variable, but low, recovery. The same decade witnessed devastating downturns in the economies of the former Soviet bloc countries, which averaged –4.3 percent annual growth rates. After 1997, several of the high-performing Asian economies grew more slowly. Only South Asian countries appeared to do well during both decades.

At the end of the decade of the 1990s, more than eighty countries had lower per capita incomes than they had ten years earlier.[6] Table 8-1 demonstrates the disappointing performance of countries in different regions of the world in improving per capita income during these two decades of reform. Of course, regional statistics hide the fact that some countries in every region performed well during this period; nevertheless, overall economic performance remained disappointing. Equally troubling, the impact of the financial crisis of 1997 led the World Bank to warn that developing country growth between 2002 and 2008 was likely to be lower than it had been between 1990 and 1996.[7]

Not only have many countries not seen much improved growth, but expert opinion on what needs to be done to promote growth has become more complex. In the early 1980s, when the current era of reform began, economists largely agreed on the list of measures that needed to be taken to stabilize economies and introduce the makings of a market economy. Often referred to as the "Washington consensus" because of their origin in international financial institutions located there, these policies, once adopted, were expected to enable developing countries to turn around their flagging economies and initiate sustained growth.[8] To grow, developing countries needed to "get the policies right."

Table 8-1. *GDP per Capita, 1975–97*
U.S. dollars 1987

Country categories and regions	1975	1980	1985	1990	1997
All developing countries (N = 124)	600	686	693	745	908
Least developed countries (N = 43)	287	282	276	277	245
Sub-Saharan Africa	671	661	550	542	518
Arab states	2,327	2,941	2,252	1,842	...
East Asia	176	233	336	470	828
East Asia (excluding China)	1,729	2,397	3,210	4,809	7,018
Southeast Asia and Pacific	481	616	673	849	1,183
South Asia	404	365	427	463	432
South Asia (excluding India)	857	662	768	709	327
Latin America and Caribbean	1,694	1,941	1,795	1,788	2,049
Eastern Europe and the CIS	...	...	...	2,913	1,989
industrialized countries	12,589	14,206	15,464	17,618	19,283

Source: UNDP, *Human Development Report, 1999* (New York, 1999), p. 154.

As the decade wore on, however, development experts began to argue that getting the policies right was not sufficient to produce dynamic market economies; institutions, such as those mentioned above, were also needed to stimulate market-based growth.[9] At about the same time, specialists in economic development who in the early and mid-1980s had demonstrated a strong antistate bias in their reform proposals began to discuss the need for capable states to manage macroeconomic policies and carry out a series of essential activities if market systems were to generate growth.[10] Institution building, a byword in much development practice in the 1960s and 1970s, reemerged as an essential ingredient of development in the 1990s.[11] The data presented by Elaine Kamarck in this volume suggest how widespread institution building initiatives have been. In the mid-1990s, development experts added human resource development and the provision of social safety nets to the list of factors that needed to be in place for markets to do well and generate growth.[12] Then, in the wake of the Asian financial crisis, experts became more concerned about how to protect poor countries from volatile global financial markets. The crisis brought to light institutional weaknesses in the countries affected and stimulated debate about optimal exchange rate regimes, capital controls, fiscal constraints, and institutional structures.

Growth, it seemed, depended on a wide variety of conditions. Along with this increased complexity, expert opinions began to diverge much more on what needed to be done and the sequence in which it needed to be done.[13] Indeed, the *World Development Report,* widely regarded as the bellwether for mainstream development thinking, acknowledged in 1999 that "governments play a vital role in development, but there is no simple set of rules that tells them what to do," beyond abiding by general principles for sound macroeconomic management.[14] Thus, not only had the list of what needed to be done to generate growth increased over time, the policy prescriptions of experts had become less definitive.

Despite poor growth performance, developing countries did become more integrated into the world economy during the 1990s. Overall, trade grew at higher rates than national income in these countries.[15] In 1990 developing countries accounted for 23 percent of world trade in goods and services; in 1997 they accounted for 29 percent. By 1999, 110 developing countries had joined the World Trade Organization (WTO). Foreign direct investment in low-income countries increased by a factor of 10 between 1990 and 1997; for middle-income developing countries, it increased five and a half times. Net private capital flows increased from less than $43 billion to almost $299 billion in low- and middle-income countries in the same period.

But with this increased integration, developing countries became more vulnerable to fluctuations in international capital flows and trade. While most of them have always been affected by changes—often radical—in the prices of primary commodities, Mexico's peso crisis of late 1994 signaled the extent to which rapid capital flows could devastate a national economy, virtually overnight. If that message was not fully convincing, the Asian financial crisis of 1997 and its contagion in Brazil, Russia, and other countries marked a new era in vulnerability. This crisis was remarkable for the extent to which it affected countries that had been considered among the stars of rapid and sustained development—Indonesia, Thailand, Malaysia, and South Korea. These countries lost $12 billion in 1997 to reverse capital flows, about 11 percent of their pre-crisis gross domestic products (GDPs).[16]

The combination of new trading relationships, financial volatility, and low commodity prices in the 1990s emphasized that many developing countries still have boom and bust economies, a condition often associated with low growth.[17] Moreover, the ease with which local currencies can be converted to dollars or other international currencies exacerbates capital flight when domestic interests lose confidence in national policies or when economic downturns threaten. Trade agreements limit the range of responses that governments can employ to manage such problems. In addition, global production networks can limit the capacity of poor countries to negotiate with transnational companies, and they constrict the range of economic policies that can be adopted without the potential for financial and trade retaliation. Debt burdens are extreme in some countries, further limiting options for economic and social policies. Indeed, without major debt relief efforts, some countries are likely to face prolonged economic crises and stagnant or declining growth. In many ways, then, globalization is introducing a more risk-filled world to developing countries, even for those that have readily taken on the tasks of policy and institutional reform.

Pervasive Poverty

Pervasive and persistent poverty is a defining characteristic of almost all countries in the developing world. The number of people living in poverty, defined as living on $1 a day or less, increased slightly from 1.17 billion in 1987 to 1.19 billion in 1998.[18] Moreover, while the proportion of poor in the population declined in some regions, it increased in Latin America and in eastern Europe and Central Asia. The proportion of poor remained almost the same in Africa. Table 8-2 provides a broad picture of the population in each region of the world that lived below the international poverty line in 1987 and 1998. These data mask the range of differences among and within countries but nevertheless indicate the extent to which poverty continues to be a persistent and massive phenomenon in developing countries. Equally disturbing, World Bank projections using a scenario of slow growth and rising inequality indicate that the number of poor in developing countries is likely to increase to 1.24 billion by 2008, incorporating 21.9 percent of their populations; even with a more positive scenario of "inclusive" growth, poverty would continue to affect 695 million people (12.3 percent of the population).[19]

At the end of the twentieth century, the human costs of widespread poverty were great. According to the 1999 *Human Development Report*, illiteracy affected 850 million adults, malnutrition afflicted some 840 mil-

Table 8-2. *Population Living on $1.00 a Day or Less*

	1987		1993	
Regions	Millions	Percent of population	Millions	Percent of population
East Asia	417.5	26.6	278.3	15.3
Eastern Europe and				
Central Asia	1.1	0.2	24.0	5.1
Latin America and Caribbean	63.7	15.3	78.2	15.6
Middle East and North Africa	9.3	4.3	5.5	1.9
South Asia	474.4	44.9	522.0	40.0
Sub-Saharan Africa	217.2	46.6	290.9	46.3
Total	1,173.2	28.3	1,198.9	24.0

Source: World Bank, *Global Economic Prospects and the Developing Countries, 2000* (Washington, 2000), p. 29.

lion people—160 million of them children—as many as a billion people were unable to meet basic consumption needs, and 340 million women were expected to die before reaching the age of 40.[20] Life expectancy improved in most of the world between 1980 and 2000, but declined—by as much as 14 percent—in a number of countries—in Kazakhstan, Zimbabwe, Uganda, Rwanda, and Zambia, for example.[21] Poverty afflicted some groups of people more frequently than others—women, children, and those who lived in rural areas. Inequality increased in the 1980s and 1990s in some parts of the world.[22]

Economic growth that creates productive jobs is essential for alleviating such conditions, but so too are public investments in physical and social infrastructure to address the concomitants of poverty—lack of education and access to medical care, poor health, high infant and maternal mortality rates, lack of sanitation, and access to potable water. The task to be undertaken is immense, as suggested in table 8-3, which compares the conditions in which people in poor and rich countries live. Table 8-4 indicates some of the shortfalls in human capital in developing countries, compared with those of rich countries and contrasts their public expenditures targeted on health and education.

Although major strides were made after 1960 in lowering rates of poverty and improving life expectancy, education, and health standards, the tragedy of the 1980s and 1990s was that progress was halted and even reversed for many countries, as economic crisis and stagnation eroded the

Table 8-3. *Life Conditions in Rich and Poor Countries, 1997*

	Country categories		
Item	All developing countries	Least-developed countries	Industrialized countries
Life expectancy at birth (years)	64.4	51.7	77.7
Infant mortality (per 1,000 live births)	64	104	6
Under 5 mortality rate (per 1,000 live births)	94	162	7
People not expected to survive to age 60 (percent of total population)	28	50	11
Maternal mortality rate (per 100,000 live births)[a]	491	1,041	13

Source: UNDP, *Human Development Report, 1999*, p. 171.
a. 1990.

gains of past decades. Moreover, measures taken to deal with the crisis heightened the problems of escaping from poverty by significantly reducing budgets for health, education, and physical and social infrastructure. Insecurity grew as formal sector jobs disappeared and were replaced by ones created in the informal sector, pension systems were restructured, endemic diseases spread, petty and organized crime grew, and communal conflict increased.[23]

Among the more distressing data to emerge in the last years of the decade of the 1990s are those that indicate the number of "new poor" in Asia—those who fell into poverty as a result of the 1997 financial crisis. Indonesia was the clearest example of how a financial crisis could reverse decades of development progress. During the 1990s, Indonesia received plaudits for a broad-based development strategy that diminished the number of people living in poverty from about 60 percent of the population in 1970 to about 15 percent in 1990.[24] However, the *Human Development Report* of 1999 estimated that 20 percent of the population, some 40 million people, were reduced to poverty as a result of the crisis. The UNDP also estimated that 12 percent of the populations of South Korea and Thailand were similarly affected, accounting for 5.5 million people and 6.7 million people respectively.[25]

Domestic conditions of deprivation translate into significant increases in international inequalities in an era of globalization. Although developing

Table 8-4. *Human Development Needs in Developing Countries*

Item	*All developing countries*	*Least-developed countries*	*Industrialized countries*
Adult illiteracy rate (percent of adult population, 1997)	28.4	51.6	1.3
Population without access to safe water (percent of population, 1990–97)	28	41	...
Population without access to sanitation (percent of population, 1990–97)	57	63	...
Public expenditure for education as percent of GNP, 1996	3.6	...	5.1
Public expenditure for health as percent of GNP, 1996	1.8	1.6	6.3

Country categories (spanning the three right columns)

Source: UNDP, *Human Development Report, 1999*, pp. 137, 148, 191.

countries made progress on a range of human development indicators, discrepancies between these and industrial countries were striking in the 1990s, as shown in table 8-4. Moreover, according to the World Bank, between 1970 and 1995, the average GDP per capita of all countries in the third of all countries in the lowest-income group declined from 3.1 percent to 1.9 percent of that of the third of countries with the highest income; average incomes for middle-income countries declined from 12.5 percent to 11.4 percent of those of the richest third.[26]

Other data confirm the extent of the gap between North and South. In the late 1990s, the 20 percent of the world's population in the richest countries controlled 86 percent of global GDP; those who made up the populations of the poorest 20 percent controlled 1 percent; 68 percent of foreign direct investment was concentrated in the richest 20 percent of countries; the poorest 20 percent received 1 percent.[27] Moreover, among developing countries in 1997, China received 31 percent of all foreign direct investment (FDI), Brazil 13 percent, Mexico 7 percent, and Indonesia 5 percent; six additional countries shared about 18 percent, and some 147 countries composing the rest of the developing world shared about 27 percent of all FDI.[28] The debt service obligations of the least developed countries increased from 62.4 percent of gross national product

Table 8-5. *Official Assistance to Developing Countries*

| | Net official development assistance | | | |
| | As percent of GNP | | Per capita (U.S. dollars) | |
Distribution	*1991*	*1997*	*1991*	*1997*
All developing countries	1.9	0.9	12.5	9.0
Least-developed countries	13.2	11.1	33.7	29.0

| | Donor assistance (as percent of GNP) | |
Source	*1986/87*	*1997*
United States	1.9	0.9
DAC[a]	13.2	11.1

Source: UNDP, *Human Development Report, 1999*, pp. 192, 196.
a. Development Assistance Committee of the OECD.

(GNP) in 1985 to 92.3 percent in 1997.[29] Meanwhile, international development assistance declined for all regions, as indicated in table 8-5.

In an international and knowledge-based economy, countries with well-educated and skilled human resources are in a better position to benefit from investment opportunities and global markets. Countries with such populations generally have higher growth rates.[30] Of course, every developing country can count on a group of citizens who benefit from globalization—the well educated, the wealthy, the globally connected, the information elite, as well as a growing middle class in many countries. But for the poor, globalization means increased marginalization. Investment in human capital is central to the capacity of countries to enter world markets at an advantage and not be stuck over time as a provider of low-cost labor. Unfortunately, the poverty of many countries—often compounded by political instability that distorts budgetary allocations toward military spending—precludes responding to the problem with the quantity and quality of resources needed.

Weak Institutions of Governance

Weak institutions of governance are also a defining characteristic of developing countries. Whether because of the artificial and partial grafting on of western institutions by colonial powers or the ravages of chronic public sector poverty, rule by corrupt leaders, or institutional incapacity and decay, government institutions in most developing countries have never worked particularly well. States have generally been highly centralized and inefficient at the same time that they have expanded to constrict the activities of nonstate actors, whether individuals or organizations; weak themselves, they also pursued policies and strategies that weakened their societies and economies.[31] Some states in Africa have virtually collapsed under burdens of economic stagnation and political strife. In many cases, the state lost legitimacy through the emergence of parallel economies and even parallel governments that they were unable to control or displace.[32] The extent of rent seeking and abuse of power in many countries increased during the 1970s and 1980s under the influence of inappropriate development policies and widespread authoritarianism. Democratization in the 1980s and 1990s did not noticeably put an end to these problems. Indeed, such conditions led Peter Evans to write of a "crisis of capacity" in much of the world.[33]

Ambitious but weak institutions of governance are a primary reason why international financial institutions insist that governments undergoing stabilization and structural adjustment radically restructure their public sectors. Much of the initial reform impetus emphasized doing away with state controls, responsibilities, and organizations.[34] As indicated earlier, only in the late 1980s did development specialists begin to emphasize that the state was an important adjunct to development, with particular roles that it must play well if both economic and political liberalization were to succeed—effective macroeconomic management, sound laws for protecting property rights and contracts, financial institutions with transparent decisionmaking and operations, and effective judicial systems, local governments, police, and many other institutions largely taken for granted in developed countries. As a consequence, throughout much of the 1990s, development specialists were concerned about building institutions for democratic accountability as well as for economic regulation and management. International financial institutions programmed large amounts of money for capacity-building initiatives at a variety of levels of government, convinced that with more effective government, development initiatives would prosper.

Although the diagnosis of weak institutions of governance as a constraint on development—whether defined in terms of growth, human development, or democracy—is clear and convincing, the prescription of institution and capacity building is not one that can be expected to demonstrate results over the short term. Indeed, most countries in the developing world continue to operate with public sector institutions that are weak, inefficient, and often ineffective. There are serious domestic consequences of these conditions. Weak institutions undermine possibilities for taking effective action in many policy areas. They strip the state of needed legitimacy to build constituencies for reform and increase contention over policy change by interjecting debates about the rules of the game into discussions of reform. They diminish the potential for turning policies into reality through effective implementation. Weak institutions, then, confront policy decisionmakers with a context loaded with the potential for failure.

There are also international consequences to the persistence of weak institutions. Developing countries lack the capacity to regulate financial markets and foreign investment; as a result the "costs of incompetence" can be high in volatile and integrated markets.[35] Most such countries are in a poor position to influence the policies or performance of international institutions as these institutions are increasingly setting standards and rules that bind states and their citizens. Organizations such as the International Monetary Fund, the World Bank, and the World Trade Organization are dominated by industrialized countries and, by definition, influential organizations such as the G-7, G-10, G-22, and the Organization for Economic Cooperation and Development exclude developing countries. When developing countries are part of international organizations or agreements, they are constrained by their inability to represent themselves effectively. In the Uruguay Round of GATT talks in 1994, for example, only twelve of the least developed countries had delegations in Geneva, and most of these delegations were significantly understaffed.[36] According to the World Bank, industrialized countries had an average of 6.8 people monitoring events at the WTO in 1997; developing countries had an average of 3.5 people to accomplish the same mission.[37] Twenty African countries sent no representatives at all, and thirteen had three or fewer representatives. Only Egypt, Nigeria, and South Africa approached the average level of representation of the developed countries.[38] In ways such as these, poverty and institutional weaknesses combine to marginalize many countries from influencing the development of new institutions of global governance.

Technology Gaps

Many developing countries are characterized by a small, highly educated, and internationally oriented elite that is fully comfortable in a world of rapidly developing and changing technology. These individuals manage large companies in the private sector, work in government ministries closely connected to economic policymaking, head nongovernmental organizations, or work within think tanks and universities on public and private sector issues. They have up-to-date computers and software, cellular phones, and palm pilots. These elites live in large urban areas, travel extensively, and interact effectively in international circles.

Members of this elite stand in great contrast to most of the citizens in their countries, many of whom continue to live in dusty villages or poverty-stricken urban neighborhoods without electricity or with only sporadic supplies of it. These populations are often illiterate or just barely literate and often lack access to telephones and have never had direct access to computers. They are disadvantaged in a knowledge-driven world by lack of access to educational opportunities, sketchy electricity grids, and lack of familiarity with the technologies that characterize the current era.[39] Enormous investments in infrastructure and education are needed before these individuals—or their children—can begin to acquire the knowledge and skills that have become commonplace in most developed countries of the world and among elites of all countries.

Of course, new technologies open up possibilities for developing countries to leapfrog over industrialized countries, saving time and money.[40] Expansion of foreign direct investment also increases the transfer of some technologies.[41] Overall, however, developing countries fall far behind developed ones in their access to information and technology. Table 8-6 presents data comparing rich and poor countries in electric power consumption, access to newspapers, radios, televisions, telephones, and computers. The gaps are impressive. At the end of the twentieth century, the richest 20 percent of the world's population living in developed countries counted on 74 percent of the world's telephone lines; in contrast, the poorest 20 percent had only 1.5 percent of such lines.[42] During this same period, one of intense expansion in the number of Internet users, 91 percent of them lived in OECD countries.[43] Some parts of the developing world suffered more than others from such technology gaps. In 1996, for example, there were more cellular phones in Thailand than in all of Africa.[44] Thirty-three percent of Mexico's manufacturing exports was of high-technology products in 1997; the comparable figure for Egypt was 7 percent, and for Madagascar, 2 percent.[45]

In addition, developing countries fall far behind developed countries in resources invested in research and development. In the period between 1990 and 1996, industrialized countries had an average of 4.1 research and

Table 8-6. *Rich and Poor Countries in the Information Age*

		Country categories		
Item	Year	Low-income developing countries	Middle-income developing countries	High-income countries
Electric power consumption	1980	188	1,585	5,783
per capita (kilowatt)	1996	433	1,902	8,121
Daily newspapers	1996	. . .	75	286
Radios	1996	147	383	1,300
Telephones, mainline	1997	162	272	552
Mobile telephones	1997	5	24	188
Personal computers	1997	4.4	32.4	269.4

Source: World Bank, *World Development Report, 1999/2000*, pp. 265, 267.

development scientists per 1,000 people in the population; developing countries had 0.4 such people.[46] According to the World Bank, in 1991, the gap between developed and developing countries in research and development expenditures was larger than the gap in GDP per capita.[47]

Although there are some areas of the developing world that are thriving in the new information economy—Bangalore, Bombay, Malaysia, and the northern border region of Mexico are good examples—technology gaps within and among countries are a serious impediment to development in an age of globalization. As knowledge is increasingly generated and spread by electronic means, as trade is increasingly managed and grows around electronic networks, as communication is increasingly instantaneous, the poorest countries and the poorest people are increasingly disadvantaged.

Policymaking in an Era of Globalization

New institutions of global governance, local control over public services and resources, private investment and privatization, and technological advances have important consequences for governments around the world. In fact, these changes are so significant that some have argued that they are "hollowing out the state," robbing it of sovereignty on the one hand and of responsibilities to its citizens on the other, making the state less central to national opportunities for development than it was in the past.[48] If anything, however, national governments are even more important to whether or not developing countries are helped or hindered by globalization.[49] Improving public policies and their implementation and creating stronger and more stable institutions of governance are essential if developing countries are to tackle the causes of the problems they face and begin to address their vulnerabilities internationally.[50]

For policymakers in developing countries at the end of the 1990s, the policy agenda for generating growth, eradicating poverty, building effective institutions and government capacity, and closing the technology gap is long, expensive, and interdependent.[51] In taking up this policy agenda, decisionmakers are implicitly acknowledging that in an era of globalization, they have lost some autonomy in determining national programs and strategies for development.[52] This is a lesson learned emphatically, of course, whenever countries experience deep economic crises and are forced to turn to international financial institutions for assistance. Under such circumstances, developing country governments are in weak bargaining positions as international financial institutions set conditions for macroeconomic management, state reform, public and private sector roles, investment priorities, and institutional structure.

Equally important, new international regimes for trade, the environment, labor, and other matters are reducing choices and discretion in these areas as well. In both cases, a presumptive template of actions constrains the decisional autonomy of policymakers, and the line between domestic and international policy becomes almost meaningless.[53] Moreover, even before new international conventions have been devised, national boundaries have been penetrated by a multitude of political and social activists playing larger roles in domestic politics, advocating for policy change, and forming alliances with domestic groups and interests.[54]

If policy agendas are increasingly influenced by pressures from outside the boundaries of many developing countries, the pressures on policymakers to act—and act rapidly—on these agenda items have also grown. Clearly, the speed with which the Asian financial crisis spread across the world was an ungentle awakening to the need for rapid reform in financial institutions and the need to move quickly to put regulatory systems in place and maintain macroeconomic stability in the midst of international volatility and national vulnerability. Adjusting to external shocks, long a concern of decisionmakers in countries with economies reliant on a few export commodities, has become a more insistent requirement for all developing countries.

Yet, taking action—particularly rapid action—has become more complex as the developing world moves toward more democratic forms of government and more active civil societies.[55] In many countries—even democratic ones—the tradition in policymaking had been for a relatively few people in centralized governments, consulting with a few politically relevant interests, to make decisions in the absence of widespread participation of citizens or even their knowledge of what decisions were being made.[56] Executives tended to set policy agendas; legislatures were frequently marginal to the policy process. Indeed, in both democratic and autocratic regimes, the adoption of major macroeconomic reforms during the 1980s and 1990s was generally managed by national leaders who centralized power in the executive branch of government, centralized that power in the office of the president or the Ministry of Finance, and relied on small groups of technocratic advisers who met behind closed doors to map out emergency policy packages. The policies were then often introduced through the decree powers of presidents rather than through laws acted upon by the legislature.[57] Often, national and international technocrats filled places at the policy table formerly filled by line ministries, party leaders, and representatives of important interest groups.[58]

As a very positive process of democratization has spread more widely, and as the policy agenda has broadened from primary concern about first-generation economic reforms to institutional and human resource development, many more voices are demanding to be engaged in policy discussions.[59] For example, as private sectors emerged and grew under the twin stimuli of privatization and liberalization, new and more diverse organizations representing business interests have also grown.[60] As labor unions enjoyed increased freedom to organize, many older, boss-controlled organizations were confronted by internal demands for greater democracy; at times they have split apart to create new unions with distinct demands and styles that are less accommodating to governments than the older organizations.[61] Citizen groups, often organized around local community issues such as police protection and environmental pollution or around commitments to identities based on ethnicity, gender, religion, or regional affiliations, are flourishing in more open political regimes.[62] Nongovernmental organizations, many of which used to eschew political activism, have become increasingly active in making demands on governments.[63]

The number of such voices has increased markedly.[64] Among the important demands they articulate, the protection of their constituencies or citizens more generally from the increased insecurity brought about by globalization and both market and government failures is central and persistent. The widespread adoption of more democratic forms of government must be applauded for bringing increased representation and transparency to public decisionmaking, but new democracies can be expected to produce newly contentious decisionmaking processes.

Besides increased pressure to take action on a variety of fronts, developing country policymakers have come under increasing pressure to be effective in implementing the policy commitments they make. The broader spread of information (itself a feature of globalization), the heightened involvement of civil society (often in alliance with international partners), and the broader and more independent role of the media (also supported and protected by international advocacy groups) have enhanced the ability of citizens to monitor the activities of government and its capacity to deliver on its promises. Thus, not only are policymakers more likely to take up, in Albert Hirschman's terms, "pressing" rather than "chosen" problems, they are more likely to be pushed into broader discussions when making decisions about these problems and to have their performance monitored when they implement policies.[65]

To add to the difficulties faced by policymakers, tangible resources for building support, compensating losers, or buying off opposition have become more limited. In the past, support for particular leaders, political parties, policies, and even the political regime was often cemented through the exchange of tangible benefits—jobs, contracts, development projects, licenses, access, and such—for votes, labor peace, or legislative support. But liberalized economies provide fewer opportunities to exchange such benefits because the state is less involved in purveying contracts, jobs, and licenses. Moreover, austerity budgets limit the possibilities for compensating losers or providing services to supporters.[66] With fewer political resources to employ to generate support and consensus around policy measures, political leaders have had to find new sources of policy support and consensus. In many ways, this implies developing new styles of leadership.

Indeed, the lot of policymakers in developing countries is a challenging one. A range of pressures constricts their choice of policies and narrows their room for maneuver within complex political environments. Decreased scope for setting policy agendas, increased pressure to make and implement decisions, heightened pressures to deal with the unwanted consequences of globalization, as well as loud voices of resistance—at the very least these conditions test the skills of policymakers in building coalitions for reform, educating diverse constituencies about the benefits of change, and managing the opposition of strongly organized groups. Governments can still make bad policy, but punishment is swift in the context of democratic politics and global markets.

Moreover, weak institutions add to the burdens on policymakers because they often increase contention over policy choices by failing to provide clear rules of the game for how conflict and debate should be managed.[67] Thus, for example, debates over economic policy easily become embroiled in debates over the appropriate roles of the executive and legislative branches of government. Efforts to reduce corruption entail debates about revising constitutions and rebuilding judicial systems. Initiatives to create new institutions lead to conflict over legal frameworks and mandates. Weak institutions also constrain what can be achieved through reform, as when efforts to devise regulatory systems are short-circuited because of corrupt and ineffective judiciaries. And weak institutions mean low levels of capacity to implement policies, as when efforts to reform national education systems fail because implementing bureaucracies lack capacity and motivation to take on the new activities required of them.

Policymakers face a difficult balancing act in responding to the dual imperative of strengthening institutions and adapting policy to the exigencies of globalization. Strengthening and creating appropriate institutions takes time, yet the challenges of globalization are current and insistent. Institutional reform can produce greater stability in policymaking and implementation, but the reform process often exacerbates political tensions. Governments are pressed to take actions, yet institutional weaknesses increase skepticism about their legitimacy to do so. As far as the responsibilities required of governments in developing countries, the state is clearly not being hollowed out. Yet in the capacity to respond to insistent sources of domestic need and international vulnerability, policymakers can easily come to believe that the state is becoming ever less competent.

What Can Be Done?

There is no question that policymakers in developing countries face particularly difficult policy, institutional, and political dilemmas in efforts to position their countries better for responding to globalization. And, as with much of life, there are no easy solutions to these dilemmas. Effective solutions to many problems must be found at international levels, as many chapters in this volume argue. Domestically, putting in place policies to create a stable macroeconomic environment, of course, is central to any possibility for sustained development. But we have seen that, increasingly, development experts agree that getting the macroeconomic policies right is necessary but not sufficient for development. They have paid particular attention to the experiences of high-performing Asian economies to garner the lessons of their sustained success.[68] Central to their findings have been the importance of investment in human capital and creating effective institutions of governance.

Turning from these three general areas—good macroeconomic management, investment in human capital, and institution building—the more specific list of factors deemed to be necessary and sufficient for development is much longer and more daunting: appropriate exchange and interest rates; increasing productivity; effective regulatory, monetary, financial, judicial, educational, health, and social security institutions; physical and social infrastructure; well-managed local government; greater efficiency in routine activities of government; transparency in decisionmaking; effective means of holding government accountable; and democratic politics.[69] Getting there from where most developing countries are remains a difficult challenge for policymakers, however. Achieving the necessary and sufficient conditions for development in an era of globalization takes time and resources.

Given the extensive list of what needs to be done and the time and resources that are necessary to do them, are there actions that political leaders, even in the midst of contentious political contexts, can take in the short term to enhance the capacity of their countries to move ahead with this task? Indeed, there are some areas in which change can be introduced fairly rapidly because, in those areas, policymakers have some scope for relatively autonomous action. They may have this room to maneuver even in highly contentious societies.

The most obvious of these areas is in improving the capacity of governments to undertake and use technical analysis of the problems confronting their countries. One of the more positive trends to emerge from the 1980–90s era of economic crisis was the extent to which political executives increased their access to well-trained technocrats and technical units within government to help analyze and form economic policy.[70] Interestingly, creating technical units within government bureaucracies and appointing well-trained technical advisers is one area in which political executives have wide scope for action. In the era of economic crisis, for example, presidents in many countries were able to bring a new generation of economists into government and provide them with important and stimulating problems to work on. Even countries with very limited human resource capacity were able to find among their citizens those who were prepared and eager to be challenged by such questions of policy. These leaders had, in most cases, the power to create new units of government— such as policy analysis units in the economic ministries or attached to the president's office—and to appoint advisers for specific purposes. Now, in the wake of the Asian financial crisis of 1997, many governments are working to increase the technical and managerial capacity of agencies charged with financial sector monitoring and regulation.

What appeared to work well for the economic ministries for the challenges of stabilization and structural adjustment can also be applied to ministries concerned about foreign affairs, commerce, and the characteristically hard-pressed social sectors. Indeed, the paucity of trained economists, policy analysts, and managers in these institutions generally stands in stark contrast to the technical expertise of the economic ministries. In an era in which international negotiation, trade, and human capital development are top priorities for government, however, there is little reason why such expertise cannot be built in these institutions. Even when such institutions prove relatively resistant to improving their performance, the capacity of political leaders to add to organizational structures and use some of their appointive powers to build appropriate technical and managerial capacity outside of recalcitrant ministries remains considerable.

A second area in which political leaders can improve the capacity of the government to respond to globalization is to make public sector access to the information revolution a focus of government initiative. Investing in computers and Internet connections, along with automating systems and training personnel in how to use information technologies, can contribute significantly to the capacity of government to have relevant information, frame good policies, provide public education about the need for reform, engage in domestic and international debates and negotiations about the content of new policies, and improve the capacity to monitor implementation of policy and its consequences. This task is somewhat more onerous than that of developing in-house technical capacity because it requires a substantial outlay of resources along with investments in training. Nevertheless, this is also an area of considerable executive autonomy and one in which there is unlikely to be strong resistance. Moreover, it comprises investments and actions that can be targeted to high-priority areas, such as organizations involved in trade or education, or to areas in which public sector personnel are eager to adopt such changes.

A third and related area is more difficult and pays off in the more distant future. This is the more general area of public sector capacity building. Nevertheless, it is similar to the preceding two areas of initiative in that public leaders can take considerable initiative in introducing organizational change. It is true, of course, that major civil service reforms undertaken in the 1980s and 1990s generated great resistance and just as frequently produced disappointing results.[71] Such reforms often included downsizing and new standards of performance, merit examinations, salary restructuring, and contractual obligations. Particularly in countries with a tradition of patronage appointments in government, these changes threatened public sector employees in almost all ministries and agencies.

But not all public sector reform needs to be addressed on such a comprehensive scale. Some countries have adopted a more modest agency-by-agency approach while others have proceeded cautiously through negotiation and public education to begin a process of change. Some have promoted an "islands of excellence" approach to alter incentive systems and managerial styles.[72] Moreover, public sector improvement is an area in which experience and research are providing new and practical insights. Some researchers, for example, have borrowed insights from work on private sector organizational development, and others have adapted the tools of economics to understand incentive systems and institutional adaptation.[73] As a result, the institutional dimensions of development and reform are less likely to be treated as a "black box" than they were in the past. In this difficult area, then, some executive discretion and the lessons of experience and research provide one way of increasing the capacity of government to respond to the challenge of globalization at the same time that it protects its citizens from its harshest impacts.

But the burden of finding ways to increase the capacity of developing countries to benefit from globalization does not fall only on the shoulders of developing countries and their public leadership. Certainly the academic community must be part of such efforts. Increasingly, researchers are attempting to understand and map patterns of change from the most microlevels of livelihoods and communities in poor countries to national policies and international markets and institutions as they are affected by insistent pressures of globalization. In this way, the problems of developing countries are being reinterpreted as global issues, relevant to the North as well as to the South. This kind of research is clearly contributing to a knowledge base about the dynamics of globalization and its impact that can be useful to policy audiences internationally and domestically. Similarly, the growth of knowledge about innovations in particular countries has become widely available through increased interest in such changes and improvements in technology that make sharing such information easier, as Fred Schauer indicates in the case of legal reform elsewhere in this volume.

Similarly, and as discussed in the chapter by Dani Rodrik in this volume, concrete proposals for international institutions have been generated in recent years in addition to ideas about how the benefits of globalization can be captured or the costs minimized. These proposals range from debt forgiveness to international standards for financial institutions, from the design of social safety nets to regulatory frameworks for public utilities, from proposals to recognize women's work in the informal sector to those focused on responding effectively to complex humanitarian emergencies, from the design of primary education systems to efforts to provide information about the environmental effects of development investments, from ideas about the contents of international trade agreements to technological advances in export crop production, and many more. Perhaps because of the seriousness of the problems, the range and creativity of the proposed solutions are extensive and provocative.

Attention to understanding the problems created by unprecedented change at the global level, as well as efforts to provide responses to them and to generate political strategies for guiding a process of change, can provide some assistance in knowing what to do and when and how to do it. The experience of almost twenty years of stabilization and structural adjustment, for example, has spawned an extensive literature on the political determinants of policy and institutional change in developing and transitional countries. This work has advanced understanding about how power is used to obstruct change, how the distributional consequences of policy change can be calculated, how crises affect the potential for policy and institutional reform, how the timing of reform is affected by electoral cycles, how policy entrepreneurs and change teams calculate strategies for introducing reform, and how ideas and leadership affect the process of change. This work does not offer a recipe for success in meeting the challenges of globalization, but it can be used to assess and reduce some of the risks of failure in undertaking reform initiatives.

Clearly, policymakers in developing countries face a difficult set of problems in efforts to position their countries to take better advantage of globalization and to protect their citizens and economies from its darker consequences. For these policymakers, and for those they represent, the future holds a long and difficult road to change. Nevertheless, current attention to problems created by rapid change at the global level, as well as efforts to respond to them, can provide assistance in knowing what to do and when and how to do it. Developing country policymakers need not be bereft of ideas, actions, or international allies when they take on the challenges of globalization.

Notes

1. The number of developing countries is based on the World Bank's 1999 classification by GNP per capita of low- and middle-income countries. The list includes all such countries that are members of the World Bank and that have populations over 300,000. Low-income countries have GNP per capita of $760 or less; middle-income countries have GNP per capita that falls between $761 and $9,360. The latter group are subdivided between lower-middle income (57 countries with GNP per capita between $761 and $3,030) and upper-middle income (37 countries with GNP per capita between $3,031 and $9,360). See World Bank, *World Development Report, 1999/2000* (Oxford University Press and World Bank, 1999), pp. 290–91.

2. Definitions, categories, and data taken from World Bank, *World Development Report, 1999/2000*, pp. 227, 231, and 290.

3. According to the World Bank, an additional 1.6 billion people were estimated to be living on less than $2 a day in 1998. See World Bank, *Global Economic Prospects and the Developing Countries, 2000* (Washington: World Bank, 2000), p. 29.

4. See, for examples of literature on institutions and capacity building, particularly in economic development, Carol Graham and Moisés Naím, "The Political Economy of Institutional Reform in Latin America," in Nancy Birdsall, Carol Graham, and Richard Sabot, eds., *Beyond Tradeoffs: Market Reform and Equitable Growth in Latin America* (Washington: Brookings and the Inter-American Development Bank, 1998); Merilee Grindle, ed., *Getting Good Government: Capacity Building in the Public Sector of Developing Countries* (Harvard University Press for the Harvard Institute for International Development, 1997); Silvio Borner, Aymo Brunetti, and Beatrice Weder, *Political Credibility and Economic Development* (St. Martin's Press, 1995); Douglass C. North, *Institutions, Institutional Change and Economic Performance* (Cambridge University Press, 1990); and Torsten Persson and Guido Tabellini, eds., *Monetary and Fiscal Policy* (MIT Press, 1994).

5. Growth statistics in this and the following five sentences are taken from World Bank, *World Development Report, 1999/2000*, p. 251.

6. Most of these countries were in Sub-Saharan Africa, eastern Europe, and the CIS. United Nations Development Programme (UNDP), *Human Development Report, 1999*

(Oxford University Press, 1999), p. 2. The UNDP classifies countries according to their level of human development, based on a composite index of GNP per capita; life expectancy at birth; and adult literacy and the combined enrollment ratio in schools. This produces categories that are similar to but not always consistent with the World Bank's country ratings. For example, Costa Rica is a high human development country (UNDP) but a lower middle-income developing country (World Bank). The UNDP ranks forty-five countries as high human development, ninety-four as medium human development, and thirty-five as low human development.

7. World Bank, *Global Economic Prospects and the Developing Countries, 2000*, p. 3.

8. The "Washington Consensus" consists of the need for achievement in ten policy areas—fiscal deficits, public expenditure priorities, tax reform, interest rates, the exchange rates, trade policy, foreign direct investment, privatization, deregulation, and property rights. It was first summarized (and named) by John Williamson in "What Washington Means by Policy Reform," in John Williamson, ed., *Latin American Adjustment: How Much Has Happened?* (Washington: Institute for International Economics, 1990).

9. This view was brought home forcefully by the rapid liberalization of the Russian economy; lacking basic institutions for a market system, liberalization contributed to a decade of economic decline, bringing with it extensive hardship for most citizens and high levels of official and private corruption. For an early discussion of the expanding agenda of economic reform, see Joan Nelson, "The Politics of Long Haul Economic Reform," in Joan Nelson and Collaborators, *Fragile Coalitions: The Politics of Economic Adjustment* (Transaction Books, 1989).

10. A significant attack on the state in the World Bank's report on Africa in 1984, *Towards Sustained Development in Sub-Saharan Africa* (Washington: World Bank, 1984), reflected mainstream thinking about the harm caused by states that intervened extensively in economic development. In 1991 the *World Development Report* contained a chapter on the state and the 1997 *Report* was about the role of the state in development, marking the "official" rehabilitation of states as important instruments of development. See Merilee S. Grindle, *Challenging the State: Crisis and Innovation in Latin America and Africa* (Cambridge University Press, 1996), especially chap. 1.

11. Grindle, *Challenging the State*, chaps. 1 and 4 for a discussion.

12. The addition of human resource development to the consensus among development experts about necessary conditions for development can be attributed to many factors, among them the work of scholars assessing the East Asian miracle economies, to the success of the UNDP's *Human Development Report* in challenging the World Bank and other institutions to take a broader view of development, and the insistence of NGOs and their networks around the world pointing to conditions of poverty and deprivation in much of the world. For assessments of the contributions of human capital to development, see Nancy Birdsall, David Ross, and Richard Sabot, "Inequality and Growth Reconsidered: Lessons from East Asia," *World Bank Economic Review*, vol. 9 (September 1995), pp. 477–508. See also Birdsall, Graham, and Sabot, *Beyond Tradeoffs*.

13. While many continued to argue for the centrality of trade to development, research carried out by Dani Rodrik suggested that this was not an optimal strategy. "Countries that have done well in the postwar period are those that have been able to formulate a domestic investment strategy to kickstart growth and those that have had the appropriate institutions to handle adverse external shocks, not those that have relied on reduced barriers to trade and

capital flows. . . . Policymakers therefore have to focus on the fundamentals of economic growth—investment, macroeconomic stability, human resources, and good governance—and not let international economic integration dominate their thinking on development." Dani Rodrik, *The New Global Economy and Developing Countries: Making Openness Work* (Washington: Overseas Development Council, 1999).

14. World Bank, *World Development Report, 1999/2000,* p. 13.

15. Data in this paragraph are all taken from World Bank, *World Development Report, 1999/2000,* pp. 5, 33, 271.

16. UNDP, *Human Development Report, 1999,* pp. 3–4.

17. See, for example, Michael Gavin and Ricardo Hausmann, "Growth with Equity: The Volatility Connection," in Birdsall, Graham, and Sabot, *Beyond Tradeoffs.*

18. World Bank, *Global Economic Prospects and the Developing Countries, 2000,* p. 29. At the same time, the *World Development Report, 1999/2000,* p. 25, estimated that the number living on less than $1 a day increased to 1.5 billion in 1998. According to this report (p. 26), "An informal rule of thumb is that a per capita growth rate of 3 percent or more is considered the minimum for reducing poverty rapidly. But the average long term growth rate of developing countries is below that level. Between 1995 and 1997 only 21 developing countries (12 of them in Asia) met or exceeded this benchmark rate. Among the 48 least developed countries, only 6 exceeded it."

19. World Bank, *Prospects for Growth and the Developing Countries, 2000,* p. 33.

20. UNDP, *Human Development Report, 1999,* p. 22. The figures given are for the global incidence of characteristics of poverty; their incidence, however, is almost exclusively concentrated in developing and transitional countries.

21. World Bank, *World Development Report, 1999/2000,* p. 26.

22. See, for example, Birdsall, Graham, and Sabot, *Beyond Tradeoffs.*

23. See UNDP, *Human Development Report 1999,* pp. 35–43.

24. Ibid., p. 33.

25. Ibid., p. 40.

26. World Bank, *World Development Report, 1999/2000,* p. 14. According to the UNDP's *Human Development Report, 1999,* p. 3, the income gap between the top 20 percent of the world's population in rich countries and the 20 percent living in the poorest countries increased from 30 to 1 in 1960 to 60 to 1 in 1990 and 74 to 1 in 1997.

27. UNDP, *Human Development Report, 1999,* pp. 2–3.

28. World Bank, *World Development Report, 1998/1999,* p. 30. The total received by developing countries was $1.04 billion, 30 percent of the world's total. World Bank, *World Development Report, 1999/2000,* p. 37.

29. UNDP, *Human Development Report, 1999,* p. 196.

30. See, for example, Nancy Birdsall and Juan Luis Londoño, "No Tradeoff: Efficient Growth via More Equal Human Capital Accumulation," in Birdsall, Graham, and Sabot, *No Tradeoffs.*

31. See, for example, James S. Wunsch and Dele Olowu, eds., *The Failure of the Centralized State: Institutions and Self-Governance in Africa* (Westview Press, 1990); Richard Sandbrook, "The State and Economic Stagnation in Tropical Africa," *World Development,* vol. 14 (March 1986); and Joel S. Migdal, *Strong Societies and Weak States: State-Society Relations in the Third World* (Princeton University Press, 1988). Such studies underscore the extent to which both authoritarian and democratic executives centralized power, often

doing so by undermining the independence of legislative and judicial institutions and obliterating the potential for local government. At the same time, these same central governments tended to grow weaker through inefficiency, corruption, and conflict over the distribution of state largesse.

32. See, for example, Grindle, *Challenging the State.*

33. Peter Evans, "The Eclipse of the State? Reflections on Stateness in an Era of Globalization," *World Politics,* vol. 50 (October 1997), p. 85.

34. Privatization, liberalization, austerity, and downsizing were the principal instruments used to reduce the size and scope of state activities in a wide range of developing countries.

35. Evans, "The Eclipse of the State?" pp. 73–74.

36. UNDP, *Human Development Report, 1999,* pp. 34–35.

37. World Bank, *World Development Report, 1999/2000,* p. 55.

38. World Bank, *World Development Report, 1999/2000,* p. 57.

39. According to World Bank figures, South Asians who lived in the largest cities had seven times the number of telephones as those who lived in smaller cities, towns, and rural areas. In East Asia and the Pacific, the ratio was about 5.5-1, in Sub-Saharan Africa, 3-1, and in Latin America and the Caribbean, about 2.5-1. World Bank, *World Development Report, 1998/1999,* p. 69.

40. For example, they can select wireless communications technologies and reduce the fixed investment needed for older technologies used. By 1993, for instance, a number of countries in the developing world were fully digitized, while the OECD countries were much more tied to older analogue technology. World Bank, *World Development Report, 1998/1999,* pp. 57, 59.

41. See D. Ernst, "Globalization and the Changing Geography of Innovation Systems: A Policy Perspective on Global Production Networks," prepared for a workshop on the political economy of technology in developing countries, Brighton, U.K., October 1999.

42. UNDP, *Human Development Report, 1999,* p. 3.

43. Ibid.

44. Ibid., p. 6.

45. World Bank, *World Development Report, 1999/2000,* pp. 266–167.

46. UNDP, *Human Development Report, 1999,* p. 178.

47. World Bank, *World Development Report, 1998/1999,* p. 2.

48. The idea of a "hollow" state was the subject of essays in *Daedalus,* vol. 124 (Spring 1995). See R. A. W. Rhodes, "The Hollowing Out of the State: The Changing Nature of the Public Service in Britain," *Political Quarterly,* vol. 65 (April–June, 1994); Susan Strange, *The Retreat of the State: The Diffusion of World Power in the World Economy* (Cambridge University Press, 1996); and Joseph Camillieri and Jim Falk, *The End of Sovereignty? The Politics of a Shrinking and Fragmenting World* (Elgar, 1992).

49. This has been the dominant view responding to those who have argued for the hollowing out of the state. See, for example, Paul Hirst and Grahame Thompson, *Globalization in Question: The International Economy and the Possibilities of Governance* (Cambridge: Polity, 1996); Jan Aart Scholte, "Global Capitalism and the State," *International Affairs,* vol. 73 (July), pp. 427–52; Evans, "The Eclipse of the State?"; and Linda Weiss, *The Myth of the Powerless State* (Cornell University Press, 1998).

50. Domestically, strong state institutions are essential to provide citizens with important insulation from the economic vulnerabilities inherent in market economies, the "embedded liberalism" that has long been enjoyed by citizens in industrialized countries. See John Ruggie, "International Regimes, Transactions and Change: Embedded Liberalism in the Postwar Economic Order," *International Organization*, vol. 36 (Spring 1982), pp. 379–416.

51. As indicated earlier, stimulating and sustaining growth requires effective macroeconomic management, policies to diversify national economies, institution and capacity building, investment in education and physical infrastructure, and measures to encourage research and development. Alleviating poverty means finding means to stimulate growth, particularly in ways that generate productive jobs, significant investment in education, health, and other social services, strengthening a wide range of institutions—those that generate policies, those that manage conflict, those that regulate and stimulate production—and investment in physical infrastructure and new technologies for enhancing agricultural and industrial productivity. Increasing the capacity of institutions to manage political and economic interactions requires significant investments in education, training, and technology as well as advances in regulatory policies and mechanisms of accountability. Remedying technology gaps requires extensive investment in infrastructure as well as education and training—investments that in turn are dependent on growth to increase the revenues of government.

52. See Scholte, "Global Capitalism and the State."

53. See Stephan Haggard, *Developing Nations and the Politics of Global Integration* (Brookings, 1995).

54. See, for examples, Margaret E. Keck and Kathryn Sikkink, *Activists beyond Borders: Advocacy Networks in International Politics* (Cornell Univesity Press, 1998); and Sanjeev Khagram, *Dams, Democracy, and Development: Transnational Struggles for Power and Water*, forthcoming.

55. In 1998, 61 percent of countries in the world had "some form of democratic government," compared with 28 percent in 1974. World Bank, *World Development Report, 1999/2000*, p. 43.

56. Even in democratic countries, conditions of poverty, illiteracy, and underdevelopment distance government decisionmaking from large portions of the population, particularly those who live in rural areas. See Merilee S. Grindle and John W. Thomas, *Public Choices and Policy Change: The Political Economy of Reform in Developing Countries* (Johns Hopkins University Press, 1991), chap. 3.

57. See, for example, country chapters in Robert H. Bates and Anne O. Krueger, eds., *Political and Economic Interactions in Economic Policy Reform* (Basil Blackwell, 1993); Stephan Haggard and Robert R. Kaufman, eds., *The Politics of Economic Adjustment* (Princeton University Press, 1992); and Grindle, *Challenging the State*. For a review and summary of this literature, see Barbara Geddes, "The Politics of Economic Liberalization," *Latin American Research Review*, vol. 30, no. 2 (1995), pp. 195–214.

58. See, for example, the role of technocrats in dramatic policy changes in Mexico in the late 1980s and early 1990s in Grindle, *Challenging the State*, chap. 5. More generally, see Jorge I. Domínguez, ed., *Technopols: Freeing Politics and Markets in Latin America in the 1990s* (Pennsylvania State University Press); John Williamson, "In Search of a Manual for

Technopols," in John Williamson, ed., *The Political Economy of Policy Reform* (Washington: Institute for International Economics, 1994); and the case studies cited in the previous note.

59. First-generation reforms are usually identified as those involved in early stabilization and structural adjustment programs. Most of these policy changes were "stroke of the pen" reforms in that they did not require extensive administrative mechanisms to be implemented. Second-generation reforms are those that require institutions and organizations for their implementation, such as, for example, an education or health policy reform.

60. See, for example, Catherine M. Conaghan and James M. Malloy, *Unsettling Statecraft: Democracy and Neoliberalism in the Central Andes* (University of Pittsburgh Press, 1994).

61. See, for example, Guillermo O'Donnell, Philippe C. Schmitter, and Laurence Whitehead, eds., *Transitions from Authoritarian Rule: Comparative Perspectives* (Johns Hopkins University Press, 1986).

62. See Manuel Castells, *The City and the Grassroots* (London: Edward Arnold, 1983); Jean L. Cohen, "Strategy or Identity: New Theoretical Paradigms and Contemporary Social Movements," *Social Research*, vol. 52 (Winter 1985), pp. 663–716; Arturo Escobar and Sonia E. Alvarez, eds., *The Making of Social Movements in Latin America: Identity, Strategy and Democracy* (Westview Press, 1992); Claus Offe, "New Social Movements: Challenging the Boundaries of Institutional Politics," *Social Research*, vol. 52 (Winter 1985), pp. 817–68; and Alain Touraine, "An Introduction to the Study of Social Movements," *Social Research*, vol. 52 (Winter 1985), pp. 749–88.

63. See, for example, Julie Fisher, *Non-Governments: NGOs and the Political Development of the Third World* (Kumarian Press, 1998).

64. There are no overall figures for the number of nongovernmental organizations in existence at the current time. Partial information suggests very rapid growth, however. In a speech delivered in China, for example, Lester Salamon stated that the creation of new associations in France averaged 10,000 annually in the 1960s and 50–60,000 a year in the 1980s and 1990s. In Italy, half of existing NGOs were created since 1985. In Hungary, 23,000 NGOs were formed between 1989 and 1993. Russia has seen more than 100,000 NGOs created since the early 1990s. Lester Salamon, "Toward Civil Society: The Global Associational Revolution and the New Era in Public Problem-Solving," keynote speech, Beijing, July 1999. I am grateful to Marty Chen for bringing this to my attention.

65. See Albert O. Hirschman, "Policymaking and Policy Analysis in Latin America—A Return Journey," in Albert O. Hirschman, *Essays in Trespassing: Economics to Politics and Beyond* (Cambridge: Cambridge University Press, 1981).

66. See, for example, Grindle, *Challenging the State*, chap. 2.

67. See, for example, Felipe Agüero and Jeffrey Stark, eds., *Fault Lines of Democracy in Post-Transition Latin America* (Coral Gables, Fla.: North-South Center Press).

68. See, for example, World Bank, *The East Asian Miracle: Economic Growth and Public Policy* (Washington: World Bank, 1993); Robert Wade, *Governing the Market: Economic Theory and the Role of Government in East Asian Industrialization* (Princeton University Press, 1990); Alice Amsden, *Asia's Next Giant: South Korea and Late Industrialization* (New York: Oxford University Press, 1989).

69. According to the "comprehensive development framework" of the World Bank, there is little that is not important in the process of development. See *World Development Report, 1999/2000*, p. 21.

70. See note 58.

71. See, for example, David Lindauer and Barbara Nunberg, *Rehabilitating Government: Pay and Employment Reform in Africa* (Washington: World Bank, 1994).

72. This approach is discussed in Barbara Geddes, *Politician's Dilemma: Building State Capacity in Latin America* (University of California Press, 1994). The World Bank has supported country efforts to develop "executive agencies" that fall outside the regular civil service and that seek to establish more professional organizations to carry out particularly important public sector work.

73. See, for example, Judith Tendler, *Good Government in the Tropics* (Johns Hopkins University Press, 1997); and Murray Horn, *The Political Economy of Public Administration: Institutional Choice in the Public Sector* (Cambridge: Cambridge University Press, 1995).

9

TONY SAICH

Globalization, Governance, and the Authoritarian State: China

THERE IS NO DOUBT that the forces of globalization are providing new challenges for international and domestic governance. Some have suggested that the challenges are particularly severe for authoritarian political regimes. The need to be increasingly accountable to liberal international trading and investment norms, and the release of the state's monopoly over the provision of information and communications (it is argued) will undermine authoritarian control and help unleash a more plural society. To compete effectively the state will be forced to cede sovereignty on certain issues upward by empowering transnational institutions, relinquish many business decisions to transnational business corporations, and be held more accountable to a nascent transnational civil society. At the same time, the state will be forced to cede sovereignty not only downward (to local administrations) but also outward (to new social actors that are crucial to national success in a global world.)

Such a scenario must be extremely troubling to authoritarian regimes. But we are far from hearing the death knell of the nation-state. There is little evidence to date that shows a correlation between membership in organizations such as the World Trade Organization (WTO) and a decline in state capacity of authoritarian regimes. Such regimes may be able to adopt a variety of strategies to limit the impact of globalization and even to turn it to their benefit. However, over the long term there is no doubt that serious new challenges will confront those regimes that continue engagement, and this will require significant amendment of previous political practice. This chapter focuses on China's integration into the global community. The November 1999 agreement between China and the United States on China's terms of accession to the WTO (following its agreement to sign the two UN covenants on human rights in 1997 and 1998) would appear to signal China's intent to join the global community. By signing these agreements, China has implicitly acknowledged that international monitoring is justifiable not only for domestic economic practice but also for political behavior. Yet in practice, while China clearly wants to be a respected member of the international community, it is deeply conflicted about how active a role to play in international governance, and few have thought about what effects globalization might have on domestic governance. That globalization has and will continue to have such effects is poorly perceived, other than in terms of the need to censure incoming information and cultural flows. Like other countries, China wishes to derive the macroeconomic benefits of globalization, but it is uncomfortable with the costs of social, political, and cultural readjustment. Foreign observers have been ambivalent about how to deal with the rise of China's economic power and its integration into global frameworks of governance. Some, taking their cue from historical parallels with the rise of new powers such as Germany and Japan at the turn of the twentieth century, see conflict as inevitable; others argue that the changed international situation makes successful accommodation feasible.[1]

In China (as in the rest of the world) writing about globalization has become a mini-industry for academics and policymakers.[2] Globalization became a hot topic after a series of lectures delivered in 1993 by the historian, Arif Dirlik, and the subsequent publication in Chinese summarizing his views. It warmed up even more with the onset of the Asian financial crisis.[3] However, the overwhelming majority of this writing concentrates on "economic globalization" with a little less attention paid to "cultural globalization," mainly interpreted as the domination of American cultural products, and virtually no consideration given to the impact on governance.[4] Those who have written about governance have tended, perhaps understandably, to be vague about the specific implications for China. For example, political theorist Liu Junning makes the case that while the shift from a planned to a market economy has promoted economic globalization, there has been a parallel shift from authoritarian politics to democratic politics that has promoted political globalization. However, he does not discuss these double processes in the context of China.[5] More specifically Xu Yong and Zeng Jun propose that a system of contracts be used to govern political and social relationships that would match those that regulate market relations. This they feel would ensure popular control of government while helping the regime to build up political capital. However, the authors do not demonstrate how this process is linked to the forces of globalization.[6]

Indeed, the impact of globalization is best seen in the economic sphere. Starting in 1979 Chinese development strategy shifted from import substitution, the privileging of accumulation over consumption, and viewing foreign trade as irrelevant to economic growth, to an active interaction with the world economy in which foreign trade and latterly, investment, were seen as major engines of growth. China entered the global markets at a fortuitous time and with its cheap and abundant labor supply benefited from the rapidly unfolding globalization of the manufacturing process, rapid strides in telecommunications, and internationalization of capital markets. The economic figures speak for themselves. The ratio of foreign trade to GDP has risen from 12.6 percent in 1980 to 39.5 percent in 1995. Between 1990 and 1998 trade almost tripled from $115 billion to $323.9 billion. (More than 60 percent of China's trade is with the rest of Asia, with the United States accounting for 21 percent of exports and 12 percent of imports).[7] Foreign direct investment in 1998 totaled $45.5 billion (with more than 60 percent coming from Taiwan and Hong Kong!), bringing direct investment to nearly 80 percent of total foreign investment in China. China's own direct investment abroad ($16 billion in 1994) was second only to Taiwan among developing countries. Foreign reserves (excluding gold) touched $149.2 billion in 1998, while external debt was $156.1 billion.[8]

Xenophobic outbursts and leadership manipulation notwithstanding, withdrawal from deeper integration into the world economy and its evolving structures of governance is impossible. This was clearly recognized by President Jiang Zemin when he noted (in March 1998), "Globalization is the objective trend for global economic development and nobody can shun it. . . . A developing nation like China should be both daring and good at engaging in the international cooperation and competitions under such economic globalization."[9]

This point was made emphatically when, despite significant domestic opposition, Jiang and Premier Zhu Rongji pushed ahead with a deal with the United States on terms of accession for the WTO. This reflected the fact that the current leadership's legitimacy to rule is tied to its capacity to deliver the economic goods, and these can only be delivered over the long term through increased trade, foreign investment, and a more disciplined domestic economy that WTO membership would bring. Entry early in 2000 not only was important for national pride and to fulfill Jiang's desire to steer China to great power status but also for very pragmatic economic concerns. With foreign direct investment (FDI) dropping, foreign interest in China waning, and domestic reforms stumbling, early entry was seen as the best way to stimulate the economy. This was compounded by fears that barriers to entry might rise subsequently, especially as the next round of talks would cover two issues of vital interest to China: agriculture and trade in services. By joining early, China might be able to forge alliances to secure policies more beneficial to its own national concerns.

Despite this more accommodating approach to foreign trade and capital, in crucial respects both Deng Xiaoping and Jiang Zemin's approach has mirrored that of their nineteenth-century predecessors in the "self-strengthening movement" who sought to import Western techniques and equipment while keeping out alien cultural and political values.[10] This previous policy of selective adaptation proved shortsighted. The Chinese did not comprehend the interrelated nature of Western societies and failed to see that Western technology could not be easily disentangled from the social and cultural matrix in which it was embedded. It remains to be seen whether the Chinese Communist Party (CCP) will be more successful in gaining the benefits of globalization without accepting its underlying premises. For example, WTO membership seems to presume not only a liberal trading order but also an independent legal system that constrains government as necessary, transparency, accountability, and a relatively pluralistic political order.

Since Mao Zedong initiated contacts with the United States and engineered the PRC's entry into the United Nations in the early 1970s, the general consensus has been that China has moved from rejection of the international status quo to acceptance. However, it is more correct to say that China has acquiesced in the international order, and while it has been a joiner, it has not been a leader in international governance.[11] Mostly this has been because China's main priority has been to develop its economic strength; membership in international organizations has been a tool for meeting this objective. This has made China reluctant to challenge the existing rules of the game unless they directly confront Chinese claims to sovereignty or economic interests.[12]

Second, China is a latecomer to all international governmental organizations, and it did not participate in the drafting of the "rules of the game." The incapacity of China to change significantly these rules to suit its national conditions has reinforced its perception that international governance is structured essentially to advance the agenda and interests of the West, especially the United States. This was apparent in the official response to the Seattle meeting of the WTO that criticized the "small number of economic superpowers" that had tried to dominate proceedings over the interests of the developing countries.[13] China's self-told history of 150 years of shame and humiliation at the hands of foreigners, the anti-imperialist thrust of Leninism, the party's legacy of distrust and betrayal, and the leaders' tendency to interpret decisionmaking as a "zero-sum" game militate against constructive engagement and interaction with the existing international governing structures.[14]

Compounding this is the fact that the CCP has never been successful in transnational governance. Its attempts in the 1960s and 1970s to lead a loose coalition of nations to oppose "U.S.-hegemonism" and "Soviet revisionism" failed, as did its attempts to fund pro-Maoist groups to destabilize neighboring governments in Asia. Not surprisingly, Deng Xiaoping's advice to his colleagues and successors was not to take the lead in international affairs, lean toward the United States, and concentrate on economic development. However, this is difficult for a nation with a psychology that emphasizes the superiority of Chinese culture and that sees an international leadership role as a right to be reclaimed.

Such sentiments can lead to instability when combined with the more strident nationalism promoted by, or acquiesced to, by President Jiang Zemin and his advisers. While China is currently open for business, distrust of foreigners and significant periods of closure have been common. As the emperor instructed Lord McCartney in 1793, China had no need for British goods. If he hoped for a good relationship, George III simply had to "act in conformity with our wishes by strengthening your loyalty and swearing perpetual obedience so as to ensure that your country may share the blessings of peace."[15] More recently, the group denounced as the Gang of Four after the Cultural Revolution (1966–76) held that foreign trade had no place in development, charging that Deng Xiaoping's first attempts to stimulate the economy through foreign trade amounted to treasonous trafficking with the imperialists.[16] The xenophobic and sudden outpouring of antiforeign sentiment following the NATO bombing of the Chinese embassy in Belgrade on May 7, 1999, revealed how close to the surface distrust of foreigners still lies.

Since 1989, the Chinese leadership has been fairly successful in manipulating public opinion to instill nationalism as a legitimizing core value.[17] While this may aid the regime's short-term stability, it presents two challenges for governance. First, it militates against constructive involvement in international organizations as rising nationalism compromises the ability of the nation-state to deal with internationalism. Second, it reinforces the outdated notion of sovereignty that still underpins the current leadership's perceptions of the world. China is essentially an empire anchored to a Westphalian concept of the nation-state trying to operate in an increasingly multilateral world. In fact, what China wants is an economic order that is international in the benefits it brings but not necessarily global in the sense of diluting the decisionmaking autonomy of the nation-state. China has displayed a basic suspicion of multilateral frameworks and has generally preferred to lock discussions into bilateral diplomacy. Thus, on joining the WTO China quickly asserted that the organization stipulated that "regardless of size, all member countries enjoy equal rights."[18] This suspicion is even more acute on political and social issues. China was quick to condemn President Bill Clinton's attempts to bring labor standards into WTO considerations, declaring that the "so-called labor standards were nothing but a covert form of trade protectionism." Labor conditions, it affirmed, were nobody else's business; there should be no interference on this issue "by other countries in the name of protecting human rights."[19]

These trends explain the seeming contradiction in China's international behavior. China wants to be taken seriously. President Jiang Zemin, in particular, has sought a role in global governance through what he has called "great power diplomacy" and the forlorn objective of creating a multipolar world in one that will clearly be unipolar in real power well into the twenty-first century. At the same time, the notion of the paramount nature of the sovereign state and the equality of all nations, irrespective of size and status, leads to the almost embarrassing procession of leaders that troop through Beijing to meet with the president. The smallest island-state receives the same treatment in the *People's Daily* and on Central Television as a major industrial power or Asian nation. The dedication to sovereignty and a territorial definition of China that is the most expansive in history, and China's reluctance to move discussions out of bilateral frameworks, causes uncertainty in the region. It also means that China is more willing to join regimes that govern the international economy but is less enthusiastic about those regional or global frameworks that would place real restrictions on Chinese military capabilities.[20] The CCP and the military have been adamantly opposed to any attempts to establish an Asian collective security system, primarily because they do not wish to give Southeast Asian nations a forum in which to criticize collectively its claims to sovereignty in the South China Sea.[21]

It can also lead to decisions that are described as principled in China but that appear petty to others. Of particular importance is China's concern to deny international space to Taiwan and to punish those countries that show sympathy toward Taiwan's views. This also underlies the excessive praise and attention that China lavishes on small Polynesian, Micronesian, or Central American states that recognize China or it fears may switch recognition to Taiwan. One extreme example was China's veto in the Security Council (February 1999), something almost unprecedented, against the continuation of the UN Preventive Deployment Force in Macedonia because of the latter's switch of diplomatic recognition to Taiwan the previous month.[22]

One example of China's poor understanding of international governance is its decision to sign the two UN covenants on human rights.[23] China does not seem to have appreciated that by signing the covenants it is accepting that there are international norms concerning the freedom of organization, right to work, procession, formation of political groupings, and other things that transcend national boundaries. China's leaders appear to have thought that they could sign on and then hold off implementation by retreating behind sovereign borders and talking about different histories and national conditions. China has been a strong advocate of the right to development and has stressed that providing food and livelihood for its people takes precedence over rights of political expression and demonstration.

China has been particularly adamant in preventing monitoring of human rights by international agencies from leading to criticism of its domestic practices. It was stung by the critical resolution in August 1989 adopted by the UN Subcommission on the Prevention of Discrimination and Protection of Minorities, the first time that a permanent member of the Security Council had been censured on human rights grounds in a UN forum. Subsequently, it fought a hard battle to escape criticism in the annual Geneva meeting of the UN Commission on Human Rights over the objections of the United States and the European Union. To escape this possible avenue of censure, China has moved to situate discussion of its human rights record in less intimidating bilateral forums.

Yet China's leaders have (haltingly and grudgingly) acknowledged to the international community and their own people that certain UN-defined rights are universal and (like it or not) subject to international scrutiny. Not only does this open up China to evaluation in terms of international norms, but it also legitimizes debates on human rights domestically. Legal reformers in China have seized on the signing of the two covenants to motivate reform of some of the most problematic areas of domestic law, including the excessive use of the death penalty, bypassing courts by sentencing people to reeducation through labor, and the lack of basic protections in criminal law such as the right to remain silent.[24]

China needs to be able to feel comfortable with the framework for international governance that it seeks to join. Many important issues beyond the directly political and economic, such as environmental protection, drug smuggling, trafficking in women, and AIDs, needs its active participation to resolve. In turn, other major nations need to incorporate China as a more equal partner and to build China's reasonable concerns into the architecture of international governance. China needs to reduce its suspicion of hostile foreign intent and adjust its outdated notion of sovereignty to accept that some issues need transnational solutions and that international monitoring does not have to erode CCP power. Without accommodation on both sides, China will remain a rather grumpy, unpredictable player in international governance.

China's decision to open up its economy during the 1980s and the pressures of globalization have inevitably led to or exacerbated political differentiation within China. Certain regions and groups and new industries are being privileged by engagement with the world economy, while the pillars of CCP power in the state-owned sector are being eroded by increased international competition. Four interrelated aspects that provide challenges to domestic governance are discussed here. First, the legal system has expanded rapidly to accommodate international capital and trade. Second, international economic engagement has contributed to new inequalities that have emerged as a by-product of the reforms. Third, these reforms have created new challenges in providing public goods and services.[25] Fourth, the CCP is confronted by how to accommodate the social forces that will benefit from further globalization while disentangling itself from elements of the traditional power base. These trends are not solely or even primarily the products of globalization, but globalization will intensify them.

To deal with the regularization of its domestic economy and its engagement with international capital and trade, China has undertaken one of the most extensive crash programs in the history of legal development. Throughout the 1980s China made significant changes to both its trade policies and the institutional structure for dealing with foreign trade and investment.[26] However, as most foreign investors would attest, inadequate implementation, lack of transparency (especially with internal regulations that foreigners are not meant to see), and a tangle of local administrative regulations detract from the effectiveness of the system.

To limit the impact of foreign engagement on governance and Chinese society as a whole China initially set up special economic zones (essentially export processing zones). During the past ten years the borders around these zones have steadily broken down as more of the country has been opened to investment and trade, or localities have jumped the gun and declared attractive deals for foreign investors. This has led to unpredictable governance of foreign investment with unclear lines of authority and jurisdiction between the center and the localities. The zones did, however, allow space to experiment with much of the legislation that now governs China's modern economy and work force relations.

WTO entry will deepen the process of regulatory design for international trade but also will have a broader impact on the functioning of the domestic legal system. The major challenge confronting the CCP will be to accept that membership presumes that disputes will be resolved by an independent rules-based supranational body rather than by party fiat or through the mediation of local political connections. Within China, pressure will mount for a more independent judiciary to adjudicate on economic issues and for greater transparency on transactions. This runs counter to current practice and will be hard to change. The practice noted above of internal regulations that foreigners are not allowed to see but that govern transactions will have to be stopped.[27] An even bigger challenge will be to enforce laws and regulations passed at the national level. While such laws and regulations may represent policy intent, they are contravened and often undermined by a myriad of ministerial regulations and locally generated rules that provide the real operating context for activities. As the saying of local officials goes, "They have their policies and we have our countermeasures" *(tamen you zhengce, women you duice)*. Last but not least, it is unlikely that there will be genuine judicial independence anytime in the near future.

There has also been great institutional adaptation as a result of increased economic engagement. Initially, several new commissions were set up to deal with foreign investment, imports, and exports and in March 1982 the State Council decided to bring all foreign trade administration under one organization by forming the Ministry of Foreign Economic Relations and Trade (MOFTEC). In turn, in 1984 MOFTEC gave up its centralized monopoly over foreign trade by expanding the number of foreign trade corporations from a dozen to several thousand and allowing them independence for fiscal and planning purposes.[28] The ministry has remained paramount, however, in policy in this field and was the front organization for the discussions with the United States and other countries on China's terms of entry into WTO. Together with those sections of the Ministry of Finance and the People's Bank of China that are engaged in foreign affairs, it has prospered most within the state bureaucracy from globalization and has consistently supported China's further economic integration.

The concentration of foreign direct investment has exacerbated regional inequalities, with greater wealth concentration in the coastal areas in the East. In 1998 Guangdong alone received 26.5 percent of foreign direct investment, the three major municipalities of Shanghai, Beijing, and Tianjin received 17.5 percent, and Jiangsu province 14.6 percent. By contrast, the nine provinces and one municipality in the Northwest and Southwest of China received only 3 percent of all foreign direct investment.[29] While annual growth in per capita rural income from 1988 to 1995 averaged 4.71 percent for China as a whole, it was 11.66 percent for Jiangsu, 9.33 percent for Beijing, and 7.11 percent for Guangdong. In the Southwest it was only 0.72 percent for Guizhou, 0.62 percent for Sichuan, and 1.26 percent for Yunnan.[30] As a result, the average 1998 rural income for the coastal areas was about twice that of the Southwest, and Shanghai was three times higher. In urban areas real income was also consistently higher, with Shanghai enjoying real income approximately twice that of the Northwest and 60 percent higher than that in the Southwest.[31]

These trends have caused major migration flows, with 80 to 120 million people moving to find work on a temporary or more permanent basis. Significant numbers have been attracted to the employment opportunities offered in the special economic zones, along the coast, and in major municipalities in the manufacturing sectors that have developed with foreign investment. This has led to a breakdown of the old residence control system that kept the farmers out of the cities and protected an intricate system of benefits and allowances that favored the urban over the rural. Currently, the government does not provide welfare or education for these migrant families, and they are not integrated into local government service provision. As China opens itself to greater foreign investment, labor mobility will increase, and this will require a major rethinking of traditional government service provision that can no longer be based on place of birth. Already, in the urban areas, native place association is becoming the main organizing principle for the migrant communities, many of which have set up their own governing and welfare structures outside of the state.[32] This does not sit well with the CCP's desire to control all social space and to lock organizations into existing systems of regime patronage.

While the central government has continually stressed that more attention has to be paid to the poorer interior, this has not translated into a coherent policy approach, and the powers that the coastal provinces have won will not be given up easily. China is pursuing an extremely inegalitarian development strategy, especially in comparison with its East Asian neighbors that it seeks to emulate.[33] There is enormous inequality in the provision of public goods and services, and the main incentives at the present time are for local governments to stress revenue mobilization at the expense of other distributional and growth objectives. This has had all the usual perverse effects: orphanages struggle to meet costs by operating karaoke bars. Doctors rely on kickbacks from pharmaceutical concerns and concentrate on expensive curative interventions rather than preventive care. Nature reserves struggle to restrain poaching by villagers only to turn around and contract out extraction to logging, fishing, or mining concerns. The most important development causing this has been the de facto decentralization of the fiscal system. A successful resolution of this dilemma lies not only in increasing the tax base of the government (a solution explored by the World Bank and favored by the Chinese central government) or squeezing the rural poor through levies and fees (a strategy often favored by local authorities) but also a rethinking of the kinds of work in which the government should be engaged. Without a more open political system the only alternatives for the losers are to suffer in silence, or to riot (as they are increasingly doing).

In addition to the regional impact of globalization, there is also a sectoral impact that will undermine further the state-owned sector of the economy and current agricultural practices and favor the growing joint venture, foreign owned, and nonstate sectors. Jiang Zemin's and Zhu Rongji's extraordinary efforts to enter the WTO during 1999 will have major consequences for governance and will heighten social tensions over the short to medium term. The terms of entry agreed upon with the United States will help formalize market structures in China, develop the internal market (most provinces trade more externally than with one another), and develop more effective institutions to govern and finance the market. Some have surmised that Zhu Rongji and fellow reformers have decided that WTO entry may be the only way to discipline domestic enterprises. This would have major consequences for corporate governance while the fallout will set new governance challenges. WTO entry is clearly contested with opposition from those sectors of the economy and regions that feel they will lose out.

In 1997–98 the Chinese leadership announced ambitious reforms to rationalize the economy, a number of which were designed to reduce the noneconomic burdens of state-owned enterprises (SOEs) that would also help meet WTO entry criteria. WTO entry should preclude continuation of massive subsidies to this sector and the considerable noneconomic role performed by the SOEs.[34] This will make it extremely difficult for the CCP to pursue its current social welfare and industrial policies, something that reformers might well favor.

World Bank figures suggest that no more than 10 percent of China's 100,000-plus industrial SOEs are fundamentally viable. SOEs absorb 60 percent of national investment; receive total subsidies amounting to one-third of the national budget; and net credit to SOEs reached over 12 percent of GDP in 1995. Importantly, 50 to 75 percent of household savings, mediated and directed by state banks, currently goes to finance SOE operations. Were a number of SOEs to go under and the state did not guarantee their losses, there would a lot of unhappy urban families who had lost their life's savings. The World Bank estimates that in 1996, 50 percent of SOEs lost money (and unofficial estimates are higher).[35]

It has become increasingly apparent that over the long term government resources would be insufficient to pay depositors and bondholders if SOEs are unable to service bad debts. At the same time, with a declining revenue base the state was unable to offer the same kind of bailout and subsidies declined from 6 percent of GDP to 4 percent in 1994. This made it virtually impossible for many SOEs to meet their full range of social obligations, even salary payments, in turn speeding up the need for pension, medical, and housing reform.[36] Thus, the leadership began to accept bankruptcies and more open unemployment; this indicates why WTO entry is important. It is important not only as a disciplining mechanism but also as an external force that reformers can blame for the pain that will be inflicted on the privileged urban working class during restructuring.

However, the full political effects of this process are unpredictable. To become viable and to conform to WTO norms, the medical, housing, and pension obligations of the enterprises need to be removed and taken over by a mixture of individual and government service provision, with the employee contributing in a manner more comparable to firms in the West. Yet, if implemented fully, these reforms would reduce further the intrusive role of the state and sponsor far greater social differentiation. In their totality, the policies would amount to a "revolution" in the relationship between state and society in terms of taking the former out of crucial areas of the life of the latter. With individuals increasingly responsible for their own work, housing, pensions, and consumption choices, inevitably they will wish to have a greater political voice, accountability over officialdom, and as a result will develop new organizations to fulfill their desires and objectives.

The consequent increase in the pace of layoffs will provide challenges for government reemployment policy while revealing the weakness of the Chinese system to provide the necessary extra social security and welfare support. This is contributing to significant discussion about the role of government. Government revenues during reforms have fallen from 36 percent of GDP in 1978 to around 11 percent in 1998. China needs to think about which functions to retain, which to let the market handle, and which to delegate to the nascent, but highly restricted, third sector. Government control over the third sector derives from both the Leninist culture that is suspicious of any activity that takes place outside of its control and fears that a thriving sector would be open to influence from the international community.[37]

This does not necessarily mean that the forces of globalization will buffet the CCP out of existence. Indeed, they may be harnessed to give it a new lease on life. With legitimacy based on economic criteria, the CCP has to maintain high levels of economic growth to sustain social stability. As deflation continues and infrastructure investments fail to provide sufficient boost to the national economy, the leadership needs to consider alternatives. The gamble is that WTO entry will not only help discipline the domestic economy but will also give a boost to growth rates in China. This explains the optimistic articles that appeared in the Chinese press after the U.S.-China agreement, arguing that WTO entry will provide more jobs than will be lost and that it could add 3 percentage points to growth over the next few years.

This requires the CCP to lower the expectations of the urban working class—which it has been doing quite successfully. Given that the CCP rejects any independent political or labor organizations, there is no one to represent their interests effectively outside of the party apparatus. In addition, the CCP must find ways to integrate the newly emerging social forces into the economic and, ultimately, political power structures. This has been especially contentious for the private business sector, much of which is concealed as collective or state enterprises. The CCP has steadily ceded more ground to the private sector of the economy, recognizing that it has been one of the main driving forces for economic growth and that it will benefit further from greater international economic integration. Thus, in March 1998 article 13 of the State Constitution was amended to elevate its status from a "complementary component to the socialist public economy" to an "important component."[38] On January 4, 2000, the chair of the State Development Planning Commission announced that the private sector would be put on an "equal footing with the SOEs" for the first time since 1949.[39] The private sector has found it difficult to obtain credit, has been vulnerable to the predatory behavior of local officials, and has not been able to list on the stock markets. This will not change customary practice overnight but should provide better political protection for the sector.[40]

Ceding political power or even drawing the new entrepreneurs into the existing power structure has been much more contentious. Conservative ideologues such as Deng Liqun have resisted recruiting wealthy private entrepreneurs into the party, and the CCP has stopped admitting entrepreneurs in practice (without adopting any formal policy of exclusion.)[41] (In Wuxi City I met with one of the wealthiest local business people who had first been encouraged to join the party and then requested to withdraw. He was not unduly bothered, since his economic power meant that local party leaders still paid him due homage and consulted with him regularly.)[42] CCP leaders' training in Marxism should have convinced them that political power will be constructed on the economic base. As globalization continues the privileging of new groups, the CCP will be presented with a major challenge of political accommodation.

The advent of the information revolution poses another problem for China's governance. The Chinese government has traditionally practiced a system of information control and censure with an intricate grading process regarding who is allowed to see which kinds of information. The CCP has tried to channel information flows so that they are vertically linked and has eschewed the horizontal flow of information. This has meant that access to information in the Chinese system has formed an important basis for power, and the ability to provide the correct interpretation of the past has provided the legitimacy to decide on current policy.[43] Under such a system the real basis of exchange is secrets and privileged access to information.

This system can starve leaders of the reliable information they need to make appropriate policy decisions. The more coercive the regime, the more what passes up is what leaders want to hear. Negative information is suppressed and its agents repressed. What globalization demonstrates better than at any point in the past is that at a certain developmental point—that is where the need for information becomes very great—it becomes extremely difficult to reduce coercion without inviting vast structural change. In the Soviet Union prolonged coercion and bureaucratization so deprived the state of the capacity to innovate that eventually it broke apart. What appeared at the top as rational public planning was based on a jerrybuilt system of deals and private negotiations.[44]

In the Soviet Union not only did little accurate information filter to the top, the top rejected and suppressed what little it got. Nor could the directors of such a highly centralized state system trust one another or their party representatives. Once the move was made to make the Soviet Union a high-information, low-coercion system, the entire organizational structure unraveled. This is precisely the problem that the current leadership in Beijing is trying to grapple with. It is not surprising that the rapid spread of the Internet and new information technology has caused unease among those managing the system as it threatens their monopoly over the flow of information.

In a number of respects, the leadership of the CCP has treated the Internet in the same way as it has traditional print forms. It has tried to institute a system of controls that will allow it to participate in the benefits of faster information flows without having to open up the information system and allowing in the disadvantages of views and information that may challenge the CCP's interpretation of events. First, it has only authorized four networks for international access in order to control information flows. Besides pornographic materials, it has also blocked access to the websites of publications such as the *New York Times*, CCN, and those human rights' organizations that are critical of China. Since 1996 it has required all Internet users to register with the police or face punishment. More recently, the state has forbidden China-based websites from using news derived from websites that are situated outside of the mainland. Consequently, a number of service providers in China have dropped news services from their menu and concentrated on "safe" areas of information provision such as sports and entertainment. In addition, traditional media forms are prohibited from using material derived from any website. To gain better control over the sector the Ministry of Information Industry was created in 1998 and includes the former ministries of posts and telecommunications, radio, film and broadcasting, and the "leading group" on information policy. The ministry is the primary regulator for this sector and reports directly to the State Council.

The ministry and its head, Wu Jichuan, have been hostile to allowing foreigners market access for both political and commercial reasons. In principle, the agreement on WTO should significantly alter this stance; China has ceded that the Internet is open to foreign investment and that telecommunication companies will be able to control up to 49 percent of telecommunication service companies upon accession to the WTO and 50 percent after two years. However, cases will be dealt with on a one-by-one basis and it is the ministry itself that will make the decisions on granting licenses. This, in combination with political sensitivities and the local protectionism, would suggest that a concerted attempt will be made to restrict foreign access in the Internet sector.

The Chinese leadership clearly is aware that it cannot control completely the flow of information or access to forbidden sites by its citizens. Its intention is to lay down warnings about the limits of the permissible and to deter the casual browser from becoming too inquisitive about the world outside. In this limited respect, it may be successful. Even though China has become extremely porous in information flows, there is scant evidence to suggest that this alone has challenged the CCP's monopoly on political interpretation for the majority. It should be remembered that as China enters the new century 90 percent of its households are still without telephones, and 99 percent of the population does not have access to networked computers in any case.[45]

It is likely that China's response to the Internet will be differentiated with much stricter controls on news and political information and practices and controls that match more clearly international practice for e-commerce dealings. Indeed, there are new opportunities for the Internet for China. Chinese will be the second language of the Internet and may even become dominant. This provides propagandists in Beijing with untold new opportunities to try to shape a Chinese political culture that stretches well beyond its physical boundaries.

However, even in the commercial area there are security concerns that can be played upon by ministries and other groups in China to restrict foreign access. For example, in January 1996 the State Council announced that the Xinhua News Agency, run by the government, would in the future be responsible for the distribution of all on-time economic information that was disseminated by agencies such as Dow Jones and Reuters. This would totally defeat the purposes of such services. The official reason given was to check content to ensure that there were no inaccuracies in the information provided or nothing that was hostile to China. The real reason was the manipulation of leaders' fears of unrestricted information flows to use the argument of state security to obtain an economic monopoly. Xinhua was apparently feeling left out of the spoils of the new technology and saw this as a good way to make money.[46]

It will take enormous skill on the part of the current leadership to prevent the challenges of globalization from undermining further the power and legitimacy of the CCP. To date, while the leadership has shown itself to be adept at adapting to economic change, it has not displayed the necessary skill at confronting the social and political consequences that arise from this change. Each time that the need for far-reaching political reform is floated, the senior leadership has backed away, hoping that its authoritarian power structures will enable it to crush any overt opposition and ride out any unrest.[47] However, it is clear that the forces of globalization will require a considerable shift in the way the CCP governs the system and will require political reform that not only seeks to make the system more transparent but also more accountable. Given its record to date this will be a significant hurdle for the current leaders to overcome. Thinking that they have learned the lessons of their fast developing neighbors in the region, political coercion has been applied in fits and starts, combined with growing economic liberalization. However, the requirements for China for continued high growth are high information, declining coercion, less hierarchy, and more accountability by means of representative institutions and a marketplace in which priorities of goods and services in the economic sphere are balanced by needs and wants in the political sphere. Whether the Chinese leadership can deal with this challenge of governance will attest whether it can retain its leadership over China's development in the twenty-first century.

Notes

1. The strongest expression of the conflict school is Richard Bernstein and Ross H. Munro, *The Coming Conflict with China* (Knopf, 1997); a more balanced assessment is presented in Andrew J. Nathan and Robert S. Ross, *The Great Wall and the Empty Fortress* (W. W. Norton, 1997). For an insightful overview of different policy preferences for dealing with China based on whether one is accommodationist or confrontationalist, see Michel Oksenberg and Elizabeth Economy, "Introduction: China Joins the World," in Economy and Oksenberg, eds., *China Joins the World: Progress and Prospects* (New York: Council on Foreign Relations, 1999), pp. 7–15. Certainly it has been the approach of all presidents from Nixon on that the more China could be engaged with the international community the better.

2. The Translation Bureau of the Central Committee of the Chinese Communist Party publishes one of the most informative series. Seven volumes have been published to date, covering topics such as globalization and Marxism, globalization and socialism, and globalization and China.

3. See Yu Keping, "Chinese Views on Research on Globalization," in *Zhanlue yu guanli* (Strategy and Management), no. 3, 1999, p. 96.

4. See, for example, Guo Shuqing, "Economic Globalization and China's Opening Up," in *Guoji jingji pinglun* (Review of International Economics), nos. 5–6, 1999, pp. 21–26; and Liu Li, "Economic Globalization," ibid., nos. 11–12, 1997, pp. 32–34.

5. Liu Junning, "Globalization and Democratic Politics," in Hu Yuanzi and Xue Xiaoyuan, eds., *Quanqiuhua yu Zhongguo* (Globalization and China) (Beijing: Central Compilation and Translation Press, 1998), pp. 67–71.

6. Xu Yong and Zeng Jun, "Globalization, Contracts, and Political Development," ibid., pp. 72–81.

7. Only in 1993 did China surpass its 1928 level of two-way trade, which constituted 2.6 percent of the world total. The total had fallen to only 0.6 percent in 1977. *Economist*, November 20, 1999, p. 25. Remember that China has only just taken over from Luxembourg as the world's number 10 trader and still ranks below Belgium and the Netherlands.

8. These figures are calculated from information in *Zhongguo tongji nianjian, 1999* (State Statistical Yearbook, 1999) (Beijing: State Statistical Publishing House, 1999).

9. "China: Jiang Zemin Praises HKSAR Government," Xinhua, March 9, 1998. My thanks to Nancy Hearst for finding this quotation and for other bibliographical help.

10. The commonly used formulation is "Chinese learning for the essence, Western learning for practical application."

11. From 1977 to 1996, China's membership in international government organizations rose from 21 to 51 and in international nongovernmental organizations from 71 to 1,079. See Samuel S. Kim, "China and the United Nations," in Economy and Oksenberg, eds., *China Joins the World*, pp. 46–47.

12. As it came out of a period of self-imposed exile, China lacked administrative personnel who could work in international organizations to advance effectively China's interests.

13. Ma Shikun and Zhang Yong, "What Is the Meaning of the Seattle Meeting?" in *Renmin ribao* (People's Daily), December 6, 1999, p. 7.

14. For an example see Jiang Zemin's comments greeting the new millennium, when he refers to how China suffered from the "bullying and humiliation of world powers" before Mao Zedong and the CCP led the nation to liberation. For the full text see *Xinhua* in English, December 31, 1999. For the role of narrative and its relationship to power in the CCP see David E. Apter and Tony Saich, *Revolutionary Discourse in Mao's Republic* (Harvard University Press, 1994).

15. Quoted in Stephen White and others, *Communist and Postcommunist Political Systems* (Basingstoke: Macmillan Press, 1990), p. 73.

16. Similar accusations were made against Premier Zhu Rongji once the United States published the details of what it claimed he had agreed to on terms for WTO entry in April 1999.

17. The CCP has been careful to set limits to the ramifications of a strident nationalism that might challenge its own position. Thus, it was ambivalent about the publication of the nationalist tract *The China That Can Say No* because of the authors' criticism of the regime's nationalist credentials, has blocked the pursuit by Chinese citizens of war reparations from Japan, and while initially supportive of the anti-U.S.demonstration in May 1999 quickly reined them in once they began to criticize the ineptitude of the government's response.

18. Ma Shikun and Zhang Yong, "What Is the Meaning of the Seattle Meeting?" in *Renmin ribao*, December 6, 1999, p. 7.

19. Ibid.

20. On this point see Oksenberg and Economy, "Introduction," p. 21; and Michael D. Swaine and Alastair Iain Johnston, "China and Arms Control Institutions," ibid., pp. 90–135.

21. See Kim, "China and the United Nations," p. 56. More generally on the issue of engaging China see the essays in Alastair Iain Johnston and Robert S. Ross, eds., *Engaging China: The Management of an Emerging Power* (New York: Routledge, 1999).

22. From the early 1980s, China stopped using the veto, claiming that it was an example of hegemonic behavior. As a result, China prefers to abstain. The only subsequent time that China exercised the veto was in January 1997 to block the mandate of a UN mission to Guatemala, also in protest against the country's diplomatic links with Taiwan. Virtually all of the earlier veto votes had been against recommendations for the secretary general. One notable exception was in 1972 concerning the entry of Bangladesh following its establishment after the war. Clearly this move was related to China's notion of sovereignty, with it not wishing to support the creation of new states through a war of secession.

23. On October 27, 1998, right after UN Human Rights Commissioner Mary Robinson's visit, China signed the International Covenant on Civil and Political Rights and on October 5, 1997, China signed the International Covenant on Economic, Social, and Cultural Rights just before President Jiang's visit to the United States.

24. Interviews with Beijing-based members of the legal profession and legal academics, June 1999.

25. For a lucid general analysis of the potential conflict between globalization and social infrastructure see Dani Rodrik, *Has Globalization Gone Too Far?* (Washington: Institute for International Economics, 1997).

26. On this process see Jude Howell, *China Opens Its Doors: The Politics of Economic Transition* (Boulder: Lynne Rienner, 1993); Margaret Pearson, *Joint Ventures in the People's Republic of China: The Control of Foreign Capital under Socialism* (Princeton University

Press, 1991); and Susan Shirk, *How China Opened Its Door: The Political Success of the PRC's Foreign Trade and Investment Reforms* (Brookings, 1994).

27. Indeed China signed a memorandum of understanding with the United States stating that all trade legislation would be public and that those regulations that were not published would not be enforced. Implementation has not been completed.

28. Margaret Pearson, "China's Integration into the International Trade and Investment Regime," in Economy and Oksenberg, eds., *China Joins the World,* p. 188.

29. Calculated from figures in *Zhongguo tongji nianjian 1999,* p. 599.

30. See Azizur R. Khan, *Poverty in China in the Period of Globalization: New Evidence on Trends and Patterns* (Geneva: International Labor Organization, n.d.), p. 36.

31. Per capita net annual income for rural households in Shanghai was 5,406.87 yuan, for Beijing 3,952.32, Jiangsu 3,376.78, Sichuan was 1,789.17, Guizhou was 1,334.46 Tibet 1231.50, Xinjiang 1,600.14, and Gansu 1,424.79. For urban residents the real income per capita was 8,825.26 yuan for Shanghai, 8,520.61 for Beijing, and 6,064.45 for Jiangsu. For Sichuan it was 5,159.97, Guizhou 4,580.48, Xinjiang 5,041.67, Gansu 4,034.26, and Qinghai 4,257.50. See *Zhongguo tongji nianjian 1999,* pp. 339 and 325.

32. See Xiang Biao, "How to Create a Visible 'Non-State Space' through Migration and Marketized Traditional Networks: An Account of a Migrant Community in China," paper delivered to the International Conference on Chinese Rural Labor Force Migration, Beijing, June 1996.

33. For a Chinese account that displays alarm at this inequality and proposes that the disparities be swiftly remedied see Wang Shaoguang and Hu Angang, *The Political Economy of Uneven Development: The Case of China* (M. E. Sharpe Inc., 1999).

34. Showing the range of their activities, SOEs employ fully one-third of China's medical staff and some 600,000 teachers and administrators. Neil C. Hughes, "Smashing the Iron Rice Bowl," *Foreign Affairs,* vol. 77 (July–August 1998), p. 78.

35. World Bank, *China's Management of Enterprise Assets: The State as Shareholder* (Washington: World Bank, 1997), p. 1.

36. The cost of social insurance and welfare funds as a proportion of the total wage bill rose from 13.7 percent in 1978 to 34 percent in 1995. UNDP, *China Human Development Report. Human Development and Poverty Alleviation 1997* (Beijing: UNDP, 1998), p. 65.

37. See Tony Saich, "Negotiating the State: The Development of Social Organizations in China," *China Quarterly,* no. 161 (March 2000), forthcoming.

38. "Quarterly Chronicle and Documentation," *China Quarterly,* no. 158 (June 1999), p. 535.

39. John Pomfret, "China Gives Broad Rein to Economy's Private Sector," *Washington Post,* January 5, 2000, p. A1.

40. For example, those in the banking system, especially at the local levels, have no experience with making loans on a commercial basis. They are used to listening to the local party boss and feel more comfortable lending to SOEs, figuring that eventually someone will pay them back.

41. For criticisms of the current policy course see the four "10,000 character manifestos" reprinted in Ma Licheng and Ling Zhijun, *Jiaofeng: Dangdai Zhongguo Sanci Sixiang Jiefang Shilu* (Crossing Swords: An Account of the Three Thought Liberations in Contemporary China) (Beijing: Today Publishers, 1998).

42. Interview, Wuxi, May 1999.

43. On this see Tony Saich, "Writing or Rewriting History? The Construction of the Maoist Resolution on Party History," in Tony Saich and Hans van de Ven, eds., *New Perspectives on the Chinese Communist Revolution* (M. E. Sharpe Inc., 1995), pp. 299–38.

44. See Apter and Saich, *Revolutionary Discourse in Mao's Republic*, chap. 9.

45. Shao Wenguang, "China: Reforms and Impact of Globalization," unpublished manuscript, May 1998, p. 12.

46. Interviews with representatives of foreign companies engaged in these negotiations.

47. The most recent occasion was at the National People's Congress meeting held in March 2000. An initial draft of the Government Work Report contained reference to the need for political reform, but this was dropped from the version finally presented by Premier Zhu Rongji. See "Political Reform Not on the Agenda," in *South China Morning Post*, March 7, 2000.

10

ELAINE CIULLA KAMARCK

Globalization and Public Administration Reform

A T THE BEGINNING of the twenty-first century a large number of national governments around the world are engaged in efforts to reform their bureaucracies. These countries have different histories and different electoral systems; they are at different stages of development and yet, to a surprising degree, they are employing a set of reform concepts and strategies that are remarkably similar. Many of these concepts come from a reform movement known as "new public management" or "reinventing government," which began in Great Britain and New Zealand in the 1980s and expanded to other countries, including the United States, in 1993. This chapter surveys the largest 123 countries in the world and charts their efforts at reform. It also attempts to explain why there is a convergence in government management reform efforts at this point in history and how these efforts are related to globalization.

But before we begin, a caveat is needed. Whether or not similarities in the language of reform will result in real governmental similarities remains to be seen. Distinguishing between political rhetoric and governmental

The author thanks her research assistant, Rob Taliercio, for his diligent research on the countries in the survey discussed in this chapter.

reality is difficult enough in one country—the work of doing this across many countries and many cultures is daunting indeed and just beginning.[1] Therefore this chapter has more modest ambitions: to lay out the reasons that so many countries have embarked on a program of governmental reform and to lay out some of the common elements of those reforms. This chapter surveys the largest 123 countries in the world, searching for government reform movements that dealt with the actual operations of the state or the traditional ground of public administration. The results of that survey and some initial observations on the causes of similarities and differences across countries are included here.

Background

Most students of governmental reform give credit for beginning this movement, sometimes called the "new public management," to Margaret Thatcher, who came to office in Great Britain in 1979 after she ran a campaign in which the heretofore sacrosanct civil service became fodder for the political debate. Her election was followed by the election of Ronald Reagan in 1980 in the United States and of Brian Mulroney in 1984 in Canada—both of whom, like Thatcher, ran campaigns highly critical of the bureaucracy. That the supposedly neutral civil service became a political issue in each of these countries came as an enormous shock to many civil servants who had seen themselves as apolitical administrators of the law. Furthermore, the emergence of the issue of government administration on the political scene meant that in some countries at least, the resulting reforms would be nonincremental.

(It is worth noting that the reform movements in Britain and the United States had ideological roots that began with the Thatcher-Reagan revolutions. These movements were then adopted and modified by the left of center party in the form of New Democrats in the United States and New Labour in Great Britain. In contrast, compared to public management reform movements in these countries, public management reform movements in other countries such as the Netherlands and Sweden have been remarkably nonideological and more practical.)

The most recent global government reform movement has had two distinct phases. Stage one took place primarily during the 1980s. In that decade governments concentrated on economic liberalization and on privatizing industries that had previously been state owned. According to Graham Scott, former Treasury Secretary of New Zealand, for most of the world the first stage of governmental reform revolved primarily around getting government out of businesses—airlines, telephones, and so on, that the United States was never in to begin with. "The United States was never really trying to solve the problem that most of the rest of us began with," said Scott at the Global Forum on Reinventing Government held in Washington in January of 1999. While Ronald Reagan shared in Thatcher's antibureaucratic rhetoric he never had the targets that Thatcher and others had for privatization and hence privatized very little. In sum, the first stage of government reform should be seen in the context of the transition to free market economies that began all over the world in the 1980s and accelerated in 1989 with the fall of the Berlin Wall.

The second decade of this movement—beginning in the 1990s—focused less on privatization and more on the administrative reform of core state functions. In this decade states have sought to cut the size of their governmental bureaucracies while simultaneously making government more efficient, more modern, and more responsive to the citizen. And, in this decade, the United States, under President Clinton, promised to "reinvent" government and thus added its own power and prestige to the governmental reform movements that were beginning in many other countries. A variety of strategies have emerged and spread from one country to another, often without even changing the terminology. In the introduction to a volume on public sector management in Europe, the editors state, "In some reports we found that the language had not even been translated from the American to the local language."[2]

Don Kettl has defined the two stages of the global reform movement as the Westminster reforms, which refer to the "pathbreaking efforts of the New Zealand and the U.K. governments" and "American-style reinvention, which was more incremental and ironically, more sweeping than Westminster-style reform."[3] In this survey of the world's largest governments both elements of reform are present and counted. In fact, in some countries the American and the British terminology conflated. For instance, the Westminster countries adopted Citizen's Charters in order to improve service delivery; the Americans adopted Customer Service. In several countries the term Customer Charters is used. But before we look at the common elements of reform it is worth taking a moment to understand the common causes.

Causes of National Reform Movements

Four factors seem to have converged to make administrative reform central to the goals of so many disparate countries around the world:
— Global economic competition,
— Democratization,
— The information revolution, and
— The performance deficit.

Not surprisingly, the pressures of international economic competition are creating new networks among subgovernments, which are moving governments toward greater uniformity.[4] As countries are forced to cooperate with one another pressures mount to synchronize activities at the subgovernmental unit. The sheer volume of transactions increases the incentives to simplify and standardize activity in a wide variety of areas from customs to bankrupcy.

The desire to attract international business and investment has also led countries to try and reform their governments in order to create a better investment and business climate. The World Bank conducted a survey that asked 3,600 international businesses to rate countries around the world in credibility and reliability. It then constructed an index consisting of measures such as predictability of rulemaking, political stability, and freedom from corruption and regressed this measure against economic performance. Not surprisingly, there was a high correlation between economic performance and reliable governmental functioning. In a comment heard increasingly in the global economy Jeff Garten says, "The world needs to walk away from countries unwilling to make serious changes."[5] In the best seller *The Lexus and the Olive Tree,* Thomas Friedman puts the need for government reform in the global economy even more starkly: "And the Supermarkets and the Electronic Herd really don't care what color your country is outside any more. All they care about is how your country is wired inside, what level of operating system and software it's able to run, and whether your government can protect private property."[6]

Global economic competition has also placed a high premium on getting deficits down. Among western European nations the primary driver has been the desire on the part of EU governments to meet the objectives of the Maastricht Treaty, which required states to reduce their debt down to a fixed percentage of GDP. Hungary, Greece, and Italy are examples of countries where explicit pressures to conform to EU entry rules precipitated government reform movements.

But even without an external factor such as the need to meet treaty requirements, in the past two decades many other states began large-scale governmental reform efforts as the result of economic crisis. Perhaps one of the most dramatic stories of economic crisis, and of government reinvention, comes from New Zealand. In the early 1980s New Zealand was, in the words of current Prime Minister Jenny Shipley, "the sick dwarf of the OECD." "We had frozen, fixed or frightened all the main indicators of the New Zealand economy. Wages, rents, exchange rates and interest rates were all controlled. Through subsidies we were picking winners but losing innovation. We were binding our human and physical resources into a straight-jacket of economic inefficiency. We were fooling ourselves, but no one else."[7]

A Labor government in New Zealand started the country along a dramatic road to recovery. It cut subsidies, reduced taxes, and opened its economy to trade. Not only did it privatize previously state owned industries— it did not stop there. New Zealand has gone further than any other country in the world in privatizing its government. "Ministers represent the taxpayers' ownership interests, and they purchase a specified set of services, annually, from the Chief Executive of a government department or agency who is personally accountable for meeting the owners' goals."[8]

In Canada efforts at governmental reform contributed to fairly impressive economic results. In its report on government reform "Getting Government Right" Canada boasts, "By 1998–99 the percentage of the Gross Domestic Product needed to support all Federal Government Programs will be at its lowest level since 1949–50."[9]

As the theory and practice of economic development matured, it became clear that "good government" was part and parcel of healthy economic development. Thus, in addition to the reasons outlined above, major national reform movements in the developing world have frequently been imposed as conditions of international or bilateral aid.[10] The World Bank, for instance, has made governance a key piece of its development work in the 1990s, and the International Monetary Fund has required significant state sector restructuring as part of its loan and bailout packages.

The second driver of governmental reform is democratization. In South Africa an important part of the transition from apartheid has been the transformation of the bureaucracy. In the words of the Honorable Zola Skweyiya, "Because of its previous rule, which was oriented to control rather than service delivery, the public bureaucracy was faced with a crisis of legitimacy. Across the board, rewards and benefits were distributed on the basis of racial and gender discrimination."[11] In South Africa an important aspect of ending apartheid is reform of the government's bureaucracies.

Democratization inevitably includes some measure of decentralization—one of the most common themes in government reform. In Poland, the government reform movement has its roots in the Solidarity movement, which began the democratization program in 1989. The hallmark of communist governments was their excessive centralization, so one of the main efforts of innovators in Poland has been decentralization and the creation of local government. In January 1999, Poland created a large number of new local governments as part of a systematic effort to shrink centralized bureaucracies and create a government founded on the subsidiarity principle shared by other western European countries. Similar efforts to decentralize are also taking place in Hungary, the Czech Republic, and in some Latin American countries such as Brazil and Chile.

A third driver of government reform is the information revolution. On the most obvious level, the information revolution allows countries to share instantly the rhetoric and reality of their reform movements. The OECD's web page, www.oecd.puma.org, provides exhaustive information on reform developments in OECD countries. When Vice President Al Gore's National Performance Review published its first report, copies were downloaded from Moscow, Russia, sooner than they were downloaded from Moscow, Idaho. There is no doubt that information technology is a major driver in the creation of a common, global language of administrative reform.

However, the information revolution is also creating a demand for governmental reform simply by exacerbating the distance in performance between the private sector and the public sector. In the United States in the 1950s, doing banking was not very different from an interaction with the government. One had to go to an office at a certain time, stand in line, and deal with a functionary. By the time the information revolution allowed the private sector to cater to the customer and deliver service through automated teller machines at any hour of the day, the governmental sector looked and felt far behind.

The same was true in Europe. "In the early 1980s, service industries in Europe became more competitive. Relaxation of restrictive practices in industries such as banking and airlines forced companies to compete for customers, not just through price but also through customer service. This had two impacts on the public sector. First it started to raise the expectation of citizens about how well services could be provided . . . secondly, it showed that there were better ways of providing services than simply having bureaucracies working for their own convenience."[12]

Thus the information revolution in the private sector raised expectations on the part of the public and made rule-bound, paper-based governmental bureaucracies seem old fashioned and unresponsive. At mid-century the organization of the Pentagon and the organization of General Motors were not terribly different. But as organizational theory in the private sector evolved and produced a new information age theory of organizations, public sector insistence on traditional bureaucracy seemed all the more obsolete.

Finally, government reform movements have been driven by deficits in governmental performance—deficits that are as often perceived as real. For all the evidence available indicating that government has actually performed well in many areas during the past few decades, publics in many countries around the world have been highly critical of the way in which their institutions have functioned.[13] In the United States this opinion has been expressed by presidents from Reagan to Clinton. Reagan maintained often that government had become "part of the problem, not part of the solution." Clinton admitted that most people think "the government could screw up a two car funeral."

Pippa Norris's book *Critical Citizens* makes the point that while democratic values have triumphed over the globe, confidence in the institutions of representative democracy has suffered an enormous erosion. Arthur Miller and Ola Listhaug, writing in that same volume, conclude that "government performance is not simply gauged by material standards or economic conditions. . . . citizens expect government to operate in an honest, competent and efficient manner."[14]

As capitalism and market mechanisms gained popularity throughout the world, the contrast between the perceived clarity and efficiency of a competitive market and the multiple, obscure goals and inefficiency of government monopolies no doubt added to the general belief that government was not performing as it should. This perspective led many countries to try and reform their governments by measuring the results of government activity (figure 10-1).

Common Elements of Governmental Reform Movements

The research for this chapter was conducted during the last six months of 1999. The dates are important since reform movements often come and

Figure 10-1. *Reasons for Starting a Public Administration Reform Movement, Examples from Various Countries*

Economic crisis/budget deficits	Economic crisis paired with a change in political leadership	Desire to meet standards imposed by European Union	Desire to meet standards imposed by international development organizations	Transition to democracy	Desire for greater efficiency
Ireland	Jordan	Hungary	Moldova	Georgia	Switzerland
New	Nicaragua	Greece	Benin	Zambia	Austria
Zealand	Denmark	Italy	Kenya	Hungary	
Benin	Bulgaria		Brazil	Czech	
Dominican	Zambia		Ukraine	Republic	
Republic	Portugal			Chile	
Sweden	Hungary			Kenya	
Netherlands	Uganda			South Africa	
Peru	Venezuela			Poland	
Canada	South Korea			Russia	
Argentina	Spain				
Italy	Japan				
United					
Kingdom					
France					
Mexico					
Brazil					
United					
States					

go, and countries that had vigorous national reform movements in 1999 may not have them in 2000 and vice versa. We decided to look at every country in the world with a population of more than 3.4 million people in order to limit the universe and get some sense of the type and frequency of reform movements in the world's 123 largest countries. Thus the universe for this study took in a wide variety—from countries like Rwanda that barely have functioning governments, to the emerging nations of Latin America, to the mature democracies of the European Union. The author and research assistant coded for eleven variables using primarily English and Spanish sources. The results are as follows.

Table 10-1. *Public Management Reform Movements in the 1980s and 1990s*

Two or more major reform movements during this period	One major reform movement during this period	Some public management reforms but no national-level reform initiative	None
31	49	19	24
25%	40%	15%	19%

Source: All of the tables and figures in this chapter show data based on our survey of the 123 largest countries in the world. See text.

Public Management Reform Movements in the 1980s and 1990s

Since public management reform movements come and go and come back again we counted the number of reform movements within each country during the past two decades. For the purpose of table 10-1 we looked for countries that had specific, well-defined reform movements at the national level. Twenty-five percent of the world's largest countries had two or more major reform movements during this period—often coming and going with a change in the government. For instance, in the United States, the Reagan administration created the Grace Commission, a large-scale, executive level effort to focus on deficiencies in the management of government. The Grace Commission had some impact on the operations of government but was hampered by a hostile attitude toward government in general, which only increased the anticipated bureaucratic intransigence. It was followed, in 1993, by the National Performance Review, an executive branch creation of the Clinton-Gore administration, which remains in operation, as of this writing, as the National Partnership for Reinventing Government.

Forty percent of the world's largest countries had at least one major reform movement during this period, and 15 percent of the world's largest countries had some public management reforms but no reform initiatives at the national level.

Germany, for example, falls into this last category. Unlike its European neighbors during this time, Germany underwent a "reform moratorium." As it moved to reintegrate the East, "the old well-proven administrative

238 ELAINE CIULLA KAMARCK

Table 10-2. *Location of Innovation*

Traditional central control agency such as Treasury or Interior Ministry	Special unit created to oversee governmentwide reform efforts
8	25
24%	76%

structures from the West were directly imported to the East."[15] But public sector management reform at the local level was quite robust, perhaps because of the Speyer Quality Competition Award, which rewards local governments for innovations. Although the national government is not known for having participated in the "new public management" sweeping much of Europe, at the local level governmental reform was characterized by a concept known as the "new steering model."

Overall, table 10-1 shows that more than half of all of the world's largest countries during this period had large-scale reform movements at the national level. This number is very high, especially considering that many of the countries surveyed had, for all practical purposes, no functioning governments.

Institutional Location of Public Management Reform Units

Increasingly, reform movements have come to be located in special units of government created for the specific purpose of achieving wide-ranging bureaucratic reforms as shown in table 10-2. The significance of these specially created units is twofold. Often they are located in the office of the chief executive, thus emphasizing the new political importance of management reform. Some nations, such as Bolivia, Argentina, and Ghana, have followed the example of the United States and given their vice presidents control over the reform movement. Second, as important as where these reform efforts are located is where they are *not* located. They are *not* located in the Finance Ministry or in the traditional budget office, places where budget cutting is a priority and where because of that priority the larger, nonfinancial missions of government reform would be lost.

Although it was difficult to ascertain the location of the reform units in many countries, we were able to ascertain the physical location of the reform effort in thirty-three countries. Most of these reform units were in specially created units. The creation of special, nonbudgetary units for

Table 10-3. *Devolution or Decentralization of Central Government Powers and Authorities*

Decentralization movement	Recentralization
49	1
40%	. . .

reform speaks to the larger goals of many of these national efforts. In other words, modern public management reform is as much about performance as it is about saving money. While the two goals sit side by side in many reform movements—the title of Vice President Al Gore's first report on reinventing government was "Creating a Government That Works Better and Costs Less"—the attempt to make these efforts about more than money means that they end up, more often than not, in specially created units and not in the traditional budget unit of national governments as table 10-2 illustrates.

Devolution or Decentralization of Central Government Powers and Authorities

Devolution is a key element of government reform in many countries, as evidenced by the fact that fully 40 percent of the world's largest countries have made devolution a key element of their government reform movement. For many countries emerging from socialist, totalitarian pasts, the creation of local government and local power bases is the critical operational element in democratization, after the achievement of free and fair elections. Recognizing this fact, the democracy project of the U.S. Agency for International Development announced that in the 1999–2000 funding cycle it would support efforts aiding local government and support the continued enhancement of decentralization.[16]

The promotion of decentralization by a central government often involves a great deal of political altruism by those at the top (table 10-3). Only one country, Peru, went through what could be called recentralization during this time. In many countries a central government elite is essentially creating potentially competing political elites every time they devolve power to local units. This explains why in so many developing countries various elements of reform—including and especially decentralization—are imposed from the outside by development agencies.[17] And it also explains why, in countries such as Poland, the creation of local government units in 1999 marked a key, important step on the journey from totalitarianism to democracy. By 1999 Poland had managed to pass a law sharing tax revenues between the national and the new local governments and to create a series of county and regional governments.

But devolution is not merely a phenomenon of public management reform in emerging democracies, it is prevalent in mature democracies as well. The states of the European Union have seen an interest in the principle of subsidiarity. Borrowed from Roman Catholic social thought, subsidiarity means that government should be as close as possible to the governed. In the first chapter of this volume Robert Keohane and Joseph Nye point out that globalization seems to be accompanied by a simultaneous urge to relocalize many governmental functions. In the United States this has taken the form of a new interest in that old constant—federalism, the most recent example being the enactment of the 1996 welfare reform law that devolved power over welfare to the states.

In 1992 Japan, a country known for its highly centralized and rigid bureaucracy, initiated a Special Scheme for Promoting Decentralization. This plan involved the designation of thirty pilot municipalities and aimed to promote greater involvement of local governments in the design of social services. In 1995 Japan passed the Decentralization Promotion Law, which established an office in the prime minister's office designed to consult on a decentralization plan due in the year 2000.

Privatization of Enterprises That Had Been Owned by the Government

For many countries privatization is the starting point in government reform efforts as table 10-4 so clearly illustrates. Privatization and decentralization are the strategies adopted most frequently by countries that had strong communist or socialist pasts. Together they form the necessary first steps toward becoming participants in the democratic, global economy. Between 1979 and 1993 nationalized industries in Great Britain fell from 11 percent of GDP to 2 percent of GDP. The story of privatization as it relates to major industrial portions of the economies of different countries has repeated itself frequently throughout the past two decades of the twentieth century and does not need to be repeated here.

But while privatization has occurred largely in the sale of state-owned enterprises in Latin America and in the former communist countries,

Table 10-4. *Privatization of Public Services*

Privatization initiatives	Contracting out of pubic services in addition to privatization	None
74	7	49
60%	9% of the privatization initiatives	40%

another form of privatization has emerged—the privatization of what used to be regarded as core governmental services or contracting out. As more and more governments shed the "socialist hangover," privatization spread beyond the industrial arena to what used to be purely state functions. In 1995 in the newly democratic Republic of Georgia, the government set up an independent health care agency funded by mandatory employer and employee contributions. In the Netherlands, once the central government cut subsidies to municipalities, they had to figure out a less costly way of delivering services. This led to a wave of privatizations in municipal services and the end of practices such as the "truck system" in Amsterdam whereby all municipal services were obligated to use one another's services.[18] In the United States, passage of the 1996 welfare reform bill opened up the welfare-to-work grants to private, for-profit contractors. This has resulted in private industrial giants such as Lockheed-Martin getting into the welfare-to-work business.

Downsizing in the Public Sector

As often as government reformers protest to the contrary, what public management reform means in many countries is a significant downsizing in the public sector. Downsizing of the public sector is not, of course, unrelated to privatization. In country after country the most immediate effect of privatization has been to transfer thousands, if not millions, of workers from the public payroll to private payrolls. For instance, Hungary went through massive dismissals in state-owned enterprises between 1990 and 1992. About 1.7 million workers, constituting 8.7 percent of their labor force, were separated.[19]

Since so much of the more dramatic data on public sector downsizing appears to be a direct result of privatization we coded downsizing in three

Table 10-5. *Countries That Have Gone through One or More Periods of Downsizing in the Public Sector*

Countries where public sector down-sizing amounted to 25% or more of the work force	Countries where public sector down-sizing amounted to less than 25% of the work force	Countries that saw an increase in public sector employment	No change or no data available
13	28	12	70
11%	23%	10%	57%

ways. Some countries had a period of public sector downsizing that amounted to more than 25 percent of the work force. More common, however, as shown in table 10-5, were downsizings that amounted to less than 25 percent of the work force. And many countries did not change at all. Although the actual figures for many countries do not show massive declines in public sector employment, some argue that what is happening around the world is a significant slowdown in the rate of growth.[20]

Downsizing is fueled not only by privatization but by efforts to combat corruption in developing countries. A common feature of corrupt governments is to place "ghost workers" on the public payroll. Often downsizing is part and parcel of the requirements placed upon a government for aid. For instance, although the World Bank does not provide direct assistance for public sector retrenchment programs, they often include public sector downsizing in their umbrella agreements. Two authors who have studied these agreements write, "Under umbrella agreements, public sector retrenchment may be part of the overall package. In our survey, about 65 percent of the programs had this umbrella connection to World Bank financing."[21]

But public sector downsizing, especially in the developing world, is very difficult to achieve. Peru reduced its civil service by more than 100,000 people between 1991 and 1993 only to rehire 163,000 workers several years later.[22] In many countries there are no private sector jobs for public sector employees who are laid off. Officials in many developing countries envy the "buyout" provisions and other cash incentive plans that have been used in the United States and in other first world countries to downsize. However, they find that in spite of the long-term savings they lack the cash to offer downsizing incentives.

Table 10-6. *Countries with Civil Service Reform Initiatives*

Countries with civil service reform initiatives	No data
27	96
22%	78%

While downsizing is tied, most often, to a need to reduce overall government expenditures, it can be part and parcel of the democratization process as well. In South Africa, downsizing the largely white civil service so that it can be replaced with a more racially balanced civil service is key to the creation of a postapartheid state.

Downsizing of the state sector is prevalent in first world countries as well as in developing countries. In these countries we can anticipate even more rapid downsizings in the years ahead as the public sector catches up with the private sector in its use of information technology and proceeds to reap the productivity gains that are now commonplace in the private sector.

Civil Service Reform Efforts

Getting rid of "ghost workers," rooting out other forms of corruption, and dealing with the inefficiencies that lead to excess personnel is only the beginning for many national reform movements. As these movements mature, it is clear that many countries are looking for ways to fix the civil service system itself so that civil servants are motivated, trained, and held accountable. Much of the world inherited some version of the Anglo-American civil service—pioneered in Britian in the mid-nineteenth century and in America in the late nineteenth century. Increasingly, this old model of how government employment should operate is coming under fire. As tables 10-6 and 10-7 illustrate, nearly one-quarter of the world's largest countries are trying one or more reforms in the civil service. Most of these reforms attempt to tie employment more closely to performance, thus making the government work force more like the private sector work force. In fact, in the Netherlands, the civil service reform process is explicitly referred to as the "normalization" process, a reference to the attempt to make the civil service more like the "normal" workplace.

In another example of the trend toward "normalizing" the civil service, Brazil created a 1998 administrative reform package that allowed for the

Table 10-7. *Types of Civil Service Reforms in Various Countries*

Cleaning up personnel rolls, hiring freezes	*Making it easier to hire and fire civil servants*	*Pay systems linked to performance*	*Flexibility in hiring and job descriptions*	*Collective bargaining reforms*	*Profession-alization and intro-duction of merit systems*
Costa Rica	Australia	Denmark	Ireland	New	Portugal
Togo	Netherlands	Hong Kong	Spain	Zealand	Hungary
Benin	Brazil	Austria		Australia	Poland
Bulgaria		Zambia		Canada	
South Korea				United	
South Africa				States	
Brazil					

dismissal of public workers when their performance was inadequate, capped the civil service wage bill, and enabled the public sector to hire workers under conditions similar to the private sector. However, in a story all too familiar to those who have tried to enact civil service reform, the enabling legislation did not pass. In 1999 Brazil did pass, however, the Camata Law, which limits personnel expenditures at all levels of government to 50 percent of current revenues at the federal level and 60 percent of current revenues at the state and municipal level. Governmental entities that do not comply cannot increase salaries, create new positions, or fill existing positions, and transfers from the federal government can be suspended.

Civil service reform in the United States, at the federal level, has not progressed very far, although with every passing year agencies of the federal government get legislation removing them from Title V, the civil service statute. However, the state of Georgia, in a move being watched by many other states, abolished its civil service system in 1996 and began hiring new workers on a performance system. Other states will clearly be tempted to do the same thing. It is probably fair to say that the civil service system of the nineteenth century will not survive too far into the twenty-first century without significant reform.

Service to the Citizen

Like civil service reform, an emphasis on service delivery is another reform that does not have immediate financial implications. Most countries have

Table 10-8. *Reforms in Service Delivery Such as Customer Service or Citizen Charters*

Service delivery reform initiatives	None
26	97
21%	79%

been influenced by the efforts in the United Kingdom to establish, in the late 1980s, Citizen Charters, which articulated explicit performance standards for everything from waiting times at the National Health Service to expectations for the punctuality of the railway system.

Efforts to improve service to the citizen appear in many countries, as table 10-8 illustrates. Portugal has established Quality Charters for public services, which contain explicit service commitments to customers. In Ireland, citizen service has been at the core of its most recent government reform movement, as indicated by its title, Delivering Better Government. They state that the goal of the movement is to view "the public as customers, clients and citizens of the state." One-stop shops, the creation of ombudsman's offices, and other improvements such as the 50 percent drop in waiting times at Argentina's social security office, reflect an emphasis on reform that goes beyond the financial. In Italy, one-stop shops exist where citizens can do everything they need to start a new business or expand an old one in one place.[23] In the United States, the telephone service offered by the Social Security Administration was rated above the telephone service of such marketing giants as L. L. Bean.[24] Australia's Centrelink progam has been studied by many other countries. It is the ultimate in one-stop shopping for the citizen, integrating customer access to government services.

As table 10-8 illustrates, nearly a quarter of the world's largest countries have made service to the citizen part and parcel of their reform efforts. This reform is not limited to first world countries only. In 1999 the Republic of Mali created one-stop investment windows for new businesses. At its core citizen charters—or customer service, as the American reinventing government movement dubbed it—is about restoring trust in government. Batho Pele is a Sesotho adage meaning "People First." It is also the title of a South African government "White Paper on Transforming Public Service Delivery." Published in September of 1997, under the leadership of Zola Skweyiya, the paper is testament to the importance of

Table 10-9. *Countries with Financial Management and Budgetary Reforms*

Countries with financial management and budget reform initiatives	No data available
37	86
30%	70%

administrative reform and citizen service in the creation of a postapartheid South Africa.

Budget and Financial Management Reform

While the initial impetus for large-scale national reform movements is often a financial crisis that requires some immediate and dramatic shrinking in the size of the public sector, another sign that modern reform movements are about more than budget cutting is the interest in financial management reforms. In addition a variety of experiments in public sector budgeting seem to be going on around the world. For some of the countries counted in table 10-9, financial management reform is simply the creation of basic systems, but for other countries such as those listed in table 10-10, the reforms resemble the reform attempts in the arena of the civil service. Performance-based budgeting, the use of new accounting systems, and the general interest in accountability exhibited by some of these reform movements are part and parcel of an effort to bring the public sector's financial management more in line with commonly accepted practices in the private sector. Like civil service reform, many of the experiments in

Table 10-10. *Examples of Financial Management and Budget System Reforms in Various Countries*

Performance management and budgeting	New accounting systems such as accrual accounting	New accountability systems such as inspectors general or comptroller general
Costa Rica, Ireland, Finland, Sweden, France, United States	Austria, Portugal, Australia, South Africa, Italy	Greece, Mexico

financial management reform seek to close the gap between the public and the private sector.

Regulatory Reform Initiatives

Nearly one-quarter of the world's largest countries have tackled the difficult problem of regulatory reform. For some developing countries the challenge is to create a regulatory structure that is honest and reliable. In addition, many countries find themselves having to create regulatory systems to oversee newly privatized sectors of the economy. Other countries find that they need to have some process for calculating the cost of regulations, lest regulations become an undue burden on a developing economy. And still others find that they need to get rid of an unhealthy amount of over-regulation in order for business to thrive. In 1998 in the Ukraine, a presidential decree reduced the need for licensing, simplified registration procedures, limited inspection and control procedures, and established the State Committee of Ukraine on Entrepreneurship Development.

Regulatory reform is one area in which a clear distinction tends to be made between mature free market democracies and developing countries. For many developing countries, the regulatory sector is the locus of governmental corruption. For them, the challenge is the creation of an effective system in the first place. In first world countries, regulatory reform efforts tend to be about simplification and to involve efforts to change the regulatory paradigm from an emphasis on enforcement to an emphasis on compliance. In a system that is more corrupt than honest, this paradigm shift sounds like an invitation to more corruption. In countries with traditions of public honesty, however, the move to encourage voluntary compliance meets a variety of goals having to do with making the regulatory process more efficient. Tables 10-11 and 10-12 summarize the presence of regulatory reform initiatives among the world's largest countries and gives some examples of the types of regulatory initiatives found.

Injecting Competition into Government

If devolution, privatization, and downsizing are all part and parcel of efforts to shrink the size of the state, and in particular its central bureaucracy; civil service reform, customer service initiatives, budget and financial reform and regulatory reform are about efforts to improve the quality and

Table 10-11. *Countries That Have Regulatory Reform Initiatives*

Countries with regulatory reform initiatives	No initiatives or no data available
30	93
24%	76%

accountability of governments. The final two elements of reform are ones that have the potential to move a nation's public administration beyond the traditional bureaucratic paradigm.

For example, the notion of injecting competition into government is a relatively new concept, but one that is being watched the world over (table 10-13). Essentially it is an attempt to bring the discipline of the market to the public sector. The leading innovator in this field is New Zealand, whose dramatic efforts to open its public services to competition and to separate, in the language of Osborne and Gaebler, "steering and rowing" have made government reform nearly as popular an export as sheep. In the United Kingdom the creation of next-step agencies, which evolved into executive agencies, constituted an admission by Prime Minister Thatcher that not all of government could be privatized and that something had to be done to reform the public sector. In the United States the effort is to create performance-based organizations—or PBOs. By creating internal competition or executive agencies, governments hope to bring innovation and efficiency to the public sector. It is but one more step in closing the gap between public and private sector management.

Table 10-12. *Types of Regulatory Reform Initiatives Found in Various Countries*

Laws initiated requiring that the costs of regulations be calculated	Regulatory systems created to oversee newly privatized sectors of the economy	Survey and review of regulations with goal of reduction and simplification
New Zealand, South Korea, Mexico	Bolivia, Chile, Ghana, Brazil	Portugal, Netherlands, Australia, Canada, Italy, United States, Ukraine

Table 10-13. *Injecting Competition into Government; Creation of Internal Government Markets, Creation of Executive Agencies*

Creation of internal government markets	No data available
7	116
Ireland, New Zealand,	94%
Guatemala, Australia, United	
Kingdom,Tanzania, United States	
6%	

Making Use of Information Technology

Nothing, however, has the potential to change public administration as much as the increased use of information technology. In almost all countries, the public sector is way behind the private sector in this area. The use of information technology as an integral part of government reform is not limited to first world countries. Burkina Faso has a computerized system that tracks every stage in the expenditure process from commitment to actual payout. In Honduras, a simplified automated system allows for faster processing of documents and reduces the discretion of customs agents—a big help in the fight against corruption. Nevertheless, as table 10-14 shows, information technology is still not as common as it could be.

Conclusion

This survey of the world's 123 largest countries shows that significant government reform is going on around the world and that, to a remarkable

Table 10-14. *Countries Making the Use of Information Technology an Explicit Part of Their Public Management Reform Efforts*

Countries making information technology a part of reform	No data available
14	109
11%	89%

degree, similar kinds of reform efforts exist in very different countries. That Tanzania purports to have created "executive agencies"—a concept borrowed directly from British reform efforts—and that the United States adapted its PBO concept from the same British reform effort shows considerable global imitation.

Besides "demand-pull" imitation there is, no doubt, much "supply-push" promotion going on around the world, led in large part by development agencies who have realized that state capacity is a critical element in economic development. According to Merilee Grindle in this volume, "Specialists in economic development, who in the early and mid-1980s had demonstrated a strong antistate bias in their reform proposals, began to discuss the need for capable states to manage macroeconomic policies and carry out a series of essential activities if market systems were to generate growth."

American cultural dominance also plays a large role in the adoption of administrative reforms around the world. And for those who, as Fred Schauer points out in this volume, purposely avoid copying the United States, there are other countries to emulate, such as Great Britain, New Zealand, Canada, and Australia, who have pioneered significant public administration reforms.

Finally, many countries are making governmental adjustments to the new global economy. Throughout the first world even left of center parties, which used to view the state as the solution to many problems, are now more willing to go along with demands for a smaller, more streamlined state. In Sweden, for instance, Flynn and Strehl write, "Whereas public spending and state intervention were previously seen as 'solutions' they were now, for the first time, perceived as problems."[25]

There does seem to be a pattern to government reform at the beginning of the twenty-first century. For many countries, government is barely functioning, and reform efforts are aimed at bare basics, such as establishing the rule of law. For others, reform means first and foremost adapting to the new global economy, mostly through privatization of state-run industries. For others privatization is followed by a concern for building state capacity sufficient to support a new private economy. And for still others, mostly advanced industrial democracies, reform is about moving beyond a twentieth-century bureaucratic paradigm and creating governments that are closer in their efficiency and capacity for innovation to the private sector. These stages are summarized in figure 10-2.

Figure 10-2. *Stages in Government Reform*

Level 1	Level 2	Level 3	Level 4
Establish the rule of law	Privatize state industries and move to a market economy	Build the capacity of the state to support a market economy	Reform the state beyond the bureaucratic paradigm

There is, no doubt, much more work to be done on this topic. Determining the extent to which the self-reports of governmental reform efforts are true is a project in itself. There can be no doubt, however, that for several reasons the end of the twentieth century has seen a revolution in public administration that is every bit as profound as that which occurred at the turn of the nineteenth century, when Weberian bureaucratic principles began to influence many governments around the world. How real, and how extensive, this revolution in government reform is remains to be seen.

Notes

1. For example, according to Flynn and Strehl, France is a good example of reform rhetoric masking a traditional reality where a strong central government, politicians, and a grands corps of civil servants have a shared interest in maintaining their power. Norman Flynn and Franz Strehl, eds., *Public Sector Management in Europe* (Hempstead, Prentice Hall Europe, 1996), p. 123.

2. Flynn and Strehl, *Public Sector Management in Europe*, p. 1.

3. Donald F. Kettl, "Management Reform for the 21st Century: Challenges for Governance, a Report of the Brookings Institution" (Brookings, 1999), p. 9.

4. See Ann Marie Slaughter, "The Real New World Order," *Foreign Affairs*, vol. 76 (September–October 1997), pp. 183–97.

5. Jeff Garten, "A Glass Half Full," *Foreign Affairs*, vol. 78 (July-August 1999), pp. 112–15.

6. Thomas Friedman, *The Lexus and the Olive Tree* (Farrar, Straus, Giroux, 1999). p. 201.

7. Prime Minister Jenny Shipley speaking at the opening session of the Global Forum on Reinventing Government, Washington, January 1999.

8. Shipley, Global Forum.

9. Governing Treasury Board of Canada for Canadians, "Getting Government Right" (Ottawa, 1997), p. 1.

10. See Mary E. Hilderbrand and Marilee S. Grindle, "Building Sustainable Capacity in the Public Sector: What Can Be Done?" in *Getting Good Government, Capacity Building in the Public Sectors of Developing Countries* (Harvard University Press, 1997), pp. 31–62.

11. Global Forum, Washington.

12. Flynn and Strehl, *Public Sector Management in Europe*, p. 3.

13. For an excellent catalogue of governmental successes, see Derek Bok, "Measuring the Performance of Government," in Joseph S. Nye, Philip D. Zelikow, and David C. King, eds., *Why People Don't Trust Government* (Harvard University Press, 1997), pp. 55–75.

14. Arthur Miller and Ola Listhaug, "Political Performance and Institutional Trust," in Pippa Norris, ed., *Critical Citizens: Global Support for Democratic Governance* (Oxford University Press, 1999), p. 216.

15. See Franz and Strehl, *Public Sector Management in Europe*, p. 140.

16. http://www.info.USAID.gov/democracy/ee/nis.html.

17. See Grindle, "Getting Good Government."

18. See Flynn and Strehl, *Public Sector Management in Euope*, p. 99.

19. John Haltiwanger and Manisha Singh, "Cross Country Evidence on Public Sector Retrenchment," *World Bank Economic Review*, vol. 13 (1999), 23–66.

20. Andres W. Marinakis, "Public Sector Employment in Developing Countries: An Overview of Past and Present Trends," *International Journal of Public Sector Management*, vol. 7 (1994), pp. 50–68.

21. Haltiwanger and Singh, "Cross Country Evidence," p. 31.

22. Ibid., table A1.

23. Kettl, "Management Reform," p. 42

24. Vice President Al Gore, *The Best Kept Secrets in Washington* (Government Printing Office, 1996).

25. Flynn and Strehl, *Public Sector Management in Europe*, p. 37.

11

FREDERICK SCHAUER

The Politics and Incentives of Legal Transplantation

L AW HAS TRADITIONALLY been among the least global of social phenomena. Largely because the very concept of law has historically been
associated with national sovereignty, the idea of law without that sovereignty has been accepted only with the greatest of difficulty.[1] Indeed, the
prevalence in so many of the jurisprudential debates of the twentieth century of the question whether international law is law at all is important tes-
timony to the fact that for many people law and globalization are inherently contradictory ideas.[2]

The association of law with sovereignty has been steadily eroding in the
academic discussions of the philosophy of law but less so in popular understanding, or so it seems.[3] In many parts of the world, of which eastern
Europe, South Africa, and the republics of the former Soviet Union provide the best examples, the fact of political transformation has been coupled with a desire on the part of the transformed republic to have a legal
regime whose chief characteristic is its "indigeneity." To cast off the past is

Earlier versions of this paper have been presented at the Kennedy School's Visions of
Governance Conference on Globalization and Governance, Bretton Woods, New
Hampshire, at the Rule of Law Seminar Series at the World Bank, and as a research seminar paper at the Center for International Development, Harvard University, which also
provided generous research support.

253

to cast off the law of the past, so it often appears, and to cast off a colonizing (or dominating, as in the case of Eastern Europe) power is to cast off
all of the residue and emanations of the colonizing or dominating power's
legal structure and legal institutions.

The previous paragraph puts things too starkly, for there are as many
counterexamples as there are examples to the claims I have just announced.
Nevertheless, recalling the special political and social situation that legal
systems have, as symbols as much as anything else, is a useful preface to the
idea I wish to put forward here. And that idea is that the transnational and
cross-border spread of law and legal ideas is not, as it may be for scientific,
technical, and economic ideas, largely a matter of the power and value of
the ideas themselves but may instead be substantially dependent, both on
the supply side and on the demand side, on political and symbolic factors
that may have more explanatory power in determining how law migrates
than do factors that relate to the intrinsic or instrumental value of the
migrating law itself.[4] In this brief chapter I offer a series of testable
hypotheses about various factors, other than the factors of inherent value,
that may influence the patterns of legal migration and legal transplantation
and thus of legal globalization.[5] I do not set out to test the hypotheses, but
I offer a small bit of evidence for believing each of them plausible enough
to be deserving of more rigorous testing and examination.

Hypothesis One

Hypothesis 1: The effect of political, cultural, and social factors
extrinsic to legal or economic optimization is greater in determining
the patterns of transnational migration of legal ideas, institutions,
and structures than it is in determining the patterns of transnational
migration of scientific, technical, or economic ideas, institutions, and
structures.

As I suggested above, law making is commonly thought of as a central
feature of national sovereignty. What is significant is not whether this is in
fact the case, as a matter of the theory of sovereignty and the theory of
nationhood, but rather the very fact of the *belief* that this is so. For insofar as this belief prevails, nations, especially new and transforming nations,
may believe that indigenous law making is an important marker of a successful transformation. As a consequence they may choose to reject extra-

national influence, even when the extra-national influence is perceived to be valuable and well meaning. The new nations favor "doing it themselves," even if that means doing it less well.[6] Especially in developed but transforming countries, as, for example, most of eastern Europe, the larger of the former Soviet republics, and South Africa, relying too heavily on external advice in law making appears to be perceived as a sign of weakness and a lack of sophistication or a lack of capacity for independent governance. When nations have a desire to send the opposite signal, and thus to signal a capacity for independent and sophisticated governance, therefore, what we often see is at best a grudging willingness to accept external advice and models and a desire to engage in indigenous law making even when the product of that indigenous law making may otherwise be suboptimal.

This is not to say that indigeneity may not sometimes be related to legal effectiveness or to the end-states, usually economic, that legal effectiveness is thought to help produce. Research by Stephen Cornell and Joseph Kalt on constitution making in the American Indian nations and by Daniel Berkowitz, Katharina Pistor, and Jean-Francois Richard on cross-national legal transplants provides strong support for the conclusion that the fact of legal transplantation, independent of and controlling for the content of what is transplanted, may be causally related to various measures of legal or economic effectiveness.[7] As Cornell and Kalt demonstrate, what I have referred to as indigeneity may serve not merely a symbolic function and have not merely a symbolic effect, but may instead (or may as a consequence of the symbolic effect) be efficacious in producing economic success. Insofar as an indigenous process of law making and constitution making may foster and reinforce the social and political conditions and institutions that are themselves conducive to economic success,[8] indigeneity may be conducive rather than extrinsic to economic success.[9]

In similar fashion, Berkowitz, Pistor, and Richard demonstrate that legal effectiveness (and economic development, insofar as legal effectiveness is conducive of economic development) is not merely a function of the characteristics of formal law but is also a function of various potential inefficiencies of implementation when law is transplanted into an "alien" implementing or enforcing environment. This effect, which Berkowitz, Pistor, and Richard label the "transplant effect," appears to have substantial negative consequences on the effectiveness of laws and legal institutions.[10] As with the Cornell and Kalt findings, therefore, these results indicate that it would be a mistake to treat the distinction between indigenous law making and transplanted law as entirely extrinsic to the question of legal effectiveness and thus of the optimality of any law or legal regime.

Nevertheless, the point of this first hypothesis is a different one. Even fully taking into account the transplant effect or any of its variants, it may still be the case that various factors extrinsic to legal optimization broadly conceived will influence the final choice between indigenous law making and borrowing law from abroad. Insofar as these factors, factors relating to the symbolic importance of indigenous law making as well as to the national self-esteem produced by indigenous law making, play a role in determining the extent of legal globalization, and in determining the patterns of legal globalization, a model that looks only to optimization will remain necessarily incomplete. For if it is true that indigeneity for its own sake, as a form of national self-expression, a method of increasing national self-esteem, and a form of signaling to the world, is a goal that nations pursue in addition to and not as a part of legal optimization, then it will almost always be true that these goals and the goals of legal optimization will be in at least some conflict. Moreover, there is some reason to believe this phenomenon is greater for law than it may be for indigenous technical, scientific, or economic development. This first hypothesis, therefore, posits that the image of law as specially related to sovereignty, national self-expression and self-determination, national reputation, and national self-esteem will produce pressures toward indigenous law making that are greater than the pressures toward indigenous institution-creation in nonlaw domains.

Hypothesis Two

Hypothesis 2: Political, social, and cultural factors are more important in determining the patterns of legal migration for constitutional and human rights laws, ideas, and institutions than they are for business, commercial, and economic laws, ideas, and institutions.

Although there is reason to believe that what I have called "extrinsic" factors are at work throughout the realm of legal development and legal migration, there is also reason to suspect that the phenomenon of preferring indigenous law making for its own sake is especially true in the making of constitutions.[11] Nations and their political and legal leaders may perceive bankruptcy, securities, and other corporate and commercial laws as largely technical and nonideological, being largely instrumental to economic development,[12] and thus capable of being borrowed or copied from the analogous laws of other nations.[13] But this perception is rarely held in the case of constitutions.[14] For Estonia to have an American bankruptcy law (which it does, drafted largely by faculty and students of the Georgetown University Law School)[15] seems to most Estonians not much different from drinking French wine and from owning German cars, Japanese televisions, and Taiwanese bicycles.[16] But to have an American constitution is quite different and would suggest a loss of sovereignty, control, and much of the essence of what helps to constitute a nation as a nation in the first place.[17] For this reason, among others, the Estonian constitution is largely an internally drafted and internally conceived document, even though some of its drafters recognized at the time and still concede that as a technical legal instrument it leaves much to be desired, and even though those same drafters acknowledge that using a model from some other country would have produced a written constitution that was better structured, more internally coherent, and less likely to be in need of subsequent amendment.[18] Similarly, the new constitution of South Africa, created under conditions in which non-South African observers were omnipresent and non-South African assistance readily available, is almost an entirely indigenous document, bearing occasional parallels in certain provisions to the European Convention on Human Rights but otherwise remarkably free from external influence.[19] Indeed, in almost none of the new constitutions drafted in the past ten years has there been the kind of extra-national influence and imprint that one sees frequently in a wide range of economic and commercial laws.[20]

Probably the same pattern would exist for other laws that reflect central political values, including laws dealing with human rights, immigration, and voting and the other structural devices of political decisionmaking.[21] Although ordinary (nonconstitutional) laws on these subjects are not as central to the idea of nationhood as is constitution making, even ordinary laws on these subjects are, like constitutions, more likely to be perceived as political and thus more immune from influences that nations are likely to see as irrelevant or intrusive. While this is again a hypothesis and not a demonstration, it seems plausible to hypothesize that the family consisting of laws relating to individual rights, national identity, and political structure would be less influenced by external forces than the family of economic, business, securities, and commercial laws, just as it seems plausible to hypothesize that constitutions would be less influenced by external forces than would so-called ordinary legislation.

Hypotheses Three and Four

Hypothesis 3: The political reputation of the donor country, both internationally and in the recipient country, is a causal factor in determining the degree of reception in the recipient country of the donor country's legal ideas, norms, and institutions, even holding constant the host country's evaluation of the intrinsic legal worth of those ideas, norms, and institutions, and even holding constant the actual legal worth of those ideas, norms, and institutions.

Hypothesis 4: The desire of a country to be received or respected or esteemed by a particular group or community of nations bears a causal relationship to the degree to which that country will attempt to harmonize its laws with those of the group or community of nations, and also bears a causal relationship to the extent to which the country's laws will eventually resemble the laws of that group or community of nations.

Although politics in the broad sense may thus influence the decision whether to look abroad or not in the search for law in new and transforming nations, politics is even more apparent in the decision about where to look when it is decided that looking abroad may be useful. The experience of Canada as a successful "donor" nation of constitutional ideas provides a useful example. In many countries throughout the world, especially ones with an English language and common law legal tradition, the ideas and constitutionalists of Canada have been disproportionately influential, perhaps more influential than those of the United States.[22] One reason is that Canada, unlike the United States, is seen as reflecting an emerging international consensus rather than existing as an outlier. On issues of freedom of speech, freedom of the press, and equality, for example, the United States is seen as representing an extreme position, whether it be in the degree of its legal protection of press misbehavior and of racist and other forms of hateful speech or in its unwillingness to treat race-based affirmative action as explicitly constitutionally permissible.[23] People can of course argue about whether the United States is right or wrong, internally, to take these positions, positions that much of the rest of the world sees as extreme, but that is not the point here. Rather, my point is twofold. First, ideas that are seen as close to an emerging international consensus are likely to be more influential internationally. Second, nations seeking to have more international legal influence may at times, recognizing the first point, create their laws to maximize the likelihood of this extraterritorial influence. Canada appears to be a plausible example of both of these ideas, and the influence of Canadian constitutional ideas in many parts of the world appears to be partly a function of the extent to which Canada has the virtue of not being the United States.[24] But such weight is also a function of the extent to which following Canada, or at least being influenced by Canada (as in South Africa, for example), is seen as a wise route toward harmonization with emerging international norms.[25]

The importance of harmonization exists in other legal domains as well. Those nations who wish to join Europe, literally and figuratively, appear increasingly to believe that having legal systems that look European will increase the likelihood of their successful entry into the European community.[26] And given that Germany is the most legally and economically significant of the European nations, we have seen in the Baltics and in eastern Europe a substantial effort by various nations to design their laws on German models. Most commonly, this effort is not based on a belief that German law is superior in any way but rather on the belief that harmonization with Germany will itself make the harmonizing nation look more European and will itself produce a legal regime that is already coordinated with the transnational community that the nation wishes to join.

Much the same applies to a larger international community. The new constitution of South Africa, unlike any other constitution in the world, explicitly mandates that the South African Constitutional Court and other courts take into account public international law and explicitly encourages courts to take into account "comparable foreign case law" in interpreting the constitution of South Africa.[27] As is clear from the debates leading up to the adoption of this provision, the motivation was only partly the desire to have South African judges learn from experiences elsewhere. Much more was it a reaction against South Africa's recent history as an outcast or pariah nation, and thus this provision appears to reflect a South African desire to have its judges bring South Africa into harmony with international standards, independent of a normative judgment about the intrinsic desirability of those international standards.[28]

This goal of harmonization for the sake of harmonization was especially apparent in the South African debates about whether speeches or publications that incite racial hatred should be subject to punishment, as they are in much of the industrialized world, or whether instead even these utterances should be protected by the ideas of freedom of speech and freedom of the press, as they are in the United States and a small number of other nations.[29] But although there was in South Africa clear knowledge of the American model, and although the American point of view was forcefully presented by a large number of South Africans, at the end of the day it was clear that it was simply politically unacceptable for South Africa, given its history, to refuse to join an international consensus on the importance of restricting communications that would incite or foster racial hatred.[30] In the final analysis, it was not the superiority of the idea that determined the outcome but the fact that the outcomes had vastly different political implications, internally and externally.

It is worthwhile to pause and reflect on the symbolic effect of legal transplantation. Clearly, in some political quarters, avoiding American influence just because it is American often appears to be a driving force. In other countries the politics and symbols may be different. In interpreting the constitution of the Republic of Ireland, Ireland's Supreme Court appears to go out of its way to use American precedents, and to go out of its way to avoid English law if at all possible.[31] Possibly concerned about the symbolism of being perceived as the "fifty-first state" of the United States, a worry of many Canadians, the Supreme Court of Canada also relies less heavily on American precedents than one might have predicted if the predictions were based solely on geographic proximity, cultural similarity, or even legal cross-fertilization. In looking for legal models and sources of legal influence, the Vietnamese appear studiously to avoid the French, while at the same time embracing the help of Denmark, which actively attempts to cultivate its legal influence in Vietnam, and Sweden, which maintained a strong diplomatic presence in Vietnam even throughout what the Vietnamese refer to as the "American War." In contrast to Canada, we see that Israel, even though having a quite different legal system from the United States, relies heavily on American precedents, while much of eastern Europe relies equally heavily on the German.[32] While membership in a common legal family (common law, civil law, Commonwealth law, and so on) explains some of the pattern on which countries rely, these and other examples suggest that the patterns may be far more politically and culturally complex and that membership in the same legal family is only one small part of the full story.

Because the citation practices of courts, unlike other forms of legal transplantation, contain an explicit record of what the sources were and where they came from, it is not surprising that judicial citations are especially susceptible to the phenomenon of symbolic effect.[33] Moreover, dramatic changes in the technology of legal information are making it remarkably easy for courts and lawyers to have access to the decisions in other countries.[34] Thus, the very ease of access is a factor in legal transplantation, as well as what might be called the politics and sociology (and incentives) of database design. Which countries have put their decisions and laws on the Internet? Which have put their decisions and laws on standard databases such as LEXIS and WESTLAW? Which countries have the database designers at LEXIS and WESTLAW selected for inclusion? Which countries have made their laws and decisions available in languages other than the language of the home country, most commonly English but occasionally French and German? And so on. All of these factors, and more, are likely to influence patterns of citation and patterns of influence, as much as, if not more than, the inherent persuasiveness or authority of one decision rather than another.[35]

Hypothesis Five

Hypothesis 5: The existence of self-interested and self-protective strategies of institutional influence, whether by governments, non-governmental organizations (NGOs), or private sector entities, plays some causal role in determining the patterns of transnational legal proliferation.

Laws do not have wings. The process of legal migration is not a function of actions by laws themselves or even by some invisible hand. Rather, the transmission of legal ideas is a function of human action, and the humans that are taking the action have their own incentives, motivations, and norms. And this applies much more strongly to organizations and institutions. When the Georgetown University Law School becomes heavily involved in the making of Estonian commercial, bankruptcy, and securities law, this involvement is, one can assume for the sake of argument, good for Estonia, but it is also good for the reputation of Georgetown University Law School. And if this is true for the Georgetown University Law School, one would expect much the same for the American Bar Association, the U.S. Information Agency, the U.S. Agency for International Development, the Reporters Committee for Freedom of the Press, and a panoply of other public sector, private sector, and nonprofit organizations, to say nothing of parallel organizations in other countries. To ignore the effect of the motivations of such organizations on legal migration seems a clear mistake.

We might hypothesize a bit about what that effect might be. For one thing, it might be an effect that inclines toward overtransplantation or oversupply. Whatever complex incentives the various law-supplying entities might have, holding down the supply does not appear to be among them. Moreover, in some cases the same entities that have the ability to supply laws also have the ability to create incentives for other countries to adopt them. The government of the United States, through the U.S. Agency for International Development, the U.S. Information Agency, and numerous other governmental or quasi-governmental institutions, can provide assistance to countries that are looking for legal models. But the government of the United States, through the Department of State, evaluates, among other things, the laws of other countries on various human rights dimensions. And although there is no reason to believe that there is close collaboration between the supplying function and the evaluating function, it would also be surprising if having an American-style law was not relevant to the evaluation or at least what the recipient country perceived to be relevant to the evaluation. To the extent that a country preferred to be praised rather than condemned in the Department of State's human rights report, then it is not implausible to suppose that that country might believe, whether correctly or incorrectly, that modeling its human rights laws on those of the United States would be helpful in achieving this goal.

It is also possible that this effect would be one in which less influential players, actively trying to create their place and the esteem in which they are held in the international community, would expend greater efforts than would more established donor nations.[36] When Danish authorities talk about "positioning themselves" to maximize their contribution to planned Vietnamese constitutional revision, it is no insult to the Danes, but merely an observation about normal human (and national) incentives and motivations, to infer that Denmark is concerned not only about Vietnam but also about Denmark, and that Denmark's self-interested concerns have something to do with the possibility that a small country not generally thought of as a major player in international circles could have a serious impact on constitutional development in a large and potentially important nation.

Much the same might apply to nongovernmental entities. Freedom House, created by the Gannett Foundation, provides the index by which democratic liberties throughout the world are commonly evaluated, and Freedom House is active in assisting various countries with press laws and press freedom. Transparency International sponsors conferences to assist countries in achieving transparency and avoiding corruption and publishes a highly influential international index of perceptions of corruption. These indexes are good for researchers, they are good for the causes of civil liberties and the fight against corruption, but they are also good for Freedom House and for Transparency International.

None of this is pernicious, and I do not mean to be taken as suggesting some grand conspiracy theory. Rather, and benignly, I mean only to suggest that the human and institutional agents of the cross-border transmission of legal ideas and models are more or less well funded, more or less politically connected, and more or less concerned with preservation of their own reputation, influence, power, wealth, and pleasure. No more but no less than any other institution, the institutions of legal migration are institutions whose own incentives and structures are likely to be causally relevant to which legal ideas are spread, how often, with what force, by whom, and to whom.

Conclusion

The foregoing impressions, anecdotes, and observations suggest one large hypothesis and numerous subhypotheses. The large hypothesis, so obviously true as to be hardly worth examining, is that factors other than the receiving nation's own evaluation of the worth of legal ideas, and other than an objective assessment of the worth of legal ideas, are significant determinants of the patterns of legal transplantation and legal globalization. The subhypotheses, however, seem plausibly correct but look to be ripe candidates for testing. These subhypotheses are the ones that I have listed above, and there are no doubt more theories, and they are the ones whose systematic and rigorous testing might well provide new information about how legal ideas, legal institutions, and legal structures find their way from one country to another.

Notes

1. This is an idea most closely associated with John Austin, especially in H. L. A. Hart ed., *The Province of Jurisprudence Determined and the Uses of the Study of Jurisprudence* (London: Noonday Press, 1954). See also Jeremy Bentham, *Of Laws in General* (London:

Athlone Press, 1970); A.V. Dicey, *Introduction to the Study of the Law of the Constitution*, 10th ed. (London: Macmillan, 1959), pp. 39–85; Thomas Hobbes, *Leviathan* (1651); and W. J. Rees, "The Theory of Sovereignty Restated," in Peter Laslett, ed., *Philosophy, Politics and Society* (Oxford: Basil Blackwell, 1956).

2. H. L. A. Hart, *The Concept of Law*, 2d ed. (Oxford: Clarendon Press, 1994), pp. 213–37; R. W. M. Dias, "Mechanism of Definition as Applied to International Law," *Cambridge Law Journal* (1954), pp. 226–31; and Glanville Ll. Williams, "International Law and the Controversy concerning the Word 'Law,'" *British Yearbook of International Law*, vol. 22 (1945).

3. See Hart, *The Concept of Law*, pp. 236–37.

4. For an admirable but unfortunately rare attempt to confront some of these issues, see the various papers in Markku Suksi, ed., *Law under Exogenous Influences* (Turku, Finland, Turku Law School, 1994).

5. On the concept of legal transplants, see generally Alan Watson, *Legal Transplants* (Edinburgh: Scottish Academic Press, 1974); Alan Watson, "Legal Change: Sources of Law and Legal Culture," *University of Pennsylvania Law Review*, vol. 131 (1983), pp. 1121–46; Alan Watson, "Legal Transplants and Law Reform," *Law Quarterly Review*, vol. 92 (1976), pp. 79–96. See also T. B. Smith, "Legal Imperialism and Legal Parochialism," *Juridical Review (New Series)*, vol. 10 (1965), pp. 39–54.

6. I exclude from my discussion cases of outright coercion, as with the post–World War II constitutions of Japan and West Germany. See David P. Currie, *The Constitution of the Federal Republic of Germany* (University of Chicago Press, 1994).

7. Stephen Cornell and Joseph P. Kalt, "Where Does Economic Development Really Come From? Constitutional Rule among the Contemporary Sioux and Apache," *Economic Inquiry*, vol. 33 (1995), pp. 402–16; Stephen Cornell and Joseph P. Kalt, "Reloading the Dice: Improving the Chances for Economic Development on American Indian Reservations," in *What Can Tribes Do? Strategies and Institutions on American Indian Reservations* (University of California at Los Angeles, 1992). Daniel Berkowitz. Katharina Pistor, and Jean-Francois Richard, "Economic Development, Legality, and the Transplant Effect," Working Paper (Harvard University, Center for International Development, November 1999).

8. One explanation for the phenomenon may be that indigenous law making operates as a kind of focal point for cooperative law-making behavior that can then serve as the focal point for cooperative economic behavior. Another is that the institutions themselves are necessary for economic development, and that indigenous institutions function better than transplanted ones. On these and related issues, see Douglas North, *Institutions, Institutional Change, and Economic Performance: The Political Economy of Institutions and Decisions* (Cambridge: Cambridge University Press, 1990); Robert Barro, "Determinants of Economic Browth: A Cross-Country Empirical Study," Working Paper 5698 (National Bureau of Economic Research, August 1996); Richard A. Posner, "Creating a Legal Framework for Economic Development," *World Bank Research Observer*, vol. 13 (1998), pp. 1–11.

9. In the case of American Indian nations within the United States, the alternative to indigeneity has been law produced in implanted and pre-packaged form by U.S. federal authority, in particular the production of generic constitutions by the U.S. Department of Interior pursuant to the Indian Reorganization Act of 1934, 73 P.L. 383, 48 Stat. 984, ch. 576, 25 U.S.C. 461 (1996).

10. Berkowitz, Pistor, and Richard conclude that legality is approximately one-third lower in transplant effect countries than where there is no transplant effect, controlling for an impressive range of other variables. For a similar suggestion, but without the same degree of empirical testing, see A. E. Dick Howard, "The Indeterminacy of Constitutions," *Wake Forest Law Review*, vol. 31 (1996), pp. 383–406, esp. pp. 402–04.

11. On a potentially large array of factors that might make constitution making different from ordinary law making, see Jon Elster, "Forces and Mechanisms in the Constitution-Making Process," *Duke Law Journal*, vol. 45 (1995), pp. 364–81.

12. See John J. A. Burke, "The Economic Basis of Law as Demonstrated by the Reformation of NIS Legal Systems," *Loyola International and Comparative Law Journal*, vol. 18 (1996), pp. 207 ff., offering an account of legal development that is "derivative" of straight economic objectives.

13. This is not to say that such perceptions are correct, for there are ideological and political assumptions built into even the most technical of commercial laws. The decision to choose as a model the highly technical securities laws of California rather than the highly technical securities laws of many other states (and the U.S. federal securities laws) is to choose a model of substantive regulation over a model of full disclosure, a choice that goes directly to the center of debates about the role of the state and the limits of its authority.

14. On the specially political nature of constitution making, see Stephen Holmes and Cass R. Sunstein, "The Politics of Constitutional Revision in Eastern Europe," in Sanford Levinson, ed., *Responding to Imperfection: The Theory and Practice of Constitutional Amendment* (Princeton University Press, 1995).

15. J. Peter Byrne and Philip G. Schrag, "Law Reform in Estonia: The Role of the Georgetown University Law Center," *Law and Policy in International Business*, vol. 25 (1994), pp. 449ff. Similarly, the bankruptcy law in Armenia is largely a product of the University of Maryland, and the non-Romanian, but international consulting company, Deloitte and Touche had a substantial influence on Romanian bankruptcy law. See Samuel L. Bufford, "Bankruptcy Law in European Countries Emerging from Communism: The Special Legal and Economic Challenges," *American Bankruptcy Law Journal*, vol. 70 (1996), pp. 459ff.

16. Cultural products such as movies, books, and art are different, and many countries treat the indigenous production of these products (and occasionally the indigenous production of culturally significant food products) as being more of an embodiment of national identity than is the case with other products. This is perhaps most true for the mass media, where not only the mass media but also the laws controlling them, are taken to be of particularly national concern and thus least susceptible to transplantation. See, for example, "Mass Media Law and Practice: Lithuania, Latvia, and Estonia," in *Post-Soviet Media Law and Policy Newsletter*, vol. 55 (May 1999), pp. 1–8.

17. On a seemingly similar phenomenon in Poland, see Wiktor Osiatynski, "The Constitution-Making Process in Poland," *Law and Policy*, vol. 13 (1991), pp. 125–43; and Wiktor Osiatynski, "Perspectives on the Current Constitutional Situation in Poland," in Douglas Greenberg and others, eds., *Constitutionalism and Democracy: Transitions in the Contemporary World* (Oxford University Press, 1993), pp. 312–20.

18. Conversation with Eerik-Juhan Truuväli, Tallinn, Estonia, August 1992.

19. The South African experience suggests that another variable may be at work as well. Constitutions, now if not in 1787 when the fifty-five framers of the American Constitution

were literally locked in a room and sworn to secrecy, are often created in extremely public conditions. This circumstance produces not only very lengthy constitutions, as in South Africa and Brazil (114 and 229 pages respectively), but, it might be hypothesized, constitutions less externally influenced. Indeed, it might be hypothesized that publicity and political involvement reduces external influence and that secrecy and bureaucratic and technical control of the process increases external influence.

20. Moreover, as Katharina Pistor has suggested to me, constitutions may be especially immune from the effect on legal migration of being a member of the same legal "family." Thus, insofar as one might expect common law countries to follow models from other common law countries, civil law countries to follow models from other civil law countries, former French colonies to follow models from other French colonies, Spanish-speaking countries to follow models from other Spanish-speaking countries, and so on, one might hypothesize, plausibly, that this effect would be less pronounced in the case of constitutions than in the case of other sorts of laws from the pertinent countries.

21. For a general overview of patterns of American influence and American noninfluence, see Jacques deLisle, "Lex Americana? United States Legal Assistance, American Legal Models, and Legal Change in the Post-Communist World and Beyond," *University of Pennsylvania Journal of International Economic Law*, vol. 20 (1999), pp. 179ff.

22. The phenomenon appears to be strong not only in countries with a British Commonwealth background but also in countries as culturally removed from the British Commonwealth as Vietnam.

23. Largely because of the efforts of American journalists, itself a phenomenon worthy of careful investigation, media lawyers throughout the world know of *New York Times Co. v. Sullivan*, 376 U.S. 254 (1964), and its role in immunizing virtually all criticism of public officials and public figures, even factually false criticism, from legal liability. Interestingly, recent court decisions in Canada, South Africa, Australia, Spain, India, New Zealand, and the United Kingdom have made explicit reference to the American approach, but none has chosen to follow this approach.

The 1965 Convention on the Elimination of All Forms of Discrimination requires signatory nations to prohibit the "incitement to racial hatred." Largely because of the effect of First Amendment decisions such as *Brandenburg* v. *Ohio*, 395 U.S. 444 (1969) (protecting the speech of the Ku Klux Klan) and *Collin* v. *Smith*, 578 F.2d 1197 (7th Cir. 1978), cert. denied, 439 U.S. 916 (1978) (protecting the speech of neo-Nazis in Skokie, Illinois), the United States has consistently "reserved" (refused to sign) on this provision, for that which international law and international treaty requires remains under current doctrine plainly unconstitutional in the United States. See Mari Matsuda, "Public Response to Racist Speech: Considering the Victim's Story," *Michigan Law Review*, vol. 87 (1989), pp. 2320 ff.

In the United States, race-based affirmative action programs are increasingly being evaluated according to the same stringent standards as other race-based classifications (see *Adarand Constructors, Inc.*, 115 S. Ct. 2097 (1995); *Hopwood* v. *Texas*, 78 F.3d 932 (5th Cir. 1996), cert. denied, 116 S. Ct. 2581 (1996)), but the international trend, as witnessed in sec. 15(2) of the Canadian Charter of Rights and Freedoms and sec. 8(3) of the Constitution of South Africa, is to create explicit constitutional authorization for race-based classifications designed to "ameliorat[e] [the] conditions of disadvantaged individuals or groups" (Canada) or to "achieve the adequate protection and advancement of persons or groups or categories of persons disadvantaged by unfair discrimination" (South Africa).

24. But not, as noted above, constitutional structure or exact text.

25. See Kent Greenawalt, "General Principles of Free Speech Adjudication in the United States and Canada," in *Fighting Words: Individuals, Communities, and Liberties of Speech* (Princeton University Press, 1995), pp. 11–27.

26. "The Hungarian Constitutional Court may have held the death penalty unconstitutional at least in part because Hungarian political and legal elites believed that doing so was a precondition for entry into association with the European Union." Vicki C. Jackson and Mark Tushnet, *Comparative Constitutional Law* (Foundation Press, 1999), p. 171. See also George P. Fletcher, "Searching for the Rule of Law in the Wake of Communism," *Brigham Young University Law Review* (1992), pp. 145–63.

27. Constitution of the Republic of South Africa, §35(1).

28. For discussion of a possibly similar phenomenon in Turkey, see Paul J. Magnarella, "The Comparative Constitutional Law Enterprise," *Willamette Law Review*, vol. 30 (1994), pp. 509–32, esp. p. 516.

29. See note 16.

30. As exemplified in the 1965 Declaration on the Elimination of All Forms of Discrimination, 660 U.N.T.S. 195. See generally Matsuda, "Public Response to Racist Speech," pp. 2320–74, esp. pp. 2345–48.

31. A noteworthy example, not as unrepresentative as one might at first think, is the contraception case, *McGee v. Attorney General* [1974], Irish Reports 284.

32. See Dafna Sharfman, *Living without a Constitution: Civil Rights in Israel* (M. E. Sharpe, 1993). Israel, New Zealand, and the United Kingdom are the only industrialized democracies without written constitutions.

It is intriguing that in the raft of constitution making that has taken place throughout the world in the past decade, not a single country has chosen to follow the model of these countries. Every transforming country has chosen a formal written constitution, despite what one might think would be a desire on the part of those newly in power to avoid the external constraints that come from written constitutions. This choice suggests that the very idea of a written constitution has become an international norm, and that the unquestioned political stability of the United Kingdom and New Zealand, even if not Israel, has had remarkably little effect on the globalization of constitutional ideas.

33. On national differences in citation practices, see Elisabeth Holzleithner and Viktor Mayer-Schönberger, "Das Zitat als grundloser Grund rechtlicher Legitimität," in *Norm und Entscheidung* (Berlin: Springer Verlag, 1999).

34. This parallels the same computerization and database expansion that has dramatically increased access by courts to social science data, newspaper articles, and other forms of "nonlegal" information. See Frederick Schauer and Virginia J. Wise, "Legal Positivism as Legal Information," *Cornell Law Review*, vol. 82 (1997), pp. 1080–1110; and Frederick Schauer and Virginia J. Wise, "Non-Legal Information and the Delegalization of Law," *Journal of Legal Studies*, vol. 29 (January 2000), pp. 495–515.

35. Much the same could be said about interpersonal influence. Increasingly, lawyers, prosecutors, judges, and other legal officials find themselves personally interacting in various international forums with their foreign counterparts. And increasingly the connections

and alliances that develop not only influence the development and migration of law across borders but also have a quasi-legal status in themselves. So although in the text I stress the more formal indexes of law, everything I hypothesize likely applies as well to the patterns of interpersonal cooperation and thus to the migration of legal ideas that are the consequence of this interpersonal cooperation.

36. On esteem as a motivating force, see Richard H. McAdams, "The Origin, Development, and Regulation of Norms," *Michigan Law Review,* vol. 96 (1997), pp. 338–403.

PART III

The Governance
of Globalism

L. DAVID BROWN
SANJEEV KHAGRAM
MARK H. MOORE
PETER FRUMKIN

12

Globalization, NGOs, and Multisectoral Relations

THE RECENT MEETING of the World Trade Organization (WTO) in Seattle produced a remarkable spectacle for those interested in "globalization" and "governance" and in particular the role of nongovernmental organizations (NGOs) on the international scene. One key actor was the WTO: an emergent international institution that convened the world's economic ministers to negotiate the trade agreements that would allow money, goods, and people to flow across international boundaries. Much was at stake in these agreements for the world's countries and their citizens. Their structure would channel the courses of Joseph A. Schumpeter's "gale of creative destruction" across the world.[1] The economic, cultural, and political fortunes of countries and their inhabitants would be buffeted by the powerful transnational forces. Traditional cultures would flourish or be shoved aside. Natural resources would be preserved or extracted. The poverty of billions might be alleviated or intensified by the distribution of expanding wealth and opportunity.

Despite the magnitude of the stakes and the range of the stakeholders affected, the meetings had few of the distinguishing characteristics of democratic policymaking. The WTO itself was simply a collection of governments that had come together to negotiate economic trade agreements. There was no sovereign power or authority to be wielded; only the pressure to collaborate for mutual advantage as perceived by the participants. If any important decisions were made, they would be made through negotiation, not voting. The discussions would be highly technical—of intense interest to some but mostly opaque to ordinary citizens. It was expected that the ministers would do their business and then go home.

And then, the citizens of the world showed up. Some 1,300 groups—committed to varied visions of the public interest—assembled in Seattle to ask questions, make protests, and impose demands on the conferees. By the time the tear gas cleared, a reality recognized by many international actors for years had become highly visible to the U.S. public and the rest of the world: NGOs have become players in international governance.

Of course, neither globalization, nor a form of international governance, nor the emergence of a kind of transnational civil society undergirded by NGOs is entirely new. Globalization (understood as the thickening of the networks of interdependence spanning international boundaries that accompanies increasingly rapid and inexpensive movement of information, ideas, money, goods, and people across those boundaries) has been increasing for centuries.[2] NGOs and civil society alliances have also been active in international governance and policymaking for many years. Antislavery and women's rights advocates, for example, have built international NGO alliances to shape national and international policies for many decades.[3]

What *is* new is the recent explosion in numbers, activity, and visibility of international initiatives by civil society actors on a variety of issues, at least in part linked to the rapid expansion of globalization of communication, transportation, and production. Indeed, accelerated globalization has apparently coincided with the blossoming of civil society groups across the globe. The talent and instinct for voluntary association to address social problems is increasingly visible in the developing countries of Asia, Africa, and Latin America, and in the transitioning countries of eastern Europe and the former Soviet Union. Citizen associations have emerged to solve local problems, provide needed services, press for better government, ally with like-minded groups from other societies, and reshape the emergent processes of international governance.

An important question is whether the blossoming of civil society at national and international levels is merely coincident with globalization or whether there is something about the processes of globalization that spawns these enterprises. An equally important question is what impact these enterprises can be expected to have on the processes of globalization themselves. Will they tend to accelerate globalization by effacing national boundaries and uniting people in common ideological commitments? Or will they impede globalization by allowing those who feel pressured by the process to develop new enclaves that can be defended against global trends? A third question is what impact these organizations can be expected to have on the quality of governance at the national and international level. Will such organizations strengthen democratic accountability and make governments more responsive to the will of their peoples, and can they help citizens deal with the growing power of corporate actors? Or will they become agents for the more or less idiosyncratic goals of the social entre-preneurs who found NGOs and the aid organizations and foundations that support them?

This chapter begins an attempt to understand how a new class of eco-nomic, cultural, and political actors—civil society organizations—are being shaped by, and are themselves shaping, the processes of globalization, and what their implications might be for the quality of governance at national and international levels. We argue that globalization processes have contributed to the rising numbers and influence of NGOs in many countries, particularly in the international arena. We also briefly consider whether the emergence of domestic and international NGOs as important policymakers strengthens or weakens the future of democratic account-ability, and we suggest several patterns of interaction among civil society, government, and business in future governance issues.

Globalization as a Multifaceted Process

The thickening networks of interdependence created by increasing flows of ideas, goods, and people across geopolitical boundaries "shrinks the world," not only physically (by bringing us into more immediate, insistent contact with one another) but also psychologically (by making us more aware of our similarities and differences and our complex interdependencies).[4] This "shrinking world effect" shapes individual consciousness and action. And, as importantly, it shapes the ways in which individuals combine together in collective efforts to manage their lives and their circumstances. It attacks and undermines some institutional arrangements that have in the past done the work of providing to individuals an individual identity and some kind of satisfactory collective response to their circumstances. It stimulates the need and provides the opportunities for individuals to form new col-lective processes and institutions that can complement or replace the old institutions. In these respects, globalization is affecting the demand for and the supply of governance. Globalization has intensified with changes in the international political system, the international market economy, and transportation and information technologies. The collapse of the Soviet Union and the end of the cold war has spawned an international movement toward democracy. Formerly totalitarian regimes that had sustained themselves at least in part by acting as allies to either the United States or the Soviet bloc were suddenly exposed by the collapse of the Soviet Union and the end of the cold war. They were suddenly vulnerable to their own citizens and their long-suppressed demands for democratic regimes and could find no help from the powers that had once competed for their favor to secure cold war advantages. The internationalization of the market spurred by the free movement of capital and technology created new wealth and optimism throughout the world. But it left those at the bottom of the economic and social ladder vulnerable to exploitation even when things were going well and to dashed hopes when business cycles or economic mismanagement undercut economic growth. The rapid movement of people and information across the globe accentuated the grossly unequal political and material conditions in which the world's populations were living and stimulated a widespread demand for greater political and economic equality, as well as a broader sense of our economic, political, and moral interdependence.

These changes have contributed to a shifting balance in the roles of the state, the market, and the civil society, in individual countries and in the international political economy. In the past, when one looked at the international political economy, one would have concluded that obviously the dominant actors were sovereign states. They seemed to be in charge of what happened within their borders. What happened across their borders—in the international commons—emerged from interaction among individual states. In the past decade, however, the power of the market has expanded, and the role of the state has been reduced in many countries, in the West and North as well as the East and South. The shift to open macroeconomies has reduced the power of individual states to manage their own economic destinies. And since economic destinies were often important in influencing the stability of political regimes, the vulnerability of domestic governments to the international economy has been accentuated. In the face of powerful economic forces that were shaping the world, and the inability of states to offer much protection, movements have arisen to provide some kind of collective response. Sometimes these have been grassroots movements in certain parts of particular developing countries.

Other times, local grassroots movements have spread to become national movements. Still other times, local movements have made alliances with international organizations to help them achieve national purposes or to lend their weight to international efforts.[5]

Globalization provides information and perspectives never before available to many people, transporting them to new possibilities of international and cosmopolitan consciousness. The increased flows of information and people contribute to a global homogenization ("Americanization"?) of tastes, norms, and concerns. McDonald's hamburgers are available in Beijing and Buenos Aires, and language and music imports raise the hackles of cultural guardians in Paris and Singapore. At the same time, the assault of external ideas and values can inspire fierce defense of traditional values and styles of life. The NGOs may express and help to create cosmopolitan and international perspectives, and they may also express and defend the values and concerns of citizens alienated from globalized perspectives and cultural "imports." Thus NGOs may express or enable globalization, and they may also ardently resist globalization in a kind of sectarianism within and across national boundaries (for example, militant Islamic movements).

Civil Society and NGOs as Emerging Actors in the International Political Economy

The concept of "civil society" has been defined in many ways.[6] For the purposes of this chapter we focus on civil society as an area of association and action independent of the state and the market in which citizens can organize to pursue purposes that are important to them, individually and collectively.[7] Civil society actors include charitable societies, churches, neighborhood organizations, social clubs, civil rights lobbies, parent-teacher associations, unions, trade associations, and many other agencies.

Civil society actors can be distinguished from the government and business sectors on several dimensions.[8] While government seeks to provide public order and public goods, and uses its authority to raise the money and create the desired public conditions, and business works to provide private goods and services through the mechanisms of voluntary exchange, civil society actors seek to give force to citizens' values and purposes through their independent voluntary efforts, as well as through the influence that citizen groups can exert on business and government. If governments mobilize resources through legitimate coercion and taxation and businesses mobilize resources though resource exchanges, civil society organizations mobilize resources through appeals to values and social purposes. While businesses are oriented to private interests and governments are oriented to public interests, civil society actors focus on the interests of social groups within the society—including those groups disadvantaged by existing arrangements.

We are primarily concerned with civil society agencies, often referred to as NGOs, that focus on poverty alleviation, human rights, environmental degradation, and other issues of social, economic, and political development. These NGOs carry out a range of activities, such as providing services to poor populations, building local capacity for self-help, analyzing and advocating policies that support disadvantaged constituencies, or fostering research and information sharing.[9] Some NGOs concentrate on serving their members, and others focus on serving clients outside the organization. Some operate domestically, working on projects whose impacts may be felt from the village level to national policy to international arenas. Examples from the developing world include

—The Grameen Bank, which began as a Bangladeshi NGO experiment in microlending to poor entrepreneurs who had no collateral for bank loans. After demonstrating that small groups who shared responsibility for the loans had a repayment rate vastly superior to ordinary borrowers, the Grameen Bank expanded its operations to serve more than 2 million poor people, mostly women entrepreneurs in Bangladesh, and catalyzed an international microcredit movement supported by major donor institutions around the world.[10]

—The Narmada Bachao Andolan, an organization representing thousands of people "ousted" from their land by India's Narmada Dam project, has successfully challenged the decisions of central and state governments of India and the World Bank to build the dam in violation of Bank policies for resettling the ousted. The transnational alliance organized by the NBA has contributed to worldwide rethinking of the value of large dams, changes in policies and practice at the World Bank, and the establishment of the World Dams Commission to review the performance of large dams around the world.[11]

Both these examples describe initiatives launched by NGOs in developing countries that have expanded to affect international policies and programs. The microcredit movement promises to foster grassroots participation in developing economies, and the struggles over large dams have produced changes in international policies and decisionmaking institutions that have effects far beyond any single country or region.[12]

Many other international NGO initiatives have been launched from the industrialized world. Recent efforts by an international coalition to ban landmines succeeded in creating an international treaty in the teeth of resistance by many governments. A long struggle over sales of infant formula to mothers in the developing world eventually produced a near-unanimous UN agreement on a code of conduct for baby food sales. Wherever they were initiated, all four initiatives ultimately involved active participation by NGOs and civil society actors from developing and industrialized countries and so tapped a wide range of information and perspectives on the issues in question.

NGOs that seek to expand their impacts beyond local and national initiatives face significant organizational problems. One option is the establishment of an international NGO (INGO) that is organized to work across national boundaries.[13] Transparency International, for example, has member organizations in more than thirty countries that provide national support to the international initiative to identify and reduce corruption. A second way to organize for international action is to create a *transnational network* whose members share values, information, and a common discourse that enables them to coordinate their actions.[14] An example of a transnational network is the emergence of widespread linkages among NGOs and other actors concerned with environmental issues during the past two decades. Such networks allow exchange of information and strategies, but they are less useful for sustained coordination of activity or mobilizing large numbers of people for contentious politics. A third option is the creation of transnational coalitions among actors to coordinate shared strategies and tactics for influencing intentional decisionmakers. A coalition among national and international environmental NGOs and directors of the World Bank produced a reform in the Bank's information access policies as well as the creation of an Inspection Panel to investigate complaints about impacts of Bank projects.[15] Finally a fourth organizational form, transnational social movement organizations, links actors with shared purposes across countries to mobilize members for action. This is the most demanding form of international civil society organization and remains relatively rare.[16] The international women's movement comes close to being a transnational social movement, at least on some issues on which it can mobilize members to challenge opponents in several countries. The different organizational forms offer different capacities for international action as well as increasing demands for coordination of resources and commitments.

While civil society organizations are not a new phenomenon, a dramatic increase in their importance has occurred in many arenas during the past two decades. This change has been characterized by at least one researcher as a "global associational revolution" that may be as important to the end of the twentieth century as the rise of the nation-state was a century earlier.[17] By the count of the *Yearbook of International Organizations,* the number of international NGOs has grown more than fourfold in the past decade.[18] Although a great deal of variance in the size and activity of the civil society exists across countries, the sector is growing rapidly in many countries and regions. It is estimated, for example, that more than 100,000 civil society organizations have emerged in eastern Europe since the fall of the Berlin Wall, and more than 1 million NGOs are operating in India.[19] In part the rise of civil society organizations, especially development-oriented NGOs, is related to the availability of resources to support them. The growing interest of foundations, international donors, and even governments in supporting nongovernmental agencies has made funds available and created incentives for entrepreneurs to create NGOs that can make use of those funds. The result in many countries has been a proliferation of NGOs that are organized more to take advantage of those resources than to accomplish their nominally value-based missions. Not all civil society actors are equally serious about achieving social missions or public purposes, nor do all subscribe to the values of tolerance, reciprocity, and nonviolence that some argue are central to the definition of civil society.[20] As it has grown, civil society has spawned a great diversity that is now pushing in a multitude of different, even competing, directions. Civil society actors can easily become confused about their legitimacy and accountability; they can focus on single issues to the exclusion of understanding the larger context; and they may be better at blocking than implementing large-scale initiatives. But they are increasingly influential actors.

Globalization's Impacts on NGOs and Civil Society

In what ways does globalization affect NGOs and civil societies within nations and across national boundaries? While our main focus is on international NGOs and the evolution of transnational civil society, we begin with a discussion of the impacts of the globalization on domestic NGOs and national civil societies. The reason is that international initiatives often have their roots in national issues around which civil society actors first organized—and then these actors found that international initiatives were required to attack the problems involved. Even when international movements begin with international NGOs, they often need domestic NGOs to give them the political base and legitimacy they need to survive and be effective. And it may well be that some of the most important effects of international NGO activities are their impacts on domestic civil societies.

Globalization and National NGOs

Countries vary considerably in the extent to which civil society organizations are active in national life as well as how open they are to the impacts of globalization.[21] Some regimes appear determined to remain isolated from external influences (for example, North Korea or Burma), while others are committed to control any nonstate agencies that might be a threat to state power (for example, China). When national doors are opened to information, trade, and travel, however, the impacts on civil society and its organizations may be profound. The torrent of information now available through media, videos, faxes, and the Internet can very quickly raise the awareness of people at all levels of the society about how others live, spread ideas about factors that constrain their own and their neighbors' lives, and disseminate many alternatives to past practices. Increased consciousness about the wider world is almost inevitable.[22]

Exposure to this flood of information can challenge old beliefs and expectations, reawaken loyalties to old values and social identities, or provoke intense discussions of highly charged concepts like "women's liberation," "land to the tiller," or "ethnic cleansing." Information flows that resonate with core social values can be the basis for the emergence of civil society organizations or social movements that speak with powerful new voices in national policy and governance processes.[23] Contact with the larger world may also exacerbate the fact and heighten the awareness of economic discrepancies. Economic integration can provide more goods at decreased costs to individuals with resources, and it may offer new jobs as corporations relocate to use cheap labor. But it may also result in layoffs of government employees in response to structural adjustment programs, marginalize groups dependent on declining exports, or demonstrate through business failures how difficult it is to meet the standards of global competition. When the "poor get poorer," the clients to be served or mobilized by NGOs expand in number and in needs.

Globalization forces at the national level can reduce state controls over the economy, increase pressure for democratic accountability, or raise questions about state sovereignty. These developments can create political space for civil society organizations as alternative sources of services once provided by the state, watchdogs over and advocates for government policy formulation and implementation, policy entrepreneurs or implementers with state partners, and social innovators to guide improved services. When globalization expands political space, civil society actors may emerge to respond to the concerns of impoverished and marginalized groups that remained voiceless under prior regimes.

It is not immediately obvious that political, cultural, and economic facets of globalization will necessarily covary or reinforce one another. Globalization will not simultaneously highlight the importance of core cultural values or open more political space for civil society initiatives or create economic consequences that exacerbate poverty. Governments may open doors to international markets while trying to control the political implications of globalization or vice versa. They may also close their boundaries to cultural impacts. In general, however, the more open the country is to globalization, the more one would expect civil society organizations to become important national actors. This is a function of three factors: globalization has impacts on consciousness that are likely to be expressed through civil society organizations; globalization is likely to place enhanced emphasis on the political ideologies of individualism, freedom, and equal rights for which NGOs are both a product and an exemplar; and globalization invites in international actors (INGOs, international agencies) that actively promote and strengthen the emergence of national civil societies.

Globalization and International NGOs and NGO Alliances

The increases of information flows, human travel, and trade associated with globalization have on the whole made the formation and operation of international NGOs and NGO alliances easier and less expensive. The costs of international organization and coordination have been drastically reduced by the shrinking globe.[24] Globalization has also contributed to the rise of new problems to which international NGOs and alliances may be relevant. The rise of transnational environmental problems, such as global warming, ozone depletion, and cross-border pollution, has sometimes severely taxed the capacities of interstate institutional arrangements.[25] International NGOs and alliances have emerged to respond to problems associated with globalization in several arenas: delivering services and responding to disasters, analyzing and advocating policy alternatives, and promoting learning.

International NGOs and NGO alliances have been *responding to disasters and delivering services* for many years, and this is still the most common international NGO role. Most of these organizations originated in industrialized countries; many have branch organizations and large projects in developing countries. A recent conference of the eleven biggest international relief and development organizations (for example, CARE, OXFAM) identified several challenges associated with globalization.[26] The end of the cold war, for example, increased the frequency of intrastate conflicts and internal refugee flows, and public cutbacks have reduced the ability of state agencies to deal with conflicts and humanitarian crises. Globalization has increased poverty in many regions, and declining development assistance funds have increased competition among international NGOs for resources. An important consequence of these trends is significantly increased demand for assistance and seriously reduced capability to meet that demand. In short, for international service delivery NGOs, globalization is escalating needs for service while resources are declining. Many of these agencies also feel pressure from private and public donors to become more "businesslike" and "results oriented" in response to widespread emphasis on market-based approaches to management.[27] The rise of civil society organizations in many developing countries is also pressing international service NGOs to turn over local operations to southern NGOs. This change threatens to redefine their primary tasks and render their staffs largely obsolete. The effects of globalization are thus pressing many international service NGOs to undertake fundamental changes.

For international NGOs and alliances that focus on *policy analysis and advocacy*, the thickening networks of global interdependence created by globalization have raised a variety of issues that affect civil society. Sometimes initial organizations form at the international level and then build alliances with NGOs at the national and local levels. Transnational advocacy networks concerned with the environment, corruption, and human rights, for example, have often been launched by international NGOs that later allied with national and local partners.[28] In other cases, national

NGOs and social movements have built coalitions with international allies to influence national and international policymakers. For example, the indigenous peoples' movement in Ecuador sought international allies in a struggle over land reform, and similar groups in Brazil allied with international actors to stop proposed dam construction.[29] In both top-down and bottom-up alliances, the processes of globalization have built awareness of alliance possibilities, enabled easy exchange of information, and contributed to personal contacts among key actors. The targets of advocacy campaigns (for example, the World Bank) have often challenged the legitimacy of international NGOs that claim to represent grassroots constituents and so contributed to building genuine coalitions across large differences in wealth, power, and culture.

A third focus for a growing number of international NGOs and alliances is *interorganizational learning and problem solving*. In part these alliances and INGOs have emerged to respond to the emergence of global problems whose solutions depend on input from many different perspectives. The World Dams Commission, for example, is drawing on the perspectives of many different interested actors in assessing the impacts of large dams in economic and social terms. The International Forum on NGO Capacity Building has generated assessments of the capacities and needs of NGOs on three continents and proposed joint problem-solving initiatives with donors and governments to respond to those needs. Easy exchange of information and engagements in consultations enabled civil society actors to identify and agree on the nature of problems, explore causes, assess options, and agree on solutions and implementation plans— across geopolitical and cultural boundaries that would have seriously impeded such undertakings a decade ago.

Such cross-cultural contacts often involve managing divergences in norms and values that can set off misunderstandings and conflicts. As value-based organizations, international NGOs and NGO alliances are often highly sensitive to such conflicts. They can play critical roles in articulating and synthesizing issues across value differences and so help to mobilize publics on international concerns and problems. The Global Network on Violence against Women, for example, has helped to identify and illuminate the common themes in movements focused on violence problems around the world—dowry deaths in India, female genital mutilation in Africa, spouse abuse in North America, and rape and torture of political prisoners in Latin America.

Civil Society and International Governance

Globalization processes are clearly having an impact on civil societies and NGOs at national and international levels. Do those impacts have consequences for international governance and policymaking? Recent research suggests that international NGOs or NGO alliances are helping to formulate and implement many international decisions and policies.[30] They have shaped international events in at least the following ways:

—Identifying problematic globalization consequences that might otherwise be ignored;

—Articulating new values and norms to guide and constrain international practice;

—Building transnational alliances that advocate for otherwise ignored alternatives;

—Altering international institutions to respond to unmet needs;

—Disseminating social innovations that have international applications;

—Negotiating resolutions to transnational conflicts and disagreements; and

—Mobilizing resources and acting directly on important public problems. In these activities, international NGOs and NGO alliances have been building the attitudes and institutions for a transnational civil society that makes a different kind of international governance possible.

Civil society actors are often the first to use global information networks to identify international problems that are not raised or resolved by existing international arrangements. International NGOs involved in service or advocacy activities are often in close touch with otherwise voiceless populations and so recognize problems that remain invisible to other actors. Since their financial support depends on public visibility of problems, they also develop linkages to media to raise public awareness of critical problems. Transparency International, for example, raises awareness about problems of corruption around the world and its impact on development. The World Watch Institute publishes a "State of the World" report that helps global audiences to recognize threats to the global environment. Raising public awareness of problems is often a prerequisite to action, and international NGO initiatives can create global discourse on emerging problems.

A second role for NGOs in the global arena is to help construct international values and norms that can guide future international policies and

practices.[31] Thickening interdependencies are raising issues whose normative implications are unclear or diverse across cultures. International NGOs
and civil society alliances can help articulate values and norms to interpret
new problems, such as the issues of environmental sustainability, and in
articulating practices, such as environmental impact assessments, to guide
future policies.

Increasingly during the past decade, transnational civil society alliances
have been central to campaigns to formulate and enforce global public
policies in response to critical problems.[32] These campaigns have often
been mounted where existing institutional arrangements would not or
could not respond to emerging problems. For example, the International
Baby Food Campaign produced a code of conduct adopted by the United
Nations, and the International Rivers Network has been critical to assessing the impacts of dams and pressing for global policies to limit their
destructive impacts.[33] The alliances organized for these campaigns often
bacame important resources to future campaigns on other issues.[34]

A fourth role for international NGOs and NGO alliances is to create or
reform international institutions to improve response to global problems.
The World Bank, for example, has been the target of transnational alliances
concerned with reducing the secrecy of their operations and creating
avenues for local stakeholders to protest Bank projects that violate its own
policies.[35] These campaigns can create more responsive institutional arrangements for the future. In other cases campaigns have created new institutional arrangements to solve emerging problems. The World Dams
Commission, for example—the product of a series of campaigns against
large dams—is systematically evaluating actual dam performance.

International NGOs may affect the impact of globalization by creating
and disseminating social innovations that affect international governance
processes. The demonstrations at the WTO meeting in Seattle are only the
latest manifestation of "NGO forums" that have brought hundreds or
thousands of NGOs to high-visibility international meetings in the past
decade, such as the earth summit in Rio or the women's meeting in Beijing.
These efforts place the discussions at these meetings under a global spot-
light and afford opportunities for dialogue and advocacy to international
publics as well as government representatives.[36] Expanded and thickened
webs of interdependency across national and regional boundaries have
facilitated the dissemination of microcredit innovations from the Grameen
Bank or strategies to influence policy from the indigenous people's movement of Ecuador.

In contrast to their roles as spark plugs for change and confrontation, NGOs may also act as mediators or catalysts for resolving conflicts at national and international levels. NGOs have played a part in trying to manage serious conflicts with regional effects in Guatemala and Sri Lanka as sources of early warning or preventive action.[37]

More generally international NGOs and NGO networks have demonstrated the capacity to mobilize people and resources for international action on important public problems. In some cases NGOs play primary roles in identifying problems or articulating value positions; in others they take direct action to invent or press for problem solutions. NGO alliances were central, for example, in mobilizing support for the adoption of the international ban on landmines, in spite of resistance from many national governments.

International NGO and NGO alliance engagement in global decision-making and institution building expands the variety of actors who are aware of and active in international governance. The civil society actors who went to Seattle broadened the issues to be discussed by the WTO by pressing for more attention to labor rights and environmental regulations. Civil society actors may also help articulate the values, norms, and critical inceptions of a shared global culture. International governance in a globalized world is increasingly responding to a wide range of actors and interests.[38]

Civil Society and Future International Governance

We have argued that globalization has contributed to the dramatic rise of civil society organizations around the world, though their impacts have been uneven across countries and issues. Some countries have been particularly open to developments associated with globalization—rapid communication and wide dissemination of information, quick travel and transportation, political democratization and fragmentation, economic dynamism and concentration of wealth, or cultural homogenization and polarization—that support the emergence of civil society organizations as important actors. We also argued that international NGOs and civil society alliances have demonstrated the capacity to engage in debates that affect international governance. Past initiatives have increased access for international NGOs and NGO alliances to policy debates and institutions. But their roles in these forums depend in large part on how they resolve questions about their own legitimacy and accountability.

NGO Legitimacy and Accountability

To advocates of both domestic and international NGOs there is little doubt that their emergence and growing influence are consistent with the ultimate goals of enhancing the quality of democratic governance and the democratic accountability of international governance decisions and institutions. But to many in centers of power challenged by NGOs—including international governance organizations, states, and national or international business organizations—the legitimacy of NGOs seems suspect. Behind the appearance of popular mass movements may be charismatic individuals supported by foundations with their own views of the public interest. Just whom do these NGOs represent? And should decisions that affect many interests and often billions of people be shaped or blocked by their actions?

Whether the emergence and active participation of domestic and international NGOs in policymaking processes should be viewed as an advance in the quality of democratic governance seems to depend crucially on what kind of claim they can make to holding domestic governments and international governance arrangements to account. It is probably best to think of "accountability" as a relationship: to say that an agency is accountable is to suggest that there is someone who can demand that it live up to its commitments at the risk of sanctions if it fails to do so.[39] Accountability lies in the actor's commitments to another, the substantive character of those commitments, and the means that the other has to ensure that those commitments are honored. Some accountability relationships are hierarchical (for example, principal-agent relations) and focus on the accountability of the agent to the principal; others are more "mutual" in that they imply reciprocal claims (for example, contracts that establish obligations for both parties).[40] Accountability is desirable because it increases the incentives for actors to perform as expected, and that reliability can improve performance as well as the relationships among the parties.

Accountability is at issue in at least two ways when civil society actors participate in international governance processes. First, do international NGOs and NGO alliances increase or decrease democratic accountability in their challenges to international institutions that formulate and implement international policies or problem solutions? If those alliances represent the world's citizens (or even a substantial part of them), their interventions arguably may increase the democratic accountability of the target institutions. But this representativeness is a difficult claim to substantiate.

And international NGO alliances might reduce democratic accountability if they promoted policies that ran against the interests of their constituents.

Democratic accountability might also be grounded in the claim that these organizations represent transcendental purposes rather than particular groups or individuals. In this view, there are urgent rights to freedom from political oppression, the threat of starvation or malignant illness, the darkness of illiteracy, and so on, that are fundamental to human rights. Democratic accountability has to be about a governing entity's ability to deliver on these fundamental human rights. NGOs that align themselves with these causes are advancing democratic governance. There can be no democratic governance locally or internationally when citizens lack the necessary conditions for exercising the rights and responsibilities of democratic participation.

An alternative claim to legitimacy is that the institution in question has failed to live up to its own policies and standards for practice. The transnational NGO coalition against the World Bank's Narmada Dam loan argued that the project failed to meet the Bank's policy on resettlement of people displaced by the dam, and an independent commission of investigators ultimately agreed that those standards had not been met.[41] In this case the legitimacy of the challenge grows out of the Bank policies rather than the representativeness of the coalition or its advocacy of fundamental rights, though questions may be asked about the coalition's standing to raise the issue.

A second important set of issues revolves around the institutional accountability of the international NGO or alliance itself—to what extent can other actors subject the alliance to sanctions for failure to meet its commitments? This is a complex question for international NGOs and NGO alliances, since their missions often commit them to serving multiple constituencies (donors and allies as well as clients) at different levels (local, national, international). Those constituencies often have very different capacities to impose sanctions for failures to meet commitments: grassroots groups may find it difficult to influence distant international NGOs even when they are nominally part of the same coalition. Successful international NGO alliances often build "chains" of accountability in which the influence and sanctions are transmitted across many links (for example, local to regional to national to international) to span the organizational distance between international NGOs and grassroots groups.[42]

Accountability also turns on clear definitions of performance expectations by the parties to the accountability relationship. Different forms of alliance vary considerably in how explicitly goals, strategies, and responsibilities are formulated. Networks, organized around shared values and largely focused on information sharing, create fewer focuses for accountability than coalitions, which share strategies and action plans. Social movement organizations are yet more explicit about goals, tactics, and mutual expectations in the face of contention with powerful opponents. As transnational alliances become more focused on shared strategies and tactics, we might expect their investments in mutual influence and accountability to rise.[43]

Whether the engagement of international NGOs and NGO alliances promotes democratic accountability of international multisectoral problem solving turns in part on the extent to which they develop their own capacities for institutional accountability to their members and stakeholders. The issue of civil society accountability and its importance for their future roles in national and international decisionmaking with actors from other sectors have drawn increasing attention from students of civil society and its international alliances.[44] These issues become increasingly central as civil society actors seek ways to work effectively with government and business actors.

Multisector Relations: Civil Society, State, and Market

Whether NGOs can become effective agents of improved democratic accountability and international problem solving may depend crucially not only on how they develop and manage themselves but also as importantly on how they interact with other powerful sectors of society that can claim to represent public interests and to pursue public goals. The experience of the past decade suggests that international NGOs and NGO alliances are more often effective in blocking decisions than they are in catalyzing large-scale action that solves critical problems. In part this asymmetry reflects the relatively low level of resources available to civil society actors, at least as compared with actors in the state and market sectors. In part it also reflects the different comparative advantages of the sectors: the state and the market are inherently better equipped for large-scale initiatives, just as the civil society may be better equipped for small-scale local experiment and innovation.

On many issues the different sectors can go about their activities without engaging one another. But there are many other issues on which businesses, governments, and civil society organizations seek to influence one another. Unfortunately, the gulfs in interests and perspectives that separate the sectors make intersectoral misunderstanding and conflict very common. Misunderstandings are likely when the parties are also separated by perceived power differences and by ideological interpretations of difference. Civil society actors—especially those that serve disadvantaged or marginalized groups—may be especially sensitized to power differences and collisions of values.

One general pattern of intersectoral relations that may emerge from disputes over interests and values is a kind of intersectoral polarization that is characterized by value-laden stereotypes, struggles over power and resources, and resistance to joint action even when some interests are clearly shared. In this pattern, each sector emphasizes its own interests and perspectives, sees little legitimacy or relevance in others' values, aspirations, or resources, and seeks to achieve its goals in spite of or at the expense of the others even when there might be significant gains available from cooperative action.

Intersectoral polarization can produce struggles to control decisions in domains where many actors have important stakes. Governments and intergovernmental organizations may seek to exclude multinational corporations and transnational civil society alliances from input to important international decisionmaking processes, even when they have critical information about the issues or large stakes in decision outcomes. Indeed, much of international relations theory focuses almost exclusively on states as the major legitimate actors in international governance.[45] In other situations multinational corporations and financial markets may shape international decisions and seek to exclude governments and civil society actors. Some analysts have argued that the recent rise of the international market has largely established that "corporations rule the world" and that governments and civil society actors have become largely irrelevant on many critical international decisions.[46] Still others argue that international NGOs and NGO alliances now have the power to block many international decisions. While the enormous diversity and fierce autonomy of civil society actors make a coherent international hegemony of one or a few NGO actors unlikely, some observers suggest that some issues are already subject to a kind of special interest gridlock in which international NGOs and NGO alliances make international decisions and progress impossible.[47]

Some disagreement and struggle for influence among the sectors on controversial issues are probably inevitable. Indeed, some contention is probably desirable for developing a thorough analysis of issues and generating creative solutions to problems. Analysts of conflict and negotiation have described several approaches to dispute resolution, including reconciling the interests of the parties, adjudicating the rights involved, or establishing which party has the power to impose its will.[48] These approaches vary in the costs they impose: negotiations that reconcile differences are generally less costly than court battles to adjudicate rights or power struggles to establish supremacy. Adjudications and contests may be necessary when the parties disagree about what rights apply or who has more power—but those processes may also be costly in many ways.

Interest-based negotiation and problem solving across sectoral differences have been used to generate solutions to various problems in the past two decades in the industrialized world and in developing countries.[49] Multisector cooperation is characterized by mutual influence across the sectors and a willingness to negotiate agreements that take into account the concerns and capacities of many parties. In this pattern interaction among governments, businesses, and civil society actors can produce appreciation of one another's concerns and aspirations, recognition of one another's resources, and negotiated agreements that all the parties regard as fair and acceptable. Multisectoral cooperation has been useful for development purposes in very diverse settings. For example,

—In rural Madagascar access to market centers has been restricted by the lack of roads, and the government has had few resources for road building or maintenance. With assistance from international donors, the government has developed partnerships with local community organizations and commercial road construction firms to create and maintain hundreds of kilometers of rural roads. In the partnerships, private firms construct roads and instruct the community organizations in their maintenance; the government authorizes the communities to collect tolls from road users; and the community maintains the roads with their own labor and funds from the tolls. The partnership utilizes the comparative advantages of the different parties to produce gains for all of them.[50]

—The city of Cleveland, Ohio, was a notorious example of urban decline in the 1970s as a consequence of outmigration of local industries, a series of riots and ethnic tensions, power struggles between business and government actors, and a variety of other factors. Local government and business leaders organized several innovative multisectoral task forces and committees to explore ways to better understand problems, build shared commitment across many institutions and sectors to solve them, and implement the host of innovative initiatives that emerged from their deliberations. During the next decade the city, once derided as "the mistake on the Lake," emerged as an exemplar of urban renewal and reform on the basis of the joint initiatives that united actors from many different sectors, classes, ethnic groups, and cultural backgrounds.[51]

While multisector cooperation is increasingly common at the national level in many countries, it is not yet common at the international level. In part this is because cooperation across sectors is intrinsically difficult, and parties are not likely to struggle with its challenges if the issues of rights and power—the alternatives to dispute resolution by reconciling interests in multisectoral negotiations—remain ambiguous. In the international arena it is often ambiguous whether appeals to rights or to power will be more effective in serving the interests of the parties than negotiating interests. In some arenas, however, long struggles among governments, businesses, and civil society organizations have established that the costs of adjudications and power struggles are likely to be very high, and negotiating interests has become an attractive alternative. Thus the World Commission on Dams, which includes representatives of all three sectors, has become an arena in which important policies and decisions can be debated and evolved, partly because it provides an alternative to a history of struggles that has been costly for many participants. As international NGOs and NGO alliances engage in more successful campaigns to influence international governance, arrangements that enable multisector cooperation can be expected to increase as the rights and powers of civil society actors become better understood and accepted. Investigators from different disciplines are already describing the rise of intersectoral cooperation in many settings.[52]

Governance grounded in multisectoral decisionmaking may further complicate already thorny questions of performance measurement and accountability. What criteria might be used to assess the performance of multisectoral initiatives? Is it important to use criteria that reflect core concerns of each sector in this assessment? Should other criteria be used that reflect value created across the sector? The following list illustrates criteria drawn from the market, state, and civil society sectors as well as a final cross-sector possibility:

—Efficient use of resources. Does the multisectoral initiative enable efficient mobilization of resources and information for effective and sustainable problem solving?

—Democratic accountability. Does the multisectoral initiative promote responsiveness and accountability to key stakeholders in the issue?

—Actualization of core values. Does the multisectoral initiative recognize, express, and support core values and norms of stakeholders?

—Social learning. Does the multisectoral initiative promote better understanding and innovation that serves the stakeholders in the problem domain?

Multisectoral cooperation is difficult and expensive. It is not appropriate for all decisions. But it may be more expensive in the long run to try to handle some problems without multisectoral participation. Civil society organizations and alliances increasingly will challenge and obstruct international policymaking that does not take the interests and perspectives of their members into account. Multisectoral cooperation can reconcile civil society actors' interests and mobilize their comparative advantages with those of intergovernmental agencies and multinational corporations in some circumstances and contribute to more rapid and responsive social learning as well.

Conclusion

We have argued that civil society organizations are increasingly important in international arenas as well as in many nations. Their emergence in the past few decades is associated with and in part caused by the forces of globalization. The rise of civil society organizations has been uneven across countries, though openness to globalization seems in general to be associated with growing strength and diversity of NGOs and other civil society organizations. The growth of international NGOs and NGO alliances has also been shaped by globalization, with impacts particularly visible for providers of services and disaster relief, policy analysis and advocacy, and social learning and problem solving. At the international level NGOs and NGO alliances have identified emerging problems, articulated new values and norms, created or reformed institutional arrangements, fostered innovations in international practice, and helped resolve conflicts and manage differences. These contributions to international governance in turn highlight problems of democratic and institutional accountability of international NGOs and NGO alliances and the possibilities of multisectoral cooperation to solve complex problems of international governance.

The growing recognition of civil society actors as legitimate and valuable actors in international governance may be a prelude to increased use of multisectoral cooperation to grapple with international governance issues. As governments and businesses accept civil society actors as representing real rights and wielding real power, the lower costs of reconciling interests in collaborative processes may encourage much wider efforts to work together. However, the potential reach and resources of the other sectors is potentially a significant threat to the autonomy and independence of civil society actors. Finding ways for all three sectors to work together while preserving their distinct identities and capabilities is an important challenge for the future.

Notes

1. Joseph A. Schumpeter, *Capitalism, Socialism, and Democracy*, 3d ed. (Harper and Row, 1950), p. 84.

2. See Robert Keohane and Joseph Nye, "Power, Interdependence, and Globalism," in *Power and Interdependence* (Addison-Wesley, forthcoming).

3. See Margaret M. Keck and Kathryn Sikkink, *Activists without Borders* (Cornell University Press, 1998).

4. Keohane and Nye, "Power, Interdependence, and Globalism."

5. Marc Lindenberg and J. Patrick Dobel, "The Challenges of Globalization for Northern International Relief and Development NGOs," *Nonprofit and Voluntary Sector Quarterly*, vol. 28, no. 4, supplement (1999), pp. 4–24; and Jessica Mathews, "Power Shift," *Foreign Affairs*, vol. 76 (1997), pp. 50–61.

6. See, for example, Jean L. Cohen and Andrew Arato, *Civil Society and Political Theory* (MIT Press, 1997); Michael Walzer, "The Idea of Civil Society," *Dissent* (Spring 1991), pp. 293–304; and Michael Bratton, "Beyond the State: Civil Society and Associational Life in Africa," *World Politics*, vol. 41, no. 4 (1989), pp. 407–30.

7. Overviews of these perspectives have been developed by Robert Wuthnow, *Between States and Markets: The Voluntary Sector in Comparative Perspective* (Princeton University Press, 1991); Walzer, "The Idea of Civil Society"; see also Rajesh Tandon and K. Naidoo, "The Promise of Civil Society," in Naidoo ed., *Civil Society at the Millennium* (West Hartford, Conn.: Kumarian Press, 1999), pp. 1–16.

8. L. David Brown, and David Korten, "Understanding Voluntary Organizations," Public Sector Management and Private Sector Development, Working Paper 258 (Washington: World Bank, 1989); and Adil Najam, "Understanding the Third Sector: Revisiting the Prince, the Merchant, and the Citizen," *Nonprofit Management and Leadership*, vol. 7, no. 2 (1996), pp. 203–19.

9. See Anna C. Vakil, "Confronting the Classification Problem," *World Development*, vol. 25 (1997), pp. 2057–70; John Clark, *Democratizing Development: The Role of Voluntary Organizations* (West Hartford, Conn.: Kumarian Press, 1991).

10. Mohammed Yunus, "The Grameen Bank Story," in Anirudh Krishna, M. Uphoff, and Milton Esman eds., *Reasons for Hope* (West Hartford: Kumarian Press, 1997).

11. Lori Udall, "The World Bank and Public Accountability: Has Anything Changed?" in Jonathan A. Fox and L. David Brown eds., *The Struggle for Accountability: NGOs, Social Movements, and the World Bank* (MIT Press, 1998).

12. Elizabeth Rhyne, and M. Otero, "Financial Services for Microenterprises: Principles and Institutions," *World Development*, vol. 20, no. 11 (1992), pp. 1561–71; and Udall, "The World Bank and Public Accountability."

13. *The Yearbook of International Organizations* identifies INGOs as organizations with voting participation from at least three countries.

14. Keck and Sikkink, *Activists without Borders*, describe "transnational advocacy networks" that have played central roles in struggles over environmental policy, women's rights, and human rights.

15. Udall, "The World Bank and Public Accountability."

16. See Sanjeev Khagram and Kathryn Sikkink, "Restructuring World Politics: Transnational Social Movements, Networks, and Coalitions and International Norms," in Sanjeev Khagram, James Riker, and Kathryn Sikkink, eds., *Restructuring World Politics: The Power of Transnational Agency and Norms* (Cornell University Press, forthcoming).

17. Lester M. Salamon, "The Rise of the Nonprofit Sector," *Foreign Affairs*, vol. 73, no. 4 (1994), pp. 109–16. The Johns Hopkins studies of the nonprofit sector in many countries have provided the base for comparative analysis across many regions. As one of the leaders of those studies, Salamon can base this assessment on impressive amounts of data. See also Lester Salamon and Helmut Anheier, "Social Origins of Civil Society," *Voluntas*, vol. 9, no. 3 (1998), pp. 17–46.

18. *Economist*, "Citizen's Groups: The Nongovernmental Order, Will NGOs Democratize or Merely Disrupt Global Governance?" *Economist*, December 11, 1999; John Boli and George Thomas, *Constructing World Culture: International Nongovernmental Organizations since 1875* (Stanford University Press, 1999), p. 14.

19. Jackie Smith, Charles Chatfield, and Ron Pagnucco, eds., *Transnational Social Movements and Global Politics: Solidarity beyond the State* (Syracuse University Press, 1997).

20. Karina Constantino-David has described the variety of NGOs that emerged in response to changing circumstances in the Philippines. K. Constantino-David, "Scaling up Civil Society in the Philippines," in Michael Edwards and David Hulme eds., *Making a Difference* (London: Earthscan, 1992), pp. 137–48. Most analysts favor definitions of civil society actors that include many competing actors. Others, such as Tandon and Naidoo, "The Promise of Civil Society," exclude organizations that are not committed to core civil society values like tolerance, nonviolence, and reciprocity.

21. Salamon and Anheier, "Social Origins of Civil Society."

22. A major approach to adult education that has emerged from grassroots "conscientization" efforts in Brazil focuses on helping the poor conceptualize their political situation and the forces that keep them poor. See Paolo Freire, *Pedagogy of the Oppressed* (Herder and Herder, 1971). The growing omnipresence of television and other forms of information and communication technology can alter the political awareness of those who in earlier decades had no idea about happenings in the wider world.

23. Khagram and Sikkink, "Restructuring World Politics."

24. Boli and Thomas, *Constructing World Culture;* see also Keck and Sikkink, *Activists without Borders;* and Fox and Brown, *The Struggle for Accountability.*

25. O. R. Young, *Global Governance: Drawing Insights from Environmental Experience* (MIT Press, 1997).

26. Lindenberg and Dobel, "The Challenges of Globalization."

27. See M. Edwards, "International Development NGOs: Agents of Foreign Aid or Vehicles for International Cooperation?" *Nonprofit and Voluntary Sector Quarterly,* vol. 28, supplement (1999), pp. 25–37; T. Dichter, "Appeasing the Gods of Sustainability," in David Hulme and Michael Edwards, eds., *NGOs, States and Donors* (London: Macmillan, 1997).

28. See Keck and Sikkink, *Activists without Borders.*

29. Kay Treakle, "Ecuador: Structural Adjustment and Indigenous and Environmentalist Resistance," in Fox and Brown, *The Struggle for Accountability;* and Anthony Hall, "From Victims to Victors," in Michael Edwards and David Hulme, eds., *Making a Difference* (London: Earthscan, 1992), pp. 148–58.

30. Fox and Brown, *The Struggle for Accountability;* Keck and Sikkink, *Activists without Borders;* Boli and Thomas, *Constructing World Culture;* S. Khagram, J. Riker, and K. Sikkink, eds., *Reconstructing World Politics* (Cornell University Press, 2000); and J. Smith, C. Chatfield, and R. Pagnucco, *Transnational Social Movements and Global Politics.*

31. Keck and Sikkink, *Activists without Borders;* and Khagram and others, *Reconstructing World Politics.*

32. Khagram and Sikkink, "Restructuring World Politics"; and Fox and Brown, *The Struggle for Accountability.*

33. Douglas A. Johnson, "Confronting Coprorate Power: Strategies and Phases of the Nestle Boycott," in L. Preston and J. Post, eds., *Research in Corporate Social Performance and Policy,* vol. 8 (Greenwich, Conn.: JAI Press), pp. 323–44; and Udall, "The World Bank and Public Accountability."

34. Jonathan Fox and L. David Brown, "Assessing the Impact of NGO Advocacy Campaigns on the World Bank," in Fox and Brown, *The Struggle for Accountability,* pp. 485–552.

35. Udall, "The World Bank and Public Accountability."

36. Martha Chen, "Engendering World Conferences: The International Women's Movement and the United Nations," *Third World Quarterly,* vol. 16, no. 3 (1995), pp. 477–93.

37. Robert Rotberg, *Vigilance and Vengeance: NGOs Preventing Ethnic Conflict in Divided Societies* (Brookings, 1996).

38. See Mathews, "Power Shift"; and Keohane and Nye, "Power, Interdependence, and Globalism."

39. See Mark Moore, "Toward a Normative Theory of the Nonprofit Sector," Working Paper (Harvard University, Hauser Center on Nonprofit Organizations, 1999).

40. See E. C. Fama and M. C. Jensen, "Separation of Ownership and Control," *Journal of Law and Economics,* vol. 26 (1983), pp. 301–25.

41. Udall, "The World Bank and Public Accountability."

42. See L. David Brown and Jonathan A. Fox, "Accountability within Transnational Coalitions," in Fox and Brown, *The Struggle for Accountability,* pp. 439–84.

43. See Brown and Fox, "Accountability within Transnational Coalitions"; and Khagram, *Dams, Democracy, and Development.*

44. Edwards, "International Development NGOs."

45. See Robert O. Keohane and Joseph S. Nye, *Power and Interdependence: World Politics in Transition* (Little-Brown, 1988); and Boli and Thomas, *Constructing World Culture.*

46. David Korten, *When Corporations Rule the World* (San Francisco, Calif., and Greenwich, Conn.: Berrett-Koehler and Kumarian Press, 1995).

47. *Economist,* 1999.

48. These distinctions are explored in detail in William L. Ury, Jeanne M. Brett, and Stephen B. Goldberg, *Getting Disputes Resolved* (Harvard University Program on Negotiation, 1993).

49. See, for examples, Barbara Gray, *Collaborating: Finding Common Ground for Multiparty Problems* (Jossey Bass, 1989); and Larry Susskind and others, *The Consensus Building Handbook* (Sage Publications, 1999). See Derick Brinkerhoff, "Exploring State-Civil Society Cooperation," *Nonprofit and Voluntary Sector Quarterly,* vol. 28 (Supplement) (1999), pp. 59–86; and L. David Brown and Darcy Ashman, "Social Capital, Mutual Influence, and Social Learning in Intersectoral Problem-Solving," in David Cooperrider and Jane Dutton. eds., *Organizational Dimensions of Global Change* (Sage Publications, 1999), pp. 139–67.

50. See Steven Waddell, "Strengthening the Road Network: Madagascar, Technical Report to USAID" (Boston: Institute for Development Research, 1998).

51. See James Austin, "The Cleveland Turnaround (A): Responding to the Crisis," Harvard Business School Case 796-151 (Harvard Business School).

52. Mathews, "Power Shift,"; Keohane and Nye, "Power, Interdependence, and Globalism"; Ann Marie Slaughter, "The Real New World," *Foreign Affairs,* vol. 76 (1997), pp. 183–91; and Elaine Kamarck, chap. 10, in this volume.

13

CARY COGLIANESE

Globalization and the Design of International Institutions

$$T$$HE CURRENT PERIOD of globalization brings with it calls for international coordination and collective action. Expanding markets lead to the deepening interdependence of economies and a growing demand for coordination in a range of regulatory areas including food safety, banking, and product standards. The increasing speed and decreasing cost of global communication depends in large part on coordinated international action to ensure network compatibility. Global environmental problems such as climate change are also prominent candidates for collective action on an international scale. As the fortunes and fates of people across the globe become more closely linked, continued international action will be needed to address a variety of global problems.

Efforts to solve global problems often center on the creation of varied forms of international institutions. By "institutions," I mean both international rules and international organizations.[1] International organizations can be nongovernmental and governmental, though in this chapter my focus is primarily on governmental organizations. Conceived in terms of rules and organizations, international institutions have been the subject of a significant body of research in the field of international relations. Much institutionalist research has focused on why international institutions are created and whether they can independently affect political behavior in a world dominated by nation-states possessing unequal power, divergent interests, and complex domestic politics.[2]

In this chapter, I operate on the premise that institutions can indeed affect outcomes and proceed to raise what has been a less explored, but no less significant, question: how does the choice of institutional form influence the effectiveness of institutions in solving regulatory problems associated with globalization? My purpose is to suggest that the broad design of international institutions can affect their effectiveness in addressing global problems and, more important, their support from the nation-states that create them. All things being equal, nation-states can be expected to prefer institutional designs that impose the least constraint on their sovereign legal authority. However, some of the least constraining institutional forms will probably turn out to be ineffective in addressing particular kinds of global problems, especially those dealing with common problems or with the protection of human rights. The challenge in these cases will be to create institutional structures that provide adequate assurance to nation-states that their interests will not be abused, while at the same time vesting the institutions with the independence needed for them to be effective in promoting global well-being.

Globalization and Global Problems

The increasing intensity and extent of global interactions brings with it a variety of challenges for governance. We can distinguish three types of problems that accompany globalization and prompt calls for international action: coordination problems; commons problems; and problems of core values, such as human rights.[3]

Coordination Problems

The first type of problem is one of coordinating global linkages, or exchanges of information, products, services, and money across national borders. When crossing national borders means confronting incompatible requirements or technologies, this will restrict transnational exchanges that people otherwise want to make. Some coordination problems are comparable to deciding what side of the road motorists should use or adopting a common unit of time.[4] For example, the technological advances that have made global communication cheaper depend on the interoperability of networks and telecommunications services in different parts of the world. Another example is the current concern about so-called electronic signatures for Internet transactions. Electronic signatures allow firms to authenticate the identity of contracting partners. Already a number of authentication technologies exist, and more will certainly be developed in the future. If different countries require the use of different authentication technologies, cross-national electronic trade would become more uncertain and cumbersome than if countries adhered to a common approach.

Coordination problems are of particular concern to manufacturers who confront different national regulatory standards. National regulations govern both the design and performance of products sold within a country (product standards), as well as the processes by which products are made (process standards). Product standards can vary in terms of required design features, such as for safety or performance, and also in the testing and other procedures used to demonstrate that the product meets the substantive requirements. Different design standards can sometimes force manufacturers to vary their products for different markets, thus diminishing economies of scale. Even if design standards are similar, different testing procedures can lead to additional costs. For example, European and U.S. automobile manufacturers report that the costs associated with complying with different standards amount to 10 percent of their engineering and design costs.[5]

Of course, the additional costs associated with different standards may well be easily justified if they are offset by additional benefits. Differences in standards may reflect different conditions or preferences within nation-states, which more than justify different, even incompatible, standards. In the absence of offsetting benefits, though, variations in regulatory standards tend to reduce competition and lead to inefficiencies.[6] In these cases, variations in product standards might amount essentially to a barrier to entry, since domestic firms in markets having excessively costly standards may be at an advantage in that market over foreign firms. In other cases, firms operating in markets with unduly lax standards for manufacturing processes—such as countries with weak environmental or labor safety regulations—may in essence hold an unfair advantage over firms based in countries with higher, socially appropriate standards. In the absence of sound justifications for different regulatory standards in different jurisdictions, the costs associated with divergent standards can lead to inefficiencies in the global allocation of manufacturing and trade.

Commons Problems

A second type of problem associated with globalization is the familiar one of protecting common resources or public goods. Public goods or common resources are nonrivalrous goods, which it is impossible to exclude anyone from using. Consequently, it is not appropriate to use a pure free market system to allocate their use. For example, as greenhouse gas emissions have increased with the growing use of fossil fuels, global warming has emerged as a commons problem.[7] All countries can use the atmosphere as a place in which to release emissions, and all benefit from the reduction of greenhouse gases regardless of whether they contribute to the reduction. As a result, there is a strong incentive for free riding. In such cases, international institutions, if sufficiently designed, may be able to overcome the free rider problem.

A related problem is the transboundary effects of otherwise domestic activity. Industry in one country, for example, can generate air pollution that moves downwind to another country. Or lax law enforcement in one country may make it a haven for drug traffickers or terrorists who stage their operations in other countries. In these cases, internal action (or inaction) results in negative externalities that are imposed on outside countries. Since the costs are disproportionately borne by others, those producing them have little incentive to invest in the measures needed to prevent them. Consequently, international action may be appropriate in these circumstances as well.

Core Values

A third type of global problem involves the protection of core, or transcendent, values. Moral principles such as equality, liberty, and democracy can be said to transcend current political practices.[8] Principled claims about rights to treatment with dignity and respect inhere in human beings as human beings, and not as citizens of a particular country. Hence, ensuring at least a minimal amount of respect for human rights is almost by definition a global problem. Moreover, the current period of globalization may be creating conditions under which important social values are becoming more widely accepted across the world. Globalization brings with it the increasing ease in the spread of information and ideas, even in heretofore closed political systems. More people in the world today have access to images and ideas from outside their own country than ever before.

The increasingly widespread exchange of ideas about cultural and political values may well contribute to broader acceptance of human rights and democratic principles, notwithstanding the positive rights that are (and often are not) protected by particular countries. Since nation-states have not uniformly secured justice and protected the rights of their peoples, effective international institutions may be needed to help guarantee minimal protection of human rights across all nations.

Global Problems and the Demand for International Institutions

I have set out three main problems that in some cases might justify the establishment of international institutions: coordination problems, commons problems, and the protection of core values. To the extent that these problems increase during a period of globalization, then the need for international action can also be expected to increase. This does not mean, though, that international institutions will automatically arise whenever there is a need for them. Nation-states can still be expected to protect their sovereignty and their interests. Indeed, at the same time that the world grows increasingly interconnected on a global scale, many nations have seen a striking resurgence of interest in localism and decentralization. In a number of federal systems, there have been moves to devolve policymaking from the national to the state or local levels. In the European Union, the principle of subsidiarity has become a symbol of the national and local institutions that appear threatened by European integration. Isolationist political candidates in countries around the world stir up resistance to new international institutions. It may well be that as the pace of globalization quickens, nation-states and their domestic publics will only become more protective of local instruments of governance.

Other obstacles to international cooperation, such as the incentives for free riding, can also be expected. There are transaction costs to the creation of international institutions. Countries need credible information to decide that cooperation will serve their interests.[9] In addition, they face the time and expense of negotiating with other nations. Despite these very real obstacles, the number of international institutions has nevertheless grown dramatically during the current period of globalization. The past fifty years have witnessed dramatic growth in various measures of international cooperation and institution building, including an overall increase in intergovernmental exchange, treaties, and international governmental organizations.[10] At least in the near term, we can expect continued interest in developing and strengthening international institutions to respond to the problems of an increasingly interdependent world, even though building these institutions will not occur without difficulty or opposition.

Forms of International Institutions

How should international institutions be designed? Nation-states have choices in how they respond to global problems. They can choose not to act, leaving open the possibility that norms or other coordinating mechanisms will develop through the marketplace or through networks of nongovernmental organizations. At other times, nation-states can seek to address international problems through domestic legislation, either imposing domestic standards on products entering into trade or coordinating domestic regulations with those of other countries. Still other times, nations can work directly with other nations to develop strategies for recognizing one another's internal norms or to create mutually acceptable international norms. In addition, nations also sometimes create international organizations possessing delegated authority to study global problems, generate recommendations or policies, implement programs, or enforce rules and settle disputes.

These responses vary in the amount of authority that remains vested in the nation-state, as opposed to being transferred to other states or international organizations. Table 13-1 summarizes six major options, or institutional forms, that countries can choose to take in response to global problems, with each form listed according to how much policy authority remains with the nation-state. In crafting responses to global problems, nation-states can choose from among this range of options, and any individual country can (and will) engage in many of these options at any given time. If globalization increases the demand for international action, we should expect to see greater use of these options, especially those involving mutual recognition, consensus, and delegation. However, initially we can expect that countries will tend to respond to new global problems with options that least impose upon state sovereignty.

Nonstate Action

The first option is for nation-states to take no action whatsoever, thereby leaving a global problem unresolved or allowing nonstate actors to attempt

Table 13-1. *Institutional Forms for Responding to Global Problems*

Item	Description of institutional form	Legal authority remaining at the nation-state level
Nonstate action	Nonstate organizations or policy networks create norms of conduct.	All
Internal control	Nation-states exercise authority through internally created policies.	All
Mutual recognition	Nation-states agree to recognize under specified conditions the internally created policies of other nation-states which, in turn, reciprocate with recognition.	All, but under certain conditions the nation-state acquiesces to the authority of other nation-states.
Consensual rules	Nation-states consent to international policies created through negotiation with other nation-states.	All, but authority is constrained by bargaining process with other nation-states.
Delegation	Nation-states delegate policy authority to international institutions. Delegations can be loose or tight.	Some
Withdrawal	Nation-states abandon or cede their policy authority altogether to another state or institution.	None

to solve it. The absence of state intervention does not necessarily mean that the global problem will persist unaddressed, for markets, transnational social norms, and private standard-setting organizations may step in to try to solve or prevent certain kinds of global problems.[11]

Market dynamics can sometimes lead to coordinated action. In the absence of any formal product standards, markets may settle on a de facto industry standard. The dominance of the Windows operating system as a standard for PC software development, for example, has arisen from the market dominance of Microsoft rather than from any particular governmental standard. Even in the face of different governmental standards, though, manufacturing practices may still converge on the most stringent standard if it is cheaper for companies to meet that standard than to design different products.

Social norms can also serve a regulatory function.[12] In the international realm, networks of professionals and other elites can diffuse norms even in the absence of intervention by nation-states. Norms may also be generated or sustained by domestic publics. Current protests against labor conditions in third world clothing factories, for example, hold the potential for entrenching norms about the treatment of workers by multinational corporations operating in developing countries.

Private standard-setting organizations also promote coordination among international businesses without intervention by the state. The International Electrotechnical Commission and the International Organization for Standardization (ISO) are both international, nongovernmental standard-setting organizations. ISO standards "govern" a broad range of products and business practices from film speed to corporate environmental management systems.

Even though nonstate norms may emerge from private standard-setting bodies, markets, and social networks, this does not mean that these norms will always be followed. Without the involvement of the state and its enforcement mechanisms, norms can be relatively easy to ignore, especially when the costs of compliance get high. However, to the extent that norms penetrate throughout social networks and become internalized by leaders and publics across the world, their effects potentially could be quite significant.[13]

Internal Control

The second option is for nation-states to exercise control through their own internal lawmaking processes. This approach maintains the maximum domain of a nation-state's sovereign authority, but it is limited by the national reach of that sovereign jurisdiction and by the likelihood that different states will adopt different standards. The global problems set forth earlier in this chapter are vexing precisely because nation-states are ill-equipped on their own to promote coordination, preserve global commons, and protect core values.

This does not mean that internal control can never affect international problems. Long-arm legislation is sometimes used to extend a nation-state's domestic authority beyond its borders, regulating outside firms that engage in transactions with residents. Moreover, under some circumstances, nation-states may be able to coordinate their internally created policies by following what other nation-states do. Countries with large economies, or especially high reputations for effective governance, may function as regulatory leaders that other nations follow, thus resulting in some regulatory convergence without formal efforts at international coordination.[14] However, harmonization without international cooperation is time-consuming and cumbersome. There are hardly any guarantees that nations will align their policies with one another.

Even if internal control is limited in the face of transnational problems, the actions of national governments do remain vital to nearly every approach to addressing global problems. Even when international institutions are needed to allow states to solve global problems, these institutions almost always depend on national decisions for their implementation.[15] For example, treaties will often require implementing legislation, and national governments are often responsible for monitoring and enforcement of international rules within their borders. It would be inaccurate, therefore, simply to juxtapose internal control with international control. What distinguishes internal control from the remaining institutional forms is the absence of any international institutional coordinating mechanism, such as an agreement, treaty, or international governmental organization.

Mutual Recognition

The third form of international institutions, mutual recognition, involves the acceptance of coordinating principles by nation-states under which they recognize, under certain circumstances, the policies adopted by other nation-states.[16] This approach provides a basis for determining which rules should apply to transactions that involve firms or individuals from different countries. Two or more countries adopting mutual recognition each maintain internal control within their respective borders but agree to a set of principles that will govern situations that involve an interaction between the countries. So, for example, nation A may agree to permit the sale of certain products that meet nation B's safety standards, even though they do not meet the precise standards set by nation A for products produced within its borders. The recognition is mutual when nation B then agrees to permit the sale of nation A's products within nation B.

Mutual recognition agreements have been used most notably in Europe, where member states of the European Union recognize products manufactured in each other's jurisdictions. The EU has also pursued bilateral negotiations with Australia, New Zealand, Canada, Japan, and the United

States. At the present, mutual recognition negotiations have tended to center around bilateral negotiations on specific products, such as food, medical devices, and telecommunications equipment.[17] In these negotiations, a key issue for nations has been to ensure that there is a measure of equivalency in the regulatory standards in the nations that would fall under the mutual recognition agreement. Hence, mutual recognition is an option available mainly to those countries that have already achieved a measure of regulatory convergence.

Consensual Rules

Consensual rules—treaties—are the fourth form of international institutions. Through the creation of international treaties or covenants, nation-states commit themselves not just to recognize one another's domestic rules but to create a new set of common, transnational rules.[18] While treaties seldom are backed by a formal enforcement mechanism,[19] they remain a frequently used form of international cooperation. More than 34,000 treaties are registered with the United Nations, with more than 500 of these being major multilateral treaties.[20]

Since each nation-state must consent to the policies contained in the treaty, policy authority still remains embedded within the nation-state.[21] In practice each nation's decision will be constrained to some degree by the bargaining process, as what emerges in a treaty may not be identical to each nation's first best policy choice. Powerful states also tend to dominate weaker states. However, each state still possesses full authority to decide whether to agree to the treaty. This preservation of authority comes at its price, of course, as rulemaking based on consensus can be time consuming, subject to the lowest common denominator effect, and biased in favor of the status quo.[22]

Delegation

The fifth institutional form, delegation, is a special form of consensual rulemaking, and it theoretically holds the promise of overcoming the limitations inherent in negotiating multilateral treaties. When countries delegate authority, they consent to the transfer of authority to an international organization to take specific actions.[23] The organization can take actions of its own accord, so countries need not negotiate treaty language to govern every decision needed to address a complex problem. In this way, international organizations can provide a forum for ongoing international cooperation. By the mid-1990s, national governments had created more than 250 international governmental organizations.[24] Among these are such well-known organizations as the United Nations, European Union, and World Trade Organization (WTO), along with many lesser-known organizations including the Codex Alimentarius Commission (which issues international food safety standards) and the International Telecommunications Commission (which sets standards for telecommunications services). Nation-states have established these and other international organizations to take a range of actions, from studying transnational problems and issuing recommendations, to creating or implementing transnational policy, to enforcing policy and settling disputes between countries.

Delegation does not mean that nation-states completely give up their authority over a policy issue to an international organization. Indeed, national leaders can be expected to ensure that their countries' interests will not be undermined by any new institutions that they create at the international level.[25] As such, countries will delegate with caution, paying attention to the terms of any delegation and the decisionmaking structure of the new institution. In this respect, national leaders' concerns about delegating authority to international organizations are not unlike those of a legislature delegating authority to an administrative agency or of any private actor delegating business or other decisionmaking authority to a third party. In such cases, tensions can arise between the interests of the nations delegating their authority and the interests of the organization receiving the authority. This is the well-known principal-agent problem, where the potential exists for the agent to act in ways that do not conform with the goals of the principal. The goals of the WTO, for example, may center more on the maintenance of competitive markets than some member countries and their publics are willing to accept, especially if the promotion of free trade comes at the expense of other social values, such as perhaps the environment or indigenous cultures. For any individual country, the question arises before it gives authority to an international organization: to what extent will the decisions made by the organization diverge from the overall interests of the nation?

Since international organizations are created by the consent of those nations who will be subject to the organization's authority, we can expect the structure of international organizations to bear similarities to delegations of authority in other contexts, such as legislative delegations to administrative agencies.[26] To minimize the potential for agents to act in ways incompatible with the interests of their principals, delegations often include measures designed to allow principals to monitor and control the actions of their agents.[27]

Delegations of governmental authority are often accompanied by one or more similar features designed to constrain the discretion of the organization to which authority is being transferred. These four features can be grouped into four categories: delineation; monitoring; sharing; and reversibility.[28] Delineation refers to the standards or principles setting forth the jurisdiction of the organization—its scope, tasks, and functions. Monitoring encompasses those procedures that ensure decisionmaking is transparent and that require certain kinds of analysis and reporting to be conducted before making decisions. Sharing arrangements provide for the involvement and representation of member states in the organizational decisionmaking process. Reversibility refers to escape clauses by which countries can withdraw from the jurisdiction of the organization under certain circumstances.

The way each of these features is constructed in specific cases will affect what might be considered the tightness of the delegation. Delegations can be tight or loose, depending on the nature of their delineation, monitoring, sharing, and reversibility. Delineations can be specific or general. Monitoring can be extensive or limited. Sharing arrangements can require consent of all member states or something less than full representation or unanimity. The conditions for reversibility can be ones that can be easily met or ones that require a compelling case. The tighter the delegation, the more control countries retain over the decisions and direction of international organizations. The looser the delegation, the more discretion the organization possesses.

Withdrawal

A final institutional form is worth noting, though perhaps more for theoretical symmetry than for its use in practice. The option of withdrawal lies at the opposite end of the spectrum from options in which legal authority rests solely within the nation-states. With withdrawal, a nation-state gives up or transfers its claim to policy authority altogether. It either abandons its exercise of authority or makes a complete, irreversible delegation to another institution. The main instances of withdrawal occur when nation-states merge or are subsumed by other states, such as with the recent German reunification.[29] Otherwise, the option of withdrawal remains largely an aspiration of those who advocate a so-called world government as a replacement for a system of governance organized around nation-states.

The Choice and Impact of Institutional Form

The nations of the world have numerous options available to them for responding to global problems. As I have just set forth, nations can choose from six broad categories of institutional form. Within each of these broad institutional forms, there is also a myriad of specific policy choices. I have said virtually nothing, for example, about the *substance* of treaties: the different kinds of requirements that nations can agree on in seeking to solve different kinds of problems. The specific requirements within treaties are obviously the subject of intense negotiations, and we know that some types of requirements turn out to be more effective than others. Ronald Mitchell has shown that, in a treaty designed to prevent oil tanker pollution, provisions that required tankers to install specific equipment were more effective in inducing compliance than were provisions that specified discharge limits.[30] Choices such as these—between technology-based and performance-based standards or between any number of other types of regulatory approaches—will almost certainly matter in affecting the performance of international rules. For the sake of this analysis, though, I would like to distinguish these kinds of "operational" choices from choices about broader institutional form. After all, performance-based or technology-based standards could in principle be adopted in domestic legislation, recognized in a mutual recognition agreement, codified by treaty, or proposed by an international governmental organization. The question I want to pose here is whether these broader institutional forms matter, all things being equal, in terms of their effectiveness in solving global problems.

By the effectiveness of institutional form, I mean the extent to which the international institution's design contributes to the solution of the global problem that it was intended to help solve (policy effectiveness) and the political legitimacy of the institution and the support it garners from national governments and their domestic publics (political effectiveness). I draw attention to legitimacy as a separate conception of effectiveness because institutions that lack legitimacy are unlikely to be able to work effectively in terms of the first conception. This is particularly the case with international institutions that depend on national governments for their continued existence and for the implementation and enforcement of international rules.

Now, I seek to bring together the three types of global problems discussed in the first part of the chapter with the institutional forms discussed in the second part. I show how certain institutional forms seem to fit better with certain types of global problems and hypothesize that this fit influences the policy effectiveness of international institutions. I further suggest that the institutional form is related to the political effectiveness, or legitimacy, of the institution. As with any claims about the effectiveness of policies and institutions, these are all subject to testing with empirical research.[31] Nevertheless, an initial step along the path toward empirical testing is to generate hypotheses about how the form of international institutions may be related to policy effectiveness and political legitimacy.

Form-Problem Fit

In the first part of this chapter, I distinguished between problems of coordination, commons problems, and core values that arise acutely in a period of globalization. If institutional form makes a difference in how effectively international institutions can solve these problems, then analysts and policymakers will need to take care in selecting the institutional forms to be used in addressing the different kinds of problems. They will need, in other words, to make sure that the institutional form fits the problem that needs to be solved.

Coordination problems will probably not be easily solved by the first two forms shown in table 13-1: nonstate action and internal control. While it is possible for coordinated behavior to develop without international agreements of any kind, the problem of coordination is most salient when nation-states have already internally adopted incompatible regulations.[32] When standards are already divergent, and when the divergence is not justified, nation-states will most likely need to take some form of collective action if they are to resolve the incompatibility. Consensual treaty making would work, since agreement on treaty language (without any significant reservations) will forge a common set of standards. However, in some cases, reaching consensus on common standards will prove difficult, especially if nation-states are trying to reconcile more than two divergent standards into one common treaty. Delegating the task of coordination to a group of experts could help break a deadlock, assuming agreement could be reached on how the expert commission would be established.

A potentially more feasible approach would be for the various nation-states to negotiate mutual recognition treaties with one another. As noted earlier, mutual recognition can require an initial degree of regulatory convergence. As long as the various standards are roughly equivalent, countries may be willing to use mutual recognition to achieve coordinated trade. A mutual recognition agreement is probably easier to achieve because it does not require nation-states to change their own existing standards or testing procedures or demand that negotiators come to a complete meeting of the minds on a common set of detailed standards.

It is harder to see how mutual recognition could help address commons problems or problems of core values. Of course, internal control cannot be expected to solve these problems either because the problems stem from actions by individual nation-states either to permit the depletion of a public good or the violation of a core value. With commons problems, individual nation-states are less likely unilaterally to internalize the social costs of their actions. The most promising option for commons problems, and perhaps also for problems of core values, would seem to be treaty making, which could establish credible rules (and perhaps authorized sanctions) to facilitate cooperation. Not surprisingly, this has been the strategy nation-states have pursued recently on environmental issues such as ozone and climate change, leading with mixed results to the Montreal Protocol and the Kyoto Protocol respectively.[33] In the course of climate change negotiations, delegation (as an institutional form) has come into play with the creation of organizations such as the Intergovernmental Panel on Climate Change, which provides scientific assessment information that can be used in the course of further treaty negotiations. Delegations to organizations charged with studying and reporting recommendations may help generate information that can feed back into processes for creating other institutional forms.

As noted earlier, the internal decisions of nation-states do remain important to policy success even when international institutions are created to address global problems. In the context of human rights and other core values, nation-states may well enter into international treaties but not honor them when dealing with heated domestic conflicts or, in some cases, even in the ordinary course of affairs. These challenges certainly can arise outside the realm of human rights too, but the nature of an international system that protects national sovereignty in "internal" affairs can make it especially difficult to enforce treaties that essentially protect citizens from their own governments. For these reasons, as well as for other reasons such as the lowest common denominator problem, international institutional forms can some-times turn out to be weak and ineffectual. In such cases, it may well be that the best available option is to return to nonstate action as a potentially viable, long-term strategy. The pressures of nongovernmental actors and the accep-tance of soft law and nonstate norms by domestic elites and publics may take time and may often exhibit little progress, but this approach may ulti-mately hold the most promise for creating better conditions for solving global problems and building effective international institutions.

Form and Legitimacy

The importance of the nation-state in the creation and implementation of international institutions makes political support and legitimacy a key facet of institutional effectiveness. However, international institutions are not unique when it comes to the need to take politics into account. Domestic policymaking is also very much the art of the possible, aiming for the most effective policy among those that are politically feasible. Moreover, in both domestic and international contexts, authority will be most effective when it is perceived as legitimate authority. Although national governments have centralized police and court systems, the state cannot watch every person's every move. Compliance is certainly affected by the existence and use of monitoring and sanctions, but it is also influenced by internalized norms and the perceived legitimacy of the regulatory institution.[34]

An institution's legitimacy or public support can be both specific and diffuse.[35] Specific legitimacy refers to the acceptance of the outcomes gen-erated by that institution in particular instances. Someone who disagrees with the WTO's U.S.-Shrimp action would view the trade body as having little specific legitimacy in that case.[36] However, that same person could still view the WTO with diffuse legitimacy if she concluded that the pro-cedures used by the body were fair and reasonable, or that over the long term the outcomes are or will be generally the right ones, even if in some cases the WTO made mistakes. A major challenge for the WTO at present seems to be how to strengthen and broaden its diffuse support among the public during a time when it has been issuing decisions that have been met with substantial criticism.

More research would be needed to understand the full range of deter-minants of diffuse legitimacy of international institutions. One factor that could affect support for international institutions is the degree of sover-eignty the institution preserves or protects for the nation-state. One might predict that, all things being equal, those institution-building efforts that least impose restrictions on state sovereignty will be perceived as more legitimate. Consequently, those institutional forms that preserve sovereignty the most would tend to garner the most political support from nation-states. Hence, internal control will generally be preferred over mutual recognition, consensual rulemaking over delegation. Things are not always equal, of course, and there may be times when states will see that the benefits of delegating authority to global regulatory organizations are greater than the costs, such as presumably has happened with the WTO. Yet, rightly or wrongly, intense debate has emerged about the nature the WTO's institutional structure and whether the institution has too much independent authority. Since the effects of international institutions can be difficult to determine—since we do not have a control group with different institutional forms—the challenge is to decide whether the WTO could achieve its free trade goals as effectively if its institutional structures were more transparent and tightly linked.

The Delegation Dilemma

The recent controversy over the WTO simply highlights a more general challenge for delegation as an institutional form. In an increasingly interdependent world, the need for delegation may grow in order to respond more rapidly to global problems. Delegating authority to international organizations, however, runs into two potential limitations. The first potential limitation is that the organization will be too constrained. The more narrowly delineated an organization's authority, for example, the harder it may be for that organization to respond to problems that change over time or to address unanticipated problems that do not fit neatly into the delineated categories. Another way an organization can be constrained is in how independently it can make decisions. In organizations where authority is shared coterminously (that is, where decisions of the organization must be made with the consent of all the member states), the organization may become hobbled since fully coterminous organizations do not really possess delegated authority at all. They simply provide a forum for international consent to take place. Requiring unanimous consent of all the member states of an organization basically institutionalizes the underlying collective action problems that delegation possibly could have solved.[37] Organizations that are tightly constrained in these ways will be less capable of responding to problems in a timely, effective manner.

The second potential limitation to delegations, though, is that they will be too *un*constrained. If nation-states in fact cede a lot of unconstrained authority, international organizations will be better poised to respond effectively to new and challenging problems. But they will also be better empowered to make mistakes or act in ways contrary to the interests of some member states. International organizations that are too powerful, and which exercise their power carelessly, can lose legitimacy among the nation-states that created these institutions. Nation-states may therefore resist the work of organizations that become too powerful or may invoke reversibility provisions to withdraw from the purview of these institutions.

In other words, a tension may often exist for international governmental organizations between policy effectiveness and political effectiveness. A balance must be achieved between creating organizations that are sufficiently independent to operate effectively and maintaining the support of nation-states (and their publics) that are understandably wary of the powers possessed by new organizations. Any new organization's authority must be sufficiently unencumbered to make the organization capable of solving global problems yet also sufficiently encumbered to make the organization acceptable to the nation-states who must agree to establish and maintain it. To optimize along these two dimensions, nation-states can seek to exploit different combinations of the four features of delegation described above: delineation, monitoring, sharing, and reversiblity. For example, nation-states can be predicted to require less sharing of decisions in organizations that contain narrowly delineated jurisdictions. As a result, organizations established to address relatively narrowly defined global problems may well depend less on power sharing or monitoring. However, organizations that are established to address a broad range of policy issues—institutions like the EU—will be based on more extensive arrangements for sharing power with member states.

Conclusion

Finding the appropriate balance between control and discretion in delegating authority to international institutions will take time, experimentation, and learning. Indeed, such a balance may really never be "found" at all as new problems will arise that seem to require more control or more discretion, and ideas will change about the proper location of policy authority. Of course, it is the presence of change that will probably make the choice of institutional forms all the more important. In a world with changing problems as well as changing ideas about how to solve those problems, arrangements will be needed that allow nation-states to create international rules and organizations—as will be arrangements that give nation-states flexibility to redirect these new institutions when a change in course is required to fit better the problems at hand.

We should expect international institution building to result in a use of varied institutional forms. Such variation provides opportunities for further research, as not all institutional forms will work equally well with different kinds of global problems. A transition from a system of dominance based on nation-state authority to one based on even more complex and interdependent global relationships has already begun, but it will also continue to move in fits and starts. Although the conditions of globalization would seem increasingly to make it in states' interests to cooperate and perhaps even to delegate to international institutions, national leaders will always need to be convinced that new institutions will indeed be used to their nations' overall benefit. We might see greater importance given to mutual recognition agreements, treaties, and international organizations. But when new international institutions result in unpopular decisions that adversely affect powerful nation-states—even if these decisions are otherwise in the overall global interest—it will likely have an effect on the future development of additional international institutions. Similarly, when international institutions appear to be ineffectual in the face of pressing global problems, that too will likely have an effect on future institutional development. Any transition to a so-called new world order will not be a smooth one. However, over time, we can hope that institutional forms will be used in ways that seem to strike the appropriate balance between policy effectiveness and political effectiveness, at least for some extended period.

Notes

1. See Peter Haas, Robert Keohane, and Marc Levy, *Institutions for the Earth: Sources of Effective International Environmental Protection* (MIT Press, 1993) (defining institutions to "include both organizations and sets of rules, codified in conventions and protocols that have been formally accepted by states"), p. 5.

2. For a discussion of the impact of institutions in international politics, see John J. Mearsheimer, "The False Promise of International Institutions," *International Security*, vol. 19 (Winter 1994–95), pp. 5–49; Robert O. Keohane and Lisa Martin, "The Promise of Institutionalist Theory," *International Security*, vol. 20 (Summer 1995), pp. 39–51; and

John J. Mearsheimer, "A Realist Reply," *International Security,* vol. 20 (Summer 1995), p. 82.

3. Although these three categories seem to capture many of the major problems that arise under globalization, they are by no means exhaustive. It also bears noting that I have *regulatory* problems in mind in this chapter and expressly leave to the side consideration of other important matters such as international security.

4. For a discussion of coordination problems, see Cass Sunstein, *After the Rights Revolution: Reconceiving the Regulatory State* (Harvard University Press, 1990), p. 53.

5. See "Product Standards, Conformity Assessment and Regulatory Reform," in *The OECD Report on Regulatory Reform* (Paris: Organization for Economic Cooperation and Development, 1997).

6. Roger Noll, "Internationalizing Regulatory Reform," in Pietro Nivola, ed., *Comparative Disadvantage? Social Regulations and the Global Economy* (Brookings, 1997).

7. For an extensive discussion of the political economy of climate change, see Jonathan Wiener, "On the Political Economy of Global Environmental Regulation," *Georgetown Law Journal,* vol. 87 (February 1999), p. 749.

8. For an argument about basic political principles, which all well-ordered states would respect, see John Rawls, *The Law of the Peoples* (Harvard University Press, 1999).

9. Once institutions are created, however, they may help reduce some of these costs. Haas, Keohane, and Levy, *Institutions for the Earth.*

10. David Held and others, *Global Transformations* (Stanford University Press, 1999), pp. 52–57. However, the rate of growth for some of these institutions, particularly international governmental organizations, has not always corresponded directly to the pace of globalization. For example, the number of international governmental organizations has declined since the 1980s. See James Hawdon, *Emerging Organizational Forms: The Proliferation of Regional Intergovernmental Organizations in the Modern World-System* (Greenwood Press, 1996), p. 13; and Cheryl Shanks, Harold Jacobson, and Jeffrey Kaplan, "Inertia and Change in the Constellation of International Governmental Organizations, 1981-1992," *International Organization,* vol. 50 (Autumn 1996), p. 593.

11. See Lawrence Lessig, "The New Chicago School," *Journal of Legal Studies,* vol. 27 (June 1998), p. 661.

12. Research on social norms is vast. For recent discussion of norms in the legal literature, see Robert C. Ellickson, *Order without Law: How Neighbors Settle Disputes* (Harvard University Press, 1991); and Cass Sunstein, "Social Norms and Social Roles," *Columbia Law Review,* vol. 96 (May 1996), p. 903.

13. See Joseph S. Nye Jr., "Soft Power," *Foreign Policy,* vol. 80 (Fall 1990), p. 153.

14. See David Vogel, *Trading Up: Consumer and Environmental Regulation in a Global Economy* (Harvard University Press, 1995).

15. See Haas, Keohane, and Levy, *Institutions for the Earth,* pp. 16–17.

16. See Kalypso Nicolaïdis, "Mutual Recognition of Regulatory Regimes: Some Lessons and Prospects," in OECD, *Regulatory Reform and International Market Openness* (Paris: Organization for Economic Cooperation and Development, 1996).

17. See "Product Standards, Conformity Assessment and Regulatory Reform," in *The OECD Report on Regulatory Reform;* and National Research Council, *International Standards, Conformity Assessment, and Trade: Into the 21st Century* (Washington: National Academy Press, 1995).

18. Of course, with multilateral treaties, it is always possible for nation-states to adopt reservations to the treaty, so the precise obligations imposed by a treaty may still vary from state to state. For a discussion of the challenges created by reservations, see David M. Leive, *International Regulatory Regimes* (Lexington Books, 1976), pp. 133–52.

19. See Abram Chayes and Antonia Handler Chayes, "Compliance without Enforcement: State Behavior under Regulatory Treaties," *Negotiation Journal,* vol. 7 (July 1991), p. 311; and Abram Chayes and Antonia Handler Chayes, "On Compliance," *International Organization,* vol. 47 (Spring 1993), p. 175.

20. Thanks to advances in global communication, a database of all the treaties deposited with the United Nations can now be found online (http://untreaty.un.org/English/access.asp [August 5, 2000]).

21. Robert Keohane, "The Demand for International Regimes," in Stephen Krasner, ed., *International Regimes* (Cornell University Press, 1983), p. 141.

22. See Cary Coglianese, "Is Consensus an Appropriate Basis for Regulatory Policy?" in Eric Orts and Kurt Deketelaere, eds., *Environmental Contracts: Comparative Approaches to Regulatory Innovation in the United States and Europe* (London: Kluwer Law International, 2000).

23. In this section, I am specifically concerned with international *governmental* organizations, since nongovernmental organizations do not depend on delegated authority from nation-states.

24. Held and others, *Global Transformations,* p. 53.

25. Leaders can be expected to protect their own institutional power, and this may make them wary of creating powerful international institutions. Domestic publics concerned about a lack of sovereignty and democratic accountability may also encourage leaders to be cautious in creating international institutions.

26. See, for example, David Epstein and Sharyn O'Halloran, *Delegating Powers: A Transaction Cost Politics Approach to Policymaking under Separate Powers* (Cambridge University Press, 1999); Matthew McCubbins, Roger Noll, and Barry Weingast, "Administrative Procedures as Instruments of Political Control," *Journal of Law, Economics, and Organization,* vol. 3 (Fall 1987), p. 243; Matthew McCubbins, Roger Noll, and Barry Weingast, "Structure and Process, Politics and Policy: Administrative Agencies and Political Control," *Virginia Law Review,* vol. 75 (March 1989), p. 431.

27. For an overview, see John Pratt and Richard Zeckhauser, "Principals and Agents: An Overview," in John Pratt and Richard Zeckhauser, *Principals and Agents: The Structure of Business* (Harvard Business School Press, 1985).

28. For a discussion of these four features in the context of federalism, see Cary Coglianese and Kalypso Nicolaïdis, "Securing Subsidiarity: The Institutional Design of Federalism in the U.S. and Europe," in Kalypso Nicolaïdis and Robert Howse, eds., *The Federal Vision: Legitimacy and Levels of Governance in the US and the EU* (Oxford University Press, forthcoming).

29. International treaties disavowing sovereign claims over Antarctica and outer space are akin to a withdrawal, although in these cases no nation possessed full sovereignty over these territories in the first place. See The Antarctica Treaty, 12 U.S.T. 794 (Dec. 1, 1959); The Outer Space Treaty, 18 U.S.T. 2410 (Jan. 27, 1967).

30. Ronald Mitchell, "Regime Design Matters: Intentional Oil Pollution and Treaty Compliance," *International Organization,* vol. 48 (Summer 1994), p. 425.

31. Such tests can be difficult to make because, as Robert Keohane and Lisa Martin have noted, "Rarely, if ever, will institutions vary while the 'rest of the world' is held constant." Robert O. Keohane and Lisa Martin, "The Promise of Institutionalist Theory," p. 47.

32. Robert Axelrod, *Evolution of Cooperation* (Basic Books, 1984).

33. Montreal Protocol on Substances That Deplete the Ozone Layer, 1522 U.N.T.S. 3 (Jan. 1, 1989); United Nations Framework Convention on Climate Change, FCCC/CP/7/Add.1 (issued Mar. 25, 1998), reprinted at 37 I.L.M. 22 (1998).

34. For an extensive discussion of compliance, see Tom Tyler, *Why People Obey the Law* (Yale University Press, 1990).

35. The distinction between specific and diffuse legitimacy is a familiar one in evaluating domestic governmental institutions, such as the Supreme Court. For a recent debate on the legitimacy of the Supreme Court, see James Gibson, "Understandings of Justice: Institutional Legitimacy, Procedural Justice, and Political Tolerance," *Law and Society Review,* vol. 23 (August 1989), p. 469; Tom Tyler and Kenneth Rasinski, "Legitimacy, and the Acceptance of Unpopular U.S. Supreme Court Decisions: A Reply to Gibson," *Law and Society Review,* vol. 25 (August 1991), p. 621; James Gibson, "Institutional Legitimacy, Procedural Justice, and Compliance with Supreme Court Decisions: A Question of Causality," *Law and Society Review,* vol. 25 (August 1991), p. 631.

36. World Trade Organization, United States-Import Prohibition of Certain Shrimp and Shrimp Products, Oct. 12, 1998, WT/DS58/AB/R, reprinted in *International Legal Materials,* vol. 38 (January 1999) (adopted Nov. 6, 1998) (appellate body report), pp. 118, 121. In this action, the WTO body found that the U.S. efforts to protect endangered sea turtles violated trade rules.

37. See Haas, Keohane, and Levy, *Institutions for the Earth,* p. 417.

14

ARTHUR ISAK APPLBAUM

Culture, Identity, and Legitimacy

O NE REASON OFTEN given to dread globalization is that it threatens to destroy distinctive national and ethnic cultures. The argument goes something like this: the pervasiveness of the English language and North Atlantic values and life-styles will undermine many local languages, values, and customs, replacing a diversity of national, ethnic, and religious attachments with a sort of cultural Esperanto spoken with an American accent. Having a rich background culture of one's own is a prerequisite for living a meaningful life, making sense of one's world, and having an intact personal identity. Losing one's culture is one of the gravest injuries a person can suffer because it damages personhood itself. Since having an intact background culture is necessary for personhood, it is necessary for the realization of any other goods or liberties valuable to persons. Therefore, cultural rights have priority over individual rights. Put so, this is ambiguous between the very strange claim that cultures are entities that can have rights at all (never mind priority) and the not-so-strange claim that individuals have rights to their cultures, and that these rights to culture have priority over other presumptive rights of these and other individuals. Even if only the not-so-strange claim is correct, governments are justified in restricting at least some important individual liberties in order to protect distinctive cultural practices from the homogenizing press of globalization.

For example, to protect Québécois culture, it would be permissible for Quebec not only to promote the speaking of French but to use coercive means to prevent the dominance of English. Currently, Quebec requires that store signs be in French and that the children of non-anglophone immigrants attend francophone schools. If the argument for the priority of culture is correct, more extreme measures to discourage the spread of English might also be justified: banning anglophone schools altogether; regulating the importation of books, movies, television, and popular music in English; or restricting the educational and employment opportunities of native English speakers. Nations such as Singapore, China, Saudi Arabia, Iran, and Afghanistan have typically defended illiberal protections of their cultural practices on two grounds: first, that the conception of the good life embodied in their cultural practices is substantively superior to the values of liberal cultures; and second, that even if the first were not true, outsiders do not have the legitimate authority to interfere in the internal affairs of a political community not their own. I shall take up this second defense shortly. The argument from cultural rights offers yet a third defense, one that appeals to concepts of personhood that liberals could accept. For this reason, the cultural impact of globalization worries many conscientious liberals whose own prospects in a global culture are quite secure.

Liberals needn't worry on this score, for at almost every step the priority-of-cultural-rights argument is mistaken. This is not to say that globalization does not present worries by way of what globalization will do to cultures. Surely rapid economic and social change will impose severe and at times unjust burdens on many, and surely some of these burdens will be the result of globalization's effects on linguistic and cultural practices. Rapid movements of jobs and people away from rural areas will not only materially impoverish those who cannot or will not learn cultural Esperanto. These shifts also will undermine attachments to social institutions in ways that could cause widespread alienation and instability. I will leave it to those with expertise in such matters to predict the facts about these harmful consequences—I have no wish to discount either their likelihood or severity. What I do wish to do is deflate some of the more hyperbolic claims made about the moral standing of these harms. Contrary to the cultural rights argument, there is something worse than to be exiled from one's culture, and that is to be imprisoned by it.

Identity

*"When in Great Britain some Welsh nationalists speak of the survival of the
Welsh language as a condition for the survival of Welsh society, they manage
sometimes to convey an impression that it is a condition of the survival of Welsh
people, as though the forgetting of Welsh were literally lethal."*[1]
    I will start with what might seem to be a picky point. Though the term
"personal identity" often is used to refer to what is at stake when culture is
in play, claims about lost, damaged, or shattered identities are usually
overblown. There aren't many ways to genuinely damage personal identity,
if this is understood as one's capacity for unified agency. Catastrophic mental illness and severe brain damage will do it, and so might science fiction
scenarios involving brain replication and the like. But nearly everything
else is hyperbole. Saul on the road to Damascus changed his name, but not
even he changed his personal identity. I am well aware that in much contemporary usage "personal identity" (along with "the self") has come to
refer to attachments and commitments, rather than to the unified agent
that has (and upon reflection endorses or revises) attachments and commitments. But this shift prejudges the momentousness of both welcome
and unwelcome changes in one's attachments and commitments. I will try
to explain why this matters.
    The truth in the cultural rights view is that speaking a language and hav-
ing access to cultural understandings and practices are necessary for endors-
ing and realizing any plan of life, whatever else one holds to be good. But
speaking a language must be distinguished from speaking a particular language, and being able to make sense of the surrounding cultural world
must be distinguished from being surrounded by a particular cultural
world. Exiles and immigrants often are disadvantaged, but they rarely are
incapable of cultural adaptation in ways that allow them to make sense of
things, pursue plans and projects, and enjoy the protections and opportunities of a social life they may not have chosen but do share. Strangers in a
strange land do not revert to mute, uncivilized Caspar Hausers.
    One way to put this is that one can have a right to culture without hav-
ing a right to one's own culture. But even this concedes too much, for it
suggests a picture of cultures as fairly static, and of cultural membership
as well defined. But "one's own culture" is a moving target in two ways:
the content and boundaries of what the culture in question is often is contested and always is in motion, and what one takes to be one's own, when

varying degrees of cosmopolitan attachment and detachment are possible, often is in play. If these two dynamics were not operating, the only threats globalization would pose to culture would be the rather unsubtle and heavy-handed exogenous ones. Smallpox wiped out entire native American tribes, and so too those tribes' cultures. A collapsed banking system could cause massive unemployment, which in turn could cause massive dislocations and violent social unrest. But one doesn't need to say much about "personal identity" to grasp what damage globalization has inflicted in these cases.

The more interesting (I do not say more important) threats of globalization are largely internal—the outcomes, in equilibrium, of individual members of a cultural community adjusting to each other's actions. French in Quebec is under threat because more and more Québécois are deciding to use English in more of their interactions, read more books in English, and watch more American movies. It is crucial to accurately model the structure of the collective action problem. Nationalists would have us believe all French speakers are spiraling down in a strategic game they all wish could have been avoided. No one would use English if each didn't fear that others would do so, and almost all are made worse off by the increasing dominance of English. Religious authorities in traditional societies say the same about secularization. A more plausible game structure, however, is that, for most, participating in the global Anglicized culture is a dominant strategy. They are best off if they can free ride on the French loyalties of others, and surely they don't want to be left behind if the others go global. But more plausible still is that there are different types of Québécois: the cosmopolitan dissenters and the nationalists. Because they have no interest in pickling others in French culture, the dissenters aren't free riders. What they want is to be free to borrow cultural materials from wherever they wish, scrutinize their attachments and commitments, and participate in the shaping of what counts as shared understandings in civil society. But if the cosmopolitans are free to do so, they will in ever greater numbers do so, thereby changing the content and boundaries of the cultural practices of Quebec. The project of the nationalists therefore cannot succeed unless the cosmopolitans are in some measure suppressed through the exercise of political coercion.

What justifies this coercion? If I am right about the structure of the game, it cannot be an argument of collective self-binding (the justification for hockey helmet rules). It cannot be an argument about preventing unfair free riding (the justification for tax enforcement). So the case must be made that the losses suffered by the Québécois nationalists (or the Iranian Islamists), who will no longer be able to live what they hold to be a culturally authentic life after the invasion of Esperanto, have moral priority over the losses suffered by the cosmopolitan dissenters, whose freedoms of expression, conscience, and association are to be suppressed. But claims to culture would have priority over claims to basic liberty only if one's very personhood, one's capacity as an agent, were threatened with destruction. The forgetting of Welsh just isn't like that.

States are not only permitted but required to defend their citizens from serious threats. Globalization might very well pose serious threats, and nothing that I've said here is incompatible with monetary and trade policies that protect against economic calamity or public health policies that protect against epidemic. If globalization's threat to local culture really were like the smallpox virus, a universally unwelcome invader, then it would be fitting to combat it like smallpox. But the mechanism by which local cultural practices and language usage change is mediated through valuable and meaningful choices individuals make about what kinds of lives they wish to live and what sorts of attachments and commitments they ought to make. It is tempting to claim that the people are trapped in a game no one wants to be in and characterize the coercive protection of culture as the provision of a public good. Two other characterizations, however, are more likely: paternalism or oppression.

Legitimacy

"As the right of each sentient being to live in accordance with its normal cultural evolution is considered sacred, no Starfleet personnel may interfere with the normal and healthy development of alien life and culture. Such interference includes introducing superior knowledge, strength, or technology to a world whose society is incapable of handling such advantages wisely. Starfleet personnel may not violate this Prime Directive, even to save their lives or their ships, unless they are acting to right an earlier violation or an accidental contamination of said culture."[2]

I turn now to a defense of illiberal protections of cultural practices mentioned earlier, the claim that outsiders do not have the legitimate authority to influence the internal affairs of a political community not their own. The most implausible version of the claim, which is seriously invoked only in defense of fragile primitive societies in, say, the Amazon or the South

Pacific, is a call for a kind of Endangered Cultural Species Act or a Star Trek-like Prime Directive. Somewhat more plausibly, it is often thought that it is wrong for multinational corporations or governments to deliberately aim at changing cultural and political practices of a target country through market forces or diplomatic pressure when the local government is opposed to such change. Target governments may be mistaken about the substantive goodness of local cultural practices and may be mistaken about the damage foreign cultural influence will do to valuable local ways of life. Still, if they are legitimate governments, these mistakes are theirs to make. Just as legitimate governments have immunity from unwanted military intervention, so too, legitimate governments have immunity from unwanted cultural intervention. So regulating the importation of English books and films to protect a local language or restricting the activities of nongovernmental organizations that seek equality for women or minorities to protect local religious practices, all are proper exercises of national sovereignty. To persist in interference or criticism in the face of governmental opposition is to show disrespect for the local political institutions and so disrespect for the people they serve.

The version of this argument that I wish to consider is that immunity of a certain sort is conceptually entailed by the legitimacy of the local government. If a government is legitimate, then, necessarily, it is immune from intervention. Because immunity is built into the idea of legitimacy, to claim that a government lacks immunity is to deny it legitimacy. The force of this conceptual claim is clear: whatever the criteria for legitimacy in government are, surely they are less stringent than the requirement that governments be perfectly just and good. But if legitimate, these governments are immune from interference with their less than just or good practices.

This claim is mistaken in both of its major steps. First, legitimacy does not entail immunity, so one is not making a conceptual error in holding that a legitimate authority is not immune from interference in the exercise of that authority. The case for the immunity of legitimate governments will have to be made by substantive, normative argument, not by appeal to the meaning of concepts. Second, legitimate governments may be much more rare than commonly supposed, so that even if there are good substantive reasons to conclude that legitimate authorities are immune, there are also good substantive reasons to conclude that authorities that fall seriously short in protecting the freedoms of their subjects are not legitimate.

To start, we need two distinctions: between empirical legitimacy and moral legitimacy, and between the concept or idea of legitimacy and particular conceptions of legitimacy—its content and criteria. Following Max Weber, much contemporary social scientific writing uses the term *legitimacy* in its empirical sense, referring to the beliefs of persons about the proper exercise of authority. An authority is legitimate, in this sense, insofar as those who are subject to its command take it to be legitimate. Obviously, empirical legitimacy is parasitic on a prior idea, moral legitimacy. For when the objects of this social scientific description, the members of some society, believe that a rule or a ruler is legitimate, they are not (or not simply) engaging in their own social scientific description of each other's beliefs. What empirical legitimacy describes are views about moral legitimacy. (This is so, even if moral legitimacy does not exist, which would be so if various forms of anarchy or nihilism were true. Unicorns do not exist either, but the idea of a unicorn does.)

When Rousseau famously writes, "Man is born free, and everywhere he is in chains. . . . How did this change occur? I do not know. What can make it legitimate? I believe I can answer this question," he is using *legitimacy* in the thoroughly normative sense, a sense that is both historically and conceptually prior to Weber's. This is not to assert that the social fact of what people take to be morally legitimate cannot figure in as a condition for having moral legitimacy. It is not incoherent to hold that an authority is morally legitimate if and only if most people (for whatever reason) believe that that authority is morally legitimate. But note that this is a claim about the substantive criteria for having moral legitimacy—a particular conception—not a claim about the meaning of moral legitimacy, which is conceptually more primitive than social facts about beliefs about it. Though not incoherent, such a claim is mistaken. In most cultures over most of history, women believed that their husbands had legitimate authority over them, but that didn't make it so. Similarly, the fact that people in a society believe that their rulers have legitimate authority, or the fact that the rulers of other societies believe that the rulers of the society in question have legitimate authority, doesn't make it so. More plausibly, empirical legitimacy might be a necessary but not sufficient condition of moral legitimacy. This would be so if some measure of effectiveness were a condition for the justified exercise of coercive control, and the perception of justification were necessary for effectiveness. Henceforth, when I refer to legitimacy unmodified, I mean moral legitimacy.

The second distinction, to which I have already alluded, is between the concept of legitimacy—what it means—and particular conceptions—its content and criteria. When someone claims that a ruler is legitimate just in case he is God's anointed, and another claims a ruler is legitimate just in case she is freely and fairly elected under the provisions of a just constitution, they disagree about the criteria for having moral legitimacy, but they agree, roughly, about what the disagreement is about.

The concept itself makes no essential reference to a procedure or to pedigree, so "a government is morally legitimate if and only if it is morally good" is a possible conception. But neither does the concept make an essential reference to substantive goodness, justness, or all-things-considered moral correctness. Possible conceptions of legitimacy can refer exclusively to an authoritative text, or a line of familial descent, or the enactments of a legislative body. Particular conceptions of moral legitimacy might specify either some procedure or some substantive attribute or both as necessary or sufficient conditions. The most plausible conceptions, I believe, require both a sufficiently close connection between the rulers and the will of the ruled and the protection of at least a short list of basic substantive rights and liberties. Perhaps governments that aren't fully democratic and fully liberal can be legitimate, but not governments that are tyrannical or that violate fundamental human rights.

What is built into the concept of moral legitimacy itself? Joseph Raz convincingly has argued that the exercise of legitimate authority by an actor entails some change in the normative situation of others. Otherwise, having authority cannot be distinguished from merely having a liberty. I think Raz is right about this, but it does not follow that this change in normative situation must be either a moral requirement of those subject to authority to obey or a moral requirement of third parties not to interfere. It is a virtue in conceptual analysis to seek the least restrictive specification that is still useful, for otherwise we risk mischaracterizing real substantive disagreements as semantic misunderstandings.

To get at what I think is the correct conceptual account of moral legitimacy, we need to return to the analytic jurisprudence that Wesley Hohfeld developed early in the twentieth century. Hohfeld distinguished four legal advantages that A can have in relation to B, which, correlatively, entail four legal disadvantages of B in relation to A. If A has a *right* (or, more specifically, a claim-right) against B, B has a correlative *duty* to A; if A has a *privilege* (or liberty) with respect to B, B has *no-right* against A; if A has a *power* with respect to B, B faces a *liability* from A; and if A has an *immunity* from B, B has a *disability* with respect to A. Each legal advantage also has its negation: having a *claim-right* is the opposite of having *no-right*; a *privilege* is the opposite of a *duty*; a *power* is the opposite of a *disability*; and an *immunity* is the opposite of a *disability*. Hohfeld's elegant scheme was formulated to show the connection between legal concepts, but, with some minor tinkering, it illuminates connections between moral concepts as well: if A has a *moral* claim-right against B, then B has a correlative *moral* duty to honor the claim, and so on.

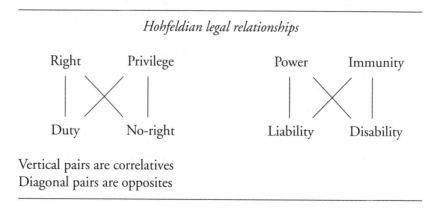

Hohfeldian legal relationships

Right   Privilege   Power   Immunity

Duty   No-right   Liability   Disability

Vertical pairs are correlatives
Diagonal pairs are opposites

On my account, legitimacy is a form of morally justified authorship: a *moral* power to create and enforce *nonmoral* prescriptions and social facts— that is to say, the moral power to author legal, institutional, or conventional rights and duties, powers and liabilities, and so on. If Hohfeld's scheme is correct, then if A exercises a moral power with respect to B, and thereby imposes upon B an institutional duty, then B must have a correlative moral liability. What is this liability? It is that B is subject to morally justified enforcement. But a moral liability is not a moral duty, and an institutional duty is not a moral duty. Raz's requirement that the exercise of legitimate authority change the normative situation of the subject of that authority is satisfied because B now is subject to a moral liability— justified enforcement. It is not conceptually necessary that, if A exercises legitimate authority in imposing upon B an institutional duty, B has a moral duty to comply.

Again, if Hohfeld's scheme holds up, having a moral power is not the same as, and does not entail, having a moral immunity. When A exercises a moral power over B, and imposes upon B an institutional duty, this imposes upon B a morally justified liability to enforcement, which is the opposite of a moral immunity from enforcement. But just because B lacks moral immunity from A, A does not have moral immunity from the interference of some third party C. There is no conceptual route from having legitimacy—having moral power—to having moral immunity. Therefore, it does not immediately follow from a judgment that the norm-generating mechanisms of a culture have legitimate authority that outsiders must not intervene in the generation and enforcement of those norms. Star Trek's Prime Directive is not a conceptual necessity, so the case for outsiders respecting illiberal cultural practices will need to be made on substantive grounds.

One such ground is that respect for less-than-just practices follows from the respect owed to members of a political community who have collectively decided, in a way collectively acceptable to them, how to govern themselves. A political community that fails to have just practices may still reasonably claim that the offending practices are *their* practices, and that, within bounds, mistakes about what justice demands are theirs to make. I said within bounds: the bounds are marked by whether interference would be disrespectful to those who are being treated unjustly—whether it is reasonable for those most burdened by illiberal cultural practices nonetheless to endorse the practices as their own. Surely, if those burdened correctly held that the burdensome cultural practices imposed upon them genuine moral duties, outsiders would have no cause to interfere for their sake.

Recall, however, that legitimate authority to impose an institutional duty does not entail a moral duty to comply. Governors (or the majority, or the powerful) can be sufficiently connected to the will and interests of the governed (or the minority, or the weak) to pass the threshold of legitimate authority, but not sufficiently connected to make the burdensome practices the practices of the burdened, and generate in them genuine moral duties to obey. Unjustly treated minorities can be forgiven if they reject a reified account of "we" in "We the People" under which their injuries are self-inflicted. When this is so, it shows no disrespect to them for outsiders to intervene on their behalf. Moral legitimacy and moral immunity can come apart, moral legitimacy and moral duty can come apart, and therefore duty and immunity can stand and fall together. When cultural minorities and dissenters aren't morally obligated to obey unjust but legitimate authority, outsiders aren't morally disabled from helpful meddling on their behalf.[3]

Notes

1. Bernard Williams, *Morality: An Introduction to Ethics* (Harper and Row, 1972), p. 22.

2. For an authoritative statement of the Prime Directive, see Starfleet Command, <<www.sfcommand.com/documents/general_orders.html>>.

3. For a leading account of cultural rights, see Will Kymlicka, *Liberalism, Community, and Culture* (Oxford University Press, 1989), and *Multicultural Citizenship* (Oxford University Press, 1995); for a leading account of legitimate authority, see Joseph Raz, *The Authority of Law* (Oxford University Press, 1979), and Joseph Raz, *The Morality of Freedom* (Oxford University Press, 1986); for a leading account of political liberty, see John Rawls, *Political Liberalism* (Columbia University Press, 1993); and Wesley Newcomb Hohfeld's work is collected in *Fundamental Legal Conceptions as Applied to Judicial Reasoning* (Yale University Press,1919).

15

DEBORAH HURLEY
VIKTOR MAYER-SCHÖNBERGER

Information Policy
and Governance

THE INCREASING AVAILABILITY of information made possible by
global information systems, including the Internet, will affect governance and the political process.[1] Governance, in turn, will affect the creation, availability, dissemination, and use of information in global information systems.

In this Information Age, the word "information" is widely used, and disparities of access to information are widely lamented—but there is no
broadly accepted definition of the term. For the purposes of this chapter,
"data" mean a representation of facts, concepts, or instructions in a for-
malized manner suitable for communication, interpretation, or processing
by human beings or by automatic means.[2] "Information" is the meaning
assigned to data by means of conventions applied to those data.[3]

Very little information has an absolute quality. At a certain time or in a
certain context, information may be very harmful, resulting in death or disaster. At another time or in another place, that same information may have
a neutral or even a beneficial effect.

Many legal systems reflect a hierarchy of information. In the United
States, for example, political speech is given special treatment, as embodied in the First Amendment, as a type of information that should be least
constrained and for which conditions should be created and sustained to

guarantee relative ease of communication. Other countries also accord political speech special consideration, in the opposite direction, as information to be closely controlled.[4]

The principal issues with regard to information are its production, access, distribution, and use. Creation of information may be encouraged, as in the case of political speech, or discouraged, as is child pornography. Access to information may be facilitated or restricted. The copyright laws of the United States provide examples of both encouraging and curtailing access to information. Documents produced by the U.S. government are in the public domain and, therefore, available without cost and for any use.[5] The U.S. copyright law grants to other creators of works a monopoly of limited duration. Similarly, other information may be made widely available, or its distribution may be strictly controlled. Finally, there may be rules to ease or inhibit the use of particular information or the use of certain information by various groups or individuals.

For each of the acts of information creation, availability, dissemination, and use, there are several issues. The first issue is the locus of control of the information and of its production, access to it, distribution, and use. Second is the issue of ownership, which may be different from control, of the information and of its generation, availability, distribution, and use. Rules may be made with regard to information production, access, distribution, and use, including restrictions, the circumstances under which rules are set, and the reasons for which rules are made, including the goals of the rules. The goals might include some combination of protection of the person, protection of property, and protection of social norms.

Information production, access, distribution, and use may be conceived, therefore, as a series of successive doors, which may swing to be more open or more closed. If, for example, the very creation of certain information is barred, then the availability, dissemination, and use of that information will also be foreclosed. Each of these doors swings on a hinge, which may be set at any point. What decides the setting of the hinge on each door?

There are usually fewer restrictions on creation of information. Examples of information that may not even be produced without sanction include political speech in some countries or circumstances, hate speech in certain jurisdictions, and, again, child pornography. Most restrictions on information center on the availability of the information and its distribution. Again, there are usually fewer restrictions on use of the information. This is a reasonable way to approach the question of information policy. It is relatively hard to implement and enforce restrictions on creation and use and relatively easier to monitor the flow of information and to close the doors more tightly on access to and distribution of the information.

In order to examine the development and state of information policy for the global network, this chapter focuses on two types of information: personally identifiable information about individuals and so-called objectionable content. These two types of information have generated considerable controversy. Polls of Internet users consistently cite concerns about their personal information online, which may hamper their participation in the global information network and e-commerce.[6] There have been several sensational cases about reactions by governmental authorities to objectionable content on the Internet.[7] With regard to personal information, there have already been three decades of international discussion and rulemaking. In contrast, while there is a lot of strong opinion about content that is "objectionable," whether it is viewed as pornographic, violent, blasphemous, dissident, or hatemongering, and plenty of national and subnational rules, there has been little inquiry or discussion at the international level about objectionable content in global information networks. These two perspectives on information policy in the global information networks— protection of personal information and regulation of objectionable content—are offered as two very different starting points from which to begin to map the global information policy landscape.

Protecting Personal Privacy in the Global Information Network

Personally identifiable information about individuals includes, certainly, information with their name or some other relatively unique identifier attached to it.[8] It would also include information about a person that, even though the name does not appear, is still identifiable to an individual.[9] Protection of personal information is often perceived to be fragmentary, uneven, and internationally variable. Yet there already exists a well-established framework, accepted at the international level and by many nations, that provides a clear set of common denominators upon which broader global consensus with regard to protection of personal information may be built. There are two international accords on protection of personal information, the 1980 OECD Guidelines on the Protection of Privacy and

Transborder Flows of Personal Data, and the 1981 Council of Europe Convention No. 108 for the Protection of Individuals with Regard to Automatic Processing of Personal Data.[10] The United States, the member countries of the European Union, and many other countries are signatories to at least one of these two documents. The OECD Privacy Guidelines and the Council of Europe Convention predate the rise of the Internet and the current and foreseeable growth in computing power and networking. Nonetheless, they are viewed as having continued validity and as providing a fundamental framework for protection of personal information. In addition to these direct and explicit privacy protections, the provisions of the principal human rights conventions, the Universal Declaration of Human Rights and the European Convention for the Protection of Human Rights and Fundamental Freedoms, are often considered applicable to the protection of personal information. Furthermore, it is asserted, the rights of freedom of movement and freedom of association in these two conventions apply to the global network, where an increasing number of transactions are identifiable and traceable, as more and more human interaction goes online. Finally, there are thirty years of experience, not only with formulating the principles of protection of personal information, but also with implementing these principles in legislation, standards, business codes of conduct, and technological design and implementation.

The development of global policy on objectionable content is similarly characterized as an impossible task. How can it ever be hoped that international consensus will be reached concerning objectionable content, and international accords developed, in a world of such political, religious, cultural, and artistic diversity? The argument is that notions of objectionable content are inherently vague and dependent on political, religious, or cultural outlook and personal perception. The same has been said, at various times, about personal information and copyrights and other intellectual property. Yet there is already lots of national and subnational regulation about objectionable content. There may actually be a greater degree of global agreement about this issue than is generally perceived. It is true that the international conversation about objectionable content is just beginning and is, therefore, preliminary and relatively inchoate. There is an absence of international discussion and written accords, both of which provide harmonizing mechanisms, exchange of experience and expertise, baselines, and more clearly articulated implementation and enforcement practices and regimes. The fact that rules do not already exist, however, does not render an outcome impossible. To the contrary, there are analogies and precedents in other informational categories, such as protection of personal information, to show the way.

Personal Information in the Global Network

When examining "governance" in the abstract one risks losing sight of the fact that the essential building block of any political system is the individual. Beginning with the individual (the condition precedent for any social, economic, or political order), this section proceeds to examine the possible effects on governance, especially in democratic political systems, of increasing availability and use of personally identifiable information.

Privacy is a necessary component of democracy. Individuals are the necessary elements of any collective, whether it be a family, nation, school, club, religious order, or Internet chat. For the individual, the collective provides a context and frame of reference, but privacy is essential for the formation of a conception of the self.[11] Individuals need to communicate,[12] but desire, at times, to limit the audience for their communications.[13] Individuals want to be able to preserve certain thoughts and activities from the wider community. In the physical world, in their diverse relationships and interactions, individuals have various zones of opacity and transparency, in which varying amounts of personal information about them are revealed.

The convergence of massive amounts of personally identifiable information with an increasingly powerful global computing and communication network of networks raises a set of significant and pressing privacy issues.

Currently, there is a variety of measures around the globe used to protect personal information, including legislation, standards, technological means, industry codes of conduct, and business practices and procedures. The particular measures employed differ significantly, depending on geographical location and technological development. This degree of variation is generally incompatible with a global network in which information, including personal, identifiable information about individuals, may travel anywhere in the network. The level of protection, for the same personal information, may be different, not because of any intent but as a result of legal, economic, technological, social, or ethical rules that happen to govern a particular part of the network. Moreover, it is often not clear which rule or rules govern various parts of the network or the information in it, leading to uncertainty, lack of clarity, forum shopping, the creation of so-called data havens, and potential inconsistency of outcomes.

The Global Trend toward Greater Protection of Personal Information

In the early 1970s, as computers began to come into wider use by government and industry, concern began to grow about the collection, use, and automatic processing of personal information.[14] The abuses of civil liberties and human rights during World War II made many Europeans especially sensitive to the potential harms of large-scale collection, manipulation, and retention of records about individuals. European countries, such as Germany, France, and Sweden, began to pass legislation to protect personal information. The United States was part of this early trend, adopting the Privacy Act, which applied to the federal government, in 1974. This trend toward adopting legislation to protect personal information has continued. Most western and central European nations, as well as other jurisdictions, such as Australia, New Zealand, and Hong Kong, now have so-called omnibus data protection legislation.[15] The United States, however, has not adopted similar data protection legislation.[16]

The culmination of three decades of European policy development is reflected in the European Union Directive 95/46/EC on the Protection of Individuals with Regard to the Processing of Personal Data and on the Free Movement of Such Data. The EU directive was adopted in 1995, with the requirement that it be implemented in national law by EU member countries by October 1998. The EU directive contains a significant extraterritorial provision that the flow of personal information from any EU member country may be halted if the jurisdiction to which it is being transferred is deemed not to have an adequate level of protection for personal information. The United States is generally viewed as lacking an adequate level of protection of personal information, owing to the absence in the United States of "omnibus" legislation. The intentions of the EU and its member countries to enforce the extraterritorial provision of the directive, and possible recourse to various international bodies by the EU and the United States or other non-EU countries that might also be affected by the directive, have triggered intense debate and inter-governmental consultation. Repeatedly, deadlines have been set for agreement on a U.S.-Europe compromise, with the tempo of bilateral negotiations increasing as each deadline approached. "In July 2000 the European Commission approved the Safe Harbor Privacy Principles proposed by the United States government as a means of offering an adequate level of protection of personal data in the United States. The European Parliament opposed the EC approval. The EC approval of Safe Harbor will be evaluated in 2003."[17] Despite the apparent schism between the EU and the United States, both have adopted the 1980 OECD Guidelines on Privacy. More recently, protection of personal information has been included in the proposed work program of the World Trade Organization (WTO) on electronic commerce, which is to be taken up in the next round of trade negotiations.

American companies doing business in Europe have had to adhere to the personal information protection laws of each of the jurisdictions in which they operated. Many American companies have proved able and willing to comply with omnibus data protection legislation for decades. The irony is that these companies are not obligated to provide the same level of protection of personal information for Americans or for individuals in other parts of the world where there is no statutory requirement.

Privacy Rules for the Information Age

The following three rules are proposed as the foundation for protection of personal information in the twenty-first century.

—Privacy must be the default. Computer and network systems and transactions on them have generally been designed to be identifiable. The history and rationales behind this condition should be examined. Instead, the global network should be designed with protection of personal information as the default.[18] The locus of control of personal information and communications should be firmly weighted toward the individual. The addition of these design criteria would provide important insights and recommendations for system design and implementation, adoption of legal norms, and the social construct.[19]

In this regard, there is a very rich and largely unexplored space between complete identity and full anonymity.[20] It would include, for example, "authorized user" and "member of the group." Many transactions in the physical world are not identifiable. Active efforts should be undertaken to make more interactions on the global network nonidentifiable.

—Claim for and return to the individual control and/or ownership of her personal information. The individual should control her personal data.[21] A third-party model predominates today, with the third party being either the government or the private sector. These entities have personal information about individuals, which they, by legal requirement or self-regulation, agree to hold and use in certain ways. These protections should continue but should be based on the rule that the control of personal information resides in the individual. In addition, there should be more effort to devise technological means to enhance privacy and personal data protection.

The key question is, "Who owns the personal data?" Today, people sometimes speak of consumers trading information for some benefit. Instead, it looks like a wholesale giveaway, with the information-gathering entity reaping a windfall, and the information provider receiving very little or nothing in return. Scams and fishing expeditions abound, such as, in the United States, so-called warranty cards, which are entirely unnecessary to invoke the consumer's rights of warranty and ask questions wholly irrelevant to the provision of the warranty, such as the income of the purchaser.

—Build a global solution. Although international rules with regard to protection of personal information are much more developed than those for addressing objectionable content, there is still more to be done to create rules that support the global network. The rules for personal information protection must be harmonious and work as a global solution. The United States should move higher up the curve Europe has already mapped and assume a role as a leader in the protection of personal information.

Privacy is often treated like a brand new issue. Yet efforts to develop rules safeguarding personal data are three decades old. A lot of work has already been done at international and national levels to establish common principles and rules, with broad acceptance by many countries. The groundwork has been laid. Now, owing to the burgeoning growth of the global information network, there is pressure and urgency to provide better protection of personal information. The current challenges are dissemination and implementation of the international and national frameworks that already exist and, as necessary, the development of new measures and practices to meet current and foreseeable privacy needs. By contrast, as the next section will illustrate, the state of information policy with respect to objectionable content remains embryonic.

Objectionable Content in the Global Information Network

The media usually depict efforts to regulate either as heavy-handed and excessive in their global reach or as inherently futile in a global network. The debate on content regulation gains little from the juxtaposition of the two extremes. The important point is the enormous pressure that the global information network places on the goals and means of content regulation.

The trial and conviction in Germany of American citizen Gary Lauck, a notorious neo-Nazi, provides an example of the reach of governmental regulation of objectionable content. For years, Lauck had been sending Nazi propaganda literature to German citizens by mail and the Internet, an activity protected in the United States by the First Amendment of the U.S. Constitution but illegal under German law. Lauck was arrested in Denmark, while he was on a speaking tour, and extradited to Germany. Similarly, the CEO of CompuServe's German subsidiary, an America Online service provider, was tried and sentenced in Munich for enabling German citizens to access Internet discussion forums within which, among hundreds of thousands of postings, pedophilic postings were also to be found.

Singapore makes futile attempts to filter the Internet, Iran has limited success in prohibiting TV satellite receivers, and China expends largely fruitless efforts to curb the inflow of information through digital networks. Serbian authorities failed to control the dissemination of political information, despite draconian measures. They had to capitulate in the face of tens of thousands of private satellite receivers, NATO TV broadcasts into Serbia by airborne information warfare units, and a dramatic swell in Internet access through conventional Serbian telephone lines.

Regulation of Objectionable Content

Content regulations generally do not attempt to forestall the creation of objectionable content. There are exceptions, such as child pornography and, in certain political systems, materials criticizing the government. Similarly, while there are prohibitions on the use of objectionable content, the great bulk of content regulation concentrates on the availability of the material and its distribution.

For many decades, nations have used this approach and regulated content by limiting its dissemination. Defamation and libel laws focus on public accusations, while an off-hand remark in a private conversation will remain unpunished. Indecency regulations permit information access only to adults, not to minors. Even the prime law school example of permissible content regulation—prohibiting someone from falsely shouting "Fire" in a crowded theatre—focuses on the specific dissemination method chosen, the "shout" directed at the public, the audience at large.

When the source of particular information and its dissemination network are within the territorial borders of a nation, the enforcement of national content regulations is comparatively easy. If specific information violates the law, the disseminators may be brought to justice and further distribution stopped.

At first glance, it may appear that the ability to enforce national content regulations would be another victim of globalization. But convictions of information providers around the globe, such as Gary Lauck and CompuServe Germany's CEO, demonstrate that content regulations survive, albeit in a different form. While enforcement becomes less likely, it also becomes more erratic, creating unexpected side effects. National authority over regulation of content is disrupted when information access and distribution are disconnected from specific geographic territories and, therefore, jurisdictional authority. For example, direct-broadcasting satellites turned information providers into international, often global, players and provided an abundance of information channels to every individual with a small and affordable satellite dish. Rupert Murdoch's satellites broadcast into China but are beyond China's jurisdictional reach.

Regulating such transborder flows of information created a novel and substantial challenge for national regulatory authorities. It has become increasingly difficult to focus enforcement on the creator of the information or the original disseminator, who may be far away. Instead, enforcement efforts may concentrate on the local provider of dissemination services, which may have very little connection to the original creator.

Enforcement of national content regulations in such a world of transborder information flows depends less on the traditional, "hard" powers of the state and much more on its softer counterparts. China was not able to take Murdoch's satellites out of the sky, but it was able to persuade Murdoch to drop the BBC from the list of channels transmitted by the satellites. In return, Murdoch gained formal acceptance of News Corp.'s TV channels in China and could actively begin to court Chinese advertisers. (This case demonstrates another feature of global information networks, namely, that network providers are becoming increasingly disconnected from the information sources they disseminate. Removing the BBC from the list of offerings posed little problem for Murdoch, who easily filled the slot with a more benign cable channel available on the market.)

Managing such transborder information flows requires governments to move from national enforcement to more cooperative engagement with other jurisdictional authorities and other players in the global information network, including international consultation, negotiation, and rulemaking. In the example of Murdoch's TV satellites as well as in other traditional media, the negotiating partners are easily identifiable, since specific types of information are limited to certain dissemination channels. This is changing rapidly. The Internet and similar information infrastructures are digital networks. All information that can be digitized—and this covers pretty much everything—can be sent across the network. The network is not limited to a specific type of information dissemination, such as audiovisual images by television and voice communication by telephony. It encompasses, instead, all elements of human communication. In this new ubiquitous information medium, the effectiveness of the old-fashioned, territorially based regulatory approach is significantly diminished. China might have been successful in jamming News Corp.'s direct-broadcast satellite if Murdoch had refused to stop broadcasting the BBC. But doing the same with digital information networks would take out not only the BBC or Murdoch's TV programs but also the entire information connection that China has with the rest of the world. Given the advanced interconnectedness of financial markets, businesses, and innumerable other networks, such as air traffic control, disconnecting a nation from the global information network, while certainly effective in enforcing content regulation, would be little short of informational suicide.

Attempts to persuade the communication network providers to cooperate with national regulatory authorities to identify objectionable content will fail because these providers themselves have no technical control over the digital information streams that flow through their networks. The provider of a connection to such a converged network is providing an information pipeline, not a specific variety of information. Even if the provider had technical control over the information flows, he might be legally barred from exerting it. According to traditional content regulation theory, private communication is free from governmental intrusion, while public communication may be regulated. While traditional information networks, such as television or telephony, may easily be placed in one category or the other, it is difficult or impossible to do so with the global information network.

The Internet defies such simple categorization because it can be used to disseminate all types of information, from private e-mails to public webcasts. Convergence causes the differentiation between private and public communication, another foundation of traditional content regulation, to crumble. The network providers in the global information network may be compared, not with Murdoch's StarTV information dissemination network, but more closely with telephone operators or mail deliverers, since all communication between the users and other content providers is private conversation between two parties. The disappearance of the public-private distinction means that governments will not be able to target network providers as possible controllers of digital information flows.

Neither the traditional method of jurisdictional authority nor the alternative model of cooperation with international information disseminators is capable of retaining governmental authority over regulation of content in the global information network. What are the options for governments?

Governments may simply continue to enforce content regulations where they can, while accepting that this domain of control will inexorably shrink. This is the Singapore approach. And although full enforcement is increasingly infeasible, the cases of Gary Lauck and CompuServe amply illustrate that episodic and uneven enforcement may continue to work in practice. The reason is the uneven network topology of the Internet. In theory, any information source prohibited in one country may move to another country and be accessible from there. On the networks, as Frances Cairncross has remarked, distances do not matter.[22] Yet, in practice, North America, Europe, and a few other countries hold a commanding height in available communication bandwidth. Being forced to move an information site from these countries to another location may not make the availability and dissemination of the information impossible, but it may seriously hamper the site's effectiveness, as a result of small bandwidth, low reliability, and substantial waiting times. Given the short attention spans in Internet time, these impediments, while not fatal in theory, may quite possibly render such information practically inaccessible. The disadvantage of this approach is its temporary nature. As overall connectivity and bandwidth increase, so will accessibility. Eventually, geographic location may not matter at all.

Governments may also work toward increased international cooperation. If nations agree on a common denominator of regulable content, that content might again be controlled at the source and enforced throughout the participating nations, leaving network providers unaffected. Even if only the nations with major backbones to the information networks agree on a common policy approach, substantial enforcement across borders may be feasible.[23] This is the current mode of thinking among the European Union member nations and the G-7. For objectionable content where national rules are already similar, as with prohibitions against child pornography, cross-border cooperation among national law enforcemnt agencies, utilizing the global information networks, may provide the first stepping-stones toward a broader regulatory framework. Though useful, a limitation of these efforts is that they generally follow the relatively slow pace of international cooperation and diplomacy, rather than dynamic, breathless Internet time.

During the last several years, a third policy option has been proposed: the use of filtering technologies to weed out objectionable content. This means of regulating objectionable content would shift the regulatory target from the creators and providers to the recipients, the users. Proponents of this so-called self-regulatory approach suggest that users "regulate" the information that flows to them by, for example, using software that filters out unwanted information. This idea, particularly if paired with a labeling system in which bits of information are labeled depending on their content, either by the creator or a third party, may sound enticing and, compared with the other options, like a relatively easy solution. Malign information would be blocked from users who find it objectionable, or whose governments find it objectionable, but reception of this same information would remain open to others.

Unfortunately, this approach has many faults. First, users hardly will turn on a software tool to filter out objectionable or illegal information that they want to access. Contrary to the term "self-regulation," in most cases the filters will be maintained by a third party, not by the users themselves. Furthermore, studies of filtering software have repeatedly shown its shortcomings, first, in filtering out objectionable information and, second, in blocking access to permissible information.[24]

Installing filters at the level of the network providers not only shifts the burden away from the recipient and back to the providers, it also creates additional problems. Who, for example, is going to create the information labels for the filters and according to what standards? If creating labels is done by third parties, a pervasive system of censorship is created, which second guesses societal standards. This purported solution will create more and worse problems than the supposed evil that it is meant to address. If, however, authors are forced to create labels for their information, what will happen if they mislabel? Some have suggested that a threat of criminal sanction is necessary to induce authors to label their information correctly. If that proposal is adopted, the end would be, not just a simple censorship system, but a truly Orwellian one, in which the author becomes her own censor.

The Way Forward

This chapter has examined the formulation of information policy in the global information networks. Dynamic information flows in global networks will affect governments and governance, as attempts are made to identify the information rules that may be helpful or necessary and the role of governments in articulating information policy as well as the participation of other stakeholders. Similarly, governmental action, especially that taken in isolation or without regard to existing norms or dominant rules or trends in other jurisdictions, may produce asymmetries, political friction, unequal treatment, and gaping lacunae. The chapter has provided a framework for thinking about information rules and policy. It then turned to examine regulation of two informational domains, personal information and objectionable content. There is a strong, international base of three decades' duration for the protection of personal information, which provides a foundation for the ever-increasing information flows on the global network and the development of rules to protect personal information by jurisdictions that have not yet done so. In contrast, while feelings about objectionable content run high, and there is a patchwork of national and subnational rules, little has been done so far to deal with objectionable content on the global information networks. In the short term, these matters may affect democratic political systems more strongly. But countries with other governance systems will not be immune from these issues and may ultimately confront them with more profound effects.

Notes

1. See chap. 6 in this volume.
2. Definition of *data* adopted by the 1992 OECD Guidelines for the Security of Information Systems.
3. Definition of *information* adopted by the 1992 OECD Guidelines for the Security of Information Systems.

4. See, for example, "Web Sites Bloom in China, and Are Weeded," *New York Times,* December 23, 1999, p. 1.

5. In marked contrast, for example, to the "crown copyright" system of the United Kingdom.

6. See, for example, the 8th WWW User Survey of the Graphic, Visualization and Usability Center (GVU), Georgia Institute of Technology, http://www.gvu.gatech.edu/user_surveys/survey-1997-10/. U.S. Secretary of Commerce William M. Daley identified privacy as "the make or break issue" for the success of the digital economy. "The Emerging Digital Economy," April 15, 1998. At a conference on the global information infrastructure (GII) at the Organization for Economic Cooperation and Development (OECD) in December 1994, the head of the delegation of the United States identified privacy, along with security, cryptography, and intellectual property, as the "showstopper" issues of the GII, which, if unresolved, would impede the development of the GII and its use to its fullest potential.

7. See the descriptions of the Lauck and CompuServe cases below.

8. But the set of personally identifiable information is actually larger than the information to which someone's name is attached. Information may be personally identifiable to an individual through the accumulation of the available information or due to the context in which it appears. If the relevant population is the whole world, then it may be difficult or impossible to identify the person involved without the name and, perhaps, without additional information, such as address. But if the relevant population is smaller, then it may be entirely possible to identify the person in the absence of her name.

9. The latter case usually arises in a contextual setting, such as a workplace, town, neighborhood, or epidemiological study.

10. The 1980 OECD Guidelines on the Protection of Privacy and Transborder Flows of Personal Data and the 1981 Council of Europe Convention No. 108 for the Protection of Individuals with Regard to Automatic Processing of Personal Data were drafted and adopted expressly to address questions of protection of personal information. These two documents are similar in content and, indeed, were drafted by international groups of experts with many common members.

11. Helen Nissenbaum, "Protecting Privacy in an Information Age: The Problem of Privacy in Public,"in *Law and Philosophy,* vol. 17, no. 5–6 (November 1998), pp. 559–96.

12. The global network is another tool for our communication with one another. It is important to bear this in mind and to develop human-centered systems and policies for the global information society. Too often, we are dazzled by the technological innovations and lose sight of their purpose. Time and again, as in the case of France's Minitel, the success of an information system is based on its use for conversation, rather than for the data and information in it, such as train schedules, telephone directories, and weather forecasts. Furthermore, it is axiomatic that, like all tools, the global network will be used in unanticipated ways with unanticipated results.

13. Coupled with our zeal to communicate is the equally strong desire, at times, to limit the audience for the communication. There are many examples of communications that an individual may wish to make, but that she does not want the whole world to be able to hear. Conversations with a husband or wife, with a boss about a new company strategy, with a coworker about the boss, or with children at bedtime are all fine communications, with nothing inherently wrong or embarrassing about them. At the same time, we do not

want everyone to be able to hear them. If everyone were able to hear or read our communications, it would very much change the nature of the interactions. Our ability to express ourselves, especially about matters closest to us, such as tenderness or competition, might be hampered.

Individuals participate in the collective in many ways—one-on-one, in a team, as part of a crowd or mob. While information and communication technologies provide many potential benefits, it is important also that communication systems are not made too transparent and that zones of relative opacity and transparency are preserved so as to permit individuals to engage in the great variety of human discourse.

14. This section does not provide an exhaustive history of the development of personal information protection laws but identifies some of the significant milestones.

The modern era of privacy and protection of personal data is generally viewed as having begun in 1890 with the article, "The Right to Privacy," by Samuel Warren and Louis Brandeis. Samuel Warren and Louis Brandeis, "The Right to Privacy," *Harvard Law Review,* vol. 4 (1890), pp. 193–220. Warren and Brandeis wrote the article in response to "recent inventions and business methods," specifically the contemporary new technologies and innovations of "instantaneous photographs and newspaper enterprises" and "numerous mechanical devices."

In the United States, four categories of privacy evolved during the twentieth century: the right to be let alone; the right to be shielded from public disclosure of private facts; the right not to be depicted in a false light; and protection from misappropriation of name or likeness. The protections available under these categories evolved as a matter of common law through judicial decisions. In some U.S. states, they were codified in statutes.

15. These laws broadly cover the personal data and information and privacy of individuals, apply to the public and private sectors, establish an independent oversight authority, usually called a data protection commission, incorporate rules governing the collection, use, and retention of personal data and information, and offer recourse and redress for violations.

16. During the past three decades, legislation at national and state levels to protect certain discrete types of personal information, such as credit records and videotape rental records, has been adopted, creating a so-called patchwork of data protection laws.

17. "Commission Decision pursuant to Directive 95/46/EC of the European Parliament and of the Council on the adequacy of the protection provided by the Safe Harbor Privacy Principles and related Frequently Asked Questions issued by the U.S. Department of Commerce."

18. As a parallel, as the global network evolved from a small, collegial research network to a worldwide agglomeration of computers, networks, and individual users exchanging all kinds of information, the IP protocol was revised to add security requirements.

19. Efforts in this direction have begun to be made. See, for example, "Design for Values," Princeton University, 1998, and the Workshop on Freedom and Privacy by Design, Toronto, Ontario, Canada, April 2000 (www.cfp2000.org/workshop/materials/ [April 16, 2000]).

20. See, for example, "Anonymity," Washington, CATO Institute, December 1999. The notions of identity, anonymity, and the spectrum between these two endpoints would benefit greatly from additional study. The spectrum might include many types of nonidentifiable transactions or pseudonymous interactions, which, as necessary or desirable, would be able to provide the appropriate level of verifiability or authentication. In the physical world,

for example, all transactions are not identifiable to the individual. A great many, in fact, are nonidentifiable, such as buying a newspaper at a kiosk or a cup of coffee in a shop, riding the subway or a bus, or reading in a library.

21. The question of the locus of control of information and communication is central. Most people, for example, have identity or credit cards with chips or magnetic stripes, which they carry with them and freely give out. Yet they do not know or have any influence over the information that is encoded on them. Increasingly, intelligence is being added to the endpoints of information systems, which gives the end user the possibility of more control, owing both to the availability of more information and to the possibility to create, manipulate, and use the information.

22. Frances Cairncross, *The Death of Distance* (Harvard Business School Press, 1997).

23. See, for example, Viktor Mayer-Schönberger and Teree Foster, "A Regulatory Web: Free Speech and the Global Information Infrastructure," in Brian Kahin and Charles Nesson, eds., *Borders in Cyberspace* (MIT Press,1997), pp. 235–54. Another example is provided by the Asia-Pacific Economic Cooperation (APEC) Forum deliberations on objectionable content.

24. David Sobel, *Filters and Freedom: Free Speech Perspectives on Internet Content Controls* (Washington: Electronic Privacy Information Center [EPIC], 1999).

16

DANI RODRIK

Governance of Economic Globalization

THE MIXED ECONOMY stands as the crowning economic achievement of the twentieth century. If it was the nineteenth century that unleashed capitalism in its full force, it was the twentieth century that tamed it and boosted its productivity by supplying the institutional underpinnings of market-based economies. Central banks to regulate credit and the supply of liquidity, fiscal policies to stabilize aggregate demand, antitrust and regulatory authorities to combat fraud and anticompetitive behavior, social insurance to reduce lifetime risk, political democracy to make the above institutions accountable to the citizenry—these were all innovations that firmly took root in today's rich countries only during the second half of the twentieth century. That the second half of the century was also a period of unprecedented prosperity for western Europe, the United States, Japan, and some other parts of East Asia is no coincidence. These institutional innovations greatly enhanced the efficiency and legitimacy of markets and in turn drew strength from the material advancement unleashed by market forces.

Parts of this chapter are drawn from Dani Rodrik, "How Far Will International Economic Integration Go?" *Journal of Economic Perspectives*, vol. 14 (Winter 2000), pp. 177–86.

Globalization—by which I mean enhanced trade and financial integration—poses both opportunities and challenges to the mixed economy.[1] On the plus side, the global expansion of markets promises greater prosperity through the channels of division of labor and specialization according to comparative advantage. This is of particular significance to developing countries, since it allows them to gain access to state-of-the-art technology and cheap capital goods on world markets.

But globalization also undercuts the ability of nation-states to erect regulatory and redistributive institutions and does so at the same time that it increases the premium on solid national institutions. Social safety nets become more difficult to finance just as the need for social insurance becomes greater; financial intermediaries increase their ability to evade national regulation just as prudential supervision becomes more important; macroeconomic management becomes trickier just as the costs of policy mistakes are amplified. Once again, the stakes are greater for the developing countries, since they have weak institutions to begin with.

The dilemma that we face as we enter the twenty-first century is that markets are striving to become global while the institutions needed to support them remain by and large national. I argue in this chapter that the implications of this discrepancy are twofold. On the one hand, the existence of jurisdictional boundaries, drawn largely along national lines, restricts economic integration. This inhibits efficiency. On the other hand, the desire by producers and investors to go global weakens the institutional base of national economies. This inhibits equity and legitimacy.

Taken together, the two processes drive us toward a no-man's world. Exporters, multinationals, and financiers complain about impediments to trade and capital flows. Labor advocates, environmentalists, and consumer safety activists decry the downward pressures on national standards and legislation. Broad sections of the populace treat globalization as a dirty word while happily devouring its fruits. And government officials vacillate, trying to please each group in turn while satisfying none.

In the long run, the way out of the dilemma is to envisage a world in which politics is as global as economics. This would be a world of global federalism, with the mixed economy reconstructed at the global level. In the short run, the continued existence of nation-states forces us toward more realistic and practical arrangements. I argue that a sound intermediate architecture has to combine international harmonization and standard setting with generalized exit schemes, opt-outs, and escape clauses. This allows most of the efficiency gains from integration to be reaped while still leaving room for a range of divergent national practices. This kind of architecture would reconstitute the "compromise of embedded liberalism" for the realities of the early twenty-first-century economy.[2]

How Global Is the Global Economy?

A common view of today's world economy is that of a global marketplace in which goods, services, and assets flow across national boundaries without friction. This is the picture that one finds, for example, in the popular accounts of Greider and Friedman—two works that are divergent in all other respects.[3] Both authors write about a seamless world market in which nation-states have been stripped of virtually all powers, while drawing very different conclusions about the desirability of this state of things.

How global is the global economy in reality? The natural benchmark for thinking about economic globalization is to consider a world in which markets for goods, services, and factors of production are perfectly integrated. How far are we presently from such a world? My answer—which is broadly consistent with Jeffrey Frankel's assessment elsewhere in this volume—is that we are quite far. Contrary to conventional wisdom and much punditry, international economic integration remains remarkably limited. This robust finding comes across in a wide range of studies, too numerous to cite here.[4] National borders (such as the U.S.-Canadian one) seem to have a significantly depressing effect on commerce, even in the absence of formal tariff or nontariff barriers, linguistic or cultural differences, uncertainty about the exchange rate, and other economic obstacles. International price arbitrage in tradable commodities tends to occur very slowly. Investment portfolios in the advanced industrial countries typically exhibit large amounts of "home bias," that is, people invest a higher proportion of assets in their own countries than the principles of asset diversification would seem to suggest. National investment rates remain highly correlated with and dependent on national saving rates. Even in periods of exuberance, capital flows between rich and poor nations fall considerably short of what theoretical models would predict. Real interest rates are not driven to equality even among advanced countries with integrated financial markets. Severe restrictions on the international mobility of labor are the rule rather than the exception. And even the Internet, the epitome of technology-driven internationalization, remains parochial in many ways.

While formal barriers to trade and capital flows have been substantially reduced over the past three decades, international markets for goods, services, and capital are not nearly as "thick" as they would be under complete integration. Why so much trade in goods and capital has gone missing is the subject of an active research agenda in international economics. The answers are not yet entirely clear. But whatever these may be, it is clear that economic globalization has far to go before the full efficiency benefits of economic integration are reaped.

The International Division of Labor Is Limited by the Scope of Political and Legal Jurisdictions

At some level there is no mystery about the "border" effects noted above. National borders demarcate political and legal jurisdictions. Such demarcations serve to segment markets in much the same way that transport costs or border taxes do. This is because exchanges that cross national jurisdictions are subject to a wide array of transaction costs introduced by discontinuities in political and legal systems.

These transaction costs arise from various sources, but perhaps the most obvious relate to the problem of contract enforcement. When one of the parties reneges on a written contract, local courts may be unwilling—and international courts unable—to enforce a contract signed between residents of two different countries. National sovereignty interferes with contract enforcement, leaving international transactions hostage to an increased risk of opportunistic behavior. This problem is most severe in the case of capital flows and has the implication that national borrowing opportunities are limited by the willingness of countries to service their obligations rather than their ability to do so. But the problem exists generically for any commercial contract signed by entities belonging to two differing jurisdictions.[5]

When contracts are implicit rather than explicit, they require either repeated interaction or other side constraints to make them sustainable. Both of these are generally harder to achieve across national borders. In the domestic context, implicit contracts are often "embedded" in social networks, which provide sanctions against opportunistic behavior. One of the things that keeps business executives honest is fear of social ostracism. The role played by ethnic networks in fostering trade linkages, as in the case of the Chinese in Southeast Asia, is a clear indication of the importance of group ties in facilitating economic exchange.[6]

Ultimately, contracts are often neither explicit nor implicit; they simply remain incomplete. Laws, norms, and customs are some of the ways in which the problem of incompleteness of contracts is alleviated in the domestic sphere. To borrow an example from Jean Tirole, what protects a consumer from the small likelihood that a soda pop bottle might explode is not a contingent contract signed with the manufacturer but product liability laws.[7] International law provides at best partial protection against incomplete contracts, and international norms and customs are hardly up to the task either.

The presence of separate national monetary regimes provides another example of trade-restricting transaction costs. Andrew Rose has recently found that countries that share the same currency trade with each other three times as much as countries that have separate currencies.[8] Moreover, this effect is much larger than the effects of exchange-rate volatility per se. The trade consequences of the latter are comparatively minor. Hence the jurisdictional discontinuity introduced by national currencies has a large negative effect on trade even when currency values are stable.

This line of argument has important implications for the question of how far international economic integration can go. If the depth of markets is limited by the reach of jurisdictional boundaries, does it not follow that national sovereignty imposes serious constraints on international economic integration? Can markets become international while politics remains local? Or, to ask a different but related question, what would politics look like in a world in which international markets had nothing to fear from the narrower scope of political jurisdictions?

Caught in an International Trilemma

A familiar result of open economy macroeconomics is that countries cannot simultaneously maintain independent monetary policies, fixed exchange rates, and an open capital account. This result is fondly known to the cognoscenti as the "impossible trinity," or in Obstfeld and Taylor's terms, as the "open-economy trilemma."[9] The trilemma is represented schematically in the top panel of figure 16-1. If a government chooses fixed exchange rates and capital mobility, it has to give up monetary autonomy.

Figure 16-1. *The Trilemma*

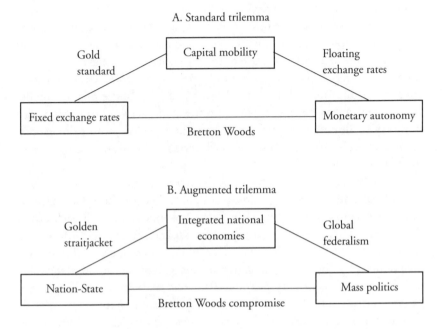

A. Standard trilemma

Gold standard — Capital mobility — Floating exchange rates

Fixed exchange rates — Bretton Woods — Monetary autonomy

B. Augmented trilemma

Golden straitjacket — Integrated national economies — Global federalism

Nation-State — Bretton Woods compromise — Mass politics

If it wants monetary autonomy and capital mobility, it has to go with floating exchange rates. If it wants to combine fixed exchange rates with monetary autonomy (at least in the short run), it better restrict capital mobility.

The bottom panel of figure 16-1 suggests, by analogy, a different kind of trilemma, one that we might call the *political* trilemma of the world economy. The three nodes of the extended trilemma are international economic integration, the nation-state, and mass politics. I use the term "nation-state" to refer to territorial-jurisdictional entities with independent powers of making and administering the law. I use the term "mass politics" to refer to political systems where the franchise is unrestricted; there is a high degree of political mobilization; and political institutions are responsive to mobilized groups.

The implied claim, as in the standard trilemma, is that we can have at most two of these three things. If we want true international economic integration, we have to go either with the nation-state, in which case the domain of national politics will have to be significantly restricted, or else with mass politics, in which case we will have to give up the nation-state in favor of global federalism. If we want highly participatory political regimes, we have to choose between the nation-state and international economic integration. If we want to keep the nation-state, we have to choose between mass politics and international economic integration.

None of this is immediately obvious. But to see that there may be some logic in it, consider our hypothetical perfectly integrated world economy. This would be a world economy in which national jurisdictions do not interfere with arbitrage in markets for goods, services, or capital. Transaction costs and tax differentials would be minor; product and regulatory standards would be harmonized; and convergence in commodity prices and factor returns would be almost complete.

The most obvious way we can attain such a world is by instituting federalism on a global scale. Global federalism would align jurisdictions with the market, and remove the "border" effects. In the United States, for example, despite the continuing existence of differences in regulatory and taxation practices among states, the presence of a national constitution, national government, and a federal judiciary ensures that markets are truly national.[10] The European Union, while very far from a federal system at present, seems to be headed in the same direction. Under a model of global federalism, the entire world—or at least the parts that count the most economically—would be organized along the lines of the U.S. system. National governments would not necessarily disappear, but their powers would be severely circumscribed by supranational legislative, executive, and judicial authorities. A world government would take care of a world market.

But global federalism is not the only way to achieve complete international economic integration. An alternative is to maintain the nation-state system largely as is, but to ensure that national jurisdictions—and the differences among them—do not get in the way of economic transactions. The overarching goal of nation-states in this world would be to appear attractive to international markets. National jurisdictions, far from acting as an obstacle, would be geared toward facilitating international commerce and capital mobility. Domestic regulations and tax policies would be either harmonized according to international standards, or structured such that they pose the least amount of hindrance to international economic integration. The only local public goods provided would be those that are compatible with integrated markets.

It is possible to envisage a world of this sort; in fact, many commentators seem to believe we are already there. Governments today actively compete with each other by pursuing policies that they believe will earn them market confidence and attract trade and capital inflows: tight money, small government, low taxes, flexible labor legislation, deregulation, privatization, and openness all around. These are the policies that constitute what Thomas Friedman has aptly termed the Golden Straitjacket.[11] The price of maintaining national jurisdictional sovereignty while markets become international is restricting politics to a narrow domain. "As your country puts on the Golden Straitjacket," Friedman notes:

> Two things tend to happen: your economy grows and your politics shrinks. . . . [The] Golden Straitjacket narrows the political and economic policy choices of those in power to relatively tight parameters. That is why it is increasingly difficult these days to find any real differences between ruling and opposition parties in those countries that have put on the Golden Straitjacket. Once your country puts on the Golden Straitjacket, its political choices get reduced to Pepsi or Coke—to slight nuances of tastes, slight nuances of policy, slight alterations in design to account for local traditions, some loosening here or there, but never any major deviation from the core golden rules.[12]

Whether this description accurately characterizes our present world is debatable. But Friedman is on to something. His argument carries considerable force in a world where national markets are fully integrated yet politics remains organized nationally. In such a world, the shrinkage of politics would get reflected in the insulation of economic policymaking bodies (central banks, fiscal authorities, and so on) from political participation and debate, the disappearance (or privatization) of social insurance, and the replacement of developmental goals with the need to maintain market confidence. The essential point is this: once the rules of the game are set by the requirements of the global economy, the ability of mobilized popular groups to gain access to and influence national economic policymaking has to be restricted. The experience with the gold standard, and its eventual demise, provides an apt illustration of the incompatibility: by the interwar period, as the franchise was fully extended and labor became organized, national governments found that they could no longer pursue gold standard economic orthodoxy.

Note the contrast with global federalism. Under global federalism, politics need not, and would not, shrink: it would relocate to the global level. The United States provides a useful way of thinking about this: the most contentious political battles in the United States are fought not at the state level, but at the federal level.

Figure 16-1 shows a third option, which becomes available if we sacrifice the objective of complete international economic integration. I have termed this the Bretton Woods compromise. The essence of the Bretton Woods-GATT regime was that countries were free to dance to their own tune as long as they removed a number of border restrictions on trade and generally did not discriminate among their trade partners.[13] In the area of international finance, countries were allowed (indeed encouraged) to maintain restrictions on capital flows. In the area of trade, the rules frowned upon quantitative restrictions but not import tariffs. Even though an impressive amount of trade liberalization was undertaken during successive rounds of GATT negotiations, there were also gaping exceptions. Agriculture and textiles were effectively left out of the negotiations. Various clauses in the GATT (on antidumping and safeguards, in particular) permitted countries to erect trade barriers when their industries came under severe competition from imports. Developing country trade policies were effectively left outside the scope of international discipline.[14]

Until roughly the 1980s, these loose rules left enough space for countries to follow their own, often divergent, paths of development. Hence, western Europe chose to integrate within itself and to erect an extensive system of social insurance. Japan caught up with the developed economies using its own distinctive brand of capitalism, combining a dynamic export machine with large doses of inefficiency in services and agriculture. China grew by leaps and bounds once it recognized the importance of private initiative, even though it flouted every other rule in the guidebook. Much of the rest of East Asia generated an economic miracle relying on industrial policies that have since been banned by the World Trade Organization (WTO). Scores of countries in Latin America, the Middle East, and Africa generated unprecedented economic growth rates until the late 1970s under import-substitution policies that insulated their economies from the world economy.

The Bretton Woods compromise was largely abandoned in the 1980s for several reasons. Improvements in communication and transportation technologies undermined the old regime by making globalization easier. International trade agreements began to reach behind national borders; for

example, policies on antitrust or health and safety, which had previously
been left to domestic politics, now became issues in international trade discussions. Finally, there was a shift in attitudes in favor of openness, as many
developing nations came to believe that they would be better served by a
policy of openness. The upshot is that we are left somewhere in between
the three nodes of the augmented trilemma of figure 16-1. Which one shall
we eventually give up?

In what follows I suggest two different paths, one appropriate for the
short to medium term and the other for the long term. The first path consists of recreating the Bretton Woods compromise: under this scenario, we
would accept the continued centrality of the nation-state and therefore
combine international rules and standards with built-in opt-out schemes.
The rationale of such a system, and what it may look like, is laid out in the
following section. The long-term path is one of global federalism. Since
this scenario obviously lies far in the future, it allows our imagination to
run considerably more freely.

Generalized Opt-out Schemes in the Short Run

As long as the nation-state remains the decisive actor, any stable regime of
international economic governance has to be consistent with national preferences. Since national policymakers always have the option of going it
alone, the regime must contain incentives for them not to do so. Therefore,
the challenge of international economic governance is twofold. On the one
hand, we must have a set of rules that encourages greater convergence of
policies and standards on a *voluntary* basis. This helps narrow the effect of
jurisdictional differences and thereby encourages greater economic integration. At the same time, sufficient flexibility needs to be built into the
rules that govern international economic relations to allow selective disengagement from multilateral disciplines. The latter is needed to allow for
exceptions owing to divergence in national norms or preferences.

Consider as an example the Agreement on Safeguards in the World
Trade Organization. This agreement allows a member state to impose temporary trade restrictions following an increase in imports but under a very
stringent set of conditions. My argument is essentially that there is a
generic case for such "escape-clause" action, and that it should be allowed
under a much broader range of circumstances and in areas going beyond
trade. As I show below, building opt-outs into the rules generally does bet-

ter than the alternatives, which are either not to have rules or to have rules that are frequently flouted.

—*The Analytics of Temporary Opt-Outs.* When will governments give up some of their sovereignty and choose to empower intergovernmental organizations? There is a simple answer in game-theoretic terms: when the long-run benefits of "cooperation" outweigh the short-run benefits of "defection" (that is, unilateral action).[15]

More concretely, consider cooperation between two countries in the context of a repeated game, where the one-shot Nash equilibrium is all-around defection. Let tariffs be the policy action in question (bearing in mind that the logic applies to any aspect of international economic policy). Both countries would prefer to be in the low-tariff equilibrium, but the one-shot Nash equilibrium entails high tariffs in both countries. (This is the case of a prisoner's dilemma applied to trade policy.) We know that cooperation can be sustained in an infinitely-repeated setting under certain conditions. In particular, cooperation will be the equilibrium strategy for any player at time t if at that time:

$$\textit{short-term benefits of defection} < \textit{(discount term)}$$
$$\times \textit{(future net benefits of cooperation).}$$

Hence, for cooperation to be sustainable, the short-term benefits of defection must be small, the discount rate low, and the future benefits from cooperation high. One form of such cooperation is the case in which each player employs a trigger-strategy of the form: "start by cooperating, cooperate if the other side cooperated last period, defect for k periods otherwise." In a static environment, that is the end of the story. Either the underlying parameters produce cooperation, or they do not.

But consider what happens when conditions change. Think of the tariff game analyzed by Kyle Bagwell and Robert Staiger, where there are exogenous shocks to the volume of trade.[16] When the trade volume is (unexpectedly) high, the benefits to short-term opportunism (imposing a tariff for terms-of-trade reasons) are also high. The left-hand side of the above expression increases, while the right-hand side remains unchanged. At that point, cooperation may no longer be an equilibrium strategy, even if it had been one previously. We will therefore get defection by both parties (a trade war) for at least k periods.

It would have been far better to allow for this possibility by altering the strategies to read: "start by cooperating, cooperate if the other side cooperated last period or if the other side defected when the trade volume exceeded a certain threshold, and defect for k periods otherwise." The outcome with these strategies is that long periods of trade wars are avoided. The game now explicitly allows for an "escape clause." A government is not penalized for withdrawing from the rules when there is insufficient incentive for it to have played by the rules. The outcome is better for all parties because unnecessary trade conflicts do not take place.

The point of this example generalizes beyond surges in trade volumes and the use of tariffs for terms-of-trade reasons. Whenever conditions change and free trade becomes incompatible with domestic social-political objectives, the system is better off allowing "defections" than treating the "defections" as instances of rule breaking. Thinking in these terms makes it clear that escape clauses ("safeguards," "opt-outs," and so on) are an integral part of sustainable international agreements.

—The Analytics of Permanent Opt-Outs. The opt-outs in the discussion above were temporary. There is also a strong case for permanent opt-outs when national preferences differ. For example, there is no reason why all countries should have identical environmental standards, labor rules, product-safety standards, or tax regulations. In cases such as these, giving national authorities some latitude makes a lot of sense. However, a free-for-all is unlikely to be optimal, since there will be spillovers across countries. By establishing less stringent labor standards or lower taxes on capital, some countries can divert trade and capital flows in their direction. In general, whenever there are externalities involved in setting standards (whether of the standard or network kind), we know that decentralized behavior will result in suboptimal outcomes.

An important paper by Thomas Piketty develops a useful guiding principle for such situations.[17] Piketty proves that a two-stage procedure of the following kind always improves on decentralized behavior among nation-states.

—In stage one, countries collectively vote on a common standard.

—In stage two, each country that wishes to depart from the common standard can do so by paying a cost.

This scheme Pareto-dominates the Nash equilibrium in which each nation behaves independently.

A small model helps illustrate how this works. Denote by t_i a policy that is under the control of national authorities. (This could be a labor standard, a tax on capital, or financial regulation.) We express the welfare function for country i as follows:

$$W_i = -\frac{1}{2}(a_i - t_i)^2 + b(\bar{t} - a_i)^{1/2},$$

with $b > 0$. This formulation captures two ideas: first, each country has a distinct ideal standard, here denoted by a_i; and second, each country's welfare is also affected by the "average" standard maintained in the other countries (denoted by $\bar{t}$). In particular, the second term has the interpretation that country i suffers a utility loss whenever other countries maintain (on average) a lower standard than country i's most preferred level. (Think again of capital taxation or banking standards for concreteness.) I assume that there is a continuum of countries, indexed by their ideal policies, and that a_i is distributed uniformly in the interval $[0, 1]$. In the decentralized, noncooperative equilibrium, each country would select its ideal policy without regard to the externality imposed on the others. This yields the noncooperative ("nc") solutions $t_k = a_k$ for all k, and $\bar{t}^{nc} = 1/2$.

In principle, the first-best outcome can be achieved by implementing a Pigovian tax/subsidy scheme to counter the externality in the choice of t. But this would require knowledge of the entire distribution of national preferences, as well as an international tax authority. I show that an alternative modeled after Piketty's suggestion is guaranteed to be Pareto-superior to the noncooperative, Nash equilibrium, with minimal informational requirements.

The alternative scheme consists of the following rule. In stage one, countries select a common tc by simple majority vote (with c denoting the common standard under cooperation). In stage two, countries are required to set their $t_i \geq t^c$ or else pay a cost $k \geq 0$. This cost k is selected subject to the participation constraint that no country is left worse off than under the noncooperative equilibrium.

To show that there is always a t^c and k under which every country does at least as well, we proceed in two steps. First, we derive the cut-off level of a, denoted a_s, below which all countries will choose to pay k and depart from the standard t^c. This cut-off value of a_s is a function of t^c and k, and is defined implicitly by the equation:

$$-1/2(a_s - t_s)^2 + b(\bar{t}^c - a_s)^{1/2} - k = -1/2(a_s - t^c)^2 + b(\bar{t}^c - a_s)^{1/2}.$$

The left-hand side of the equality is the utility level when the country indexed by s selects its own most-preferred t, t_s, and pays the cost k. The right-hand side is the utility level when this country sticks with the common

Figure 16-2. *Solution to the Harmonization-with-Exit Game*

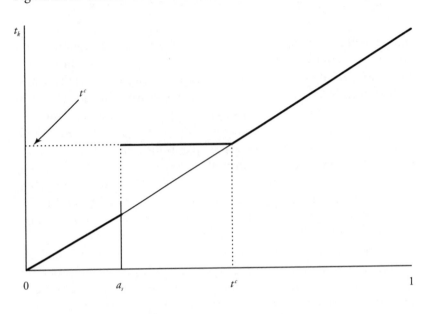

standard t^c. By assumption, country s is indifferent between the two options. Solving this equation (and noting $t_s = a_s$), we get $a_s = t^c - \sqrt{2k}$. Note that countries with $a_k > t^c$ are not constrained by the rules, so they simply pick their most preferred standards, $t_k = a_k$.

Given a certain t^c and k, the outcome is as depicted in figure 16-2. The thick line shows choices of t as a function of a. Countries with a's in the range $(0, a_s)$ pay the cost k and select their most preferred t's. Countries in the range (a_s, t^c) select t^c. And countries in the range $(t^c, 1)$ select their most preferred t's. The effect of the scheme is to lift the standards adopted in the second (middle) of these ranges. It can be shown that the average standard is thereby raised to $\bar{t}^c = 1/2 + k$, which is at least as large as $\bar{t}^{nc} = 1/2$.

In step two, we derive the equilibrium levels of t^c and k. Since t^c is selected by majority voting among countries and k by the constraint that no country is left worse off, the solutions are easy. Note first that the worst-off country under the scheme is the one with lowest a, that is, $a_k = 0$. For this country to be as well off under the scheme as under the non-cooperative outcome, it can be checked that the following criterion has to be satisfied: $k \leq b^2$. Maximizing the median country's welfare subject to that constraint in turn yields the results $k = b^2$ and $t^c = 1/2$. (The latter follows from the fact that the median equals the average, given the uniform distribution of a's.)

In fact, any k in the interval $(0, b^2)$ is a Pareto improvement compared to the non-cooperative equilibrium. So for a small enough k this scheme will always work, without requiring any knowledge of b. Harmonization coupled with an opt-out clause (the latter exercised at a cost) is a flexible way of combining standardization with diversity.

—Discussion. The analytical frameworks described above provide a useful way to think about the governance of economic globalization. The opt-out principle is in fact already in use in the WTO, albeit in a limited way. As mentioned before, the GATT and the WTO contain explicit safeguard schemes that allow countries to impose temporary tariffs in response to import surges. These safeguard measures have not been used much, because taking advantage of antidumping (AD) procedures is considerably easier. In practice, it is AD duties that have served as the safeguard mechanism of choice. The GATT also allows permanent escapes under specific conditions for nontrade and foreign policy reasons. More to the point, the GATT has recognized the need in the past for relaxing or not imposing disciplines in the areas of agriculture, textiles (MFA), and in selected industrial products (VER). Rather than viewing these as "derogations," one should perhaps view them as part and parcel of the broader logic of achieving international cooperation.

As the disciplines of the international trade and financial regimes expand into new areas, the analysis here suggests that there will be a parallel need to build reinvigorated opt-out mechanisms. As long as nation-states remain at the core of the international system, considerations of sustainability and diversity require that the rules allow selective disengagement from multilateral disciplines.

In the area of trade, one could imagine expanding the scope of the current Agreement on Safeguards to a broader range of circumstances, such as those arising from concern over labor standards, the environment, or human rights. The purpose of such an expanded escape clause mechanism would be to allow countries, under well-specified contingencies and subject to multilaterally approved procedures, greater breathing room to fulfill domestic requirements that conflict with trade. To prevent abuse, the mechanism would have to ensure that domestic proceedings would be transparent, democratic, and open to all interests (including those that benefit from trade), and that the results would be subject to periodic reviews. (These procedural requirements can be interpreted as corresponding to the k in the model discussed previously.) If this could be achieved *in exchange* for a tightening of rules on antidumping action, which have a highly corrosive effect on the world trading system, the benefits could be substantial.

In the area of international finance, we need to think of similar mechanisms. In the wake of recent financial crises, international institutions have developed a formidable list of codes and standards to which countries are expected to adhere. These cover fiscal transparency, monetary and financial policy, banking supervision, data dissemination, corporate governance and structure, and accounting standards. These codes may often be not appropriate to the needs of developing countries. They typically require a large investment in resources and administrative capability. In practice, the real question is this: will opt-outs be allowed in an informal, ad hoc manner, or will they be built into the rules explicitly? The discussion here suggests that the latter strategy is far preferable.

Global Federalism in the Long Run

Over the long run, can we envisage a world in which the reach of markets, jurisdictions, and politics is each truly and commensurately global—a world of global federalism?

Perhaps we could, based on the following reasoning. First, continuing technological progress will both foster international economic integration and remove some of the traditional obstacles (such as distance) to global government. Second, short of global wars or natural disasters of major proportions, it is hard to envisage that a substantial part of the world's population will want to give up the benefits that an increasingly integrated (hence efficient) world market can deliver. Third, hard-won citizenship rights (of representation and self-government) are also unlikely to be given up easily, keeping pressure on politicians to remain accountable to the wishes of their electorate.

Further, we can perhaps project an alliance of convenience in favor of global governance between those who perceive themselves to be the "losers" from economic integration, like labor groups and environmentalists, and those who perceive themselves as the "winners," like exporters, multinational enterprises, and financial interests. The alliance would be underpinned by the mutual realization that both sets of interests are best served by the *supranational* promulgation of rules, regulations, and standards. Labor advocates and environmentalists would get a shot at international labor and environmental rules. Multinational enterprises would be able to operate under global accounting standards. Investors would benefit from common disclosure, bankruptcy, and financial regulations. A global fiscal authority would provide public goods and a global lender-of-last-resort would stabilize the financial system. Part of the bargain would be to make international policymakers accountable through democratic elections, with due regard to the preeminence of the economically more powerful countries. National bureaucrats and politicians, the only remaining beneficiaries of the nation-state, would either refashion themselves as global officials or they would be shouldered aside.

Global federalism would not mean that the United Nations turns itself into a world government. What we would be likely to get is a combination of traditional forms of governance (an elected global legislative body) with regulatory institutions spanning multiple jurisdictions and accountable to perhaps multiple types of representative bodies. In an age of rapid technological change, the form of governance itself can be expected to be subject to considerable innovation.[18]

Many things can go wrong with this scenario. One alternative possibility is that an ongoing series of financial crises will leave national electorates sufficiently shell-shocked that they willingly, if unhappily, don the Golden Straitjacket for the long run. This scenario amounts to the Argentinization of national politics on a global scale. Another possibility is that governments will resort to protectionism to deal with the distributive and governance difficulties posed by economic integration. For the near term, either one of these scenarios should be regarded as more likely than global federalism. But a longer time horizon leaves room for greater optimism.

Conclusion

This chapter provides a framework for thinking about the governance of economic globalization. I have argued that we are presently nowhere near complete international economic integration, and that traveling the remaining distance will require either an expansion of our jurisdictions or a shrinking of our politics. We can envisage a long run in which politics and jurisdictions expand to match the scope of a truly integrated global economy. This is my scenario of global federalism. But in the short run, more realistic solutions are needed.

As Raymond Vernon put it, "We are being challenged to think of the means of governance that can embrace comfortably the global aspirations of cosmopolitans, the national aspirations of nation-bound groups, and even the local aspirations of subregional interests. How to bridge these very different perspectives is not obvious. Neither the ideas nor the institutions for reconciling these perspectives are yet evident."[19]

I have argued that we need to scale down our ambitions. Augmenting the efficiency benefits of international economic integration requires the further empowering of multilateral institutions and greater reliance on international standards. As long as nation-states predominate, neither is likely to be sustainable unless escape-clause or opt-out mechanisms are explicitly built into international economic rules.

In *The Economic Consequences of the Peace*, John Maynard Keynes drew a vivid picture of an integrated world economy at the pinnacle of the gold standard. Writing in the aftermath of a devastating world war and anticipating a period of economic turbulence and protectionism—correctly, as it turned out—Keynes considered this a lost era of great magnificence.[20] Will we experience a similar recoiling from globalization in the first decades of the twenty-first century? The answer depends on our ability to devise domestic and international institutions that render economic globalism compatible with the principles of the mixed economy.

Notes

1. See Robert O. Keohane and Joseph S. Nye in this volume for a discussion of various aspects of globalization, as well as some useful conceptual distinctions between some relevant terms: globalization, globalism, interdependence, sensitivity, connectivity, and vulnerability. Robert O. Keohane, and Joseph S. Nye, "Power, Interdependence, and Globalism," unpublished paper, November 16, 1999.

2. The term quoted is from John G. Ruggie "Trade, Protectionism and the Future of Welfare Capitalism," *Journal of International Affairs*, vol. 48 (Summer 1994), pp. 1–11.

3. William Greider, *One World Ready or Not—The Manic Logic of Global Capitalism* (Simon and Schuster, 1997); and Thomas L. Friedman, *The Lexus and the Olive Tree: Understanding Globalization* (Farrar, Straus and Giroux, 1999).

4. See in particular Martin S. Feldstein and Charles Horioka, "Domestic Saving and International Capital Flows," *Economic Journal*, vol. 90 (June 1980), pp. 314–29, the results of which have been confirmed in numerous subsequent studies. See also John F. Helliwell, *How Much Do National Borders Matter?* (Brookings, 1998).

5. See James E. Anderson and Douglas Marcouiller, "Trade, Insecurity, and Home Bias: An Empirical Investigation," Working Paper 7000 (Cambridge, Mass.: National Bureau of Economic Research, March 1999) for empirical evidence that suggests that inadequate contract enforcement imposes severe costs on trade.

6. Alessandra Casella and James Rauch, "Anonymous Market and Group Ties in International Trade," Working Paper W6186 (Cambridge, Mass.: National Bureau of Economic Research, September 1997) were the first to emphasize the importance of group ties in international trade, using a model of differentiated products.

7. Jean Tirole, *The Theory of Industrial Organization* (MIT Press, 1989), pp. 113–14.

8. Andrew K. Rose, "One Money, One Market: Estimating the Effect of Common Currencies on Trade," Working Paper 7432 (Cambridge, Mass.: National Bureau of Economic Research, December 1999).

9. Maurice Obstfeld and Alan Taylor, "The Great Depression as a Watershed: International Capital Mobility over the Long Run," in Michael D. Bordo, Claudia D. Goldin, and Eugene N. White, eds., *The Defining Moment: The Great Depression and the American Economy in the Twentieth Century* (University of Chicago Press, 1998), pp. 353–402.

10. However, Holger C. Wolf, "Patterns of Intra- and Inter-State Trade," Working Paper W5939 (Cambridge, Mass.: National Bureau of Economic Research, February 1997), finds that state borders within the United States have a deterrent effect on trade as well.

11. Friedman, *The Lexus and the Olive Tree.*

12. Friedman, *The Lexus and the Olive Tree,* p. 87.

13. John Ruggie has written insightfully on this, describing the system that emerged as "embedded liberalism." Ruggie, "Trade, Protectionism, and the Future of Welfare Capitalism."

14. Robert Z. Lawrence, *Regionalism, Multilateralism, and Deeper Integration* (Brookings, 1996) has called the model of integration followed under the Bretton Woods-GATT system as "shallow integration," to distinguish it from the "deep integration" that requires behind-the-border harmonization of regulatory policies.

15. This discussion draws on Dani Rodrik, "The Debate over Globalization: How to Move Forward by Looking Backward," in Jeffrey J. Schott, ed., *Launching New Global Trade Talks: An Action Agenda,* Special Report 12 (Washington: Institute for International Economics, 1998).

16. Kyle Bagwell and Robert Staiger, "A Theory of Managed Trade," *American Economic Review,* vol. 4 (September 1990), pp. 779–95.

17. Thomas Piketty, "A Federal Voting Mechanism to Solve the Fiscal-Externality Problem," *European Economic Review,* vol. 40 (January 1996), pp. 3–18.

18. See Bruno Frey, "FOCJ: Competitive Governments for Europe," *International Review of Law and Economics,* vol. 16 (1996), pp. 315–27, on some intriguing ideas for the design of federal political systems.

19. Raymond Vernon, *In the Hurricane's Eye: The Troubled Prospect of Multinational Enterprises* (Harvard University Press, 1998), p. 28.

20. John Maynard Keynes, *The Economic Consequences of the Peace* (Harcourt, Brace, and Howe, 1920).

Contributors

All contributors, except for Robert Keohane, are at the John F. Kennedy School of Government, Harvard University.

Graham Allison
Douglas Dillon Professor of Government at Harvard University and Director of the Belfer Center for Science and International Affairs

Arthur Isak Applbaum
Professor of Ethics and Public Policy

L. David Brown
Visiting Professor of Public Policy and Associate Director of International Programs, Hauser Center for Nonprofit Organizations

William C. Clark
Harvey Brooks Professor of International Science, Public Policy, and Human Development

Cary Coglianese
Associate Professor of Public Policy

John D. Donahue
Raymond Vernon Lecturer in Public Policy and Director, Visions of Governance for the 21st Century

Jeffrey Frankel
James W. Harpel Professor of Capital Formation and Growth

Peter Frumkin
Assistant Professor of Public Policy

Merilee S. Grindle
*Edward S. Mason Professor of
International Development*

Deborah Hurley
*Director, Harvard Information
Infrastructure Project*

Elaine Ciulla Kamarck
*Director, Innovations in American
Government, and Special
Adviser, Gore Presidential
Campaign*

Robert O. Keohane
*James B. Duke Professor of
Political Science, Duke
University*

Sanjeev Khagram
Assistant Professor of Public Policy

Viktor Mayer-Schönberger
Assistant Professor of Public Policy

Mark H. Moore
*Daniel and Florence Guggenheim
Professor of Criminal Justice
Policy and Management and
Director, Hauser Center for
Nonprofit Organizations*

Pippa Norris
*Associate Director and Lecturer Joan
Shorenstein Center on the Press,
Politics, and Public Policy*

Joseph S. Nye Jr.
*Don K. Price Professor of Public
Policy and Dean of the Kennedy
School*

Dani Rodrik
*Rafiq Hariri Professor of
International Political Economy
and Director, Center for
International Development*

Neal M. Rosendorf
*Adjunct Lecturer in International
Relations and Dean's Research
Specialist*

Tony Saich
*Daewoo Professor of International
Affairs*

Frederick Schauer
*Frank Stanton Professor of the First
Amendment and Academic Dean
of the Kennedy School*

Index